# Modern/Postmodern

Also available from Continuum:

*Deconstruction and Critical Theory*, Peter V. Zima
*Philosophy of Modern Literary Theory*, Peter V. Zima
*What is Theory?*, Peter V. Zima

# Modern/Postmodern

## Society, Philosophy, Literature

Peter V. Zima

**continuum**

**Continuum International Publishing Group**

| | |
|---|---|
| The Tower Building | 80 Maiden Lane |
| 11 York Road | Suite 704 |
| London SE1 7NX | New York, NY 10038 |

www.continuumbooks.com

Updated version of *Moderne/Postmoderne. Gesellschaft, Philosophie, Literatur*, Tübingen-Basel, Francke, 2001 (2nd ed.) Used by permission.

**British Library Cataloguing-in-Publication Data**
A catalogue record for this book is available from the British Library.

ISBN:  HB: 978-0-8264-2402-0

**Library of Congress Cataloging-in-Publication Data**
Zima, P. V.
 [Moderne/Postmoderne. English]
 Modern/postmodern : society, philosophy, literature / Peter V. Zima.
  p. cm.
 ISBN:  978-0-8264-2402-0
 1. Postmodernism. 2. Postmodernism (Literature) 3. Modernism (Literature)  I. Title.

B831.2.Z5513 2010
149'.97–dc22

                                                                    2010003799

Typeset by Newgen Imaging Systems Pvt Ltd, Chennai, India
Printed and bound in Great Britain by CPI Antony Rowe, Chippenham, Wiltshire

In memory of my parents

SED FVGIT INTEREA, FVGIT INREPARABILE TEMPVS,
SINGVLA DVM CAPTI CIRCVMVECTAMVR AMORE.

Pvblivs Vergilivs Maro
(*Georgica* III, 284–285)

# Contents

# Preface

The constructions of modernity, modernism and postmodernity proposed in this book came about in a coordinate system whose vertical axis presents the postmodern critiques of modernity and modernism in a historical perspective, while the horizontal axis presents them in a conceptual context where they oscillate between universalism and particularism, indifference and ideology. Depending on one's perspective, the space between the two axes appears as the *modern, modernist* or *postmodern problematic,* whose relative coherence should not hide its contradictions and disparities.

The complexity of the vertical or historical dimension is partly due to the fact that the sociological and philosophical critiques are aimed at a *rationalist, Enlightenment modernity* (since about 1600), whose universalism is denounced as repressive, whereas the literary critiques turn against *aesthetic modernism* (since 1850 or 1880), whose representatives are blamed for being elitist, esoteric or utopian. This complexity should not induce anybody to suggest that modernity in the philosophical and sociological sense (in the sense of 'Enlightenment, rationalization and progress') has nothing to do with aesthetic modernity or modernism.

On closer inspection, *literary modernism* appears to be a *late modern self-criticism of modernity* which has numerous parallels in philosophy and sociology. Baudelaire's, D. H. Lawrence's and Robert Musil's critiques of the bourgeoisie, of Enlightenment rationalism and of a naïve faith in progress has philosophical and sociological counterparts in the works of Marx, the Young Hegelians, Nietzsche, Alfred and Max Weber or Georg Simmel (cf. Chapter 2). As a late modern self-criticism of modernity, modernism is also inherent in Adorno's and Horkheimer's Critical Theory and announces postmodern theories whose authors believe that this self-criticism does not go far enough. It is not by chance that contemporary British and American philosophers tend to read Adorno as a postmodernist or a 'proto-postmodernist' and that Habermas believes that Adorno's particularizing thought goes over into poststructuralism (cf. Section 3.5).

In the eyes of postmodernists, the modernist or late modern critique does not go far enough because they can no longer endorse key concepts of (late) modernity such as 'subjectivity', 'truth' or 'utopia' which were of great importance to modernists in the sense of Proust, Musil, Eliot, Simmel or Adorno. It becomes clear at this point that, although postmodernity emerges from the late modern or modernist problematic, it also breaks with it. In what follows, various aspects of this break will be considered in detail, but a certain continuity will also be taken into account.

Lyotard can only argue that postmodernity is not a new epoch (cf. Chapter 3) because he does not acknowledge the dialectic between continuity and discontinuity and because (as a post-Marxist) he tries to avoid the modern and modernist idea of a new era in the revolutionary or utopian sense at all costs. However, it seems futile to cling to the vision of an unending, self-perpetuating modernity in a situation where key modern concepts are questioned or rejected by philosophers (like Lyotard himself), by sociologists and literary critics alike; in a society which takes on plural, polymorphous forms due to market-based indifference.

At this point, the complexity of the horizontal axis comes to its own. On the one hand, postmodern sociologists, philosophers and writers reject modern, rationalist universalism which they relate – quite rightly – to the principle of domination and the rule of the exchange value; on the other hand, they plead in favour of the particular and the plural, both of which guarantee, in their eyes, a certain amount of non-conformism and non-identity vis-à-vis the powers that be. In this respect, they continue Adorno's particularizing tendency (as expressed in his 'thinking in models' and his 'parataxis').

Their – very different – arguments have one element in common: the tendency to hide the dialectical nexus between the particular, the plural on the one hand and indifference as interchangeability on the other. In a situation where beauty, truth and reason are only recognized in their particular and plural form – as competing beauties, truths and reasons – there is a real danger that indifference as interchangeability of values will ultimately prevail. If I am daily confronted with countless conflicting truths, ethics and aesthetics, I have two options (as a non-theorist or non-scientist): shrug my shoulders tolerantly at this excess of values and value judgements or decide in favour of a single ideology and declare it to be the only legitimate one. As a theorist I have the possibility to react dialogically to the problem of diversity and plurality (cf. Chapter 6).

Indifference as interchangeability in the sense of the exchange value can therefore elicit two contrary reactions: apathy and ideological engagement. The postmodern problematic evolves between these two extremes: between the tolerance of an unlimited pluralization geared towards the laws of the market and ideological fanaticism. The main problem of some postmodern thinkers – from Rorty to Lyotard and Bauman – seems to consist in their inability to perceive the *ambivalence* of pluralism and particularization. They do not perceive it because, unlike Baudrillard, they are not familiar with the concept of *indifference*. They may be right in assuming that particularization and pluralism resist the repressive mechanisms of a universalism governed by the principle of uniformity, but they overlook the fact that an extreme pluralism in the political, religious, ethical and aesthetic sense tends to confirm the interchangeable character of the particularities in question – and that it provokes ideological reactions.

This is the reason why an attempt is made in the last chapter – certainly not for the first time in the history of philosophy and the social sciences – to reconcile the particular and the universal. A reconciliation of this kind is most likely to prove satisfactory in a situation where none of the parties concerned is obliged to give up vital interests. Therefore a dialogical theory is mapped out whose moments of truth come about in a lasting interaction with heterogeneous theories: with otherness or alterity in the ideological and the epistemological sense. Whenever two discourses originating in heterogeneous groups of scientists overlap, one can speak of an *interdiscursive search* and an *interdiscursive moment of truth* temporarily endorsed by scientists who otherwise disagree. (The intersubjective critique *within* an ideologically and theoretically homogeneous group is *not* to be questioned or devalued – although it has its limitations and drawbacks.)

Naturally, 'truth' means something different here from what it meant in the philosophical systems of Plato, Descartes or Hegel, especially since the 'moments of truth' mentioned above have a provisional or heuristic character. Nevertheless, the concept of truth is defended here against all brands of relativism which tend to reject even the idea of true hypotheses obtained in dialogue. Its defence does not mean, however, that alterity and particularity are sacrificed; on the contrary, the dialogue envisaged in the last chapter presupposes the radical alterity of my discussion partner whose particular otherness guarantees a genuine search for truth based on ideological and theoretical difference.

The attempt to reconcile the particular and the universal, particular and general interests, is not a purely theoretical or speculative project, as the numerous political critiques of Rousseau and Hegel show. This is why the final section of the book introduces a political turn by evoking the interaction of the particular and the general within the European integration process. At the same time, it raises the question concerning the critical and dialogical potential of this process. It is a question rather then a thesis or a theory, for it goes without saying that an analysis of the critical and dialogical components inherent in European integration would require a thorough study of its own.

That part of the book is also an attempt to imagine an alternative to the negativity of Adorno's and Horkheimer's Critical Theory and to that of some postmodern philosophies and to replace this negativity by a dialogical approach, which is not only a theoretical project, but seems to gain momentum in the politics of European integration. It is by no means certain that this idea will be welcomed with enthusiasm at a time when 'Euro-scepticism' is fashionable among many European intellectuals. Many of them (who never expected a common currency to emerge) indulge in a rhetoric of resignation, while others keep looking across the Atlantic where they still locate the 'new world'. It could now be developing on this side of the ocean: in a Europe where a polyphonic and genuinely multicultural identity is being institutionalized beyond the monolingual nation state. – This is possibly a thought *à rebours* and may go against the grain in some intellectual circles. But even they are not immune to change as developments since 1989 have shown.

# Chapter 1

# Modernity – Modernism – Postmodernity: Attempting a Definition

Should sceptics turn out to be right, then this book deals with an object which does not exist, a *proton pseudos* not worth commenting on. Time and again, sceptical remarks concerning the concept of 'postmodernity' are to be heard, relegating it to the realm of human errors and chimeras. The common sense idea according to which 'postmodernity' cannot possibly be a chimera, since a vast array of authors keep discussing it, turns out to be deceptive, for it will be remembered that humanity has frequently been attracted by nebulous concepts such as 'providence', 'fate', 'world spirit' or 'phlogiston'.

The way out of this dilemma seems to be the more plausible consideration that the concept in question is not an object in the traditional sense, but, as Brian McHale pointed out some time ago,[1] a *construction*. One might add that this construction is symptomatic of the present situation of European and North-American societies.

It is symptomatic in the sense that advocates of a 'postmodern turn' such as Zygmunt Bauman in Britain, Gianni Vattimo in Italy and Wolfgang Welsch in Germany seem to believe – for quite different reasons – that the development of their respective societies has arrived at a significant turning point. Even sociologists like Anthony Giddens, Alain Touraine and Ulrich Beck, who do not consider themselves as postmodern, are inclined to believe that the social changes, which have been taking place since the Second World War, have yielded something qualitatively new.

Even an American Marxist like Fredric Jameson, who tends to take a critical view of postmodern trends, believes that in post-war North America and Western Europe global cultural transformations are taking shape which warrant the notion of 'postmodernism': 'The point is that we are *within* the culture of postmodernism to the point where its facile repudiation is as impossible as any equally facile celebration of it is complacent and corrupt.'[2] It ought to be added that both conservative and critical sociologists confirm this diagnosis on a different, more general level when they refer to the *postindustrial society* (Daniel Bell) or the *société postindustrielle* (Alain Touraine).

When, in a somewhat different context, Ulrich Beck opposes the new 'risk society' to the old 'industrial society',[3] while Zygmunt Bauman and Alain Touraine distance themselves (after Adorno and Horkheimer) from the rationalist Enlightenment tradition of modernity, it may well be asked whether the word 'postmodernity' (as opposed to 'modernity') does not signal real changes in society, politics, philosophy and art. Steven Best and Douglas Kellner refer to such changes in order to justify the notion of 'postmodernity': 'For us, the "postmodern" highlights what is singular and original in the contemporary era.'[4] In other words: the innovations and particularities of modern society distinguish it from (late) modern society.

Even if one starts from this very general idea of postmodernity, one may attempt to disentangle the problems caused by the coexistence of heterogeneous theories and definitions of the postmodern condition. The aim of such an attempt cannot be a final definition that puts an end to all discussions (a goal that is neither desirable nor possible to attain), but, more realistically, a clarification of the terminology involved. Clearer conceptual premises might provide a more reliable framework for future discussions.

For it can be quite frustrating, especially for those unfamiliar with the subject, when somebody like John O'Neill argues that 'nothing much is to be gained from definitions of postmodernism',[5] when a Marxist like Alex Callinicos insists on 'the intellectual inadequancy of postmodernism',[6] while the Croatian author Mladen Kozomara considers postmodernity as a 'pseudo-concept' and a 'misleading perspective'.[7] Such diagnoses are particularly irritating in view of the fact that philosophers and sociologists such as Zygmunt Bauman, Scott Lash or Wolfgang Welsch seem to take the existence of a postmodern society for granted, while Heinrich Klotz draws the conclusion: 'Although the concept of postmodernity has become a source of wrong ideas, we are unable, for the time being, to replace it by a better one.'[8]

Those who believe that a more concrete definition of postmodernity ought to be aimed at, will agree with Frank Fechner who sees modernity as part of the terminological problem: 'It is thus necessary to elucidate the concept of modernity underlying a particular discourse on postmodernity.'[9] This idea is the starting point for the following chapters, all of which are attempts to understand postmodernity in correlation with and in contrast to modernity.

## 1.1 Problems of Construction: Modernity and Postmodernity as Epochs, Ideologies, Styles and Problematics

One need not be an unconditional supporter of Radical Constructivism in order to realize that we can only perceive reality as our construct. Where the ecologist discovers a valuable biotope, the farmer may see a piece of useless land or even an obstacle to the optimal cultivation of the soil; where the Marxist–Leninist describes exploitation and class struggles, the liberal economist speaks of a competitive market society; where the admirer of classical music turns his back on dissonance and chaos, the modernist or postmodernist discovers innovative art.

Hence 'postmodernity' as such, as a 'thing in itself' in the sense of Kant, does not exist. Only competing constructions exist which may or may not be comparable. Brian McHale quite rightly reminds us of 'the discursive and constructed character of postmodernism',[10] comparing the latter with other theoretical (and at the same time ideological) constructs such as 'Renaissance', 'American literature' or 'Shakespeare'. For even the seemingly neutral object 'Shakespeare' is constructed very differently by a literary critic such as Northrop Frye and a Durkheimian sociologist in the sense of Jean Duvignaud.

This also applies to the concepts of 'modernity' and 'postmodernity', whose semantic content not only depends on chance and individual idiosyncrasies, but also on ideological engagement. It is hardly surprising that a conservative advocate of postmodernity like Peter Koslowski presents a construction which differs substantially from that of contemporary Marxists such as Callinicos and Jameson or from the one underlying this book in which the author develops Adorno's and Horkheimer's Critical Theory as a dialogical theory in the sense of Bakhtin.[11]

There is nothing to 'unmask' in this case, for it is perfectly legitimate to start from conservative, liberal, Marxist, feminist or critical premises in order to construct an object like 'postmodernity'. It seems essential, however, that theoretical discourse be open to empirical testing and that it should not preclude critical dialogue by relying on monologue (identification with the object), dualism (good vs. evil) and the elimination of self-reflection.[12] Such tendencies towards monologue and discursive closure often make themselves felt in conservative (Koslowski) and Marxist theories (Callinicos) – and especially in National-Socialist and Stalinist discourses whose object constructions can hardly be called 'theoretical'. As sources of cultural theories, ideologies are by no means equal or equally 'true', as some brands of relativism would have us believe.[13] However, a theory of culture or society cannot be refuted by arguments aiming at its conservative, liberal or Marxist origins.[14] This fact is amply illustrated by F. H. Tenbruck's moderately conservative approach which is enlightening in many respects and will be dealt with in the second chapter.

It is not surprising that, more often than not, notions such as 'modern' and 'postmodern' are considered as chronological constructions: as *periods* or *epochs*. For the prefix 'post' can only be taken to mean that we are dealing with a period of time which follows modernity and departs from the latter in spite of all continuities that may still exist. This is how Manfred Hennen views the matter when he argues that, in the case of modernity, one 'should distinguish an historical period from a global social diagnosis'.[15] However, it will become clear in the second chapter that all social diagnoses presuppose the existence of historical periods and a corresponding historical classification. Moreover, it is obvious that this kind of classification is not merely based on logical and semiotic criteria, but also on ideological ones (cf. Chapter 2). The intricate links and relations between periods such as *modern times, modernity, modernism* and *postmodernity* will be discussed in some detail in the next section.

At this stage, it seems important to consider the difference between epoch (period) and ideology because, in the debates concerning modernity and post-modernity, it is often unclear whether our interlocutors refer to ideologies as systems of values and ideas or to historical periods. When Habermas, in his frequently quoted article on 'Modernity – an unfinished project' (1980), identi-fies modernity with the Enlightenment and its heritage, thus ignoring modern counter-currents such as romanticism, he tends to use the concept of moder-nity as a metonymy. For he reduces a heterogeneous epoch stretching over centuries to one of its philosophies or ideologies (cf. Section 3.5).

In a similar fashion, but pursuing quite different political goals, Linda Hutcheon and Nicholas Zurbrugg oppose a popular and critical postmodernity to a conservative modernism (1850–1950). While Zurbrugg considers postmo-dernity as an aesthetic and refers to 'variants of postmodern aesthetics',[16] Hutcheon speaks of 'modernism's ideologically and aesthetically motivated rejection of the past'.[17] In both cases, modernism and postmodernism are constructed as relatively homogeneous ideologies – albeit with historical connotations.

A completely different stance is adopted by the French Marxist Henri Lefebvre who defines 'modernism' or 'modernity' (he uses both concepts) as a phase of social development inaugurated by the failed Russian revolution of 1905.[18] At this point, the conceptual intricacies appear: 'modernism' or 'modernity'?

While 'modernism' in the sense of 'late modernity' is identified by most authors with the expansion of modern literature and art since 1850 (Benjamin, Adorno) or since 1890 (Bradbury, McFarlane), Lefebvre has his 'modernism' begin half a century or a quarter of a century later: with the Russian revolution of 1905. This is somewhat unusual, especially since he does not really make his construction plausible.

Does literary modernity or modernism not begin with Baudelaire and the European revolutions of 1848? Or does it begin with the work of Nietzsche whose *Morgenröte* (1881) is as heavily symbolic as the revolution of 1905? Questions of this kind do reveal the difficulties inherent in all attempts to clarify the concepts involved, but are hardly conducive to concrete answers or results. For isolated dates or events do not provide a reliable base for con-structions such as 'modernity' or 'postmodernity'.

Attempts by literary critics to define these units predominantly or exclusively on a stylistic level are particularly vulnerable to criticism. A well-known attempt is Ihab Hassan's analysis of stylistic features in the most general sense of the word: *indeterminacy, fragmentation, dissolution of the canon, irony, carnivalization,* etc. are considered as salient features of postmodern literature. The informed reader, who is familiar with romantic irony, will be puzzled to come across it in Hassan's model of postmodernism, especially since irony is also one of the basic characteristics of modernism. Is fragmentation not one of the main features of Proust's and Musil's novels? Is carnivalization not omnipresent in the novels of Dostoevsky, Céline and Joyce?

Why is Hassan's analysis unconvincing? One reason is that Hassan tries to define postmodernity without (late) modernity, thus ignoring Frank Fechner's rule according to which modernity, modernism and postmodernity ought to be related to one another; the other reason is his focus on *stylistic analysis*. The latter tends to bracket out historical, social, political and philosophical developments whose dynamic interrelatedness accounts for literary evolution (cf. Section 4.1). This is why modernity and postmodernity will not be constructed here (in Section 1.3) purely chronologically as periods, as ideologies or stylistic systems, but as *problematics*: as *compounds of problems*.

## 1.2 Key Concepts: Modernity, Modernism, Postmodernity, Postmodernism, Posthistoire and Postindustrial Society

It hardly makes sense to enumerate all the meanings of these ambiguous and ill-defined concepts, thereby increasing the present confusion. In a first step, it seems useful to distinguish the concept of modernity from that of modernism, especially since 'modernity' is frequently used as a synonym of 'modernism' or of 'modern times'.

While many philosophers and sociologists (Bauman, Giddens, Habermas, Touraine) tend to treat 'modernity' and 'modern times' in the Enlightenment sense as synonyms, literary and art critics tend to identify 'modernity' with 'aesthetic modernism'. When the sociologist Zygmunt Bauman equates modernity with the age of reason, opposing it to postmodernity, he adopts the first point of view: 'All in all, postmodernity can be seen as restoring to the world what modernity, presumptuously, had taken away; as a *re-enchantment* of the world that modernity tried hard to *dis-enchant*.'[19] When David Harvey defines 'modernity' with Baudelaire as the 'transient' and 'fleeting' (i.e. the fashionable and ephemeral), he adopts the second, the aesthetic point of view: ' "Modernity", wrote Baudelaire in his seminal essay "The painter of modern life" (published in 1863), "is the transient, the fleeting, the contingent; it is the one half of art, the other being the eternal and the immutable".'[20]

Hence Baudelaire's Parisian modernity[21] does not refer to the expansion of reason from 1600 onwards, but to artistic and literary forms which developed in the second half of the nineteenth century and were considered by Walter Benjamin, especially in his works on Baudelaire, as examples of modern art. Adopting a somewhat schematic point of view, one could thus distinguish an historical or philosophical concept of modernity, which refers to the *age of reason* in the sense of 'modern times', from a predominantly aesthetic and stylistic concept that refers to *artistic forms in late modernity*, i.e. in the second half of the nineteenth century and beyond.

The identification of 'modernity' with 'modern times' has a long philosophical tradition which begins with the disintegration of Hegel's philosophical system in the critical philosophies of the Young Hegelians. In one of his attempts to complete and to save Hegel's system, one of Hegel's disciples, Friedrich Theodor Vischer (1807–1887), mentions the 'great crisis (. . .) which separates modern times from the middle ages'.[22] Departing from Hegel, who views the middle ages and modern times as a homogeneous Christian epoch, Vischer adopts a more advanced point of view and defines modernity (modern times: since about 1600) as an independent unit. This new philosophical definition, which upgrades the new era around 1850, is not due to chance, but to a changing conception of history brought about by the crises of the nineteenth century. This change of consciousness could be considered as *late modern* or *modernist*. It enables us to relate the concepts of *modernity* and *modernism* to one another: for in this context, *modernism or late modernity could be defined as an auto-criticism of modernity, of the spirit of modern times* (cf. below).

In British philosophy and sociology, the expression 'modern thought' is usually taken to be identical with 'thought in modern times'. In his well-known *History of Western Philosophy* (1946), Bertrand Russell refers to a 'modern philosophy' which, favoured by the rise of individualism and secularization, gradually supersedes medieval thought.[23] The sociologist Anthony Giddens is somewhat more concrete when he makes the beginning of modernity coincide with the seventeenth century ('from about the seventeenth century onwards')[24] when the works of Francis Bacon (1561–1626) and other Enlightenment thinkers begin to make an impact. The German sociologist Friedrich H. Tenbruck adopts a similar stance when he relates the secularization process to the 'scientific revolution of the seventeenth century'.[25]

How can modernity in the sense of 'modern times' and modernism be related to one another? As was already pointed out in conjunction with Vischer's constructive critique of Hegel, 'modernism' could be globally defined as *the self-reflexive and self-critical turn in modernity*. 'Modernism always also constituted, in a sense, a *critique* of modernity',[26] as Roy Boyne and Ali Rattansi explain in their introduction to *Postmodernism and Society*.

They are right in the sense that modernist philosophers and writers such as Nietzsche, Dostoevsky, Musil, Kafka and Pirandello cast doubts on the validity of some key concepts and ideas of modernity: e.g. on the notion of *truth*. Moreover, these authors begin to question the possibility of organizing society on the basis of Enlightenment rationalism and its unconditional trust in progress. Although they continue Nietzsche's and Kierkegaard's critique of religion in a new context, they also begin to doubt the established authority of science, thus anticipating the critique of science in postmodernity – for example in the works of Lyotard, Vattimo and Bauman. However, as a self-criticism of modernity, modernism (or late modernity) still *belongs to the modern period*, to the era known as 'modern times'.

In the Spanish-speaking world, the word 'modernism' evokes the Spanish-American concept of *modernismo*, an aesthetic and literary current whose most prominent representatives are Juan Ramón Jiménez in Spain (1881–1958), José Martí in Cuba (1867–1895) and Rubén Darío in Nicaragua (1867–1916). Contrary to a cherished belief according to which Hispanic *modernismo* has nothing to do with modernism in the European and North-American sense, with the modernism of T. S. Eliot, Faulkner, Musil or Gide, *modernismo* and *modernism* do overlap. For in many of Martí's and Darío's texts, the influence of European modernists such as Nietzsche, D'Annunzio or Puvis de Chavannes can be detected. It seems to confirm the hypothesis that *modernismo* is part and parcel of the Euro-American *modernist problematic.*[27]

This hypothesis re-appears in Gilbert Azam's book *El modernismo desde dentro*, where literary *modernismo* is related to the modernizing tendencies in Spanish and French Catholicism[28] as well as to the literature and philosophy of the *Generación del 98*. Azam speaks of the 'internal continuity that can be detected between the generation of 1898 and *modernismo*'.[29] Apart from the philosopher and writer Miguel de Unamuno (1864–1936), authors such as Azorín (José Martínez Ruiz: 1873–1939), Pío Baroja (1872–1956) and Antonio Machado (1875–1939) belong to this generation which never tired of emphasizing the European vocation of Spain. It can be called 'modernist' in a general sense because one of its starting points was the crisis of cultural values and that of the individual subject and because it had been strongly influenced by Nietzsche, Schopenhauer and Kierkegaard, as well as by European and Latin American modernists (Darío, Martí).

More intricate than the affinity between *modernism* and *modernismo* seems to be the relationship between *modernism* and the *avant-garde*. While some authors assume a coexistence of two unrelated or even incompatible artistic currents, others recognize in the European avant-garde movements harbingers of a postmodern constellation. Matei Calinescu is convinced that modernists like Proust, Kafka or Joyce have hardly anything in common with avant-garde movements such as Futurism, Dadaism or Surrealism.[30] Although he departs from this assessment, the sociologist Scott Lash also tends to regard modernism and the avant-garde as two *separate* entities and to define the avant-garde movements as postmodern because they destroy the auratic autonomy of artworks and address the masses rather than elites: 'I take the avant-garde of the 1920s to be postmodernist.'[31] If this assessment were correct, Brecht, Breton and Khlebnikov would have to be considered as postmodern . . .

There is no need, at this stage, to anticipate the fourth chapter and to comment on Lash's theses in detail; it seems more urgent to define the relationship between modernism and the avant-garde and to show that they should not simply be identified. In the fourth chapter, it will be suggested, however, *that the various avant-gardes can be understood as particular aspects of modernism*: partly because avant-garde techniques are to be found in certain modernist novels

and dramas, partly because the avant-gardes are rooted in the modernist problematic and hence share political, existential and aesthetic *problems* with the
great modernist works of art.

The perspective adopted by Lash implies that postmodernity in general can
be conceived as a new problematic which goes beyond modernity (as 'modern
times') and beyond modernism as a self-reflection and self-criticism of modernity. One could choose to speak of 'postmodernity' whenever the latter is
opposed to 'modernity as modern times' (in the philosophical and sociological
sense defined above) and of 'postmodernism' whenever the latter is opposed to
'modernism as self-criticism of modernity' (especially in the aesthetic or literary
sense).

A concrete example of the first opposition is to be found in *The Sociological
Imagination* (1959) by C. Wright Mills, probably the first sociologist to use the
word 'postmodern': 'We are at the ending of what is called The Modern Age.
(. . .) Now The Modern Age is being succeeded by a postmodern period.'[32]
The second opposition is commented on by Brian McHale: 'In *Postmodernist
Fiction*, I told a story about how, through a change in the structuring of texts,
the modernist poetics of fiction gave way to postmodernist poetics.'[33]

Although the concept of postmodernism as we know it today was first used
in the North-American *debates on literature which took place in 1959 and 1960*
(cf. Section 4.2), it did appear prior to these debates in contexts analysed by
Wolfgang Welsch. He quite rightly points out that the concept was not adopted
in architecture until 1975 and that, contrary to a wide-spread opinion, it does
*not* originate in this discipline.

Welsch found out that the English expression 'post-modern' was first used
around 1870 by the English drawing room painter John Watkins Chapman who
tried to go beyond French impressionism. A completely different meaning was
attributed to the polysemic signifier in 1917 by Rudolf Pannwitz (1881–1969), a
writer and philosopher, who saw man as a being capable of 'completing the
cosmos' and, following Nietzsche, demanded a postmodern effort to overcome
nihilism and decadence by 'superman'. Like Nietzsche, this philosopher envisaged a postmodern redemption from the shortcomings and confusions of
modernity. However, his concept of modernity does not refer to 'modern times',
but to the period of crises and of 'decadence' which begins roughly in 1850.[34]

In the present context, Welsch's hint at the pejorative *postmodernismo* concept
of the Spanish philologist Federico de Oníz is of some interest. By *postmodernismo* Oníz means the self-critical revision (1905–1914) 'which followed the
*modernismo* period (1896–1905) before the latter rejuvenated itself in the *ultra-
modernismo* (1914–1932)'.[35] A parallel development was detected in religion by
Gilbert Azam who investigates the numerous links between literary and religious *modernismo*.[36]

In the sociological and political context, it is worth having a closer look at the
way the historian and philosopher Arnold Joseph Toynbee (1889–1975) constructs postmodernity, because it continues to be relevant for contemporary

discussions. Toynbee starts from the premise that modern national thinking is
being superseded by supranational, global thought. Although this idea sounds
quite plausible because it does anticipate political and cultural developments
in the 20th and 21st centuries, it is also problematical because it does not
take into account counter-developments – e.g. tendencies towards regionalism,
new nationalism and religious fundamentalism. Trends towards globalization
in economics, ecology, politics and technology are certainly a topic within the
postmodern problematic, but the counter-tendencies towards social and cultural particularization, which are so prominent in postmodern philosophy,
seem to be as strong if not stronger.[37]

These extraordinarily heterogeneous uses of the adjective 'postmodern'
show to what extent a polysemic word can yield a vast array of constructions
which overlap, contradict each other or even turn out to be incommensurate.
Each theory, each ideology can get hold of the word in order to turn it into an
object of hope, admiration or hatred. As a social construct, theoretical discourse
cannot possibly avoid this kind of social and psychic impulse. However, the subject of theory[38] should see to it that the impulse is recognized as an historically
contingent force that should not be allowed to eclipse theoretical reflection –
and (self-)irony.

Theory as a self-reflexive, ironical discourse fails whenever a concept such as
modernity or postmodernity is simply discredited, loaded with pejorative connotations and turned into a caricature for ideological reasons. The German
philosopher Wolfgang Welsch is quite right in objecting to the caricature of
*postmodernity* as *posthistoire.* 'Postmodernity has nothing whatsoever to do with
the notion of *posthistoire* propagated by the sociologist Arnold Gehlen since the
fifties.'[39]

What exactly does Gehlen mean by *posthistoire?* In 1952 he revives this concept
introduced into the debates by the mathematician and philosopher Antoine
Cournot (1861) and the sociologist Célestin Bouglé (1901)[40] and argues, following the right-wing Hegelians and Nietzsche, that history has come to an end.
This idea should be considered against the backdrop of the global stalemate
within which the USA and the USSR seemed to condemn themselves and history to immobility: 'If we now return to the topic of the two hemispheres with
their basic ideologies, then it will hardly come as a surprise when I conclude
that there is nothing new to be expected in the history of ideas (. . .).' Several
lines further, he adds 'that the so-called developing countries will not find a
positive third ideology'. Thus history – or at least the history of ideas – has come
to an end:

> For global ideologies of this kind, including those which have become obso-
> lete, like fascism, or those which have never flourished, like Rousseau's or
> Nietzsche's doctrines of salvation, are exclusively European products, not to
> be found elsewhere. I therefore venture the prognosis that the history of
> ideas has ended and that we have arrived at posthistoire (. . .).[41]

In the present context, this conclusion, which reminds us of Daniel Bell's 'end of ideology',[42] has to be rejected as premature, especially since Bell had to revise his thesis. The post-war stalemate was broken up after the fall of the Berlin Wall in 1989, and the history of ideas was revived by the ideological use or abuse of Islam[43] in those developing countries which Gehlen relegates to the eternal periphery of history.

Nevertheless, Gehlen's speculative diagnosis, later adapted to postmodern times by Baudrillard (cf. Section 2.6), is by no means useless, because the atrophy of grand ideology (fascism, National Socialism, Marxism–Leninism) seems to be a widely perceived fact underlying Jean-François Lyotard's theory of the *postmodern condition*. After the collapse of fascism and the fading of Marxism–Leninism, whose decline seems to have discredited all secular doctrines of salvation, Lyotard defines the postmodern 'as incredulity toward metanarratives'.[44]

Lyotard's approach will be dealt with in detail in the third chapter; but it should be pointed out at this stage that the incredulity he proclaims comes quite close to Gehlen's assertion that the history of ideas has come to an end and to the early Bell's thesis about the 'end of ideology'. (Although Gehlen does speak of the 'end of the history of ideas', he also mentions the 'end of history' – which is obviously not the same thing. In this respect, his theory is ambiguous).[45]

Although *postmodernity* and *posthistoire* should not be treated as synonyms (in this respect, Welsch is right), Welsch's assertion that the two concepts have nothing to do with one another can hardly be justified because it obliterates their *affinity*. What does this affinity consist in? In the incredulity towards 'grand ideologies' which both concepts articulate and which – long before Lyotard – sociologists like Gehlen and Bell detected in society.

Much later, the somewhat conservative sociologist Friedrich H. Tenbruck, who does not use the concepts 'postmodernity' and 'posthistoire', confirms their diagnosis. In an article published in 1976 (i.e. 3 years before Lyotard's *La Condition postmoderne*), he writes about social science: 'The grand ideas, which it used for writing the historical credo of modernity, are exhausted.'[46] In contrast to the early Bell and Lyotard, he does not proclaim the end of all ideologies or metanarratives, but believes that an ideological renaissance is possible, accompanied by an exhaustion of cultural energies in market society. Science had to revoke its messianic promises, but: 'The revocation of these promises does not only clear the terrain for fanatical and destructive counter-movements; it might also lead to an atrophy of energies, of imagination, of resolution and discipline all of which are part of our culture.'[47]

This loss of cultural energies is also considered as a danger by Daniel Bell who, along with Alain Touraine, coined the expression *postindustrial society*. In view of the fact that this concept will be commented on in some detail in the second chapter, only its relevance to the postmodernity-discussion will be explained here. In Bell's work, it refers to certain scientific and technological developments which lead to structural changes in the production process. One of these changes is the decreasing importance of the production of goods and the concomitant increase in services (e.g. in health, education and leisure). Another – related – change is the growing importance of professional groups (technicians, teachers, trainers) and the concomitant decline of the working class. In a global perspective, science and technology (and not industry) appear as the driving forces of contemporary economic and social change which becomes increasingly dependent on 'intellectual' technologies such as computer science.

These developments end up by undermining the capitalist ethic defined by Max Weber primarily as an ascetic orientation towards productivity and profit. In postindustrial society, Bell believes, this orientation is gradually superseded by a leisure-oriented hedonism that is incompatible with the capitalist production ethos. This kind of hedonism favours an individualization and atomization of society and an orientation of individuals towards consumption and pleasure (cf. Section 2.3).

In this particular context, Bell describes postmodern society as a society in which narcissistic individuals are mainly driven by the desire for self-fulfilment and in which social values, moral convictions and ideological or religious utopias become increasingly marginal. Again, postmodernity appears as marked by the crisis of the modern industrial system of values and by the necessity to initiate a general reappraisal of this system. It becomes increasingly reflexive, calling not only modernity as 'modern times', but also late modernity as modernism into question. As postmodernity *and* postmodernism, it is marked by the consciousness of an historical transition which will be reconstructed in the following section.

## 1.3 Modernity, Modernism and Postmodernity as Problematics

It stands to reason that a chronological or historical dimension of modernity and postmodernity exists and that it cannot be ignored simply because Lyotard points out on several occasions that postmodernity is not a new epoch.[48] For in history and sociology these concepts refer to social and cultural *developments, transitions* and *transformations*. In spite of this, it seems dicey to consider postmodernity as a completely new era which supersedes late modernity or modernism (treated here as synonyms). Even in present-day society, pre-modern, modern, modernist and postmodern phenomena coexist in politics, science and art, and it would be nonsensical to argue that all traces of the modern and late modern past have been eradicated after 1950 or 1960.

Considering the coexistence of past and present cultural phenomena, postmodernity can be constructed both as an innovative continuation of modernity and as a break with the latter. Dietmar Kamper, who argues along these lines, speaks of a unity of opposites: 'Hence the two contrasting theses are both valid: postmodernity is a radicalized modernity which remains faithful to itself, and postmodernity betrays the essence of modernity.'[49] This idea of a dialectical unity of opposites implies a rejection of ideological dualism: it is crucial to avoid considering postmodernity as *either* a betrayal of modernity (as Habermas or Eagleton do) *or* as a pluralist re-enactment of it (as Welsch does). For this kind of ideological dualism usually leads to a confrontation of mythical instances or 'actants',[50] one of which represents 'evil' while the other represents all that is 'good'.

This mythical opposition comes about when Stephen Crook associates 'postmodernism's radical pretensions'[51] with nihilism, using global expressions such as 'postmodernism attempts',[52] 'postmodernism regards',[53] 'postmodernism requires'[54] and 'modernism requires',[55] which turn the two concepts or constructions into 'villain' and 'hero'. They come to represent hostile ideologies whose uncompromising quest for truth is somewhat naïvely narrated by Linda Hutcheon, who refers to 'the obscurity and hermeticism of modernism',[56] and concludes that 'postmodernism challenges some aspects of modernist dogma'.[57] Within this dualist scheme based mainly on T. S. Eliot's modernist work, she identifies literary modernism with a hermetic style and an elitist attitude – as if Auden, Joyce, Brecht, Malraux, Hesse, Heinrich Mann, Camus and many others had never existed. (The second half of Joyce's *Ulysses* is considered to be postmodern by authors such as Brian McHale and Willy Erzgräber.)[58]

However, modernity and postmodernity, modernism and postmodernism can hardly be understood as ideologies, philosophies, rival aesthetics or stylistics. To the observer, who has a sense of complexity, they appear as *problematics*: as *social and linguistic situations* within which conflicting answers to certain questions or incompatible solutions to certain problems are proposed. *The homogeneity of the problematic consists in the affinity of its problems and questions, its heterogeneity in its divergent answers and solutions.* Questions, which, in a particular historical constellation, seemed relevant and meaningful and were situated at the centre of the problematic, are relegated to the periphery of intellectual life in a new problematic – or forgotten altogether.

Thus the question concerning the identity, the freedom and the responsibility of the individual subject, a question situated at the centre of existentialist debates during the interwar period, seems hardly relevant anymore. It is disregarded or explicitly dismissed by the postmodern Nouveau Roman. The related Marxist question regarding the relationship between revolutionary tactics and ethics, which George Lukács was so concerned about, is hardly talked about these days.[59] Critical intellectuals, heirs to the 1968 movement,[60] may still remember with nostalgia or melancholy the question of the late Sixties: 'How many working class children are there at this university?' The *new question* concerns the number of women at all levels of the institution.

In this case, the rise of new professional groups and elites[61] and the actions of social movements (e.g. women's movements) are responsible for the shifts in the old problematic and for its gradual transformation into something new. In the course of this transformation, which, far from being a mutation, is a gradual, almost imperceptible process, new questions appear and require new answers. While late modernity or modernism inherited the question of subjectivity and identity from romanticism and realism (from Shelley, George Eliot, Balzac), this question becomes marginal in postmodernism and is often superseded by the question concerning reality as environment.

Question and answer cannot be concretely understood as long as they are not related to particular *group languages* (*sociolects*)[62] within a particular *social and linguistic situation*. While the modernist question concerning the political engagement of intellectuals cannot be understood independently from existentialist and Marxist sociolects and discourses of the interwar period, postmodern questions concerning the global risks society is exposed to[63] or male domination in language are more closely related to pacifist, ecological and feminist groupings. It goes without saying that such groupings are less concerned with the religious, political or aesthetic preoccupations of male individuals ('dead white men') such as Kierkegaard, Unamuno, Proust or Kafka. Their thinking evolves in a different problematic whose problems are not only due to shifts in social structures and power relations, but also to new developments in economics, technology and science.

It need hardly be emphasized that the construction of modernity, modernism and postmodernity is part and parcel of this problematic and at the same time an attempt to answer some of its most pressing questions. In other words, it belongs to the social and linguistic reality it is meant to explain. Conscientious sceptics, who advise us to postpone a possibly premature answer, because they believe that a greater historical distance is needed for a clear assessment of the present situation, may find that the (re-)construction of a distant past is not any easier. In the 1970s, the literary critic Ulrich Weisstein rejects Paul Van Tieghem's attempt to locate Villon and Rabelais in the middle ages and to consider Montaigne and the Pléiade poets (Ronsard, Du Bellay) as Renaissance writers – thus limiting the Renaissance to a period of merely 40 years. According to Weisstein's own construction, it extends over 300 years: from the fourteenth to the sixteenth century.[64]

The hermeneutic idea that the problematics mentioned here can only be (re-)constructed within the contemporary social and linguistic situation leads to the question regarding the position of the subject of discourse: of the author responsible for the construction. Although he starts from Adorno's and Horkheimer's post-war Critical Theory, which is firmly rooted in *late modernity* or *modernism*, i.e. in a critical self-reflection of modernity, he envisages a socio-semiotic and dialogical re-definition of this theory in view of the postmodern constellation (cf. Chapters 2 and 6).

It is not by chance that, in the course of the discussions, postmodern perspectives were discovered in the works of Walter Benjamin and Theodor W. Adorno.[65] In the USA, Steven Best and Douglas Kellner even refer to 'Adorno's

proto-postmodern theory'.[66] Although Adorno's thought cannot possibly be
called postmodern (and this is not what Best and Kellner are trying to do), the
postmodern aspects of post-war Critical Theory should not be overlooked: they
account for the affinities between this theory and the postmodern problematic
as a whole. Once these affinities have been acknowledged, it becomes more difficult to construct a Manichean opposition between the late modern problems
tackled by Adorno or Horkheimer and those of postmodernity.

How can modernity, modernism and postmodernity be constructed as cultural problematics? First of all, it should be remembered that modernity,
defined as 'modern times', and postmodernity (beginning after the Second
World War, roughly in 1950) are almost incommensurate historical units. For
modernity, which is frequently identified by philosophers and sociologists with
the age of reason, i.e. with a period stretching over almost three centuries (from
1600 to 1850), is too long and too heterogeneous to be compared with postmodernity, a period of 50 or 60 years. This is the main reason why in this book –
especially in Chapters 4 and 5 – mainly *modernism as late modernity* (1850–1950)
is compared and contrasted with the *postmodern problematic*.

However, in the next two chapters, modernity as 'modern times' and Enlightenment will also be considered because authors such as Bauman, Touraine and
Giddens, Lyotard and Habermas use the word in this particular sense – and
because it is not easy to avoid the impact of accumulated knowledge. What is at
stake here, is not only a dubious construction (almost three centuries on one
side, half a century on the other), but also the plausible thesis according to
which the postmodern problematic breaks with the entire modern tradition –
from Francis Bacon to the *Dialectic of Reason* (1947), whose authors tried to save
what was left of modern rationality after the war.

In the realm of cultural values, which are at the same time linguistic values
(meanings of words), modernity, modernism and postmodernity appear as
constellations[67] that are structured by three central social, psychic and aesthetic
problems to which all political, psychological, philosophical and aesthetic questions and answers can be related: *ambiguity, ambivalence* and *indifference*. This
somewhat compact summary has the following implications: philosophy and
literature of the 18th and the early 19th centuries are characterized by an ambiguity that can be dissolved by the theory of knowledge, by philosophical psychology or the narrator's explanations. In most cases, such theoretical or literary
explanations restore the contrast between essence and appearance, truth and
lie, good and evil, etc. Thus reality appears as comprehensible, as transparent –
in spite of all the difficulties subjects have to overcome. In literature, writers
such as Jane Austen, Balzac, Pérez Galdós and Gottfried Keller describe this
process in the course of which appearances are dissolved, masks fall and the
true character comes to the fore (cf. Chapters 4 and 5).

Their divergent conceptions of realism are synthesized in Hegel's aesthetic,
where art fulfils the function of dissolving appearances and of overcoming
ambiguities or contradictions in the sensual representation of truth. Far from

being a distorted reflection of reality, art appears to Hegel as superior, i.e. more realistic and more informative than the reality of everyday life itself, the truth of which is frequently masked by ambiguities and misleading, fleeting phenomena.[68] Hegel's system is possibly the last philosophy inspired by the idea of Reason's superiority[69] and by the complementary modern idea that all entropies, disorders and irrational impulses can be integrated into a coherent grand design. Hegel's 'unity of opposites' can also be conceived as an overcoming of ambiguity in the syntheses of higher knowledge.

In modernism (late modernity), this epistemological optimism turns out to be an illusion, and the crisis of literary realism, accompanied by the disintegration of the Hegelian system in the theories of the Young Hegelians, announces an era of *ambivalence* marked by a *unity of opposites that resists all attempts at synthesis*. Good and evil, truth and lie, essence and appearance are inextricably related so that it becomes impossible to discover essence behind appearance and to overcome ambivalence.

The thinker of ambivalence, the modernist challenger of Hegel is – along with Dostoevsky – Friedrich Nietzsche whose prominent role in the works of D. H. Lawrence, Italo Svevo, Robert Musil, André Gide and Hermann Hesse is a sign of the times and a symptom of fundamental typological affinities.[70] '*A general insight: the ambiguous* character of our *modern world*',[71] remarks Nietzsche in one of his posthumously published writings. Nietzsche's philosophy and Kafka's novels depart radically from rationalism and Hegelianism by insisting on the impossibility of dissolving appearances and by calling into question the concepts of truth and essence. Unlike Hegel, who expects art to make philosophical truth accessible to the senses, Nietzsche defines art as 'the *good* will to appearance',[72] thus turning his back on the metaphysics of essence.

Moreover, he anticipates the postmodern problematic by considering the possibility that ambivalence as unity of incompatible values, such as good and evil, truth and lie, eventually leads to *indifference*, defined as interchangeability of values.

> It might even be possible that *what* constitutes the value of those good and honoured things resides precisely in their being artfully related, knotted and crocheted to these wicked, apparently antithetical things, perhaps even in their being essentially identical with them.[73]

If, however, we are led to believe that those 'apparently antithetical things' do not even exist, because 'in reality' they are identical with their opposites, then an *era of indifference* begins: good and evil, truth and lie, love and hatred tend to become indistinguishable.

The theory of value developed by the young Marx completes and clarifies Nietzsche's critique of metaphysical value and truth in many respects. For Marx also anticipates the *interchangeability of values* or *indifference* when he writes about money that it converts and transforms everything and that it is the 'general *confusion* and *conversion* of all things' ('die allgemeine *Verwechslung* und *Vertauschung* aller Dinge'): 'Whoever can buy courage is courageous, even if he is a coward. (. . .) It [money] is the reconciliation of incompatibilities, it forces contradictions into an embrace.'[74]

It is in conjunction with these complementary arguments put forward by Marx and Nietzsche that the *transition from late modernity to postmodernity and from ambivalence to indifference* is considered here – parallel to the transition from ambiguity to ambivalence – in relation to the intensified mediation by the exchange value, to the concomitant social differentiation and the ideological fragmentation of society. Postmodern currents in philosophy and literature confirm Marx's and Nietzsche's fundamental idea that, in a society governed by the economic principle, there is no cultural (political, moral or aesthetic) value that could successfully and durably challenge the *indifference of the exchange value.*

Hence postmodernity, as analysed in the chapters to come, is the *era of indifference:* of exchangeable individuals, relations, values and ideologies. This should not be taken to mean that in postmodern market society no religious, moral or aesthetic values exist; it does mean that those who act in their name do so in the face of the dominant exchange value whose influence increases from decade to decade.

If one adopts this theoretical perspective, one should not lose sight of the central nexus between indifference (interchangeability), pluralism, particularization and the ideological reactions to indifference and pluralism. Where moral, aesthetic and political values (and entire ideologies such as the fascist or communist ones) appear as contingent, interchangeable entities, their implicit or explicit claim to universal validity is disputed. There is no specifically Christian, liberal, socialist or nationalist value judgement that could claim universal acceptance within a particular society. *The tendency towards particularization and the complementary trend towards political and cultural pluralism thus become the salient features of a postmodern problematic based on indifference.* However, violent ideological ('fundamentalist') reactions are always possible within this indifferent and pluralist complex (cf. sections 2.5 and 2.6).

In order to avoid a mimetic misunderstanding which might confuse the construction of the postmodern problematic proposed here with reality, it seems appropriate to conclude this chapter with a critical reflection on the construction process. To begin with, it should be pointed out that the construction – from ambiguity to ambivalence, from ambivalence to indifference – is based on relevance criteria and classifications, most of which are derived from the value problematic: the religious dualism of the feudal era (*faith/heresy*)[75] is followed by the structural ambiguity of individualist market society, the latter is radicalized in the late modern era of ambivalence which is eventually superseded by postmodern indifference (as interchangeability of values: not as affective indifference of individual subjects). One should also bear in mind the narrative structure of this construction which comes about on at least three complementary levels. The development 'from modernity to late modernity, to postmodernity' runs parallel to the development (i.e. narrative structure) 'from ambiguity to ambivalence and indifference' – and the latter is closely related to the evolution of capitalist and late capitalist society.

Whoever proclaims, as Lyotard does, that our era is marked by a general 'incredulity toward metanarratives'[76] and agrees with Robert Musil that we 'don't want to listen to narrations anymore'[77] will also tend to consider the author's narration with a certain scepticism. The author will be sympathetic: for his ambition is not to persuade and to proselytize in the ideological sense, i.e. to identify his discourse with reality, but to have his constructions tested in an open dialogue (cf. Chapter 6). Moreover, sceptics ought to consider the fact that even Lyotard narrates, within an impressive metanarrative, how to relate modernity and postmodernity to one another, and that even Musil narrates why narration is no longer possible. The point is not to deny or gloss over the narrative structure of theoretical discourse, a structure thoroughly analysed by Greimas and other semioticians, but to consider the narrative character of cultural theory in a constructivist and dialogical perspective.

# Chapter 2

# Modernity and Postmodernity in a Sociological Perspective

Founded as an autonomous discipline in the second half of the nineteenth century by Emile Durkheim, Vilfredo Pareto, Max Weber, Ferdinand Tönnies, Georg Simmel and others, European sociology is a science marked by crises that induce modern thought to adopt a reflexive, self-critical stance. Like some writers of the incipient twentieth century, who are generally being considered as *modernist* (i.e. *late modern*), like Proust, Gide, Kafka, Svevo or Musil, the founders of sociology reacted to the crisis of cultural values in an advanced market society. Although they adopted – very much like the writers – different and often contrasting points of view, their diagnoses tended to overlap. They continue to be debated by contemporary sociologists such as Anthony Giddens and Alain Touraine in Europe, Daniel Bell and Amitai Etzioni in the USA.

1. They all seem to start from the hypothesis that a permanent tension exists between the cultural (religious, ethical, aesthetic) values of modern societies and the market-oriented processes of rationalization which have a growing impact on individual thoughts and actions.
2. This idea is completed by the assumption that the systematic and technocratic character of progressive rationalization could result in a paralysing 'steel armour', as M. Weber put it, and seriously hamper individual and collective initiatives.
3. At the same time, the mediation by the exchange value, so vividly described by the young Marx, casts doubts on all cultural values in late capitalism and leads to a situation where *value-oriented* (*wertrational*) action is gradually replaced by *goal-oriented* (*zweckrational*) action[1] in the Weberian sense.
4. This development tends to weaken the kind of collective consciousness analysed by Durkheim and his followers (Mauss, Fauconnet) in conjunction with the social division of labour and to engender a narcissistic individualism commented on by Bell, Giddens, Etzioni and others.

In the introduction to this chapter, it is of course impossible to deal in detail with such fundamental social issues which could become the object of a theoretical work on modern sociology.[2] Here, it seems more important to describe

their impact on the reflexive turn of modernity in order to understand contemporary critiques of modernity as continuations of the sociological critiques
around 1900.

The first point mentioned above was thoroughly commented on by Max
Weber in many of his writings, where he shows to what extent Protestantism,
considered as an inner-worldly asceticism geared towards material success, contributes to the rise of capitalist rationality and to the secularization of religion:
'Life-orientations are no longer related to persons, but to "material", rational
goals; charity itself [is turned] into a materially conceived nursing organization
designed to enhance the glory of God.'[3] Objectification and rationalization in
the sense of goal-oriented rational action are thus considered in Weber's work
as essential aspects of European and North-American modernity.

Not only his postmodern heirs, but Weber himself was conscious of the fact
that secularization, rationalization and goal-orientation tend to free individuals
from religious and traditional bonds and at the same time impose new constraints upon them which are not easily shed. When Georg Weipert points out,
during the 15th Congress of German Sociologists, that according to Weber 'the
rationalized bureaucracy is not only a nightmare, but also a genuine political
menace',[4] he reveals the self-critical impulse of modernity in its late-modern
phase – an impulse that gains momentum in the postmodern constellation.
The irrational aspect of this impulse is revealed whenever Weber presents the
charismatic leader as an antidote to the inertia of bureaucracy. It is an antidote
which reminds the literary reader of Musil's 'utopia of the other state' and of
the fact that, within the modernist problematic, rationalization and irrationalism are twin phenomena – both in sociology and in literature.

Nowhere is the Weberian self-criticism of modernity as conspicuous as in the
discussion about 'Max Weber and the Project of Modernity' which took place in
1987 between Dieter Henrich, Claus Offe and Wolfgang Schluchter. While
Henrich reminds us of the fact that, according to Weber, 'Enlightenment can
only be continued as long as it renounces its high hopes,'[5] Schluchter insists
on Weber's critique of the notion of progress: 'In this perspective, the notion of
progress, which Weber so meticulously analysed in various parts of his work,
becomes quite ambivalent.'[6] Like in Thomas Mann's *Doctor Faustus*, it becomes
ambivalent because progress as rationalization and domination over nature
implies the risk of a relapse into barbarism.

The fact that rationalization and technical progress are linked – for better or
for worse – to market laws that tend to erode the cultural foundations of society,
is time and again emphasized by Alfred Weber. Long before Bell and Etzioni,
he seeks to defend cultural values against the utilitarianism of technical civilization: 'But only at a point (. . .) when life is freed from all necessities and utilities
and is thus enabled to rise above them, *do we have culture.*'[7] This plea in favour
of culture and value-oriented action, that could hardly be encountered in
Max Weber's work, is typical of a situation where the orientation towards
market laws and the exchange value is no longer considered as progress by all

observers, but diagnosed as a fatal trend by an increasing number of critical spirits.

Some remarks by Werner J. Cahnmann concerning the North-American reception of Ferdinand Tönnies's work are particularly characteristic of this self-critical analysis of modernity as Enlightenment and progress:

> One should add that the 'secular' society's centre turns out to be the market, where people meet 'not because they are similar, but because they are different'. The central value of the market is efficiency in view of the expected success and not respect and a deferential attitude towards tradition.[8]

This detachment of the individual from tradition described by Tönnies and his followers is reminiscent of Durkheim's key arguments in his work on *The Division of Labour in Society*, where *organic solidarity*, engendered by the division of labour, is made responsible for the various forms of anomie, but at the same time considered as a prerequisite of individual freedom. In societies marked by a *mechanical solidarity* that strongly resembles Tönnies's *community* or *Gemeinschaft*, individuals may find affective security among their kind. In this case, however, 'our individuality is nil',[9] as Durkheim aptly points out. For mechanical solidarity is marked by resemblance or even uniformity, whereas organic or functional solidarity is based on interdependence, differentiation and hence *individualization*.

Although Durkheim refuses to take sides in this conflict between a pre-modern mechanic and a modern organic solidarity, he does favour a democratic form of socialism and the foundation of professional associations capable of consolidating collective consciousness and its values and of checking the rise of radical individualism in market society. (In recent years, Niklas Luhmann developed Durkheim's idea of social differentiation, i.e. the systemic division of labour, when he defined postmodernity as a type of society consisting of autonomous and competing systems and world views.)[10]

The ambivalent character of the late modern problematic can be observed in most writings of modern sociologists. It consists in the fact that the founders of sociology refuse to adopt a dualistic stance when it comes to deciding in favour or against secularization, progress, the market or the concomitant process of individualization. Most of them try to relate the benefits of this development to its tragedies.

This also applies to Georg Simmel: on the one hand, he describes the destructive effects of mediation by the exchange value, on the other hand, he emphasizes the fact that individuals owe to the market their freedom, their emancipation from traditions, rituals and dogmas. He never overlooks the destructive force of money:

> By eliminating all distinctions between things, by translating all the qualitative differences that separate them into quantitative differences, by imposing itself, its colourlessness and its indifference and by becoming the common

denominator of all values, it appears as the most terrible leveller: it deprives things of their particularity, their specific value, their incomparable character.[11]

But at the same time, he emphasizes, in his *Philosophie des Geldes* (1900), the 'importance of monetary economy for individual freedom'.[12]

Social ambivalence, and possibly the tragedy of modernity, seem to be due to the fact that market laws, technical progress and general rationalization both favour and endanger the development of democracy, welfare and individual freedom. In the following sections, it will be shown what this tension between emancipation and domination, progress and catastrophe amounts to in contemporary sociological theories, some of which adopt and develop the concept of postmodernity (Bauman, Etzioni), while others criticize or reject it. However, they all continue the *reflexive process of late modernity* which was triggered off by the critiques of 'classical' sociology: by Marx, Durkheim, Max Weber and Simmel.

## 2.1 Critiques of Modernity: Universalism, Particularization and Social Movements

Ambivalence in the sense of late modern sociology is also a salient feature of Max Horkheimer's and Theodor W. Adorno's *Dialectic of Enlightenment* (1947, Engl. 1973) which is the starting point of this and the following chapter. On the one hand, the authors recognize the emancipating effects of enlightened thought, but show, on the other hand, to what extent the principle of domination is inherent in all brands of enlightened rationalism – even in the most recent ones. Their critical project does not oppose the Enlightenment tradition, but pleads in favour of an innovative reform: 'The accompanying critique of enlightenment is intended to prepare the way for a positive notion of enlightenment which will release it from entanglement in blind domination.'[13] The aim underlying this approach is a thought delivered from the rationalist and positivist principle of domination over nature. The authors envisage a way of thinking that also resists mediation by the exchange value which admits individuals and things only as objects of manipulation. Time and again, the notion of ambivalence underlying late modern sociology comes to the fore in Horkheimer's and Adorno's analyses. Modernity is both, liberation and servitude:

> The blessing that the market does not enquire after one's birth is paid for by the barterer, in that he models the potentialities that are his by birth on the production of the commodities that can be bought in the market.[14]

The decline of the individual subject, alluded to in this passage and related by Adorno and Horkheimer to the rise of monopoly capitalism and the parallel growth of bureaucratic trade unions, is an aspect of the domination over nature.

'Subject and object are both rendered ineffectual,'[15] the authors of the *Dialectic of Enlightenment* point out. They are reduced to 'nothingness' (the key word in the original is: *nichtig*), because the subject's domination over nature and its objects eventually reduces the subject to a self-controlling and self-negating mechanism. The principle of domination over individuals is inherent in enlightened rationalism: 'Enlightenment behaves toward things as a dictator toward men. He knows them in so far as he can manipulate them.'[16] Similarly, the positivist scientist is only interested in objects in so far as he can manipulate them instead of understanding them for their own sake.

But what exactly is the 'positive concept of enlightenment' Adorno and Horkheimer have in mind? They propose a theory that starts from the critical premises of Enlightenment philosophy, but at the same time heeds Schelling's dictum about art as 'the prototype of science'.[17] The latter ought to incorporate the mimetic moments of art when approaching its objects. '*Ratio* without mimesis is self-negating,'[18] Adorno remarks roughly two decades after the *Dialectic of Enlightenment*, in his posthumously published *Aesthetic Theory* – which is also inspired by Walter Benjamin's notion of mimesis.[19]

In the third chapter, it will become clear that Jürgen Habermas does not accept this self-critical continuation of Enlightenment thought, a continuation geared towards artistic mimesis, because he believes that it is too particularistic and too hostile towards the social sciences. He is not the only one to voice this kind of criticism, for it is true that Adorno's post-war orientation towards essayism, parataxis and mimesis amounts to a break with the theories and methods of the social sciences.[20]

However, Habermas's critique did not discourage other philosophers and sociologists from resuming and radicalizing some of the key arguments of the *Dialectic of Enlightenment*. Thus Alain Touraine's *Critique de la modernité* uses Adorno's and Horkheimer's early work as a starting point and keeps returning to it – albeit critically. In some respects, Touraine confirms Ulrich Beck's theory of a society marked by global risks: a theory which evokes the possibility of a domination-free modernity. But it is feminism in its many forms that gave the particularizing tendency of the *Dialectic of Enlightenment* its most radical turn, thus calling into question the very possibility of a critical theory which, as Habermas knew, cannot do without concepts. Taking a global view, one may conclude that Adorno's and Horkheimer's critique of Enlightenment thought is the starting point of the theories commented on below.

It is not by chance that the sociologist and philosopher Zygmunt Bauman, who will play an important part in the ethical debates dealt with in the next chapter, agrees with Adorno's and Horkheimer's critical theories, while rejecting Habermas. 'I don't like Habermas, however',[21] he explains in an interview. Why not? Because Habermas, as will be shown later on, strongly disagrees with the penchant for particularization underlying the *Dialectic of Enlightenment* (thus provoking feminist criticism), while Bauman espouses and radicalizes this penchant by working out a particularistic sociology and a corresponding ethic.

His critique of modernity tends to confirm Adorno's and Horkheimer's rejection of a rationalism based on the domination over nature and to reinforce their polemic against 'the subjection of all reality to logical formalism'[22] and to the abstraction of numbers mediated by the exchange value. Bauman considers conceptual universalism and universal domination as two sides of a coin or two aspects of a problem that can only be solved by postmodern particularization:

> I take here the concept of 'modernity' to stand for a perception of the world, rather than (as it has been misleadingly intimated) the world itself; a perception locally grounded in a way that implied its universality and concealed its particularism.[23]

This anti-universalistic critique of modernity (as Enlightenment) is not only to be related to Bauman's postmodern reading of the *Dialectic of Enlightenment*, but also to his consternation in view of the barbaric anti-Semitism that swept across Europe during the Second World War. For Bauman, the modern Jew is the non-conformist par excellence, the different one who is made to adapt by dominant thought in its rationalist, universalist or totalitarian form. This repressive adaptation corresponds to a modern urge to overcome ambivalence in order to restore universal transparency and identity. Bauman goes one step further – and probably too far – by making modern universalism and rationalism responsible for the atrocities of National Socialism and Stalinism – without considering the fact that German National Socialism can and should also be viewed as an historical reaction to Enlightenment values, to the values of Lessing, Börne and the young Marx.

It is not surprising, in this context, that he keeps pleading in favour of the particular and the singular and in favour of a radical, irreducible cultural pluralism whose conceptual integration he rejects. All measures aiming at universalization, for example the attempt to present certain values or concepts as being universally valid, is viewed by him as a symptom of domination or the kind of hierarchical thought he combats. If taken seriously, Bauman argues, the expression 'postmodern culture' is an oxymoron, a contradictory unit, because the postmodern world is marked by a radical, irreducible plurality, whereas the notion of culture implies hierarchy and a tendency towards unification.

Postmodern society appears to him and to the German philosopher Wolfgang Welsch (cf. Section 2.5) as 'incurably pluralistic',[24] as 'composed of an indefinite number of meaning-generating agencies'[25] and 'a plethora of multiple realities and universes of meaning'.[26] One can hardly go further in the direction of particularization and pluralism. European or 'Western' culture, Bauman argues, can only be saved if it admits its geographic and historical particularity – one could also say: its contingent character.

Bauman's approach becomes one-sided when the postmodernist praises the market economy for promoting variety and individuality. 'Contrary to the anguished forebodings of the "mass culture" critics of the 1950s, the market proved to be the arch-enemy of uniformity,' he points out and adds: 'The market thrives on variety (. . .).'[27] It may be true that, unlike the planned economy of the Soviet type, market society produces a vast array of ever-changing products, including cultural ones. However, Pasolini formulated the antithesis to Bauman's thesis long before the sociologist began to show interest in postmodernity: relying heavily on commercialized media, on the formation of trusts and 'chains' (hotel chains, supermarket chains, restaurant chains, etc.), the market also tends to delete cultural, national and regional differences, turning individuals into jeans, Coca Cola and hamburger consumers and into living adverts for particular 'brands'.[28] Bauman, the thinker of ambivalence,[29] thus neglects the ambivalence of the market and the dialectic between the general and the particular in a market society which frees individuals from traditional bonds in order to impose an almost totalitarian control upon them as consumers.

As Adorno and Horkheimer already pointed out, early market society favours the autonomy of the individual and of art, whereas late capitalist society accelerates the atomization of individuals by dissolving class and group solidarities and by obliterating regional differences. The market thus abolishes what it previously encouraged: the uniqueness of the individual by a commercialized and unifying social communication (especially in the media) and the autonomy of art by its commodification in the culture industry.

Bauman seems to ignore this dialectic of the market when he insists on the variety generated by market society, but at the same time deplores – in a separate train of thought – the dependence of individuals on the market and the destruction by market laws of their technical, social, psychic and existential 'skills'. In this context, he foresees that Habermas's question concerning political legitimacy might be drowned in indifference or a 'lack of interest'.[30]

The underlying problem seems to be due to the fact that both, extreme particularization (radical pluralism) and extreme universalization (rationalist unification), can result in indifference defined as *interchangeability of positions and values*. In a social situation in which every single group clings to cultural values, whose claim to universal validity is rejected by a majority, all values and truths tend to become interchangeable, *indifferent*. In view of this fact, Bauman gives up the 'project of truth'[31] which only makes sense as long as truth is recognized as universally valid. In postmodern pluralism, whose advocates deny the existence of universal truth, values such as 'freedom', 'justice', 'equality', 'democracy' or 'science' appear as meaningless as soon as they are detached from specific and contradictory meanings conferred upon them by particular cultures, subcultures and groups.

The only way out of this dilemma seems to be a rejection of the false alternative 'universalism or particularism' and a return to the post-Hegelian dialectic between the universal and the particular. In this case, what matters is not an attempt to impose democracy and freedom in an abstract and universalistic manner, but the question what concrete meanings such concepts can assume in a particular historical and social situation. It will become clear on various occasions that advocates of postmodern ethics and politics like Bauman, who defines "'modernity" from the perspective of the experience of "postmodernity" '[32] and speaks of 'the futility of modern dreams of universalism',[33] can no longer believe in this kind of dialectic. (One should not say, following some Neo-Marxists: 'are no longer capable of this kind of dialectic'.)

If one compares Bauman's postmodern reactions to the crisis of modernity as enlightenment and rationalization with corresponding critiques in the works of Alain Touraine, Anthony Giddens and Ulrich Beck, one discovers, in spite of numerous differences and contradictions, common problems and common reactions to them: i.e. *a postmodern problematic situated beyond modernity*. It is conceivable, of course, that Touraine, Beck and Giddens, who reject the notion of postmodernity,[34] trying instead to reflect upon and correct the shortcomings of *modernity*, would disagree with an interpretation which accentuates their postmodern propensities. However, it can be shown that their reactions to modernity are not so different from Bauman's.

Like the other sociologists mentioned here, Touraine recognizes in enlightened modernity a break with traditional social forms and a concomitant breakthrough of the rationalist principle, which he calls *l'idéologie moderniste*, relating it to the domination over nature and individuals. Touraine hints at Max Weber's sociology on the one hand and at the *Dialectic of Enlightenment* on the other, when he presents his sketch of modernity: 'It introduces the domination of rationalizing and modernizing elites over the rest of the world by organizing trade and industry and by initiating colonial expansion.'[35] As in the case of Bauman, Adorno and Horkheimer, modern forms of domination are called into question along with the process of rationalization and the notion of progress.

It is interesting to note that Touraine, like Foucault before him (cf. Chapter 3), believes that the crucial steps towards modernization can be observed in the seventeenth century. He praises the sixteenth century for not being dominated by a 'unitary myth' ('mythe unitaire')[36]: neither by the myth of Reason nor by that of Progress. He asks himself whether, at the end of the millennium (in 1991/92), we are not closer to the birth pangs of modernity than to its triumphs in the Enlightenment era.

Not surprisingly, his affirmative answer to this question implies a break with the idea of continuous progress. As in the case of Bauman, it also implies a break with Historical Materialism identified by Touraine with a systematic discourse irretrievably linked to domination and the idea of historical progress. For Marx and Lukács, he argues, the proletariat is not a class subject capable of autonomous action, but an executor of historical necessity.[37] The category of totality, inherited from Hegel by Marxism, continues the struggle of rationalist universalism on a different level by postulating an identity of reason, history and the subject. Unlike the Marxists, Touraine tries to show how reason, subjectivity and rationality diverge. He blames Marxist socialism for 'adopting a hostile attitude to class subjectivity, for neglecting democracy and for being less interested in social justice than in the realization of an historical project'.[38] In the third and the fourth chapter, it will be shown that some of these postmodern ideas are to be found in Albert Camus's *L'Homme révolté* (1951).

Touraine seems to agree with some of Bauman's, Adorno's and Horkheimer's basic ideas when he presents his own notion of a reflexive and self-critical modernity: 'Modernity is not a victory of the One (triomphe de l'Un), but its disappearance and its replacement by the difficult, but necessary relations between rationalization and individual or collective freedom.'[39] Here the Weberian perspective predominates: rationalization and bureaucracy are to be balanced out by the subjective factor, by subjective initiative and freedom. While Weber tends to link subjectivity to individual political initiative and the charismatic leader, Touraine associates it with the *social movement*.

From the very outset, since the seventies, when he published *Pour la sociologie* (1974), he has been focusing on the question why it is not meaningful in sociology to separate social systems from social actors: 'Whenever one analyses an economic or a political system without considering the way actors behave, one cannot hope to understand the latter.'[40] The sociologist of action[41] defines society neither as action nor as system, but as a systematic co-occurrence of social actions: 'Relations between classes, political influence, organizational roles, interpersonal relationships are the most important categories of social relations.'[42]

Following this conception of society, Touraine proposes the model of a self-reflecting modernity based on the premise that postindustrial society can be divided into four relatively independent spheres, two of which are individual, while the other two are collective in nature: *eros (sexuality)* and *consumption*; *nationalism* and *economic enterprise*.

Unlike in the Enlightenment period of modernity, when these four elements were held together by instrumental reason, especially since the nation was a vehicle of modernization and a guarantee of individual freedom, instrumental thought and action tend to turn against the actors in contemporary society which Touraine himself calls 'postmodern'.[43] In this phase of social development, the destructive forces of sexuality, consumerism, profit-orientation and nationalism come to light. Corresponding to the four spheres of a disintegrating modernity, four destructive, centrifugal and antisocial forces make themselves felt according to Touraine: 'the search for pleasure, social status, profit and power'.[44]

At this point, one is reminded of the conservative theories of postmodern and postindustrial society mapped out by Daniel Bell and Amitai Etzioni. Anticipating the third section of this chapter, which will deal with the works of these authors in some detail, it should be pointed out that the sociologists agree that profit, power and pleasure have one common denominator: *the indifference of the market* (of the exchange value). For all three of them are situated outside the sphere of religious, ethical, aesthetic and political values and outside the realm of truth and its criteria. For an action or utterance that causes an increase in power, pleasure or profit need be neither pious nor good, neither beautiful nor democratic – nor true.

In this context, it is hardly surprising that sociologists such as Touraine, Bell and Etzioni are anxious to endow social action with a new religious (Bell), ethical (Etzioni) or political (Touraine) value-orientation. The question remains, however, whether their attempts to strengthen value-oriented action can be successful in a society where most spheres of life function under the sway of market laws and where value-orientations seem to decline.

Touraine's suggestions concerning a way out of the postindustrial and postmodern crisis are particularly characteristic of the discussion about postmodernity as a whole. Like Ulrich Beck, Habermas and various feminist authors, Touraine hopes that the emergence of new collective subjects within the *life world* (*Lebenswelt*, Husserl, Habermas) will lead to a renewal of modernity by political, ecological and cultural action. Modernity, which was hitherto only half a modernity, because it tended to be identified with rationalization, technical progress and domination over nature, is now expected to take into account 'the tension between rationalization and formation of subjectivity'.[45]

What exactly is Touraine's view of the new social subjects? In conjunction with his central concept of *social movement*, he refers to workers', women's and ecological movements and to the Polish *Solidarność*. In this context, he defines the subject as social movement: 'The subject exists exclusively as *social movement*, as a challenge to the logic of order, be it utilitarian or simply aiming at social integration.'[46]

The subject is not a class in the Marxist-Hegelian sense, because it is not supposed to fulfil a mission of historical reason, but to react spontaneously to the disintegration of enlightened, rationalist modernity. It thus appears as a reaction to postmodern conditions: 'What is called postmodernity, what I call the final disintegration of the rationalizing model of modernity, is precisely what the subject revolts against.'[47] Hence the task of the subject is not to reunite the spheres of *eros, consumption, nationalism* and *economic enterprise*, but to mediate between them beyond instrumental reason.

It is by means of political action that the collective subject is expected to contest the hegemony of power and money, a hegemony also analysed and criticized by Habermas, thereby strengthening the *individual subject*:

The subject comes about both in its struggle against state apparatuses and by showing respect for the Other as subject; the social movement is a collective action defending the subject against the power of commodification, of economic enterprise and of the state.[48]

Touraine adds: 'There is no subject without social engagement (. . .).'[49] In spite of all the differences, one is here reminded of some Neo-Marxist projects, worked out by André Gorz, Serge Mallet and Lucien Goldmann, who were also scanning the post-war horizons for a new subject – the 'new working class' – that was supposed to counter commercialization, reification and bureaucracy.[50]

One is also reminded of Ulrich Beck's 'risk society', which is situated beyond industrial capitalism, because it is no longer guided by instrumental thought, by the domination over nature, by economic growth and an ideology of progress, but by a systematic scepticism towards all of these principles. As in the case of Bauman and Touraine, modernity becomes self-reflecting in Beck's approach: 'We are therefore concerned no longer exclusively with making nature useful, or with releasing mankind from traditional constraints, but also and essentially with problems resulting from techno-economic development itself. Modernization is becoming *reflexive*, it is becoming its own theme.'[51] It will become clear that this self-reflecting process, initiated by the founding fathers of sociology, is also situated at the centre of Giddens's thought.

Although Beck does not present himself as a postmodern author and does not identify 'risk society' with postmodernity, but rather with a *late modern, postindustrial era*, Frank Fechner is probably right when he remarks: 'The initial stage of postmodernity coincides with the break-up of Cartesian logic within Western thought caused by the ecological and technological dangers confronting humanity. In this respect, Ulrich Beck's "risk society" can be viewed as a postmodern diagnosis of crisis.'[52] What exactly does this diagnosis look like?

Very much like Bauman and Touraine, Beck contests enlightened universalism and, along with it, the universal validity of scientific reason in the instrumental sense: 'My *thesis* is that the origin of the critique of science and technology lies not in the "irrationality" of the critics, but in the *failure* of technoscientific rationality in the face of growing risks and threats from civilization.'[53] He shows to what extent not only modernity as a whole, but also science as part of it, become self-reflecting, because the awareness of risks resulting from modernization 'has established itself against the *resistance* of scientific rationality'.[54]

The reflexive turn of science, which inaugurates a demystification of scientific *ratio* and of scientists as humans, is brought about by supporters of ecological, pacifist movements or trade unions who rely on certain scientists in their criticism of established science. In this context, Beck mentions several '*forms of scientization of the protest against science*'.[55] He thus divides the notion of science into two halves and strips it of its Cartesian and universalist pretensions. Whoever speaks in the name of science has to reckon that his opponents will invoke this very science in order to refute him or that they will submit proofs within the framework of competing scientific theories.

Not only the faith in science and progress is thus shaken, but, along with it, the faith in traditional values and institutions such as the family, gender roles, the trade unions and the notion of class. Beck shows that progressive commercialization, individualization and a risk distribution that encompasses all classes not only endanger the family, but also tend to make the class in the Marxist sense obsolete. On the one hand, ecological catastrophes make themselves felt well beyond class boundaries, thus undermining class solidarity so much insisted on by Marxists; on the other hand, some industries benefit from certain risks, while others are threatened by them (e.g. the producers of charcoal). Such inequalities further increase the discrepancies within the working class. At the same time, economic competition and the individualization of social situations entail a disintegration of traditional male and female role patterns, of family structures and an isolation of the individual. The result, as seen by Beck, is that 'the basic figure of *fully developed* modernity is the the *single person*.'[56]

This idea that social and cultural forms of solidarity fall prey to an economically conditioned individualization and atomization, is not particularly new. For in the past, sociologists such as David Riesman in the USA and Lucien Goldmann in France developed it in a different context.[57] However, in the case of Beck and Giddens, it is the 'late modern' (Giddens) or postmodern context that matters, for the idea appears in a new light.

Both authors believe that the new ethic of self-realization, which is taking shape in different societies, should not be confused with banal egoism: 'Such new value-orientations are frequently (mis-)judged as forms of egoism and narcissism. Thus the core of the new phenomenon which manifests itself here is misinterpreted.'[58] Giddens's approach makes it possible to define this core: it is the 'reflexive project of self-identity'[59] in a society disoriented by risks and anomies (cf. below). Similarly, Beck refers to the 'process of reflexive modernization'[60] in his more recent work *Weltrisikogesellschaft*.

However, Beck's answer to the problems of risk society is not so much the self-realization of the individual, but democratization. The idea is to make decision-making in economics, politics and science 'accessible, according to the rules provided for such things in the recipe book of modernity: *democratization*'.[61] This plea for more democracy in Beck's discourse can only be understood in context if one considers the way he looks at the relationship between industrial and postindustrial or risk society. Geared towards the domination over nature and the accumulation of riches, industrial society has failed to keep some of its crucial promises: such as democratic decision-making or equality of men and women. Beck believes that postindustrial society is beginning to take these promises seriously.

In this respect, he seems to agree with the philosopher Wolfgang Welsch who defines postmodernity as the realization of modern projects of democratization: 'Thus postmodernity is a situation where modernity no longer has to be advocated, because it is being realized.'[62] Unfortunately, it is not made clear by Beck and Welsch how the process of democratization can continue or be intensified in a world dominated by increasingly corrupt party bureaucracies and globally operating banks and trusts.

Beck's reaction to this argument is reminiscent of Alain Touraine's stance. Like the French sociologist, he insists on the importance of social movements:

In this sense, on the one hand the new social movements (ecology, peace, feminism) are expressions of the new risk situations in the risk society. On the

other, they result from the search for social and personal identities and commitments in detraditionalized culture.[63]

In contrast with Touraine, who tends to exalt social movements, associating
them with a new social order ('une société nouvelle'),[64] Beck is more sceptical:
'*Social movements* – mean, taken literally, coming and going. Especially going.
For self-dissolution is their leading member.'[65] In the light of this scepticism,
which is borne out by the dissolution of a vast number of movements (from the
1968-movements to the peace-movements of the 1970s), Touraine's approach
loses some of its credibility.

In this context, it is easier to understand why Anthony Giddens, who seeks to
explain contemporary society as *late modernity*, i.e. as a radicalized, self-reflexive
form of modernity, is less impressed by changes brought about by social movements, but prefers to observe a scenario where individuals try to attune their
projects of self-realization to the social and political needs of society. Analysing
contemporary 'life-politics', he points out in *Modernity and Self-identity*: 'It is a
politics of self-actualisation in a reflexively ordered environment, where that
reflexivity links self and body to systems of global scope.'[66] This is a somewhat
vague description which – considered in context – means that the aspirations
of groups and individuals towards self-realization have to be compatible with
the interests of society and humanity as a whole. Giddens speaks of 'morally
justifiable forms of life'.[67] In concrete terms, this could be taken to mean that
the individual is expected to envisage a new life style that excludes waste and
damage to the environment.

Unlike Touraine and Beck, Giddens (very much like Locke and John Stuart
Mill) starts from the individual: presumably in the hope that the project of self-
realization can be harmonized with the problem-solving strategies of society at
large. It is a rather vague hope which reveals the perplexity of contemporary
social science rather than its critical insights.[68]

In spite of all the differences that make the theories commented on partly
incompatible, a common diagnosis does seem to exist. It can be summed up in
six points:

1. Since the rise of modern sociology, which developed along with the self-
   reflexive and self-ironical novels of Virginia Woolf, James Joyce, Robert
   Musil, Italo Svevo, Luigi Pirandello and Marcel Proust,[69] social scientists have
   been critically analysing the modern and late modern process of enlightenment and rationalization. In the works of authors such as Max Weber, Alfred
   Weber, Georg Simmel and Emile Durkheim, this critique often leads to
   scepticism, occasionally even to pessimism.
2. In contemporary sociology, there is a tendency to repudiate a modernity
   which extols an enlightened rationalism based on the domination over
   nature and on the rule of the general principle at the expense of the particular, the singular.

3. At the same time, sociologists and philosophers observe a transition from an industrial class society, geared towards the exploitation of nature, to a postindustrial society (Bell, Touraine), a 'risk society' (Beck) or a postmodern society (Bauman, Welsch).
4. This postmodern society is considered by Bauman – but also by Lyotard and Welsch – as a world of radical pluralism and multicultural polyphony. The fact that this pluralism is an aspect of postmodern indifference has been pointed out by Touraine (although he does not use the concept as such).
5. At the same time, this society is viewed (by both Giddens and Beck) as a world of extreme individualism, of anomie and estrangement, marked by the ideal of self-realization and by different forms of narcissism.
6. The sociologists commented on here seem to agree that late modern or postmodern problems such as rationalization, bureaucracy, fragmentation and environmental threats can best be solved by a radical and all-pervasive democratization. While Bauman and Giddens tend to emphasize pluralism and individual self-realization, Beck and especially Touraine insist on the importance of social movements, i.e. on collective subjects. (Here it becomes clear just how nonsensical the rejection of the concept of *subject* is – even in the present social context. It can only be endorsed by those who rely one-sidedly on thinkers such as Foucault, Derrida or Lyotard.)

The aim of the following sections is not so much a comprehensive presentation of theoretical perspectives and opinions, *but the answer to the question how feminist, Marxist and conservative theories react to the problematic mapped out by the sociologists.* For if it is true that 'classical' sociology and the contemporary approaches commented on here deal with the main topics and the most pressing questions of the modern-postmodern-debate, then it ought to be possible to understand the feminist, conservative and Marxist reactions both in a social and a sociological context. This is why the contemporary diagnosis was presented here in conjunction with four different, but complementary sociological perspectives.

## 2.2  Feminist and Eco-Feminist Critiques

The feminist approaches are not only linked here to the sociological diagnoses, because they frequently deal with topics commented on by Bauman, Touraine, Giddens and Beck, but, more importantly, because they also start from a radical critique of domination, Enlightenment thought and rationalism. This is what distinguishes them from most Marxist thinkers who find it hard to part with Hegelian historicism and with industrial society defined as class society. It will become clear that the Marxists go along with the feminists when it comes to criticizing mechanisms of domination, but that they turn against the feminists (and sociologists like Bauman) when it comes to defending historical teleology and reason's claim to universal validity.

In spite of such disagreements, in the course of which feminism and Marxism tend to appear as homogeneous entities, it seems reasonable to take into account the growing heterogeneity of feminist and Marxist positions. Hence, in what follows, both aspects will be dealt with: the strong tendency towards particularization, which distinguishes most brands of feminism from Marxist or sociological theories, and the feminist emphasis on solidarity and on the corresponding postulate of a universally valid social critique. It hardly comes as a surprise that the coexistence of these tendencies – particularization on the one hand and the postulate of a universally valid critique on the other – leads to contradictions and tensions among feminist theories.

Some feminist discourses are marked simultaneously by a critique of society and civilization that is reminiscent of the *Dialectic of Enlightenment* and by the postmodern thesis that this critique should not primarily be aimed at capitalism, but at male domination. According to the French author Françoise d'Eaubonne, the approaching political, military and ecological catastrophe is not being caused by the problems of profit-oriented capitalism, but by a male domination that has lasted for thousands of years and that is inherent both in the capitalist and in the socialist order, because in both cases sexism is the dominant power.[70] In a complementary manner, other, less general and less apocalyptic feminist studies focus on male domination and not on the perils of capitalism or the market laws. One of the key questions raised by Mary M. Talbot is: 'How do patterns of male dominance vary across different cultures, and in different contexts within cultures?'[71] In a complementary way, Sally Johnson and Ulrike Hanna Meinhof plead in favour of a 'study of the mechanisms of oppression, that is, of the specific ways in which men construct a world which so manifestly excludes and undermines women'.[72]

If one examines more carefully the discourses of these authors, one realizes that 'male domination' or 'dominance' is considered as a universal phenomenon along with 'sexism' which is presented as an all-pervading cultural mechanism. The driving force of technical civilization, which progresses at the expense of nature and humanity, is sexism. The processes of rationalization, division of labour and differentiation – analysed by Max Weber, Durkheim and Luhmann – are subsumed under this universal historical principle together with Marx's class domination. The flaw of the feminist discourses quoted here is not so much their disregard for these alternative or competing theories of domination, but their attempt to explain problems of contemporary society in a monocausal manner by relating them (almost exclusively) to universal sexism.

For it is precisely this attempt which is implicitly contested by other feminists, who question the essentialist and universalist concepts of 'traditional' philosophical theories, because such concepts transform male interests and ideas into universally valid constants. Nancy Fraser's and Linda Nicholson's oscillation between universalism and particularism illustrates the dilemmas of feminist critique.

Although they begin by repudiating Lyotard's scepticism towards all general concepts and theorems (cf. Chapter 3), when they argue in favour of a theoretically founded critique of society, they renounce the philosophical, universalist foundations of social criticism. An effective critique of male dominance, they believe, may require some of the genres rejected by postmodernists. They are necessary for social criticism in general. Among these genres might even be those 'metanarratives' considered with distrust by Lyotard and his postmodernist friends. Effective criticism, the authors (rightly) argue, 'requires at minimum large narratives about changes in social organization and ideology (. . .)'.[73]

It is all the more surprising to hear them say that they envisage a 'postmodern-feminist paradigm of social criticism without philosophy'.[74] Eventually, they plead in favour of a postmodern feminism which breaks with all variants of rationalist, Hegelian and Marxist universalism: 'Moreover, postmodern-feminist theory would be non-universalist. When its focus became cross-cultural or transepochal, its mode of attention would be comparativist rather than universalizing, attuned to changes and contrasts instead of to "covering laws".'[75] The partial plausibility of this approach is due to the fact that, in the past, authors such as Carol Gilligan[76] tended to ignore cultural and ethnic 'differences among women'[77] and thus lost credibility.

The main weakness of Fraser's and Nicholson's argument is due to their attempt to ignore the dialectic between the particular and the universal instead of practising it systematically. Very much like Françoise d'Eaubonne, whose simplifying discourse they surpass in all respects, they *presuppose* the existence of general principles – e.g. domination and sexism – but at the same time reject universalistic criteria in philosophy and social science. In the next chapter, it will appear that problems resulting from this contradiction between the particular and the universal are difficult to solve (as Adorno knew when he replaced his 'thinking in models' by a paratactic discourse) – but the authors could at least have reflected on their implicit universalistic premises.

A break with the universalistic approach of modernity and a 'particularistic turn' also make themselves felt in Anna Yeatman's feminist book *Postmodern Revisionings of the Political* (1994). Dealing with Australian and New Zealand cultures, it highlights ethnic particularities. However, the author is even less circumspect than Fraser and Nicholson when it comes to tackling the nexus between the particular and the universal.

Starting from Lyotard's highly questionable premise that there is no *reason*, but only a multitude of *reasons*, the author dismisses the idea of an historical reason inherent in rationalism, Hegelianism and Marxism: 'There being no Reason, in the singular, the utopian vision of reason bringing into being a society free from domination has lost all credibility.'[78] From this point of view, postmodern resistance to domination, rationalization and universalism turns into a resistance to modernity as a whole. 'First', explains Yeatman, 'postmodernism questions the modern construction of historical time in terms of linear *progress*.'[79]

At this point, it becomes clear that feminists and social scientists, who try to think within the postmodern and postindustrial problematic, have abandoned modern patterns of thought such as individual autonomy, classless society or the truth content of art. They set out from different norms and values. But what exactly are Yeatman's reactions to the postmodern problematic?

She presents eight theses which can be summarized here without omitting essentials: 1. a deconstructionist approach to all modern and modernist traditions; 2. a postuniversalistic way of theorizing in which the voices of minorities oppose the inevitable universalism of theory; 3. the idea that binary constructions of differences are provisional and ambivalent because frontiers not only separate, but also link what is different; 4. a perspectivism which is meant to be relational, not relativistic; 5. the complementary consciousness that theory is historically contingent; 6. the assumption that theoreticians find themselves in a particular, contingent situation in relation to institutionalized intellectual authorities and in relation to their potential public; 7. the resulting emphasis on the subjectivity of the theoretician and, finally, 8. the idea of language as a material, active and productive system.

At this point, one is reminded of Zygmunt Bauman who – as was shown earlier on – also stresses the irreducible particularity of theoretical viewpoints and the heterogeneity of cultural perspectives. Yeatman's theses seem to converge in a statement by Steven Best concerning the difference between modernity and postmodernity: 'Thus, in direct opposition to modern views, postmodernists valorize incommensurability and fragmentation as liberating.'[80] How does the feminist regard this liberation?

She sets out from the postulate of a 'politics of representation',[81] a politics which highlights the question concerning the discursive representation of reality: 'Whose representations prevail? who has the authority to represent reality? To put the question differently: who has to be silenced in order that these representations prevail?'[82] In this new context, Yeatman argues, the critical testing of hypotheses mapped out by Popper and the consensus imagined by Habermas lose their legitimacy, because 'consensus depends on the systematic exclusion of those who would dissent if they were given a voice'.[83]

Once again, the critical-rationalist (Popper) and the hermeneutic (Habermas) quest for intersubjective testing and generalization is called into question by radical particularization. On the one hand, this is understandable, because – for different reasons – Popper and Habermas apply the criterion of intersubjectivity without analysing the cultural and ideological determinants of *subjectivity*[84]; on the other hand, it is an oversimplification of the problem, because Yeatman overlooks the fact that formal logic provides the elementary framework of communication and that everyday language is the ultimate metalanguage permitting cultural and ideological idiosyncrasies to be overcome (although it does not guarantee such overcoming).[85]

Considering that the discursive contrast between universalism and particularism will recur in virtually all chapters of this book and that it is a philosophical rather than a sociological problem, it will be commented on at this stage only insofar as it is relevant to Anna Yeatman's arguments. For her it is of considerable relevance because she would like to show to what extent not only women but also ethnic and cultural minorities are excluded from a political, scientific and philosophical consensus dominated by men.

She therefore pleads in favour of an *oppositional thought* based on the perception of ethnic and cultural differences and refuses to level out such differences by 'false' (i.e. rationalist, Hegelian or Marxist) generalizations. Experience among Australian and New Zealand aborigines is quoted in support of her approach: 'The starting point of these oppressed groups is the assumption of specificity of perspective: a Maori point of view, a Pekha (. . .) point of view. There is no privileged position of generality – no god's eye view.'[86]

However, this basically correct assessment will not prevent extremely heterogeneous groups such as European, American or Japanese scientists and ecologists (e.g. 'Green-Peace-activists') from *agreeing* on scientific grounds with Polynesians and Maoris on the dangers and harms of nuclear tests. One can also assume that physicists and computer experts among Polynesians and Maoris can communicate with their European or Korean colleagues without encountering too many linguistic or cultural hurdles. It is of course the case that communication in the social and cultural sciences, where cultural, ideological and linguistic frameworks (derided as 'myths' by Popper)[87] play an important part, is frequently hampered by idiosyncrasies. But even in this area, communication is not *a priori* doomed to failure – as will be shown in the last chapter.

Yeatman's main problem seems to consist in the fact that she does not distinguish the different discursive levels – everyday language, politics, science, social science, etc. – and instead favours a perspectivism that leads to a radical particularization of language. It is not clear how this particularism is to be related to the universalistic character of the social sciences which she acknowledges. In this respect she reproduces a flaw of feminist argument which came to light in the case of Nancy Fraser and Linda Nicholson.

The hypothesis that we are dealing with a weak spot in feminist discourse is borne out by the work of Honi Fern Haber who challenges globally postmodern tendencies towards particularization in *Beyond Postmodern Politics* (1994). To her, the one-sided emphasis on difference and radical heterogeneity in cultural or sexual matters constitutes an acute threat to *solidarity* and *subjectivity*. Women's movements operating in different cultural and racial settings cannot be successful without relying on these two factors. Without solidarity and subjectivity, the author argues, 'oppositional politics'[88] are bound to fail.

In view of such arguments, it is not surprising that she eventually evokes the universal aspects of language, insisting – against feminists such as Yeatman – on the necessity of overcoming differences, at least in certain cases, in order to allow for the formation of subjects in coherent political action. In the age of deconstruction, she does not hesitate to emphasize the importance of structures:

'Because it is of the very nature of language to create structures, the repression
of difference is the fact beyond which we can never get.'[89] Honi Fern Haber's
arguments show to what extent social criticism and 'oppositional politics' need
the concept of truth as a universally valid factor: for there is no criticism without
a search for truth and without the hope to find it (cf. Chapters 3 and 6).

The postmodern tendency towards particularization weakens feminist solidarity not only by extreme differentiation, as Honi Fern Haber aptly points
out, but also by its movement towards indifference which is the final result of
the differentiation process. Where communication breaks down, because each
group insists on its uniqueness, positions and opinions become interchangeable, in-different in a situation of extreme pluralism. At best they are marvelled
at like some exotic menus of 'ethnic' restaurants in the USA; at worst they provoke rejection and violence. This destructive potential inherent in pluralism
is taken into account by Alain Touraine who envisages a 'multiculturalism'
'marked by segregation and racism' ('chargé de ségrégation et de racisme').[90]

How is the relationship between feminism and postmodernity to be imagined
in view of these arguments and counter-arguments? Probably not in agreement
with Linda Hutcheon who defines both terms as ideologies or world views:

> Feminisms are not really either compatible with or even an example of post-
> modern thought, as a few critics have tried to argue; if anything, together
> they form the single most powerful force in changing the direction in which
> (male) postmodernism was heading but, I think, no longer is.[91]

It would probably be more accurate to say that feminism as a homogeneous
movement does not exist (not even in a plural form), because there are many
*heterogeneous* 'feminisms' ('Marxisms', psychoanalyses) which, far from opposing
a homogeneous, mythical, male postmodernity, are trying to solve particular
problems *within the postmodern problematic.*

The fact that feminist questions and answers tend to coincide with those of
some contemporary sociologists (Bauman, Beck, Touraine), who oppose universalism in the name of cultural particularization, gives substance to the idea
of a 'postmodern problematic' which is common to different groups of thinkers. In what follows, it will be shown that some conservative sociologists like
Friedrich H. Tenbruck, Daniel Bell and Amitai Etzioni pose similar questions
and offer similar answers in spite of all ideological differences which separate
them from feminists, Bauman or Beck.

## 2.3  A Conservative Postmodernity?

Habermas, who tends to identify postmodernity with the conservative and
anti-enlightenment ideologies of post-war society (cf. Chapter 3), has already
answered this question. It nevertheless seems worthwhile repeating it, because

one can safely assume that – in spite of some similarities – the conservative answers compete and collide with the critical (Bauman), the feminist (Yeatman) and the Marxist (O'Neill) ones. In this perspective, all attempts to identify postmodernity with a 'male' or a conservative ideology in the sense of Hutcheon or Habermas appear as risky simplifications. From a theoretical point of view, it seems more meaningful to assume that similar *postmodern problems* are perceived in divergent ideological and theoretical perspectives.

For within the postmodern problematic, conservative sociology and political science form – very much like feminism or Marxism – a particular complex of questions that is to be situated within the polemical relationship between ideology and the market. Like the Marxists and the feminists, conservative social scientists consider with apprehension the commercialization of all spheres of life (from medicine to art and sports). With Barry Smart, who is certainly not a conservative, they observe the growing 'commercialisation of information and communications media'.[92] They might even agree with a Marxist like Fredric Jameson who relies on Baudrillard in criticizing a postmodern society in which the exchange value tends to obliterate all use values.[93]

Considering this problem, the German philosopher Peter Koslowski puts forward arguments which are reminiscent of the most conservative elements in Alfred Weber's sociology: 'The norms of the economic system are outside culture (. . .).'[94] In the same strain, he adds: 'The economic-technical paradigm tends to underestimate and delete the cultural meaningfulness of human practice.'[95] In view of such criticism, it is hardly surprising that the philosophers and sociologists commented on in this section tend to oppose the process of modernization and commercialization by advocating a religious and moral (i.e. ideological) renewal.

Unlike Koslowski and Amitai Etzioni, the German sociologist Friedrich H. Tenbruck does not use the word 'postmodernity', but nevertheless tends to view the evolution of modernity in a perspective which overlaps with that of Bauman, Touraine and Yeatman. To him, modernity and the Enlightenment appear both as universalistic and missionary – as universalistic and imperialist, Bauman and the feminists would say:

> Whatever today's social scientists may say about the social origins of modern secularism – it was the result of the mission of a universalistic concept of truth that came about during the Enlightenment and was firmly established in the nineteenth century within the religion of science.[96]

From Tenbruck's point of view – as from Bauman's and Touraine's – even Marxism–Leninism and communism appear as aspects of this new religion whenever they aspire to replace the 'universal church'.[97] It becomes clear at this point that, within the postmodern problematic, it is not so much Marx's early work that counts, but the deterministic and centralistic brands of Marxism propounded by Karl Kautsky on the one hand and the Leninists on the other.

This insight could lead to a reappraisal of both Enlightenment and Marxism to the effect that, especially their self-criticisms in the works of Rousseau and in Neomarxism, significantly depart from metaphysical universalism and heuristically map out critical and dialogical theories which investigate the very possibility of truth instead of propounding universally valid dogmas (cf. Chapter 3).

However, Tenbruck's alternative points in a different direction which seems to be characteristic of postmodernity as a whole. Having diagnosed the demystification of science by science itself ('the faith in its legitimating power has disappeared'),[98] the sociologist cannot but dismiss enlightened universalism. As with Bauman and some feminists, this dismissal leads to the discovery of a new tendency towards particularization:

> Only one *alternative* is conceivable: that the idea of universal truth leaves this world as it once entered it. Many symptoms bear witness to this kind of pluralism, in which truth would be reduced to the variably defined practical and factual correctness of individual statements. For a long time doctrines have been increasingly successful which have abjured universalistic criteria of truth. Not only religious sects or cults present themselves in their idiosyncrasies without bothering to relate themselves to other doctrines. Even contemporary youth culture is inspired by this powerful particularistic spirit (. . .).[99]

It is worth quoting Tenbruck at some length because he sums up crucial aspects of the postmodern problematic.

Relying on his social diagnosis, he concludes that science cannot prove or justify social values because 'no foundations can be discovered within the twofold universalism of freedom and rationality (. . .)'.[100] The alternative envisaged by the German sociologist is a return to the norms and values which have hitherto been recognized as valid:

> Science took the view that the hierarchy of values could only be established by way of rational proof. However, the opposite is true. For values manifest their status and their validity only in situations where they are experienced in their capacity of shaping experience.[101]

This kind of return to a culturally lived experience may seem meaningful and in agreement with some contemporary tendencies; however, renouncing all rational critique of values, a critique quite rightly demanded by Hans Albert,[102] is highly problematical. Is it conceivable that the value of a 'master race' be dealt with on the same level as values such as 'freedom', 'justice' or 'humanity'? Should it become impossible to discuss the generalization of values?[103]

In this context, the work of Peter Koslowski shows how dangerous an ideological approach to values can be. On the one hand, Koslowski denounces the universalism and the rationalism of the Enlightenment period and criticizes the domination of the human subject over nature; on the other hand, he debunks the radical pluralism of postmodernists such as Bauman, Lyotard and Welsch, because it seems to him that it implies a new polytheism. It may be the case that French postmodernism has revealed the totalitarian tendencies in Hegelian and Marxist philosophies: 'However, it exposes postmodern thought to the danger of descending into the arbitrariness of polytheism.'[104] Like Chateaubriand at the beginning of the nineteenth century, Koslowski envisages a revival of Christianity by romantic means, i.e. by a return to traditionalism.[105]

He does in fact oppose ideas of the Enlightenment by a dualistic and monological discourse dominated by mythical actors and romantic nostalgia: 'Today the romantics appear to us as the true realists who have grasped better the most pressing problems of modernity and the problematical character of social modernization since the industrial revolution than the simplifying "realists" and Enlightenment rationalists.'[106] It is not quite clear whom the word 'realists' refers to: most probably to all those who disagree with Koslowski's opinions.

It soon becomes obvious what this kind of discourse is aiming at when Koslowski links postmodernity, 'which bears the imprint of religion',[107] to the Christian Middle Ages. Oddly enough, it is not his own proposal to revive a medieval ideology that appears as a conservative step back to Koslowski, but Habermas's 'project of modernity', 'because it is an attempt to preserve left wing Hegelianism'.[108] Romanticism and the Middle Ages, however, appear to him as particularly relevant to contemporary society.

Considering this pattern of thought, it is hardly surprising that Koslowski does not appreciate the kind of pluralism advocated by Bauman, Lyotard, Welsch and Yeatman: 'Plurality is not the end of our culture, but serves a higher purpose.'[109] This 'higher purpose' turns out to be an ideological or religious normalization of society which – in the present context – can be interpreted as an ideological reaction to market-based pluralism: 'Christianity is the normal religion in Germany, Christianity as a whole, not one of its confessions.'[110]

Although the Hellenistic and Christian character of modern European thought and culture can be considered as an historical fact, it is hardly possible to agree with a prescriptive discourse which proclaims monologically a certain normativity basing itself on dichotomies and mythical agents: 'To the modern axiom, according to which "the relations determine the substance and the self", postmodernism opposes the auto-definition according to which "the self is an indivisible and original substance".'[111] Not the idealism of this sentence is ideological, but the dualism constructed by Koslowski between a functionalist modernity and a Christian postmodernity. The latter is represented by the mythical actor 'postmodern culture' considered by the author as a real historical agent.

Although Koslowski hardly contributes to a more concrete understanding of modernity and postmodernity because, unlike Tenbruck, he turns both concepts into ideological myths, his discourse is nonetheless interesting because, like the other sociological discourses, it sheds light on some aspects of the postmodern problematic. Once again, the latter is described by concepts such as

*social movement* and *self-identity*: 'The new social movements react to the crisis
of modernity and to its loss of cultural contextuality.'[112] One is reminded of
Giddens's presentation of a late modern society in *Modernity and Self-Identity*,
when Koslowski mentions the 'rediscovery of the self' and 'the task of self-
discovery'[113] as crucial points of his postmodern programme.

Symptomatic of postmodern thinking is his idea that extreme pluralism and
particularism may at any moment turn into indifference: 'In a society, where
all ways and views of life are equally valid, not tolerance but indifference in
cultural matters prevails.'[114] It becomes clear at this stage that postmodern
society appears – from a conservative, a Marxist and a feminist point of view – as
a collective balancing act between engagement, tolerance and indifference.
(This problem will be dealt with in more detail in Section 2.5.)

In order to avoid a lapse of contemporary life into market-based indifference,
Koslowski pleads in favour of a religious and ethical renewal of society. He mentions the necessity of a 'larger ethical consensus'[115] in postmodernity and concludes: 'The ethics of economics is an attempt to counter this development by
bringing about a new unity between economics and culture, the world of work
and the life world (Lebenswelt).'[116]

This attempt to bring about an 'ethical or religious turn' within the postmodern constellation is reminiscent of the well-known project of the American
sociologists Daniel Bell and Amitai Etzioni, whose diagnoses differ substantially,
but who share Koslowski's conviction that the uncontrolled mechanisms of
marketing and consumerism can only be checked by a systematic ethical and
religious renewal. They also believe that market mechanisms contribute to the
spread of indifference and at the same time provoke ideological reactions to it:
feminist and ecological attempts to avoid the worst, a religious renewal or ethical reforms, etc. (*moral rearmament, morele herbewapening*, as the Dutch company
Philips called it several decades ago).

The postmodern dialectic of indifference and ideology underlies Daniel
Bell's criticism of the late capitalist order which, according to Bell, threatens to
destroy the ascetic mentality it helped to bring about. At the centre of Bell's
well-known study *The Coming of Post-Industrial Society* (1973) is Max Weber's thesis about the 'innerworldly asceticism' of the Protestant ethic which is supposed
to underlie rational action and the search for success. To Bell, this thesis appears
as an accurate description of traditional industrial society, the very foundations
of which are undermined after the Second World War and in particular during
the turbulent Sixties. Innerworldly asceticism, the guarantee of a functioning
capitalist economy, is threatened by mutations within the capitalist system
itself.

Five factors can be identified that are responsible for this development:
1. a shift of emphasis from the production of goods to the service sector in the
economy; 2. a corresponding shift in society at large from liberal to technical
professions and a concomitant decline of the proletariat; 3. the increasing

importance of science for social innovation and political programmes; 4. an orientation towards the future defined as planning of technical progress; 5. the rise of a new 'intellectual technology',[117] as Bell puts it, geared towards computer science.

In the present context, Bell's analysis of the scientific, technological and technocratic processes is less important than his descriptions of the new social strata which are more attracted by *consumerism and services* and less interested in the *production of goods*. For this new orientation has far-reaching consequences: among other things the division of society into an economic-technological and a cultural sector. While traditional industrial society appears to Bell as an integrated system of culture, character structure and economy (which it wasn't), postindustrial society is considered by him as a hedonistic world dominated by consumerism and organized fun.

His explanation of this social order is marked by the dialectics of irony: 'Ironically, all this was undermined by capitalism itself. Through mass production and mass consumption, it destroyed the Protestant ethic by zealously promoting a hedonistic way of life.'[118] Eventually, this development leads to a split of the social order: 'In the organization of production and work, the system demands provident behavior, industriousness and self-control, dedication to a career and success. In the realm of consumption, it fosters the attitude of *carpe diem*, prodigality and display, and the compulsive search for play.'[119] Both realms are united in their ignorance of a 'transcendental ethic'.

It is interesting to observe to what extent Bell's perspective overlaps with that of Alain Touraine. In conjunction with a 'disintegrating modernity', the French sociologist also speaks of a 'search for pleasure', social status, profit and power (cf. Section 2.1). The two sociologists appear to be complementary insofar as Bell develops Touraine's thesis according to which the hedonistic culture of postindustrial society is hostile to bourgeois culture and closely related to nineteenth century *aesthetic modernism*.

In short: fashion (as dandyism) and the 'artificial paradise' in the sense of Baudelaire, both of which were accessible to a minority towards the middle of the nineteenth century, have become mass phenomena in the course of the twentieth century. Bell even speaks of the 'victory of modernism' in contemporary society and, in his book *Cultural Contradictions of Capitalism* (1976), he opposes performance-oriented modernity to a modernism defined as decaying or late modernity. John O'Neill aptly points out that 'Bell's conception of post-modernism seems to turn upon a rejection of everything in modernism except its puritanism as the matching ethic of bourgeois culture and industry'.[120]

The question is, however, whether nineteenth century industrial society can actually be viewed as an integrated system of economy and culture. Very different thinkers such as Karl Marx and Alfred Weber seem to agree that nineteenth century society is marked by strong tensions between economy and culture. One might add that the consumer orientation described by Veblen in his theory of the *leisure class* and of *conspicuous consumption*[121] could already be observed in nineteenth century capitalism. According to Bell's analysis of contemporary social developments, the consumption and leisure spheres of society keep growing so that the orientation towards consumerism can increasingly compete with the orientation towards production and profit. However, both orientations originate in the market and are dominated by the exchange value (as profit and consumerism) which tends to negate all cultural values.

Bell shows how this comes about when he describes the destruction of the Protestant ethic by the mechanisms of late capitalism. However, he tends to view this development primarily as a conflict between two competing ideologies, Puritan individualism and hedonism, without considering the fact that the nineteenth century will to profit tended to negate all cultural values, including the Protestant ethic, by its tendency to indifference and reification. This is probably the main reason why his overt and covert pleading in favour of an ethical and religious renewal of postindustrial ('modernist') society is hardly convincing.[122] Although they are more substantial than those of Koslowski, his arguments have one thing in common with the conservative rhetoric of the German author: *the attempt to give market society an orientation that is not purely economic.*

The idea that this attempt is *postindustrial* and *postmodern* at the same time is confirmed by Amitai Etzioni's *communitarian sociology* and his ethical project. Etzioni, who borrows the notion of postmodernity from C. Wright Mills in the Sixties[123] and makes the beginning of the new era coincide with the end of World War II, imagines a postmodern society capable of organizing its own future. He maps out a 'theory of societal self-control'[124] which is meant to inaugurate this kind of rational organization.

What exactly does an active postmodern society capable of 'self-control' look like? To begin with, it is a society which, unlike its less successful predecessors, takes its own norms and values seriously, instead of merely paying lip service to them. Etzioni readily admits that the scientific, technological and technical discoveries of modernity cannot be made undone, but he would like to activate them in order to ensure an optimal transition from modernity to postmodernity. This is how he envisages a successful postmodern society:

> Increased knowledge and consciousness, a deepening participation in the public sphere, a decline in the obsession with material assets and rewards, and growth in the effectiveness of societal controls – all these require a greater reliance on symbols and a smaller role for objects in societal life.[125]

This type of discourse, which, unlike Bell's global critique, does not aim at a reinstatement of Max Weber's Protestant ethic, is, like most other conservative discourses of postmodernity, anti-utilitarian, anti-hedonistic, anti-rationalist. To a certain degree it is even anti-individualist. Very much like Tenbruck, Koslowski and Bell, Etzioni pleads in favour of traditional cultural values and a revival of ethics.

It is hardly surprising that his communitarian agenda relies heavily on Kant's postulate that individuals ought to be considered as ends in themselves, not as means. The American sociologist defines the active, postmodern society as an 'association of members who treat each other as goals and non-members as if they were members (. . .)'.[126] This plea in favour of a value-oriented, ethical action is obviously meant to improve the social control of market mechanisms in a postmodern society which can turn into an 'active society' as long as it does not succumb to the dictates of its own economy: 'The "mass" sector has grown and the role of the state and the market has increased; collectivities have become less strong, less encompassing, less pervasive, and, as we shall see, less authentic.'[127] As in other postmodern (and late modern) theories of society, the contrast between market and culture (as value system) makes itself felt in Etzioni's approach.

In view of this antagonism between culture and the market, Etzioni tends to emphasize two factors: the intensification of social planning and the reinforcement of collective consciousness which he would like to be accompanied by more competition. New technologies and techniques should be used to improve the control of economic and social developments and of their influence on human environment; at the same time, democratic consensus should be encouraged whenever possible. By proposing 'more control *and* more consensus-building',[128] Etzioni tries to prevent planning from being dissociated from democratic consensus. Experts and expert cultures, he argues, ought to be integrated into democratic decision-making.

This idea and the complementary notion of *social movement*, which Etzioni considers to be a crucial factor of democratic control, are reminiscent of Ulrich Beck's and Alain Touraine's theories of society.[129] Along with a more pronounced orientation towards collective ethical values, the social movement is expected – as in Touraine's case – to strengthen subjectivity in a bureaucratic society. One is also reminded of Bell, Koslowski and Touraine when Gerard Kelly points out in a review of Etzioni's work: 'The aim is to reaffirm a sense of morality and shared duty in a society that Etzioni believes has been fatally undermined by excessive individual rights, by the pursuit of self.'[130]

In Etzioni's more recent works, it becomes clear that his argument has always evolved on two levels: on the *factual level*, where it is oriented towards the question *what is the case* and on the *prescriptive level*, where it aims at the question *what is to be done*. Since the two levels are closely interrelated, it is not always easy to distinguish the two questions. Whenever Etzioni criticizes Adam Smith's individualist and utilitarian ('neoclassical') approach for bracketing out collective and normative-ethical factors, it can safely be assumed that his 'communitarian' ideology is reflected in his methodological premises. For Etzioni believes – very much like the Marxist Lucien Goldmann – that it is not individuals who are the decisive social actors, but collectives or groups.[131] It hardly comes as a surprise that, in a general assessment of his own approach, he concludes that the latter is closer to Romanticism than to Enlightenment rationalism.[132]

Apart from being marked by the affinity to a certain Romanticism (like Koslowski's approach), Etzioni's work is imbued with the potentially harmful propensity to deal ideologically with sociological issues. The ideological tendency can hardly be overlooked in his book *The Spirit of Community*. Starting from the somewhat banal hypothesis that 'rights presume responsibilities,'[133] Etzioni confronts American individualism with his own 'communitarian agenda' and appeals to the reader by launching a postmodern slogan: 'Be a Communitarian: Join the Movement.'[134] Further on in this text, he pleads in favour of strengthening 'the communitarian elements in the urban and suburban centers'.[135] He has no qualms about advocating 'shared heroes and values'[136] whose presence is meant to set limits to cultural pluralism. In such cases, his ideological discourse encounters that of Peter Koslowski. Both discourses are symptoms of the postmodern problematic insofar as they illustrate the *need for ideology* in an era marked by indifference and radical pluralism. At this point, the image of a postmodern sociological conservatism comes into focus. We are dealing with an ideological and sociological language which confronts contemporary trends towards secularization, commercialization, scientism and technocracy by a plea for collective values and a radical ethical renewal.

Although critical theoreticians will hesitate to condemn this current of thought on 'ideological' grounds, in order to avoid a sterile ideological confrontation, they will point out an idealist element that links the various conservative approaches. They all neglect the economic factors, which have been eroding collective consciousness, thus accelerating the decay of religious, moral and political norms and values. At the same time, they neglect the virulent ideological reactions to this process which are characteristic of secularized market society. They neglect these reactions, because *they are themselves* such reactions within, on the verge of or even outside the scientific spectrum: reactions to the political and moral indifference of the market, of technological progress and natural science. It becomes clear at this stage that theories cannot afford to ignore their – always inevitable – ideological foundations without degenerating into moral or political ideologies. Self-reflection in the social context is a prerequisite of all sociological theories.

Considering the problematic as a whole, it becomes obvious that it is not meaningful to identify postmodernity with its conservative, 'neo-romantic' tendencies, as Habermas does. Postmodernity is not a conservative ideology, but a complex problematic within which feminist, ecological, critical and even Marxist discourses *interact*. It ought to be remembered, however (and this was one of the key ideas here), that the conservative, feminist and critical discourses do overlap in crucial points as they react to *common postmodern problems*.

## 2.4 The Marxist Critique: For and Against Postmodernity

Marxist reactions to the postmodern problematic are heterogeneous because a homogeneous Marxism does not exist – as little as a homogeneous existentialism or feminism. While an author like John O'Neill rejects postmodernity, to which he nevertheless reacts by proposing a non-Promethean, 'Orphic' Marxism, Fredric Jameson, Alex Callinicos and Terry Eagleton attempt to deal with the postmodern constellation within the traditional Marxist framework. Inevitably, such attempts lead to distortions, because postmodernity is not conceived as a problematic, but as an ideology or a relatively homogeneous system of values.

The fact that postmodernity is neither an ideology nor a system of values, but an open problematic or a changing socio-linguistic situation, is inadvertently revealed by John O'Neill, who tends to condemn everything postmodern, but at the same time imagines an 'Orphic Marxism' considered as a reaction to the contemporary problematic insofar as it dismisses the historical and revolutionary teleologies of modernity.

Without explicitly admitting it, O'Neill acknowledges some of the sociological diagnoses commented on here, e.g. when he points to the ambivalence of late capitalist society in which contradictory forces such as manipulation and emancipation of individuals coexist: 'Such a culture is marked by its identification of opposites, its ability to collapse contraries, to combine sentimentalism and indifference, exploitation and emancipation, to psychologize the political process while deepening its disciplinary politicizations of the psyche and its therapeutic culture.'[137] This ambiguity of postmodern culture, which (as will be shown later on) is also perceived as a chance by Marxists like Michael Ryan, is meant to empower a humanist Marxism to activate its critical potential.

O'Neill, who agrees with Foucault's and Lyotard's postmodern critique of rationalism and the principle of domination, rejects all brands of Marxist rationalism: not only Althusser's scientistic interpretation of Marx,[138] but also Habermas's idea that Marx's work contains scientistic and technocratic elements.[139] His critique of Marxist scientism yields an Orphic project: 'Marxism has itself practised scientism and a crude Prometheanism. My reformulation of Marxist humanism gives emphasis to its civility over its industrialism.'[140]

In spite of all the diatribes against postmodernity, which abound in O'Neill's work, the informed reader discerns at least two postmodern ideas: the critique of scientism and the complementary rejection of industrialism which are also to be found in Bauman's and Touraine's works. In this context, 'Orphic Marxism' appears not so much as an alternative to postmodern ideologies, but as part and parcel of the postmodern social and linguistic situation.

O'Neill's openness to deconstructionist and feminist terminologies shows to what extent he assimilates elements of postmodern theories to his non-scientistic, humanist Marxism. Marx even appears to him as a deconstructionist *avant la lettre*, who – long before the rise of deconstruction – began to doubt binary oppositions such as *spirit/body*, *masculine/feminine* or *individual/society*. One may wonder, however, to what extent the advocate of an 'Orphic Marxism' glosses over crucial differences between a Hegelian dialectic of the nineteenth century and a Nietzsche-inspired deconstruction of the 20th. (A similar problem crops up in Michael Ryan's *Marxism and Deconstruction* [1982]: an attempt to make Marx's and Derrida's critiques of metaphysics appear as two complementary aspects of a global criticism of patriarchal capitalism.)[141]

As a Marxist, O'Neill is not primarily interested in a theoretical and ideological alliance with deconstruction, but rather envisages a synthesis of Marxism and Alfred Schütz's phenomenological sociology. In this context, it is hardly surprising that he puts the concept of *life-world* (*Lebenswelt*: Husserl, Schütz), used by Habermas in his critique of 'power' and 'money', at the centre of his argument. For he is primarily interested in mobilizing ethnomethodology and Winch's linguistic philosophy against the claim of sociology to be the final metadiscourse in the realm of social science. His complementary aim is a scientific rehabilitation of common sense and everyday language. According to O'Neill, it is one of the principal tasks of the sociology of knowledge to take seriously 'its reflexive concern with the grounds of *communication* between everyday common sense reason and scientific rationality'.[142] The aim of this concern is a general improvement of the translatability of everyday language and common sense into scientific languages.

Improving social communication on this level, O'Neill believes, enables us to attain three basic goals: the 'political accountability to which experts must be held',[143] the transformation of society into a 'communicative community'[144] and the decolonization of the life-world by communicative democracy. In many respects, this postmodern Marxist project is reminiscent of the democratization proposals put forward by Touraine and Beck, insofar as it also emphasizes a closer control of expert groups and of science. However, it also leaves open the question how democratic control can be maintained in an increasingly corrupt society dominated by rationalization, computerization and bureaucratization. One might add that O'Neill adopts a somewhat uncritical stance towards common sense because he does not consider its function as a vehicle of stereotypes, prejudice and propaganda: a function critical sociology ought to reflect.

If one considers some discourses on postmodernity after 2000, one is struck by the *continuity of the problematic*. Thus Steven Best and Douglas Kellner believe that in order to counter the 'coevolution of science, technology and capitalism',[145] society has to reinforce the process of democratization and collective self-determination: 'The inherent ambiguity of current transformations demands dialectical analysis of their positive and negative aspects and a keen political vision for promoting the life-enhancing and democratizing possibilities at hand.'[146] This is not substantially different from what postmodern authors such as Wolfgang Welsch and critics of postmodernity such as Alain Touraine and Ulrich Beck have to say. Adopting Habermas's terminology, one could argue that the idea of both critical postmodernists and critics of postmodern trends is to defend the life-world against the invasive systems of 'power', 'technological reason' and 'money'. Their intellectual affinity can best be explained by the fact that they all react to a *common problematic*.

In the early nineties, Fredric Jameson adopted a similar stance, albeit within the context of a Marxist terminology which contains neither 'Orphic' nor phenomenological theorems. Starting from his article 'Postmodernism or the Cultural Logic of Late Capitalism' (1984) and from the work of the Marxist economist Ernest Mandel, he argues that liberal capitalism was superseded by monopoly capitalism towards the end of the nineteenth century and that the latter was eventually transformed into global capitalism after the Second World War. Jameson rejects Bell's and Touraine's concept of 'postindustrial society' and tries instead to develop a theory of *multinational*, global capitalism.

According to him, contemporary capitalism invades the last enclaves of pre-capitalist forms of production which up to now it tolerated and exploited at the same time.

He explains that Mandel's intervention in the postindustrial debate involves the proposition that late or multinational or consumer capitalism, far from being inconsistent with Marx's great nineteenth-century analysis, constitutes, on the contrary, the purest form of capital yet to have emerged, a prodigious expansion of capital into hitherto uncommodified areas. He adds: At any rate, it will also have been clear that my own cultural periodization of the stages of realism, modernism, and postmodernism is both inspired and confirmed by Mandel's tripartite scheme.[147]

(One can only hope that this kind of tautology – 'inspired and confirmed' – is not typical of dialectic discourse.)

It is certainly one of Jameson's merits to have abandoned simplifying chronological schemes in order to consider the postmodern form of culture as a constellation of cultural phenomena which turns into a dominant in the course of the 1950s and 60s. Refusing to reduce postmodernity to an ideology or a style, he constructs it as a system of cultural patterns that gradually supersedes late modernity. It is a system made up of heterogeneous elements which are nevertheless held together by a dominant.[148] This dominant is the exchange value which Jameson analyses without taking into account the vast array of ideological reactions to it.

Compared with the concept of problematic underlying this book, Jameson's concept of 'epoch with a dominant' has the advantage of making postmodernity appear as a relatively homogeneous whole: as *a reified constellation deprived of historical consciousness*. At the same time, it has the disadvantage of obliterating the heterogeneous ideological reactions to the problematic and its development. How is it that a certain feminism can be conceived as a response to post-modern problems along with Koslowski's conservative ideology and O'Neill's

'Orphic Marxism'? This question can hardly be answered within an approach
based on the idea that postmodernity is marked by the loss of the historical
dimension. For this diagnosis applies neither to Koslowski's postmodern conservatism nor to O'Neill's 'Orphic Marxism' – both of which open historical
perspectives.

However, Jameson is by no means guilty of reducing postmodernity to such
negative components as 'the loss of historical consciousness'. For he views
the 'postmodern constellation' (Renner) as an ambivalent situation marked by
the coexistence of reification and emancipation. Adopting the point of view of
Critical Theory, one could nevertheless argue that, in spite of this ambivalence,
the reifying factors predominate in Jameson's model.

Among them is a 'new superficiality' which involves contemporary theory as
well as a culture primarily geared towards the electronically produced image, the
simulacrum.[149] This hypothesis which, on the one hand, bears out Baudrillard's
vision of a one-dimensional, purely phenomenal media reality (cf. Section 2.6),
on the other hand, substantiates the indifference-theorem put forward here, is
made plausible by Jameson when he explains that 'the culture of the simulacrum comes to life in a society where exchange value has been generalized to
the point at which the very memory of use value is effaced (. . .)'.[150]

According to Jameson's model, this global development has at least three
negative consequences. An atrophy of historical consciousness can be observed
in the course of which the historical perspective is gradually replaced by a
spatial one. Especially the media tend to replace historical continuity by an
'unexpected juxtaposition'[151] in space. The impact of this fragmented imagery
transported by the media leads to a destabilization of sensory perception and
to a dissociation of impressions and emotions from concrete individuals.
Emotions become free floating in the imaginary space of 'world events' created
by the media. This in turn leads to Jameson's conclusion that postmodern consciousness is caught in a space dominated by technologies: a space it cannot
escape from.

Jameson's global assessment of postmodernity could be summed up as follows: the culture of electronically transmitted images and its a-historical perception undermine all faith in a collective historical goal and a better future.[152]
Adopting Marcuse's terminology, one could say that the reification of consciousness by the media deletes the 'second dimension', i.e. the ability to see
through reified reality and to perceive alternatives. This development culminates in a disorientation of individual and collective subjects that is appre-
hended by Jameson as much as by Touraine, Beck and Etzioni.

In spite of these negative aspects of postmodernity, Jameson holds on to the
Marxian dialectic according to which capitalism is to be considered simultaneously as an historical progress *and* as a catastrophe.[153] The progress, Jameson
believes, may consist in a radical democratization of the media which may
still be expected to fulfil an informative, critical and didactic function. He imagines a media aesthetic that would decisively contribute to the reorientation
of individual and collective subjects in the sense of Brecht's 'Epic Theatre'.

Such an aesthetic would take advantage of the growth and the increasing availability of information in postmodern societies: 'Our social order is richer in information and more literate, and socially, at least, more "democratic" in the sense of the universalization of wage labor (. . .).'[154] It is certainly true that a vast amount of information has been accumulated in the course of the twentieth century; but it is also true that individual subjects find it increasingly difficult to cope with the dizzying growth of information material and hence cannot take advantage of its availability. Time and again, it is revealed that people read less and that, in certain social groups, literacy is in decline.

On the whole, it becomes clear that Jameson still looks for Marxist or late modern solutions to postmodern problems. Like Touraine and Beck, he asks how subjects can be strengthened in view of a globally expanding commodification and reification. However, unlike the French or German sociologist, Jameson is less inclined to relate the problem of democratization to the notion of social movement. He prefers to establish a link between postmodern democracy and a pedagogic and political culture in the sense of Brecht. In spite of their logical consistency, such proposals seem ineffective in view of what Adorno calls the 'psychotechnical treatment of the masses'. In a highly fragmented, pluralized and atomized society, the rise of a vigorous political anti-culture or subculture seems an unlikely event.

The Marxist discussion of postmodernity is radicalized by Alex Callinicos in *Against Postmodernism* (1989), where the success of postmodern tendencies and currents of thought is linked to the failure of communism and socialism in Eastern Europe: 'Not only does belief in a postmodern epoch generally go along with rejection of socialist revolution as either feasible or desirable, but it is the perceived failure of revolution which has helped to gain widespread acceptance of this belief.'[155]

A hypothesis is confirmed here that is also put forward by Marxists such as Terry Eagleton: that the collapse of the socialist experiment in the course of the 80s helped to establish the hegemony of postmodern thought diagnosed by Jameson. The confused and disappointed intellectuals of 1968 are seen as the driving force of postmodern thinking by Callinicos. Their final rejection of Marxism, which he interprets as a *trahison des clercs*,[156] appears to him as the actual postmodern turn. Eagleton explains this reaction of the intelligentsia, which announces its disappearance as a critical force,[157] in *The Illusions of Postmodernism* (1996):

> The power of capital is now so drearily familiar, so sublimely omnipotent and omnipresent, that even large sectors of the left have succeeded in naturalizing it, taking it for granted as such an unbudgable structure that it is as though they hardly have the heart to speak of it.[158]

In contrast with O'Neill and Jameson, who agree with some of the postmodern arguments aimed at Enlightenment rationalism, Callinicos is filled with scorn for liberal critics such as Bauman who believe 'that any attempt at total social change will lead straight to the Gulag'.[159] He tries to refute Bell's theory of postindustrial society by asserting, on the one hand, that the increase in the number of white collar workers cannot be deduced from the growth of the service sector and by arguing, on the other hand, that impoverished white collar workers are to be defined as working class. He adds that, in the course of industrialization of the Third World, an 'industrial working class on a global scale'[160] will emerge – and challenge the communist party's hegemony in China, one might add.

Once again, we are confronted here with some of the fundamental questions Marxists and Neo-Marxists have been grappling with for almost 150 years. What exactly is a social class? When do we speak of a 'class in itself', and when is it possible to speak of a 'class for itself'? Is the 'new working class' in the sense of André Gorz, Serge Mallet and Lucien Goldmann a class in the Marxian sense or not, etc.?

Callinicos is probably right in criticizing Jameson's theory for dealing too summarily with global capitalism, for analysing in detail the economic boom of the 1960s, which Jameson identifies with a new, postmodern phase of social development, and for completely neglecting the recession between 1975 and 1976. However, one cannot help feeling that Callinicos's basic aim is a reformulation of the Marxist theory of *economic cycles*. In spite of his allegiance to the Marxist tradition and his rejection of postmodern ideologies, his approach can also be understood as a reaction to the postmodern problematic. Like Touraine and Beck, although in a different theoretical and ideological context, he seeks historical alternatives to capitalism in the realm of *social movements*: in the Polish Solidarność, in the Workers' Party of Brazil, in the working class movements in South Korea, etc. After the year 2000, when especially Solidarność declined because it had lost its credibility, the hopes linked to such alternatives seem to be fading.

On the whole, it becomes increasingly obvious that some of the Marxist answers to postmodern questions can only be understood within the postmodern problematic: especially when they turn against a universalism and a historicism which were part and parcel of traditional Marxism. At the same time, several arguments put forward by Callinicos can be gauged as symptoms of a discursive tendency towards inertia which ideologies find difficult to overcome.

## 2.5  Pluralism, Indifference and Ideology

Not only the Marxist, but even the sociological reactions to postmodernity – e.g. those of Beck and Touraine – imply a logic of disintegration in the sense that they focus on the contradictions of modernity. Bureaucracy and freedom, rationalization and solidarity, production and consumption, commercialization and culture are seen as irreconcilable opposites which threaten the cohesion of modern societies. However, it is good to know that not all contemporary sociologists and philosophers consider postmodern developments with such scepticism.

In spite of all their dissents, proponents of a dynamic modernity like the sociologist Richard Münch and theoreticians of postmodernity such as Wolfgang Welsch seem to share the view that contemporary society, far from being on the brink of collapse, is about to gather new momentum. While Münch dismisses the notion of postmodernity as superfluous and believes that an *interpenetration* of crucial elements of modernity – of individual freedom and rationality, participation in social change and solidarity – is possible, Welsch imagines a postmodern modernity considered as a democratic and radically pluralized society.

Both approaches are worth considering because they make it clear that it is possible to construct the object 'postmodernity' without apocalyptic connotations. Münch quite rightly refuses to identify modernity with one of its aspects or phases, with nineteenth century capitalism, industrialism or Bauhaus-functionalism: 'All of these phenomena were children of modernity who have aged in the meantime or even died and have been superseded and replaced by new generations.'[161] He partly seems to confirm Callinicos's diagnosis according to which the decline of socialism gave a boost to postmodern modes of thought, because 'socialism turns conservative and loses its progressive role to other movements'.[162]

Münch seems confident that the interpenetration of the four factors mentioned above can guarantee a dynamic continuity:

Unlike Weber's theory of rationalization which, in its ultimate consequences, yields nothing but scepticism when the future relationship between individual freedom and social order is concerned, the theory of interpenetration relates freedom, rationality, social order and involvement in social change within a voluntarist order.[163]

It is not the task of this chapter to answer the question whether Münch's approach is actually a way out of the Weberian impasse. Having dealt with postmodern and late modern arguments put forward by Bauman, Beck, Bell and Touraine, it seems more relevant to ask why Münch ignores or underplays the social contradictions, risks and crises revealed by these sociologists and why politicians, who are permanently being confronted by chronic unemployment, social protests and growing criminality, have not yet begun to apply Münch's theory of interpenetration. Is it conceivable that their hectic lives have hitherto prevented them from inserting a sociological reading pause?

Although he does not think that the concept of postmodernity is superfluous, because he believes that modernity ought to be preserved and superseded by postmodernity, Wolfgang Welsch approaches the postmodern problematic with a confidence similar to Münch's. For reasons very different from those of the Weber disciple and Weber critic Münch, he refuses to place the contradictions and pitfalls of modernity at the centre of the theoretical scene: for he views the postmodern turn as a *realization of modern and late modern promises*. It is within the postmodern constellation, he explains, that modern pluralism will be realized and the promise of democratization fulfilled:

> Plurality is the key concept of postmodernity. All the notions that have come to be associated with postmodernity – such as the end of meta-narratives, the dispersion of the subject, the de-centred meaning, the co-presence of histori-cally distant features and the impossibility to synthesize heterogeneous forms of life and reason – can all be understood in the light of plurality.[164]

Welsch keeps insisting on the radicalization of this plurality in postmodern societies and emphasizes that cultural pluralism was already a fact in modernity. He quite rightly invokes Max Weber's dictum that the modern world is marked by a 'polytheism of values' and adds: 'Even from a sociological point of view, it becomes obvious that postmodernity is a continuation of modernity which it accomplishes by radicalizing it. For modernity was geared towards plurality – a salient feature of postmodernity – like no other society before it.'[165] In agree-ment with philosophers like Lyotard and Rorty, who will be commented on in the next chapter, Welsch opposes totalizing tendencies and a mode of thought which tends to subsume competing and colliding viewpoints under a common denominator.

He is obviously aware of the danger that an undifferentiated pluralism may turn into indifference. This is probably the reason why he is so keen on dissoci-ating his notion of pluralism from superficiality and indifference. It is simply mindless, he argues, to confuse postmodernity with a 'levelling anything goes'.[166] He is nevertheless conscious of the risk emanating from radical pluralism, when he explains: 'A new arbitrariness would by no means be better than the old imperialism. And today, postmodernity should not, by resisting the latter, fall prey to the former.'[167] It should not, it must not. Who will prevent it from doing so, since Welsch himself observes – very much like Jameson – the postmodern propensity towards superficiality and arbitrariness? This kind of exorcism is not a solution, for it will never be a substitute for systematic sociological analyses.

It obliterates what Peter L. Berger and other authors call the 'discontents of modernity'[168]: the discontents that emanate directly or indirectly from a tech-nological economy and that increase as postmodernity progresses. Welsch, the advocate of pluralism, disposes too light-heartedly of Berger's diagnosis accord-ing to which 'there are also discontents specifically derived from the pluralization of social life-worlds'.[169] Hence an apology of pluralism cannot be an appropri-ate answer to postmodern problems.

One of the reasons why sociologies of postmodernity were dealt with along with postmodern sociologies was the fact that a sociological analysis of the prob-lematic, which is virtually absent from Welsch's work,[170] is an indispensable framework within which the key philosophical and literary arguments have to be understood. So far, these arguments have yielded the following insights:

1. Pluralism (very much like individualism, democratization, secularization and rationalization) is inseparable from the consolidated market economy the laws of which impose themselves on all social contexts thus threatening the autonomy of culture and art.
2. The strong tendency towards particularization, which accompanies the rise of pluralism and the fragmentation of the social world, makes political, ethical and aesthetic values look increasingly trivial and interchangeable.
3. Eventually, the exchange value, the universally recognized common denominator, which negates all qualitative, cultural values, appears to producers and consumers as the only valid criterion.

Welsch's main problem is due to his tendency to ignore *in-difference* as *interchangeability of trivialized values* and to reduce it to *one of its effects*: to superficiality and emotional indifference. However, indifference as a sociological and sociosemiotic concept does not mean the affective indifference of individuals, but refers to the insight of both ordinary people and scientists that certain values, which may mean a lot to them, are no longer shared by others, have to compete with counter-values and thus turn out to be contingent.

Most consumers, who rush to the next underground station, ignoring a handful of Jehovah's witnesses and a demonstration of Greenpeace activists, are unlikely to belittle religious beliefs or efforts to save the threatened environment; but the only pressing question that is *common to them all* concerns the state of their bank account. Thus the exchange value survives as the only universally ackowledged value in postmodernity.

Max Weber, who spoke of the 'polytheism of values', anticipated the *modern* tendency towards indifference when he wrote:

> The levelling effect of 'every day life' in the original sense of this expression consists in the fact that the individual, who is immersed in this life, is unaware of the psychologically and pragmatically caused confusion of mutually incompatible values and that he does not even *wish* to become aware of it: i.e. that he eschews the choice between 'God' and 'Devil' as well as a final decision regarding the question which of the colliding values is to be attributed to the former and which to the latter.[171]

This impossibility to choose as an active subject is characteristic of a *social situation* marked by *in-difference* which should not be reduced to emotional superficiality. (About the relationship between ambiguity, ambivalence and indifference more will be said in Section 2.6 and in Chapter 4.)

Hence these considerations should not be taken to mean that, at the end of the day, all people will be indifferent to everything. On the contrary: the problematic mapped out here implies a social anomie in the sense of Durkheim to which individuals and groups may react with *ideological dualism*. Such dualism is opposed to indifference, but at the same time functions as a *dialectical complement to the latter.* Therefore postmodernity should not only be envisaged as a post-ideological era of tolerant pluralism, but also as a world of ideological polarization and conflict. In a society where traditional religious, moral and political values have ceased to be convincing and relevant to the constitution of subjectivity, dualistic ideologies and ideological fanaticism may often fill the moral void.[172]

The fact that Welsch ignores the ideological reactions to indifference and pluralism explains his postmodern optimism which at times assumes bucolic features. His statement 'that an adequate practice of plurality will not be easy'[173] sounds like a euphemism in the context of this chapter. Münch's theory of modernity as interpenetration of individualism, rationalization, solidarity and activism is complementary to Welsch's arguments insofar as it also brackets out the growing conflict potential. Both authors tend to ignore the problems of individuals whose flight from the pluralistic world of indifference and anomie ends in ideological dualism which transforms them into active subjects: into fighters for a 'cause'.

## 2.6 The Case of Baudrillard: Indifference without Ideology

Baudrillard is a 'case' and this final section a kind of case study, because his work exposes essential aspects of the postmodern problematic and gives an extreme form to the concept of indifference. Unlike Münch and Welsch, who tend to highlight the potential of democratization inherent in late modern or postmodern societies and to overlook the pitfalls of organized capitalism, Baudrillard puts indifference as exchangeability of values, emotions and impressions at the centre of his analyses. He turns it – along with the notions of *simulation* and *sign exchange* – into a key concept of his theory of *postmodernity as posthistoire.*

In *L'Illusion de la fin*, both concepts crop up and can almost be read as synonyms:

> Production, market, ideology, profit, utopia (profit is itself a utopia), all that was modern, the capitalist economy of competition was modern – our economy, which is unreal and speculative and does not even know the ideas of production, profit and progress, is no longer modern but postmodern (elle est post-moderne).[174]

It becomes clear at this point that, from Baudrillard's point of view, Mannheim's key concepts of *ideology* and *utopia* belong to a bygone modern era and cannot be revived in postmodernity. The latter is also referred to by Baudrillard as 'our post-history' ('notre post-histoire'),[175] because he believes, as will be shown later on, that events and ideologies become indistinguishable in late capitalist media simulation. In this respect, he agrees with Jameson who borrowed some of his ideas.

This is probably the reason why Wolfgang Welsch, who tends to present post-modernism as a pluralistic idyll, condemns the sociologist of Nanterre as a 'leading figure of the diffuse, border-blurring postmodernism',[176] associating him with the negative notion of *posthistoire*. 'Baudrillard', he explains, 'is not a thinker of postmodernity, but reformulates another, an older diagnostic: that of *posthistoire*.'[177] He goes on to construct a rigid dualism between *postmodernity* and *posthistoire*. 'By contrast, the theorem of postmodernity is of a different calibre, and nothing is more confusing than a lumping together of postmodernity and *posthistoire*.'[178]

It is certainly true that a conceptual mix is not acceptable as a theoretical recipe; the question is, however, whether it makes sense to adopt Welsch's narrow definition and to exclude the conservative Koslowski (cf. Section 2.3) as well as the apocalyptic Baudrillard from an idealized postmodernity, instead of inserting their mutually incompatible perspectives into the postmodern prob-lematic. Is Koslowski's conservatism not an ideological reaction to the phenom-enon of indifference analysed by Baudrillard? Is indifference not the dominant structure within which nationalist, liberal, fundamentalist, feminist and conser-vative ideologies oppose each other?

This is not what Baudrillard thinks. He sets out from the idea that, after the collapse of Marxism–Leninism and the May-revolts of 1968, political ideologies and politics in general no longer count, because the exchange value as 'fractal value' (cf. below) turns into an end in itself and eventually obliterates all use values that point beyond the world of exchange, thus usurping reality as such. In this situation, politics and ideologies tend to disappear as independent factors, because the entire sector of material and cultural use value production is absorbed by the exchange value and by the abstraction of exchange.

In this context, Baudrillard speaks of the 'involution of the political', the 'resorption of the political'[179] and argues in *Simulacres et simulation* that political and ideological contrasts are levelled out in indifference as interchangeability of values and viewpoints: 'What has disappeared is the hostility of enemies, the reality of incompatible projects, the ideological seriousness of war.'[180] In an unprecedented complicity, European communists and socialists look after capi-talist economies, and the communist governments of China and Vietnam encourage their growth – in spite of the apparent antagonism between Vietnam and the USA.

In this social situation governed by the exchange value, even Marxist ideol-ogy and theory are condemned to aporia. In *La Gauche divine*, a chronicle of French politics between 1977 and 1984, Baudrillard shows how the French Left looks after late capitalism, thus systematically postponing revolution instead of bringing it about. In view of this stagnation, which entails an 'emaciation' of Marxism as political practice, he announces in an apocalyptic fashion 'the end of the great Marxist promise'[181] and predicts in a rhetorical sweeping blow the end of the subject, of revolution and history. In *La Gauche divine*, where not a word is said about France's limited scope of action within the EU, the OECD and NATO, he observes the 'liquidation of history' and the 'end of history'.[182]

One might suspect at this stage that Baudrillard's work articulates the kind of apocalyptic feeling which marked the rhetoric of many Paris intellectuals after the failure of the 1968 uprising and the decline of West-European Marxism. Baudrillard, who, in his early writings, pinned all his hopes on a revolt of marginal groups,[183] eventually dismisses this kind of residual Marxism and embraces a postmodern Nietzschean thought which is hostile to both ideology and the critique of ideology. For he believes that social reality, defined in relation to the use value and to critical thought, is no longer perceptible. Its essence has been absorbed by the appearance of the exchange value.

Why is it that Baudrillard's sociological model can be considered as Nietzschean and what exactly does it look like? His thought, very much like that of some poststructuralist philosophers such as Deleuze, Lyotard and Derrida, can be defined negatively as anti-Platonism and anti-Hegelianism. Christopher Norris certainly has a point when he refers to Baudrillard's 'inverted Platonism'[184] which tends to replace essence by appearance, true knowledge (as *noesis* or *epistemè*) by rhetoric and the signified by the signifier.

It is at the same time an 'inverted Hegelianism' which is only aware of appearances and therefore dismisses as irrelevant all questions concerning essence. They are a product of totalizing knowledge. The dialectical question of Hegelians like Lukács and Goldmann, how the 'appearance and the delusion of this inferior, transitory world'[185] can be dissolved even under late capitalism, is replaced in Baudrillard's theory by a vertiginous dance 'over the surface',[186] as he himself puts it. He goes on to quote Nietzsche's well-known text whose author praises the superficiality of the ancient Greeks: 'They knew how to live . . . to stop . . . at the surface, the fold, the skin, to believe in forms, tones, words. . . . Those Greeks were superficial – out of *profundity*.'[187]

Baudrillard also decides to remain on the surface out of a deep distrust of depths. For he no longer believes in the possibility of discovering essence or reality behind appearances. His representation of the epistemological shift, which came about during the transition from the nineteenth to the twentieth century, is an impressive metanarrative in the sense of Lyotard (Section 3.2) and bears witness to a growing agnosticism that is at the same time a Nietzschean bias:

> The real revolution of the 19th century, of modernity, is the radical destruction of appearance, the disenchantment of the world and its submission to the violence of interpretation and history. (. . .) The second revolution, that of the 20th century, of postmodernity, which is a gigantic process of the destruction of meaning, equals the previous destruction of appearance. Whoever strikes with meaning, is struck dead by meaning.[188]

Relying on this – thoroughly historical – interpretation of the last two centuries, Baudrillard finds that the dialectical and the critical scenes are empty: 'La scène dialectique, la scène critique sont vides. Il n'y a plus de scène.'[189]

In a situation where reality (Hegel's *essence*) has been obliterated by appearance, the central point, from where appearance could be criticized, also disappears.

This is probably why, in Baudrillard's work, the word *disparition* occurs so frequently – along with the Hegelian expression *Furie des Verschwindens* (German in: *Simulacres et simulation*, p. 231).[190] Along with reality, meaning, truth, the social, history and the individual disappear. 'Beyond everything', a title an English colleague was considering for his next book, seems a fair description of Baudrillard's way of looking at things – or rather their absence.

What does this 'fury of disappearance' look like in Baudrillard's sociological and semiotic model? In his works published in the 1960s and 70s – *Le Système des objets* (1968) and *Pour une critique de l'économie politique du signe* (1972) –, he sets out from the plausible hypothesis that, in late capitalist society, the mediation by the exchange value invades all spheres of life and that it becomes increasingly difficult to distinguish use value from exchange value and to be aware of the disappearance of use values. While Marx and the Marxists observe the process of increasing mediation, but nevertheless continue to emphasize the crucial difference between use value and exchange value, Baudrillard believes that the basic difference that structured the critique of political economy has vanished: 'The point where the Marxist analysis is most convincing, is at the same time its weakest spot: namely the distinction between use value and exchange value.'[191] In Baudrillard's perspective, objects in market societies tend to disappear in the ever faster turnover of goods and are replaced by simple signs of the exchange value.

Using Marx's critique of political economy in a subversive way, the author of *Pour une critique de l'économie politique du signe* maps out a three-tier model in order to illustrate the dissolution of the use value in the exchange value in the course of social development. In *La Transparence du Mal*, a fourth tier is added to this model: a 'natural state' ('stade naturel') of the use value is followed by a 'commercial phase' ('stade commercial'), followed by a 'structural phase' ('stade structural') which is marked by an unprecedented domination of the exchange value. This third phase was structured by a code, 'and the value expanded here in relation to a number of models',[192] i.e. it could no longer be related to concrete objects. Baudrillard calls the fourth and last phase in the development of the exchange value the 'fractal phase':

> In the fourth phase, the fractal or rather viral or, better still, radiating phase of the value, a referent can no longer be indicated: the value radiates in all directions, into all gaps without being related to anything at all – out of sheer contiguity.[193]

This is the reason why he refers to 'the value' in general, meaning the all-embracing exchange value that can no longer be distinguished or defined.

In the 'structural' or 'fractal' phase of monopoly and state monopoly capitalism, use value and exchange value, clearly distinguished by Marx, who analysed the 'commercial phase' of liberal capitalism, become indistinguishable. From *Pour une critique de l'économie politique du signe* onwards, Baudrillard speaks of a 'determining logic of the exchange value'[194] and of a 'generalization of the

exchange value'.[195] Material appearance obliterates everything, thereby excluding all questions aiming at a reality beyond appearance.

The appearance of the exchange value is reinforced on a linguistic and a
semiotic level by the signifier whose materiality and ambiguity render superfluous all questions concerning meaning or truth (the 'presence of meaning',
Derrida would say). The signifier appears as an aspect of the exchange value
when Baudrillard points out: 'The signified (and the referent) are mere *effects*
of the signifier (. . .).'[196] This idea, which Baudrillard shares with Barthes,
Derrida and other authors of the *Tel-Quel*-Group whom he quotes,[197] is a
Nietzschean attempt to equal appearance with society as such and to exclude
conceptuality, meaning, reality and truth from theory.

In *Le Crime parfait*, this point of view takes shape:

> Thus the prophecy is fulfilled according to which we live in a world where
> the original function of the sign consists in making reality disappear and in
> concealing this disappearance at the same time. Contemporary art doesn't
> do anything else. The media don't do anything else.[198]

This disappearance of reality, which comes about imperceptibly, is referred
to by Baudrillard as 'the perfect crime'. (He uses an expression from his book
*De la séduction*, where the highly discrete and hardly noticeable manoeuvring of
Kierkegaard's seducer is described as a 'perfect crime'.)[199]

The simulacrum of the media appears to him as a subtle synthesis of the
exchange value, as a signifier without a referent. Following Marshall McLuhan's
thesis 'medium is message', he tries to show to what extent the units of meaning
become self-referential: like the signifiers, like the exchange value. By produc-
ing simulacra without origin or reality, the medium refers exclusively to itself,
thus giving rise to a hyper-reality: 'The hyperreal represents a much more
advanced phase insofar as it effaces the contradiction of the real and the
imaginary.'[200]

Hyper-reality comes about as its simulacra are detached from what is commonly called the 'real world'. In *Simulacres et simulation*, Baudrillard distinguishes four kinds of images: images that can be related to a 'fundamental
reality' ('réalité profonde'); images that mask and distort this reality; images
that mask the absence of such a reality and, finally, images or pure simulacra
that are independent of all notions of reality.[201] 'The transition from signs which
hide something to signs which hide the fact that there is nothing (qu'il n'y a
rien) is the decisive turning point,'[202] the author explains.

It is worth focusing on the analogy between these four categories of images
and the four phases of the mediation by the exchange value. The first category
corresponds to the 'natural phase of the use value'; the second to the 'commercial phase', the 'capitalisme marchand', where considerable distortions can be
observed; the third corresponds to the 'structural phase' of monopoly capitalism,
where the reference to reality gradually disappears; and the fourth coincides

with the 'fractal phase' of state monopoly capitalism, where all links with reality are lost.

What is at stake here is not a simple analogy, but the fact that the world of the media is a world of simulacra and of simulation which appears to the sociologist as a world mediated by the *exchange value* defined as *sign value*:

In this way the era of simulation is announced everywhere by the commuta- bility of formerly contradictory or dialectically opposed terms. Everywhere we see the same 'genesis of simulacra': the commutability of the beautiful and the ugly in fashion, of the left and the right in politics, of the true and the false in every media message, the useful and the useless at the level of objects, nature and culture at every level of signification.[203]

Here it becomes clear what Baudrillard means by 'simulacrum': not an illu- sion that falls apart sooner or later when it collides with reality, but something unreal, chimerical that usurps the place of the real and can without difficulty, imperceptibly be replaced by its opposite.

Faithful to his rhetoric of sweeping statements, Baudrillard gives his theory of indifference an extreme turn when he writes: 'Everything becomes undecid- able, the characteristic effect of the domination of the code, which everywhere rests on the principle of neutralisation, of indifference. This is the generalised brothel of capital, a brothel not for prostitution, but for substitution and commutation.'[204] At the same time, he dismantles his theory by cancelling the opposition between use value and exchange value, thus precluding himself from distinguishing truth from falsehood: 'Everything becomes undecidable . . .' This is the end of scientific theory. Where indifference as interchangeability of items coincides with the real, it also becomes a matter of indifference whether Marx, Althusser, Baudrillard or Francis Fukuyama interprets capitalism cor- rectly – for even theory turns into an exchange of simulacra. Hence Baudrillard would be well-advised to abandon his favourite expression 'in reality'. Where reality is obliterated by total simulation, it can no longer function as a referent of discourse.

One should nevertheless avoid dismissing Baudrillard's theory as 'unscien- tific', 'elitist' (M. Billig)[205] or as 'empty rhetoric'. It is particularly important for the discussion about modernity and postmodernity because it shows the *problem of indifference* to be a crucial dimension of the postmodern problematic. Without the concept of indifference, as analysed by Baudrillard and redefined here as *interchangeability of values and positions*, postmodernity cannot be understood. Baudrillard is so often derided or attacked and provokes so many verbal aggres- sions because liberal, conservative and socialist thinkers refuse to believe in the bankruptcy of their value systems: a bankruptcy described by the French sociologist.

However, this is also the crucial point which Baudrillard neglects when he speaks of the 'end of the idea' ('fin de l'idée')[206] and, more specifically, of the end of ideology and the political. For ideology is by no means dead; on the contrary, it continues to play an important part within the postmodern problematic by enabling individuals and groups to turn into agents. In a context dominated by indifference, ideological reactions (e.g. against Baudrillard's notion of indifference)[207] are even more pronounced than in the era of modern ambiguity or of late modern (modernist) ambivalence. The era of indifference is – as was aptly pointed out by Touraine (Section 2.1) – very much an era of ideologies, all of which are relegated by Baudrillard to the realm of the simulacra – along with individual and collective subjectivities.

For this reason the concept of indifference used here is not synonymous with Baudrillard's. It is defined in relation to modern ambiguity and modernist ambivalence (which leads to indifference); at the same time it is dialectically related to the dualistic discourse of ideology which continues to oppose ambiguity, ambivalence and indifference. The decline of old international ideologies such as fascism, National Socialism or Marxism–Leninism that is partly responsible for the rise of postmodern rhetorics, by no means excludes new ideologies such as fundamentalism, eco-politics, feminism, nationalism.

The reason why Baudrillard does not take ideology as a 'discourse of meaning'[208] seriously is well known. By deleting the contrast between use value and exchange value, instead of dealing with it dialectically, he is unaware of what remains outside the realm of exchange, thereby defying the 'signifier', the 'code', as he puts it.

Although it is true that, in contemporary society, the exchange value has penetrated into all spheres of life (including religion, science, sports), it is inadmissible to narrow down the dynamics of society to its market laws: for one ceases to understand its development. Independently of Baudrillard, the German Marxist Wolfgang Fritz Haug observes: 'From the point of view of exchange value, use value is but a delusion.'[209] However, he will categorically refuse to adopt this viewpoint and thus abandon all critical perspectives which are always based on an ideological engagement. This is the crucial difference between Baudrillard on the one hand and Marxism or Critical Theory on the other.

For it is impossible to understand late capitalist economy without postulating the existence of a use value. (It goes without saying that 'late capitalism' is a discursive construction: both in Marxism and in Critical Theory.) The functioning of such an economy becomes incomprehensible if one cannot assume that most consumers take into account the use value – in spite of all publicity gimmicks.[210] It would be naïve to believe that the reason why many Japanese, Korean and Chinese products, especially cameras and computers, are more successful than their European or American rivals is simply due to advertising and packaging. The decisive factor is the combination of their technical use value with their relatively low price. From the point of view of a *competent* person using computers or cameras and interested in the storage capacity of a hard disk or the precision of a light meter, the *relationship* between use value and exchange value has to be reasonable.

It is conceivable, of course, that there are customers who buy a phallic camera with a large telephoto lens or who prefer the elegance of a small camera that fits into a *Dior* handbag, because such items transport certain connotations within the social sign system or in what Baudrillard calls the 'code'. But they do not represent the customer in general. It is probably not by chance that, in his early writings, Baudrillard's presents the car[211] as his favourite example. For the red sports car is full of mythical connotations and can be exchanged for social prestige, speed addiction, Eros and Thanatos. However, not all customers are equally immature or 18 years old. Had Baudrillard taken the trouble to leave the lofty heights of abstraction and descend into the world of empirical analysis, he might have discovered that consumers interested in computers and cameras tend to take the use value seriously and are only occasionally deceived by marketing strategies and advertising. Unfortunately, Baudrillard tends to consider the world of simulacra as being co-extensive with the social world.

As a disillusioned postmodern post-Marxist he develops an aversion towards empirical research and a concomitant propensity towards mythical thought. In his perspective, not the use value appears as an alternative to the hyper-reality of exchange value, but the *symbolic exchange* of archaic or mythical societies: i.e. the non-commercial reciprocity of gift and counter-gift as expressed in a generous action situated beyond production and capital accumulation.

Gerd Bergfleth summarizes succinctly Baudrillard's key argument:

In Baudrillard's world, symbolic exchange functions as the absolute Other: it is the principle of universal subversion which is meant to reverse and replace the principle of universal simulation. Its alterity implies above all a completely different form of exchange that cannot be dealt with in economic terms: the form of generosity that excludes equivalence and does not constitute a value, but rather guarantees social cohesion by way of reciprocity. The model of symbolic exchange is the model of social exchange among primitives as expressed in the exchange of gifts.[212]

The underlying idea is obviously an enhancement of pre-capitalist patterns of life which are presented as an alternative to the hopelessly lethal system of hyper-real simulation. Like Lucien Goldmann, a contemporary of Baudrillard, who projected the archaic *human community* (*la communauté humaine*) into a post-capitalist future,[213] the early Baudrillard opposes the archaic myth to a late capitalist system he rejects. The difference between the Marxist and the post-Marxist consists in the fact that Goldmann's *human community* is oriented towards the future and a better life, whereas Baudrillard's symbolic exchange declares its solidarity with death: 'The system itself is driven towards its nihilistic disintegration, because it devalues everything by simulation, but its real end, which even "devalues" devaluation, presupposes something completely different that comes to light along with the sacrificial character of symbolic exchange.'[214] This sacrifice, which is realized by death, finds its clearest expression in terrorism. The terrorist sacrifices his hostage and at the same time is sacrificed himself.

'In a system', Baudrillard explains, 'which adds up living and capitalises life, the death drive is the only alternative.'[215]

It may be tempting, but it is probably unjust to read Baudrillard's work as an apology of terrorism and violent death, especially since he distanced himself in the 1980s and 90s from his fundamental work which was published in 1976.[216] However, advocates of Critical Theory, who hold with Adorno that the entire social system is 'false' and therefore prefer negation to any kind of constructive or affirmative action, will notice, while reading Baudrillard, that the absolute negation of the existing order – as hyper-reality or false totality – is either ineffective (as Sartre already observed in his critique of Mallarmé)[217] or conducive to despair and violence.

This is the reason why this kind of negativity is eventually rejected here in the last chapter. It is superseded by the question of a die-hard rationalist concerning the possibilities and perspectives contemporary society still has to offer. Should it become clear at one point that humanity has no future any more (for ecological or other reasons and because both capitalism and socialism have failed), then this diagnostic is to be accepted: without recurring to post-Marxist mythologies which merely dissolve problems in nebulosity.

Baudrillard's discourse is responsible for this kind of theoretical nebulosity in spite of the fact that it sheds new light on the problematic of indifference: it finally succumbs to the indifference principle, because the French sociologist keeps putting forward ambiguous arguments which can be inverted and are immune to criticism. In what follows, seven discursive mechanisms underlying his theory will be analysed in some detail, and it will be shown to what extent they subvert this theory on the level of argument: 1. *totalization as exaggeration*; 2. *mechanisms of immunization and of discursive monologue*; 3. *polysemy*; 4. *metaphors*; 5. *associations*; 6. *mythical actants and actors*; 7. *an apocalyptic teleology inherent in the theory as a whole*. In order to avoid misunderstandings and unjust criticism, the French original will also be quoted.

It goes without saying that an exhaustive semiotic analysis of Baudrillard's discourse cannot be envisaged here; the aim of this epilogue is to put forward a few examples in order to reveal the dubious nature of his way of thinking.

1. *Totalization* and *exaggeration* often cause an argument to become invertible. 'We have moved from the Other to the Same, from alienation to identification (...).' ('On est passé de l'Autre au Même, de l'aliénation à l'identification [. . .].')[218] Unfortunately, the opposite statement seems as plausible: We may also have moved from the Same to the Other, from identification to alienation.

2. Baudrillard is a champion of *immunization* whenever he indulges in apodictic statements, as for example in *Simulacres et simulation*, where he proclaims (in 1981) that 'the deterrent excludes war' ('la dissuasion exclut la guerre').[219] Counter-arguments are monologically ignored. The apocalyptic prophecy at the end of *L'Illusion de la fin* 'that one day everything will collapse' ('un jour

tout va craquer')[220] is impossible to refute – especially since the author of that book also takes the view that history will continue as before, because everything moves in a circle: '*History will not end.*' ('*L'Histoire n'aura pas de fin.*')[221] Which of these two statements is to be considered as valid? Probably both of them, since everything is interchangeable.

3. *Polysemy* is one of the salient features of Baudrillard's discourse: 'Contemporary revolution is a revolution of uncertainty.' ('La révolution contemporaine est celle de l'incertitude.')[222] The reader may wonder whether social revolutions were ever marked by 'certainty'.

4. Like some of his postmodern colleagues, Baudrillard adopts a very generous, almost poetic attitude towards *metaphor*. Thus he writes about the unification of 'heavenly' Western Europe with 'hellish' Eastern Europe:

> Since then, the barrier that separated hell from paradise has been liquidated. And in this case, of course, liquefaction is becoming general, and it is always hell that submerges paradise. (Désormais, la barrière qui séparait l'enfer du paradis a été liquidée. Et dans ce cas, bien entendu, la liquéfaction est générale, et c'est toujours l'enfer qui submerge le paradis.)[223]

Nobody will deny the fact that prognoses concerning the reintegration of Eastern Europe into the West European system are a dicey venture. But Baudrillard's biblical and aquatic metaphors will hardly be considered relevant by sociologists or political scientists, especially since the European integration process has been reasonably successful after 2004 (in spite of economic, financial and political problems in Poland, Latvia or Hungary).

5. Baudrillard is also a champion of *association*, and it is quite astonishing to see how he manages to link topics that are apparently miles apart in a rhizome-like web: 'Aids, stock market crash, electronic viruses, terrorism are not interchangeable, but they seem to belong to one family.') ('Le Sida, le krach, les virus électroniques, le terrorisme, ne sont pas interchangeables, mais ils ont un air de famille.')[224] Although it is encouraging to hear that not *everything* is interchangeable, it remains difficult to imagine a link between the 'stock market crash' and the 'viruses' – in spite of Baudrillard's metaphoric use of the word 'contagion'.

6. A special part is played in Baudrillard's discourse by *mythical actants* (in the sense of Greimas and his followers): by instances whose empirical status is more than dubious. History, the system, the world, the media or society as a whole act like the sun or the moon in fairy tales: 'Sometime in the 1980s, history turned in the other direction.' ('Quelque part dans les années 80 du XXᵉ siècle, l'histoire a pris son virage dans l'autre direction.')[225] One almost expects to hear that Jupiter disagreed with the new direction and cruelly punished History for its deviance.

7. Finally, Baudrillard's entire discourse is governed by an *apocalyptic teleology* which is clearly expressed by the prophecy that 'all will collapse' and by most

of his more recent works. In his world, both, total simulation and symbolic exchange, end in death.

As in the case of Bauman and other postmodernists, the apocalyptic mood of Baudrillard's work can be explained as a reaction or over-reaction to the unfulfilled hopes of modernity. Postmodern disappointment with modernity is most clearly articulated in *Le Crime parfait*:

> All of modernity was geared towards the arrival of this reality, the liberation of humans and real energies that would change the world objectively and beyond all illusions (. . .). Today, the world has become real in a sense that surpasses all of our hopes.[226]

The second sentence is bitter irony: in the sense that our hopes have been realized, but at the same time perverted. The dream has turned into a nightmare.

Baudrillard, who, as was shown above, is quite happy to stay aloof from empirical research, is not very fond of details. This is probably one of the reasons why he is not particularly interested in the question whether contemporary European society carries a critical potential and how this potential could be activated. In an apocalyptic discourse marked by total negation, such a question can only appear as a meaningless foreign body.

This is why, in his book on America and in *Le Crime parfait*, he only sneers at European politics. He criticizes Europe's inability to bring about a 'federal event' ('événement fédéral')[227] and believes that modernity was only imagined by the Europeans, whereas it was realized by the USA. In *Le Crime parfait*, he blames 'Europe', a mythical actant, for being absent from the Bosnian war, from Sarajevo, and speaks of 'l'Europe introuvable'.[228]

The European Union, which still lacks a government, is often absent from the international political stage and is sometimes prevented from speaking with one voice, because there are too many apocalyptic intellectuals like Baudrillard (even among politicians) who are not really interested in European integration. In the last chapter, it will be shown that there is a critical dimension to this integration which can be considered as an alternative to Baudrillard's visions of collective death. History is not coming to an end, and the future of Europe may just have begun.

# Chapter 3

# Postmodern Philosophies as Critiques of Modernity

Time and again Jean-François Lyotard insisted on the fact that postmodernity is not a new period or a new era, but a counter-movement inherent in modernity.[1] However, the attentive reader, who still remembers Foucault, Deleuze and Vattimo, cannot help feeling that the continuity, which is supposed to link modernity to postmodernity, hides a break.[2] For it is not by chance that in his work Lyotard emphasizes the postmodern 'incredulity toward metanarratives',[3] mentions a 'decline'[4] of these metanarratives and points out that postmodernity marks the end of the people as sovereign: 'Postmodernity is also the end of the people as sovereign of the stories.'[5] In other words: Lyotard keeps presenting postmodernity as a new beginning, as a break with old modes of living and thinking.

Even if one is aware – with historians and hermeneutic philosophers – of the overlapping of historical periods[6], example of postmodern elements in modernity and modernism, one would like to know more about the historical break announced by the prefix 'post': not only in Lyotard's work, but also in the works of authors such as Eco, Rorty and Vattimo. This break becomes apparent as soon as one compares the philosophical problematic of this chapter with the sociological problematic constructed in Chapter 2.

As in sociology, where Bauman, Beck, Touraine and Giddens bid farewell to the automatism of progress, to classes and the performance principle[7], to industrial society and to what Giddens calls the 'evolutionary narrative',[8] an historical turn is announced in philosophy. Authors such as Foucault, Lyotard and Deleuze not only criticize the conceptual patterns of modern thought, of Enlightenment rationalism, Hegelianism and Marxism, but at the same time follow Benjamin, Adorno and Horkheimer by linking these patterns to the principle of domination. In the process, subjectivity not only appears as individual freedom, but is also understood as subjection or subjugation in the sense of Foucault and Althusser. This postmodern critical turn seems to confirm the hostility towards the notion of progress as expressed in Adorno's *Negative Dialectics*: 'It is not true that the object is a subject, as idealism has been drilling into us for thousands of years, but it is true that the subject is an object.'[9]

The critique of this submission or sub-jection, whose different forms are meticulously analysed by Michel Foucault, leads to a radical reckoning with idealist (rationalist, Hegelian) universalism in Adorno's work. Like Lyotard, the author of *Economie libidinale* (1974), Adorno links this universalism to the exchange value:

> The universal domination of mankind by the exchange value – a domination which a priori keeps the subjects from being subjects and degrades subjectivity itself to a mere object – makes an untruth of the general principle that claims to establish the subject's predominance.[10]

This rejection of universality in the name of a humiliated particularity, in the name of exploited nature, not only relates postmodern critiques of modernity to those of Critical Theory, but also announces an affinity between postmodern philosophy and contemporary sociology.

Like the sociologists, who ponder on the consequences of scientific, technological and technical progress, linking the latter to imminent crises rather than to a progressive emancipation of humanity, the philosophers cast doubts upon the legitimacy of Christian, rationalist, Hegelian and Marxist metanarratives. Like Camus in the 1950s, they reject the secularized eschatology of Marxism: 'The Bolsheviks thought that they had turned a page of history,'[11] Foucault remarks and thus reveals the illusory character of Marxist historicism.

Where the notion of universal history as a legitimating factor is abandoned, the faith in the universal validity of modern concepts such as 'humanity', 'human nature', 'human rights', 'truth' and 'emancipation' is shaken. Like the sociologists, who tend to defend the particular interests of movements, marginal groups and individuals against a totalitarian social administration in order to promote *critical action* in the sense of Touraine[12], philosophers declare their solidarity with the particular: with the non-compliant, the eccentric, the unassimilated, with whatever cannot be subsumed under the common denominator of universal logos. Like Bauman, Touraine and Beck, Deleuze and Lyotard plead in favour of a radical pluralism of minorities, a 'patchwork of minorities' (Lyotard) which does not follow any general rule.

However, this radical pluralism, which emphasizes the idiosyncratic and the particular, involves certain problems, as was pointed out in the previous chapter. In a situation where the manifold particularities cannot be subsumed under a common denominator, the problem of relativism surfaces again. In such a situation, the question concerning the interchangeable character of incompatible or incommensurate positions, first raised by Mannheim's sociology of knowledge, crops up once more. Unlike Mannheim's approach, which is a concession to relativism, because the 'free-floating intellectuals', who are meant to aspire towards universal knowledge, cannot fulfil this function,[13] the tendency towards particularity observable in Critical Theory does not necessarily imply indifference in the relativist sense of interchangeable positions. For Adorno and

Horkheimer presuppose the existence of certain concepts and values such as autonomy, individuality, truth and reason which appear to them as universal in character.

In the case of Deleuze, Lyotard, Foucault and Rorty, one is often reminded of the desperate situation of Diotima in Robert Musil's famous novel: 'Whenever Diotima felt almost ready to opt in favour of such an idea, she had to admit that it would also be a good thing to go for its opposite.'[14] Which ideas should be realized in postmodernity whose supporters advocate the contingency of all perspectives, along with pluralism and particularism? Why should one prefer Rorty's 'liberal democracy'[15] to Lyotard's anti-capitalist 'patchwork of minorities' or to Etzioni's 'communitarian politics'? Would it not be an equally 'good thing' to realize the opposite of whatever political ideal? In this case, of course, everything would stay as it is, and the indifference of market society would continue to function as the basis of disorientation.

The danger of incommensurability and interchangeability arising from the coexistence of heterogeneous particularities is one of the reasons why a postmodernist disciple of Lyotard such as Wolfgang Welsch does everything to avoid the undifferentiated pluralism of some postmodern philosophies. For the other side of the pluralist coin is indifference. Commenting on Deleuze's and Guattari's metaphor of 'rhizome' (cf. Section 3.3), Welsch points out: 'In this respect, rhizomatic thought is the type of thought we are looking for, because it fulfils the function of relating heterogeneity and transition (*Übergang*) which apparently cannot be reconciled, but nevertheless have to be thought of as complementary.'[16] Welsch's idea of a 'transversal reason' could be considered as a systematic, but also paradoxical attempt to save postmodern pluralism and particularism by dissociating them from an indifferent heterogeneity. His approach will be dealt with in the fourth section and in the last chapter. Instead of a 'transversal thought' in the sense of Deleuze's and Guattari's 'rhizome', a dialogical solution will be proposed there which mediates dialectically between the particular and the universal.[17]

The construction of a postmodern philosophical problematic as envisaged in this chapter is not a series of individual cases, but an attempt to structure the heterogeneous by pointing out *common questions, answers and tendencies*. In this respect, it is similar to the sociological construction in the second chapter. This means that – for better or for worse – similarities and affinities will be highlighted rather than contrasts or contradictions.

Like all theoretical schemes, the construction proposed here can easily be deconstructed: for example by arguing on the basis of particular selections and actantial (narrative) models[18] that the theories commented on have nothing in common. However, such an argument stems from the kind of postmodern particularism that is being questioned throughout this book. It will be argued against this deconstructionist nominalism that the elements common to the theories concerned are stronger than their heterogeneous contexts might suggest at first sight. Not individual works will be dealt with here, but the postmodern problematic as it manifests itself in philosophy. Although the latter might 'not exist' in the sense of a naïve realism, its (re-)construction is by no means arbitrary, especially since its Nietzschean origin is one of the main foundations most theorists agree on.

## 3.1 Nietzsche's Heirs

Virtually all of the philosophical problems and topics, which will be dealt with here, have been announced by Friedrich Nietzsche's work, if the latter is read as a reaction to European idealism. For Nietzsche's critique is aimed at concepts such as *history, necessity, the subject, essence, truth, totality, dialectics* and *work*: concepts which turn out to be the main suspects in postmodern discussions. All of them have been undermined and eroded by Nietzsche's persistent criticism – along with conceptuality as such. Whenever Nietzsche attempts to deduce historical necessity from chance, essence from appearance and truth from the accumulated figures of rhetoric, he discredits some of the most revered notions of idealism. For what is left of 'truth' if it consists of well-established but unconsidered metaphors?

'History' has been among the key concepts of German idealism ever since Hegel defined the development of humanity as a teleological process supervised by a divine or secular super-subject whose task it is to intervene as helper, judge or avenger. Nietzsche believes that this notion of history is obsolete. What is backward about a philosopher in the idealist sense? – he asks and answers: 'That he *knows* what is true, who is God, what the goal is, what the way is . . .'[19] A modern philosopher in the Hegelian sense may have known all this, late modern philosophers such as Sartre or Adorno began to doubt some of the fundamental modern truths, and the postmodernists frankly admit that questions concerning truth, God and human destiny are no longer on their agenda. They have ceased to be backward.

Virtually all of their texts are imbued with a latent scepticism vis-à-vis historical teleology and the Hegelian-Marxist notion of history. Thus Gianni Vattimo defines the postmodern era and the prefix *post* in conjunction with the present impossibility of Hegelian *Aufhebung* and of Marx's historical revolution. According to him, the dialectical overcoming or *Überwindung* is replaced by Heidegger's *Verwindung* which is of Nietzschean origin:

> The first philosopher to speak in terms of the possibility of *Verwindung* – even if, of course, he does not use the word itself – is not Heidegger but Nietzsche. It could legitimately be argued that philosophical post-modernity is born with Nietzsche's work (. . .).[20]

Lyotard projects this philosophical problematic into its political and historical context when he relates the failure of 'overcoming' to the collapse of socialism in Central and Eastern Europe. To him, Marxism appears as the last metaphysical teleology of history: 'Marxism, the last offspring issuing from Christianity and the Enlightenment, seems to have lost all of its critical potency. It has collapsed with the fall of the Berlin Wall.'[21] Even critics of postmodern philosophies are aware of a context marked by the failure of ideological metanarratives and still recall Bell's thesis (later revoked by Bell himself) according to which all ideologies have come to an end.[22] Even if one continues to use the concept of ideology[23] for sociological reasons, it is becoming increasingly difficult to conceive – with Comte and Hegel – of social development as a linear or dialectical (contradictory) process leading to ever higher forms of life.

At the same time, Nietzsche's idea prevails 'that among humans reason is a feeble force compared with powerful chance'[24] – an idea he may have come across in Young Hegelian thought. Starting from Nietzschean premises, Gilles Deleuze enhances the importance of chance, insists on its *necessity* and on the *plurality* it brings about. In an analysis of Mallarmé's *Un coup de dés*, he advocates a Nietzschean affirmation of chance:

> For, just as unity does not suppress or deny multiplicity, necessity does not suppress or abolish chance. Nietzsche identifies chance with multiplicity, with fragments, with parts, with chaos: the chaos of the dice that are shaken and then thrown. *Nietzsche turns chance into an affirmation.*[25]

This passage is completed by Deleuze's book on Nietzsche: 'Or, as Nietzsche would put it, one proclaims the necessity of chance. Dionysos is a player. The true player turns chance into an object of affirmation (. . .).'[26] Chance and game, the fragment and the manifold: these are the concepts of a new mode of thought which, after the collapse of Hegelian Marxism, no longer tries to fathom out the laws of an historical process.

Such thought is no longer inspired by a progressive and cumulative conception of history that seemed natural to the Enlightenment, to rationalists and dialecticians. It is more fascinated by Nietzsche's circular metaphor of the *eternal return*, a metaphor associated by Lyotard with the circulation of the exchange value and by Vattimo with the impact of the media which give the impression of simultaneity, of eternal repetition. Lyotard's book *Des dispositifs pulsionnels* evokes a link between the 'eternal return' and the circulation of capital: 'One can see what Nietzsche means to us today. *The regulated return is the Kapital* (*Le Retour réglé, c'est le Kapital.*).'[27] The production for the market appears to him – quite rightly – as a 'metamorphosis without an end and without a goal'.[28] Vattimo, for his part, focuses on the perception of everyday life when he points out: 'Progress also becomes routine (. . .).'[29] It is a well-known fact that routine can also be thought of as a permanent return of the same.

It is incompatible with the intentionality of a social or transcendental subject that could be made responsible for a teleology in the historical sense. The death of the divine subject in Nietzsche's philosophy entails, in most postmodern theories, the death of the human subject which Hegelian Marxists expected to replace divine providence.

Michel Foucault, considered by H. Fink-Eitel as 'Nietzsche's double',[30] stands both Hegel and Marx 'on their head', when he views history not as the self-realization of the divine or the human subject, but as its self-dissolution.

> The purpose of history, guided by genealogy, he explains, is not to discover the roots of our identity, but to commit itself to its dissipation. It does not seek to define our unique threshold of emergence, the homeland to which metaphysicians promise a return; it seeks to make visible all of those discontinuities that cross us.[31]

In another context, Foucault speaks of the 'systematic dissociation of identity'.[32]

The reader may feel that in these texts Foucault comments on Nietzsche's philosophy in order to outline his own programme of an 'archaeology of knowledge' and a 'genealogy of power', albeit indirectly and in a compressed form. For he shows why, in a social and linguistic situation where the *telos* of history turns out to be an illusion, the existence of an individual and collective subjectivity can no longer be presupposed. Only its traces, rests or fragments can still be spotted. In this context, Gianni Vattimo speaks of a 'finity of the subject' and a 'disappearance of foundations'.[33]

Within the postmodern philosophical problematic, which – like the socio-logical and the literary – is marked by a strong tendency towards particulariza-tion, the physical body as human life tends to replace the metaphysical subject. In some of his essential publications on the history of madness, criminality and sexuality, Foucault deals primarily with the political and scientific administra-tion of the human body and with the question how subjectivity is *engendered* by this kind of administration which is always also an aspect of power. How are physical individuals formed by administrative power structures (by ideology, Althusser would say) until they become what they are meant to be: feeling, thinking and acting *subjects*? In this process described by Foucault, the auto-nomous and responsible subjectivity of philosophical idealism is imperceptibly reduced to its physical substratum: 'In Nietzsche's perspective, modern culture is primarily defined by a lack of vitality,'[34] remarks José-Guilherme Merquior and adds: 'In the perspective of Foucault, Adorno and Marcuse, its salient fea-ture is its compulsive character.'[35]

In this context, Foucault's discourse appears to him as a plea in favour of the ill-treated human body: 'Our freedom is our physical life which has not been colonized by social rules.'[36] This interpretation may rest on an exaggera-tion valid only for the first volume of *Histoire de la sexualité*, not for the following volumes whose author envisages self-realization *within* certain social norm and value systems. It is nevertheless relevant, because it illustrates the postmod-ern rejection of concepts such as reason and truth which, in Foucault's work, accompanies the discovery of the corporeal. It is not by chance that *Surveiller et punir* begins with the agonizing martyrdom of Damiens who failed to assassinate the king in 1757. Its description is meant to illustrate the physical aspect of oppression: 'Le corps des condamnés' is the title of the first chapter.

In Nietzsche's thought, this tendency towards particularization in a materialist, corporeal sense was accompanied by a scepticism towards the concepts of *truth* and *essence* which claim universal validity and form the core of Platonism and German idealism. Nietzsche no longer believes that appearance hides essence: 'What does "appearance" mean to me! Certainly not the opposite of some essence – what do I know about essence except the predicates of its appearance!'[37] The question is of course in what kind of social and linguistic situation (in what kind of *episteme*, Foucault would say) Nietzsche's polemic against essence, which has endured the wear of centuries from Plato to Hegel, becomes possible. The answer could be that the discovery of language as the main tool of conceptualization inaugurated Nietzsche's and Heidegger's critique of traditional metaphysics. Foucault concludes: 'The role played by history in the past is now taken over by language.'[38] At present, one may ask at any time with Wittgenstein and Winch: Which language game does this concept belong to? What figures of speech is it made up of?

It is within the framework of this problematic that a postmodern philosopher like Vattimo can say: 'There is no liberation beyond appearances in a putative realm of real Being (. . .).'[39] This thesis is confirmed and developed by Gilles Deleuze in different parts of his work where the reader finds out that, from the point of view of the artist, truth and appearance coincide: 'Truth is appearance.'[40] In Deleuze's thought, truth falls apart, and the result is a vast array of local truths which can vary according to contexts and interests: 'We have the truths that we deserve depending on the place we are carrying our existence to, the hour we watch over and the element that we frequent.'[41] Truth in the sense of Plato, Kant or Hegel has abdicated, and we are confronted by contingent truths, the spatial and temporal relativity of which is emphasized by postmodern thinkers like Deleuze, Lyotard and Rorty.

In this context, Richard Rorty can invoke Nietzsche when criticizing the realist concept of reality according to which true thought comes closest to the real world and can therefore be considered as objective. No convergence can be postulated between thought and the real world, and truth appears to Rorty – as it did to Nietzsche – as a contingent product of linguistic traditions and rhetoric conventions which are no longer perceived as such:

> Nietzsche thought that the test of human character was the ability to live with the thought that there was no convergence. He wanted us to be able to think of truth as: 'a mobile army of metaphors, metonyms, and anthropomorphisms – in short a sum of human relations, which have been enhanced, transposed, and embellished poetically and rhetorically and which after long use seem firm, canonical, and obligatory to a people'.[42]

Thus the linguistic turn amounts to a localization and a particularization of the truth concept. If truth is purely conventional in character, it cannot claim universal validity, because it articulates particular constellations and power relations.

Along with conceptual truth, postmodern Nietzscheans dismiss the ratio- nalist and Hegelian-Marxist ideal of universally valid scientific knowledge. As Nietzsche's heirs, both Rorty and Deleuze look for authentic perception in the realm of art rather than in science. Even the author of the *Gay Science* preferred art (especially music) to a nineteenth-century science inspired by positivism and its empiricist ideals: 'Had we not embraced the arts and invented the cult of lying, we could hardly cope with the insight into the universal absence of truth or lie (. . .) which is now provided by science.'[43]

This critique of conceptual thought is later taken up by Rorty, who sides with postmodern 'textualism' against the scientific ideal of the metaphysical tradi- tion, maintaining that the 'textualism' of the twentieth century was centred on literature and set out to 'treat both science and philosophy as, at best, literary genres'.[44] It will be shown later on that this approach is entirely in agreement with Deleuze's attempt to integrate creative moments in the aesthetic sense into philosophical discourse and with Derrida's or de Man's desire to delete the institutional separation between philosophy and literature.

Where the claim of philosophy or science to unify our perception of reality by making essence and truth accessible is called into question, Hegel's *category of totality* falls apart. The result is a *multiplicity* of heterogeneous elements. In Deleuze's analyses, Dionysus appears as a tragic figure, as a guardian of creativity and multiplicity: 'Dionysus affirms all that appears, "even the most bitter suffer- ing", and appears in all that is affirmed. Multiple and pluralist affirmation – this is the essence of the tragic.'[45] Elsewhere, Deleuze speaks of the 'joy of multiplicity, plural joy'.[46] He concludes his book by giving a brief summary of Nietzsche's work which appears to him as an incessant movement of multiplic- ity, chance and play: 'The sense of Nietzsche's philosophy is that multiplicity, becoming and chance are objects of pure affirmation.'[47] The *player* is the one who practises this mode of thought by relying on *chance*: on Mallarmé's *coup de dés*.

In this setup, the antagonist and spoilsport is the dialectician, the Hegelian or Marxist, who refuses to recognize the playful aspects of chance, trying to integrate the latter into the laws of an historical progress kept in motion by human *work*. Deleuze considers dialectics as a conceptual, theoretical, 'reactive' and hence life-negating thought that is for ever linked to the Christian doctrine of salvation: 'The dialectic is, first of all, the thought of the theoretical man, reacting against life, claiming to judge life, to limit and measure it.'[48] He goes on to say that dialectics in this sense is 'the authentically Christian ideology'.[49] The opposition he sets out from and eventually returns to at the end of his book is that between Hegel and Nietzsche: 'There is no possible compromise between Hegel and Nietzsche.'[50] In this respect, Douglas Kellner and Steven Best are quite right in pointing out that Deleuze finds an alternative to dialectical thought in Nietzsche's work.[51]

However, this explanation does not only apply to Deleuze, but to most postmodern philosophers who react to the problems resulting from a rationalist domination over nature and a blind belief in progress, to the decline of Marxism–Leninism and the 'de-historicization of experience'[52] by critically dissecting the old metanarratives. The main objects of their criticism are key concepts of modernity such as *history, necessity, subject, essence, truth, totality, science, work* and *dialectics.* The alternatives they have in mind are strongly particularized non-concepts such as the *eternal return, chance, the body, language, power, multiplicity, art, play* – and in general a thought aiming at the particular, the unique and the distinctive.

This orientation is also characteristic of Adorno's late modern dialectic, especially if the latter is seen as a self-criticism of modernity. However, his dialectic differs from the postmodern approaches commented on here by its persistent refusal to sacrifice conceptual thought to the non-conceptual: 'The cognitive utopia would be to use concepts to unseal the non-conceptual with concepts, without making it their equal.'[53] By refusing to follow the (modern) dialectical movement from the concept to the non-conceptual, from the universal to the particular and back, postmodern thinkers renounce the possibility of going beyond the particular in order to mediate between heterogeneous positions. However, unmediated heterogeneity confirms the indifference of the exchange value whose levelling effects are criticized by Adorno and Lyotard alike.

In the following sections, the postmodern problematic will be examined in more detail within the contexts of social philosophy, ethics and aesthetics. It will become clear that, apart from Nietzsche, Hume and Kant have helped postmodern thinkers to reinforce existing tendencies towards particularization and pluralization.

## 3.2  Postmodern Social Philosophy and the End of Metanarratives: From Foucault, Deleuze and Lyotard to Vattimo and Rorty

Having taken part in postmodern debates about 'the end of metanarratives', one may wonder why Albert Camus is never mentioned as the first critic of these metanarratives and the initiator of postmodernity. This silence may be due to the fact that the market of culture demands permanent innovation, originality and stunning ideas. How else could one account for a situation where Lyotard explains why the grand metanarratives of the past have lost their credibility, without ever referring to Camus's radical, Nietzschean critique of the Christian and Marxist metanarratives in *The Rebel*?

It is a silence one could also explain in conjunction with Pierre Bourdieu's sociological theory of cultural capital. Had Lyotard, instead of quoting prestigious thinkers such as Kuhn, Gödel, Frege or Luhmann, naïvely announced in the preface to *La Condition postmoderne* (1979) that he intended to develop one of the central theses underlying Albert Camus's *L'Homme révolté* (1951), a book that fascinated young people after World War II, he would hardly have impressed anyone.

However, Albert Camus writes about the Christian narrative:

> From this moment, human nature becomes the subject of history, and significant history expressed by the idea of human totality is born. From the Annunciation until the Last Judgement, humanity has no other task but to conform to the strictly moral ends of a narrative that has already been written (d'un récit écrit à l'avance).[54]

As in the case of Lyotard and Deleuze, Marxism is presented in Camus's work as a secularized form of Christian teleology: 'Marx reintroduced crime and punishment into the unchristian world, but only in relation to history.'[55]

Camus, the modernist philosopher and writer of contingency, of chance and absurdity, has so far not been defined as a postmodern thinker, because he focuses on the individual and not on the 'structure', the 'construction' or the 'signifier'. From his postmodern heirs Camus is separated by the 'linguistic turn' – some would say: by the rise of the linguistic *paradigm* in the 1960s and 1970s.

However, with Michel Foucault he shares the belief that the individual is primarily to be conceived of as *physis*, as a corporeal being, not as an autonomous subject endowed with reason and spontaneously aspiring towards universal values such as truth or justice. On the contrary, the subject appears to him as an entity *subjected* by various institutions and manipulated within power structures. It is turned into a subject by a Christian, Marxist or rationalist discourse which may at any time sacrifice human life to a grand historical design. In his novel *The Outsider* (*L'Etranger*, 1942), Camus reveals the narrative mechanisms of a dualistic Christian and humanist discourse which transforms the unwitting protagonist Meursault into a responsible criminal subject who deserves capital punishment.

Like Camus before him, Foucault avails himself of Nietzsche's philosophy in order to reveal the compulsive character of Christian, humanist or Hegelian–Marxist discourse and in order to show in *The Order of Things* (*Les Mots et les choses*, 1966) to what extent Marxist humanism is part and parcel of the nineteenth-century scientific episteme which turns human beings as subjected individuals into objects of scientific knowledge. The classical (rationalist) episteme, a noetic system based on linguistic taxonomy and the correspondence of language and reality, is followed by an episteme of human sciences: '(. . .) For the whole configuration of knowledge has been modified and they came into being only to the degree to which there appeared, with man, a being who did not exist before in the field of the *episteme*.'[56] However, this appearance of man in Marxism,

sociology or psychoanalysis goes hand in hand with the subjection and fragmentation of human beings by the division of labour inherent in the new
sciences or *disciplines.*

Unlike Camus who, as a modernist philosopher of absurdity and human freedom, hoped to deliver the individual from the constraints of Christian, Marxist
and other humanist discourses, Foucault tries to show, from *L'Histoire de la folie*
to the first volume of *Histoire de la sexualité*, how the human body is being manipulated and 'normalized' by science until it turns into a socially acceptable subject. *L'Histoire de la folie* shows, on the one hand, how, in seventeenth-century
France, sexuality is regulated within the family and, on the other hand, how
contemporary psychoanalysis delivers patients from the constraints of bourgeois morality only to subject them to the discourse of the analyst. Foucault
writes about Freud: 'But on the other hand he exploited the structure that
developed the medical personage; he amplified its thaumaturgical virtues, pre-
paring for its omnipotence a quasi-divine status.'[57]

Since Foucault, the Nietzschean thinker, tends to consider knowledge as a
form of power, science can neither appear to him as a disinterested quest for
truth nor as an open discussion among free and autonomous subjects in the
sense of Habermas. He sees both science and communication as embedded
in power structures. His speculations about the end of humanity in the final
section of *The Order of Things* can be read in this context. For man as a homogeneous subject ceased to exist ever since he was divided into different parts by
his own sciences and inserted into the genetically manipulated continuum of
biology. Roddey Reid points out in this context: 'It is quite possible that we are
witness to the irrevocable death of man who is being constructed and cate-
gorized by "medical humanism".'[58] (The expression *humanisme médical* was
coined by Foucault in *Les Mots et les choses*: p. 398.)

It becomes clear at this stage that Foucault inverts Marx's thesis about the
self-liberation of humanity through historical consciousness and practice by
turning Marx's consciousness *for* itself into consciousness *in* itself. Insofar as
humans become objects of human sciences, they are subjected to the power
structures of these sciences. They no longer appear as consciously acting subjects, but as manipulated bodies. The result is a postmodern particularization
commented on in detail by Habermas in his essay on Foucault: 'From the outset, he is interested in the human sciences as media that in modernity strengthen
and promote the mysterious process of this socialization, that is, the investment
with power of concrete, bodily mediated interactions.'[59] Unlike Foucault,
Habermas stresses the universalistic tendencies of the social sciences: for example their communicative character and their contribution to intersubjective
understanding (cf. Section 3.5).

It remains to be asked what political consequences ensue from Foucault's
idea of history, his critique of the grand metanarratives and his conception of
knowledge as power. Especially in his posthumously published *Dits et écrits*, one

notices to what extent Foucault (like Camus before him) rejects the historical practice of the Marxists–Leninists, the Maoists and the Trotskyists of the 1970s.[60] All of these movements appear to him as accomplices of the human science power structures which impede the self-realization of the individual.

His postmodern sympathies go to the marginal groups of society who resist the mechanisms of power he so conscientiously describes. Steven Best and Douglas Kellner may be right when they conclude:

> For a modern concept of macropolitics where clashing forces struggle for control over a centralized source of power rooted in the economy and state, Foucault substitutes a postmodern concept of micropolitics where numerous local groups contest diffuse and decentred forms of power spreading through-out society.[61]

Unlike Marxism–Leninism (e.g. Lenin's *State and Revolution*), which aims at the conquest of state power, not at its destruction, the social philosophies of Foucault, Deleuze and Lyotard envisage a pluralizing subversion of power.

Foucault's perspective may seem one-sided as it tends to identify social power with the coercive system of psychiatric clinics and prisons, thus bracketing out the democratic use of power in post-war European and American societies. One need not be a fervent supporter of Parsons's and Luhmann's system theories in order to realize that power and money are means of collective and individual action which can be used or abused to the benefit or the detriment of the general public. Even 'green' ministers, who agitate against whaling and nuclear energy have to wield power in order to attain their political goals; even scientists, who support the foundation of a European University (e.g. in Florence/Fiesole) and organize lobbies to that effect, rely on existing power structures. The condemnation of power in general is as meaningless as a moralizing crusade against 'the evils of money'. In such cases, 'power' and 'money' are turned into mythical forces.

Foucault can hardly be said to avoid this pitfall when, in an interview with Deleuze entitled 'Les Intellectuels et le pouvoir' (1972), he denounces virtually all social functions that can be associated with power in one way or another: 'Every struggle is sparked off by a particular source of power (e.g. a boss, a warden, a prison director, a judge, a trade union leader, an editor-in-chief).'[62] Foucault calls upon the oppressed to contest, to fight power and speaks of a 'struggle against power' ('luttes contre le pouvoir').[63]

However, the point is not to denounce centres of power (a meaningless activity), but the *abuse* of power or its *dysfunctional use* by individuals and groups. For the alternative to the rule of law is not, as Foucault would make us believe, blissful anarchy, but the usurpation of power by one or two mafias – possibly in cooperation with the army and the secret services.

What Foucault has in mind in the 1970s is a struggle against power *tout court*: 'Women, prisoners, soldiers, hospital patients, homosexuals initiate different forms of struggle against structures of power, coercion and control they are subjected to.'[64] Although he explains in 1972 that such forms of resistance 'are linked to the revolutionary movement of the proletariat',[65] he hastens to add (like Deleuze: cf. below) that this struggle does not take on 'the form of totalization'[66] and that, unlike the Marxist intellectual, unlike the 'organic intellectual' in the sense of Gramsci, the present-day intellectual no longer speaks in the name of the masses: for he has ceased 'to be a representing or representative consciousness'.[67]

In this political situation in which, as Lyotard puts it, 'each individual is referred to himself',[68] one could explain the retreat of the older Foucault into the private sphere of the 'technology of the self'. What matters to him in the final stages of his development, is not the contestation of power by postmodern movements, but the question concerning the authentic life of the individual in which 'the culture of the self takes as its goal the perfect government of the self – a sort of permanent political relationship between self and self.'[69]

Foucault's *souci de soi* prompted Christopher Norris to speak of a 'near-schizophrenic' philosopher who, on the one hand, supports the cause of the oppressed and, on the other hand, seeks refuge in a dandy-like cult of the ego.[70] It was interpreted by others as a liberal propensity which in many respects continues Foucault's early writings in the sense that it confirms his revolt against all heteronomies that threaten the subject and at the same time renews his plea in favour of subjective autonomy.[71] It will become clear to what extent Foucault's postmodern search overlaps, at least in *one point*, with that of Rorty.

Gilles Deleuze, whose intellectual development owes a lot to the dialogue with Foucault, starts from four premises in his critique of modernity: from the decline of the metaphysical metanarratives of modernity, the resulting enhancement of the particular and the singular, the corresponding reappraisal of life in the sense of Nietzsche and the discovery of epistemological and political pluralism. In his book on Foucault, Deleuze tries to forge links between Nietzsche and the French philosopher: 'The superman has never meant anything but that: it is in man himself that we must liberate life, since man himself is a form of imprisonment for man. Life becomes resistance to power when power takes life as its object.'[72] Even in Deleuze's writings, the difference between power and domination is glossed over, and power appears to the reader as one of those mythical windmills postmodern Don Quixotes are so fond of attacking. In such cases, modern power is frequently identified with capitalism and its helpers. Although postmodern thinkers have abandoned Marx's idea of historically overcoming the capitalist system, some of them continue his critique in a strongly particularized perspective.

In this perspective, Gilles Deleuze's and Félix Guattari's voluminous work on capitalism and schizophrenia – *L'Anti-Œdipe* (1972/73) and *Mille Plateaux* (1980) – could be read as a major attempt to telescope Nietzsche's, Foucault's and even Wilhelm Reich's approaches into a massive critique of modern capitalism. This critique no longer starts from Marx's critique of Political Economy, but from an economy of the libido that is omnipresent in society and thus accounts for the fact that all social objects and positions can be *invested by libido* as objects of desire. In contrast to psychoanalysis, which tends to limit sexual desire to the oedipal context of the nuclear family, they develop a schizoanalysis that extends desire to all spheres of society in an attempt to turn it against capitalism and its power structures. This 'dissemination' of desire can be traced back to Nietzsche's 'will to power', Foucault's idea of 'productive power', which constitutes truth and subjectivity, Lacan's theory of a 'polymorphous libido'[73] and Derrida's Mallarméan metaphor of *dissémination*.

Deleuze's and Guattari's analysis of a schizophrenia that is produced by the contradictory libidinal orientations within late-capitalist market society is not simply a diagnosis of collective pathologies, but also – very much like Lyotard's *Economie libidinale* (1974) – an attempt *to exploit the critical potential of these pathologies*. In spite of the general obscurity of *L'Anti-Œdipe*, one thing is clear: desire is socialized and is geared towards social objects: 'Desiring-machines are in social machines and nowhere else, so that the conjunction of the decoded flows in the capitalist machine tends to liberate the free figures of a universal subjective libido.'[74] This passage, inspired by Wilhelm Reich's unorthodox psychoanalysis[75], expresses the hope that the desire released by the capitalist system will liberate the subjects, thus contributing decisively to the system's disintegration.

But what should subjective desire be liberated from? It should be delivered from the constraints of oedipal socialization within the bourgeois family. For within this family, subjects are being produced, who submit to the reality principle (*ananke*), to authority, asceticism and eventually to *Thanatos*, the drive towards death. Their socialization makes them prone to fascism. By choosing the oedipal situation within the bourgeois nuclear family as its starting point, Freudian psychoanalysis shows that it is in agreement with the bourgeois-capitalist system. Therefore it is attacked by Deleuze and Guattari in Nietzsche's name and in the name of a pseudo-Marxist discourse as a new religion and a new form of deceit: 'Psychoanalysis becomes the training ground of a new kind of priest, the director of bad conscience: bad conscience has made us sick, but that is what will cure us!'[76]

Deleuze and Guattari also tell us how it heals. What matters, they argue, is to analyse the nexus between power and the unconscious and to find out how the libido scattered throughout the system can be turned into a liberating force capable of blowing up the latter. Unlike the authors of *Anti-Oedipus*, who still try to mobilize the countless subversive schizo-subjects against the system, those of *Thousand Plateaus* hope that marginal groups will continue and intensify the liberation process: outsiders, immigrants, homosexuals, lunatics, etc. They are expected to replace the Marxist revolutionary subject, the proletariat: 'A tribe in the desert instead of a universal subject within the horizon of an all-encompassing Being.'[77]

The title *Thousand Plateaus* announces what is at stake: the pluralization and particularization of revolutionary resistance or, to put it with Steven Best and Douglas Kellner: 'a sustained celebration of difference and multiplicity'.[78] This pluralized resistance is mapped out by Deleuze in the discussion with Foucault mentioned above, where he rejects all forms of totalizing criticism:

> This global politics of power collides with local counter-movements, with active and sometimes preventive defence measures. We should not totalize this (. . .). However, it is our task to form popular groups at the basis and to relate them by a system of connecting links.[79]

Deleuze's remark that 'this is very difficult' is somewhat superfluous, because it goes without saying, but at the same time it reveals the disorientation of postmodern philosophy. For even philosophers such as Deleuze and Lyotard are bound to ask themselves whether a system, which has survived emigrations and immigrations, wars, fascism and the world revolution, can actually be dislocated by relatively small groups agitating at its outskirts. Sociological analyses of contemporary movements in the sense of Touraine or Beck seem more promising than this kind of philosophical speculation (cf. Section 2.1).

The flexible robustness of the capitalist edifice may have surprised most intellectuals in the Quartier Latin who, after 1968, began to doubt the social relevance of Marxist theory and of historical metanarratives in general. Lyotard's introductory remarks to the thirteenth chapter of his *Postmodern Fables* (*Moralités postmodernes*, 1993) are particularly characteristic of his position in the 1990s: 'The contemporary world offers a picture of liberal, imperialist capitalism after its triumph over its last two challengers, fascism and communism: so Marxism would say, were it not defunct.'[80]

This historical diagnosis is based on two ideas which accompany all of Lyotard's thought, in spite of its turns and contradictions: a growing scepticism towards the grand Marxist metanarrative ('from feudalism to capitalism, from capitalism to socialism') and the concomitant idea that the future is blocked because 'the system' cannot be overcome – an idea that relates him to Adorno.

The mere fact that Lyotard's membership in Cornelius Castoriadis's Marxist movement *Socialisme ou Barbarie* was very short-lived bears witness to the scepticism of the French intellectual of the 1960s and 1970s *vis-à-vis* the Hegelian and Marxist notions of history.[81] As an alternative to Marxist critiques of society, Lyotard proposes (in the 1970s) a policy of libidinal forces, of affective intensities and of desire. This is why his post-1968 approach is being commented on here in conjunction with that of Deleuze and Guattari. Like Deleuze and Guattari in *Anti-Oedipus* and *Thousand Plateaus*, Lyotard attempts to give libido a subversive turn in the 1970s: to divert it dysfunctionally from the capitalist mode of production and its 'goal-attainments' (T. Parsons) and make it available for subversive projects: 'One has to view the emergence of such dispositions within the body politic in the same perspective as the libidinal investments into the erotic body: as incompatible, contingent, simultaneous, interrupted impulses.'[82]

Lyotard's revolutionary hope might look like a perversion to Daniel Bell. While Bell regrets that young generations in post-war Western Europe and the United States try to adopt a bohemian way of life by imitating some modernist practices and by investing their libido in consumerism and not in production (cf. Chapter 2), Lyotard pleads in favour of a withdrawal of libido from production and a libidinal investment in a 'désir schizo': a subversive 'schizo-desire'.[83] The latter is so diffuse that it can be invested in virtually everything, thereby undermining the capitalist order.[84]

Even Marx seems far too puritanical to him and is criticized in *Libidinal Economy*:

> Marx wants an (in)organic body, does his desire enslave it to a genital model? We want a schizophrenic model and an unstable body. Marx wants to charge? We want generalized gratuity. Marx accuses? We exonerate. Marx-the-proletariat suffers and redeems? We joyfully love all that appears.[85]

This postmodern alternative to Marxian thought is not only reminiscent of May 1968, but also of Nietzsche. The fact is that Lyotard's early writings are not merely attempts to combine Marxism and Psychoanalysis, but also aim at reviving a Nietzschean, Dionysian vitalism which is turned by Foucault and especially Deleuze and Guattari into the main driving force of postmodern thought.

Lyotard's break with this kind of Nietzschean thought in *Rudiments païens* (1977) and *Instructions païennes* (1977) should not make anybody overlook a latent continuity based on a global tendency towards particularization. From *Dérive à partir de Marx et Freud* (1973) onwards, the orientation of discourse towards the individual, particular libido and the strict refusal of all brands of universal reason in the Enlightenment and the Marxist sense appear as complementary. Unlike in Adorno's and Horkheimer's case, where the critical function of reason is recognized, reason is associated in Lyotard's philosophy with the power structures of capitalism and the universal character of the exchange value. In one of his remarks about reason, Lyotard is quite explicit: 'Reason and power are one.' ('Raison et pouvoir, c'est tout un.')[86] Reason appears to him not only as a repressive, but also as a levelling force which tends to wipe out all differences.

Especially in his later works, Lyotard pleads – very much like Deleuze – in favour of such differences and an irreducible pluralism. At this stage, however, he relegates to second place the philosophy of Nietzsche and instead relies heavily on Kant's *Critique of Judgement*. This work emphasizes the qualitative differences rather than the continuities between modes of thought, and this is exactly what Lyotard is looking for in the last phase of his development. In *The Postmodern Condition*, *The Differend* and other writings of the late 1970s and early

1980s, he sets out from a strongly particularizing interpretation of the *Critique of Judgement* and from Wittgenstein's linguistic philosophy in order to prove the irreducible heterogeneity of social interests, languages and modes of thought (cf. Section 3.5).

Starting from the well-known premise he shares with Foucault and Deleuze, according to which 'we no longer have recourse to the grand narratives,'[87] he holds that conflicts between colliding collective interests and languages cannot be settled within an encompassing metadiscourse because they are incommensurate. In this situation, Lyotard believes, only two possibilities are on offer: either the incompatibility of group languages and interests are negated by their subordination to an encompassing language (mode of thought) or the incommensurate character of languages is recognized and defended. The first case boils down to a gross *injustice* (*tort*, Lyotard), while the second brings about a *paralogy* leading to the recognition of the unique or incommensurate character of group languages. Lyotard considers this state of affairs as a kind of postmodern justice.

What matters most in this case is his argument that the conflict between heterogeneous social languages in the sense of Wittgenstein is a *differend* which cannot be settled by the rules of a superior language, that is turned into a *lawsuit* (*litige*). For the latter would invariably entail an *injustice*, a *tort*:

> An injustice comes about if one and the same rule of judgement is applied to different types of discourse 'in order to settle their differend as a lawsuit (. . .). An injustice is due to the fact that the rules of the type of discourse which determines the judgement differ from the discourse(s) which is (are) to be judged'.[88]

One could also say 'from the discourses to be condemned', for in European and American law systems, most of which are organized along universalistic lines, it often happens that discourses of ethnic, linguistic or religious minorities are a priori condemned because they are subjected to heteronomous criteria.

The epistemological consequences of Lyotard's theses will be discussed in detail in the fifth section. At this stage, the social and political aspects of his particularism are at stake. They are summed up by Jacob Rogozinski in the following polemical and critical question: 'But how is a "justice of the many" ("justice des multiplicités") to be conceived of?'[89] The coexistence of a vast number of heterogeneous notions of justice, which the authors of *Postmodernity and Critical Legal Studies* are trying to relate to one another dialectically,[90] is problematical because the colliding points of view tend to cancel each other in a postmodern indifference defined here as interchangeability of values. This indifference does not only entail affective neutrality ('tolerance'), but also violence and terror. Where there are no universally valid criteria, the Other or the incommensurate appears as meaningless or even threatening, because it is seen as a danger to the identity of the One. The temptation of groups and individuals to escape from the anomie of indifference and radical pluralism by seeking refuge in ideological dualism and monologue (cf. Section 2.5) should not be underestimated.

The violent moment is also inherent in Lyotard's social philosophy insofar as he calls – together with Deleuze and Guattari – for a revolt of the particular against the universal: against Platonism, which he associates with capitalism, against reason as an instrument of state power, against all centralized, 'phallocratic' thought.[91] The forces he would like to mobilize against the state, against capital, reason and universal logic are reminiscent of the forces invoked by Foucault, Deleuze, Guattari and even Touraine: the patchwork of minorities, marginal movements and rebellious groups. He considers all of these as potential adversaries of centralized power. 'Capital gives political hegemony to the economic genre,'[92] Lyotard points out and imagines all sorts of resistance to this process of centralization: including taking hostages. It goes without saying that he does not recommend this kind of violence; however, he continues a long French tradition which – from the anarchist Proudhon to the surrealist Breton – rebels against the rationalized, absolutist centralism of the French state.[93]

Lyotard extends his postmodern revolt, which is reminiscent of the postmodern literary rebellions of Thomas Bernhard, Werner Schwab and Félix de Azúa (cf. Section 5.7), to include the social movements (feminists, homosexuals, ethnic groups) whose anti-ascetic, 'libidinal' attitudes might disrupt the process of capitalist production:

> (. . .) Loss of production, consumption without services in return, refusal to 'work', (illusory?) communities, *happenings*, sexual liberation movements, occupations, *squattings*, productions of sounds, words, colours without any pretence to 'create a work'. Are these the 'superfluous men', the '*masters*' of today: marginal individuals, experimental painters, pops, hippies and yippies, parasites, lunatics, inmates?[94]

Two points seem to be important for Lyotard. Like some sociologists, like Touraine and Beck (cf. Chapter 2), he focuses on social movements; but unlike the sociologists who avail themselves of empirical methods and tend to describe rather than to evaluate, the postmodern philosopher associates women, marginal groups, prostitutes, homosexuals and immigrants with his own metaphysical hopes and desires, some of which are strangely reminiscent of George Lukács's mystifications of the proletariat in *History and Class Consciousness* (*Geschichte und Klassenbewußtsein*, 1923). For in Lyotard's thought, the subversive, deconstructionist and negating activity is not an end in itself, but a new metaphysics which is virtually absent from the works of the sociologists.

In a somewhat different way, Gianni Vattimo's work shows to what extent heterogeneity and pluralism are promoted to the status of supreme values within the postmodern problematic. Setting out from a premise shared by most of the thinkers commented on here, he holds that it is impossible to conceive of 'universal history as unilinear'.[95] At the same time, he quotes Heidegger's term *Verwindung* in order to indicate that the utopian *Überwindung* (overcoming) envisaged by revolutionary thinkers from Marx to Marcuse has been dissolved in commercialized mass society by a pseudo-realization of utopian promises (cf. Section 3.7). According to him, the modern utopia of a universal human culture has been transformed into heterotopia, that is into 'communities that show, express and recognize themselves in different myths and formal models'.[96]

However, Vattimo, like Lyotard, has to confront a question most postmodern advocates of multiple subcultures[97] try to avoid: the question how to deal with 'the violent community of Nazis listening to Wagner' or 'that of rockers geeing themselves up for violence'.[98] His answer to this question his hardly convincing: 'In arguing that universality as understood by Kant is realized for us only in the form of multiplicity, we can legitimately take plurality lived explicitly as such as a normative criterion.'[99]

It is by no means certain that we can do this because Vattimo's premises are not clear. The particularizing postmodern philosopher, who denies the existence of universal values and criteria, cannot proclaim pluralism to be a universally valid norm. This logical contradiction is accompanied by a social one. The postmodern philosopher cannot but accept the antagonistic interests and discourses without attempting to assess their legitimacy from a metadiscursive point of view. However, a pluralism that brackets out the question concerning the universal validity of certain interests and values turns out to be a pseudo-criterion. For the key question remains: How do we know which value ought to prevail when conflicting interests and views collide?

This is also Rorty's problem. Like Foucault, Deleuze, Lyotard and Vattimo, the American philosopher starts from the postmodern idea that the world can no longer be explained within the framework of one of the major metanarratives: within Christianity, Enlightenment or Marxism. As a tenacious critic of Hegel and heir to Nietzsche as well as to American pragmatism (Dewey, James), Rorty never tires of attacking the rationalist and Hegelian thesis according to which the development of humanity obeys certain definable laws.[100]

The idea here is not to investigate the dialectic of necessity and chance in order to show that the decline of Austria-Hungary or the Soviet Union occurred for structural reasons and therefore cannot be constructed as a concatenation of contingent events. It is more important to realize that Rorty starts from premises very similar to those of the other postmodern philosophers (e.g. the decline of the historical metanarratives), but nevertheless arrives at political results some of which are diametrically opposed to those obtained by Lyotard or Bauman – although they do confirm the general tendency towards particularization. On the whole, it appears that the reactions of different postmodern philosophers to the postmodern problematic show striking similarities in spite of all the divergences that can also be observed.

At first sight, Rorty's liberal pragmatism, which frequently degenerates into an open apology of liberal-capitalist market society, seems incompatible with the anti-capitalist rhetoric of the French philosophers. Rorty speaks of the 'inevitable ethnocentrism to which we are all condemned'[101] and leans heavily – but arbitrarily[102] – on Hegel in order to replace Kant's universal approach by an historical relativism and particularism: 'The Kantian identification with a central transcultural and ahistorical self is thus replaced by a quasi-Hegelian identification with our own community, thought of as a historical product.'[103] In order to define this community, Rorty uses an expression to which most of the Rive Gauche intellectuals would react with repugnance or resentment: 'us postmodernist bourgeois liberals'.[104]

Elsewhere he specifies: 'The only "we" we need is a local and temporary one: "we" means something like "us twentieth-century Western social democrats".'[105] Considering Rorty's generous use of terminologies, it is hardly surprising that expressions such as 'bourgeois liberals' and 'social democrats' are imperceptibly turned into synonyms.

Rorty's tendency towards particularization, which relates him – in spite of all differences and divergences – to the French philosophers, ends in a paradox. On the one hand, he agrees with pragmatists such as Dewey and James that it is impossible to find universal cognitive and political criteria applicable to societies outside the liberal-democratic spectrum; on the other hand, he tends to present 'Western liberal democracy' as a generally valid norm. The first part of the paradox is illustrated by the statement 'that there are no problems which bind the generations together into a single natural kind called "humanity" '.[106] The second part of the paradox surfaces whenever the bourgeois-liberal (not the social democratic) social order is presented as a *summum bonum* and a general standard: 'Bourgeois liberalism seems to me the best example of this solidarity we have yet achieved, and Deweyan pragmatism the best articulation of it.'[107]

This open apology of liberalism, whose solidarity all unemployed and redundant individuals have been enjoying since the nineteenth century, is accompanied by a rejection of all metadiscourses (especially the Marxist ones)[108] which have persistently questioned the legitimacy of liberalism: 'Accommodation and tolerance must stop short of a willingness to work within any vocabulary that one's interlocutor wishes to use, to take seriously any topic that he puts forward for discussion.'[109]

Unlike Lyotard, who aims at maintaining the *différend* and at avoiding injustice (in the sense of *tort*), the liberal Rorty excludes a priori certain types of discourse. It sounds quite cynical when he writes about liberal society that it should see to it that writers and revolutionaries 'make life harder for others only by words, and not deeds'.[110] Breton and Marinetti might have slapped him in the face for such a remark. In this respect, the American feminist Honi Fern Haber is not altogether wrong when she criticizes Rorty because 'his politics makes room for solidarity only by imposing a form of terror (. . .)'.[111]

In the case of Rorty, as in the case of Lyotard, the propensity towards 'violent' solutions is due to the process of particularization (which has quite different political connotations in Rorty's and in Lyotard' case). By rejecting all universalistic criteria and by refusing to consider 'humanity as a whole',[112] the American pragmatist ignores the banal but useful idea that there are problems which do bridge the gap between generations: that is environmental problems on a global scale, problems dealt with by Beck in his *Risk Society* (for example the systematic clearing of tropical rain forests), the threat of wars and nuclear disasters, which liberals, Marxists, feminists and even religious zealots try to avert, the struggle against hunger, disease and death. What is missing in Rorty's thought is Habermas's notion of the generalization of interests that ought to be completed by the notion of generalization of values – or rather the *possibility* to generalize values (*Verallgemeinerungsfähigkeit*).[113]

However, it is one of the salient traits of the postmodern problematic that it excludes questions concerning the possibility of generalizing collective interests or value judgements and that it pushes the tendency towards particularization to a point where private and public interests fall apart: 'Many passages in Foucault (. . .) exemplify what Bernard Yack has called the "longing for total revolution", and the "demand that our autonomy be embodied in our institutions".'[114] This retreat into a private sphere of non-commitment is not only a symptom of radical pluralism and postmodern indifference, but also reveals the basic orientation of an American campus philosophy which thrives in a few academic oases sheltered from public life: from the commercialized reality of decaying cities and the conflicts between ethnic groups.

It is hardly surprising that this kind of philosophy divests individual self-realization of all public involvement relegating it to the private sphere: 'We should stop trying to combine self-creation and politics, especially if we are liberals.'[115] This sentence is interesting insofar as it could also be read as a summary of Foucault's intellectual development: from his revolt against power and its truths to his self-centredness which, in the context mapped out here, might appear as the final phase of particularizing thought.

## 3.3 Postmodern Epistemology I: Foucault, Deleuze, Vattimo and Rorty

In view of these postmodern tendencies towards particularization, which can be observed in the works of some contemporary authors, it might seem somewhat rash to speak of a postmodern epistemology, especially since epistemology is often associated with general validity. Rorty, who is probably right in rejecting all accusations of being a relativist, points out that a pragmatist like him does not have an epistemology at all. Since he does not have an epistemology, he cannot possibly have a relativist one.[116] If, parallel to these arguments, one considers the fact that in 1983, that is one year before his death, Foucault asks what

exactly the word 'postmodernity' means ('Qu'est-ce qu'on appelle postmodernité? Je ne suis pas au courant.'),[117] one will be inclined to regard all efforts to
reconstruct a *postmodern epistemology* with an incredulous smile.

Nevertheless, some arguments can be mustered in favour of such efforts. In
the last section, it was shown time and again that a critique of power and society
can yield a critique of particular forms of knowledge. If epistemology is not
defined as an objectivist metaphysics of knowledge, but as a critique of knowledge, then it may appear meaningful to attribute an epistemology to Rorty.
Within the postmodern problematic, the latter is complemented by Foucault's
critique, insofar as it also inquires into the historical and socio-genetic conditions of knowledge, reason and truth. 'What does a history of reason look
like?'[118] – Foucault asks and proposes, inspired by the Critical Theory of Adorno
and Horkheimer, a 'rational critique of rationality'.[119]

Hence the crucial point is not the fact that Rorty sees himself as a 'postmodernist bourgeois liberal' (cf. supra), while Foucault wonders what the word
'postmodernity' could mean. For in spite of his well-known categorical statement 'I have never been a structuralist,'[120] Foucault's work was considered by
such different thinkers as Jean Piaget and Günter Schiwy as part and parcel of
the structuralist theoretical complex.[121] The point is that essential aspects of
Foucault's, Rorty's and even Vattimo's and Deleuze's theories can be understood as heterogeneous, but comparable and complementary reactions to the
*postmodern problematic*. What exactly does this problematic look like from an
epistemological and critical point of view? 1. In the first place, it can be shown
that all of the critiques commented on here react to the socially and politically
induced *collapse of the grand metanarratives* (described here in the previous
section). In this sense, certain epistemological problems can be deduced from
those of social philosophy and sociology. For social reasons it does not seem
possible anymore to presuppose the existence of stable key concepts such as
'reason' or 'truth' within the framework of rationalist, Hegelian or Marxist
metanarratives claiming universal validity. 2. All forms of knowledge, all notions
of reason and truth are now being considered from the outside, as it were, so
that their claims to validity are limited to particular historical or cultural contexts. One of the consequences of this development is a drastic *pluralization* and
*particularization* of these concepts. 3. The human subject no longer appears as
an autonomous instance capable of recognizing truth by contemplative means
or in the course of social action, but as a *sub-ject* (*sub-iectum*) produced by power
structures whose truth and identity correspond to the truths of the authorities
wielding power. 4. As soon as reason and truth are recognized as plural and
particular forms of knowledge and challenged accordingly, there seems to be
no other solution than a postmodern proclamation of epistemological pluralism and particularism. The claims of philosophy to universal validity are lost in
the process. Henceforth, philosophy either accepts *rhizomatic thought* in the
sense of Deleuze and Guattari, thus turning into *weak thought* or *pensiero debole* in
the sense of Vattimo, or comes close to *creative writing*, as is the case in some of
Derrida's, Hartman's or Rorty's works.

On the whole, the postmodern problematic appears as a social and linguistic situation in which actors feel that, after the collapse of the rationalist faith in progress and of the Marxist metanarrative, the individual has been deprived of all landmarks, because not a single concept or value can claim universal validity. It seems important to view this problematic from the outside, *du dehors*, as Foucault would say, instead of being submerged by it.

As an heir to Nietzsche, as a critic of Hegel, Foucault no longer believes that it is possible to understand social evolution as a meaningful process governed by necessity and moving towards a definable historical or metaphysical goal. Unlike Comte and Marx, who believed in a linear and cumulative or contradictory social process leading to ever higher forms of life, Foucault perceives discontinuity, disruption and contingency. In *The Order of Discourse* (*L'Ordre du discours*, 1971), he unambiguously dismisses the rationalist-positivist and Hegelian idea of a 'continuous unravelling of an ideal necessity'.[122]

In *La Pensée du dehors* (1986), he presents the *membra disiecta* of an idealist dialectic which fell prey to Nietzsche's destruction of metaphysics. Reflection, *Aufhebung* and the unity of the subject lose their credibility after the disintegration of dialectical discourse, and the philosopher begins to scan the postmodern horizon for viable alternatives:

> Not reflection but oblivion; not contradiction, but a contestation that deletes; not reconciliation, but repetition (ressassement); not a spirit that laboriously seeks its unity, but an endless erosion coming from outside; not a truth that lights up at the end of the day but the helpless flow of a language that has always been there.[123]

This commentary to Maurice Blanchot's Nietzschean work could be read as a self-presentation of Foucault's critique of Hegelian and Marxist dialectics.

The development of our knowledge does not appear to him as a cumulative process moving towards an historical goal, but as a history of mutations and breaks. His greatest merit seems to consist in his Nietzschean discovery that human thought is not brought about in a Platonic or Cartesian manner by the spontaneous contemplation of autonomous subjects, but produced within particular power and discourse constellations. The latter cannot be integrated into a linear or dialectical metanarrative, because they turn out to be disconnected, autonomous systems as soon as they are viewed *from the outside* (*du dehors*) and recognized as particular units whose validity is limited in space and time. From this point of view, truth and reason no longer appear as *universally* and transculturally valid essences underlying an historical continuum, but as variable concepts whose *particular* character is due to their function in changing cultural contexts.[124]

What matters to Foucault, Christiane Sinding points out, is to recognize the 'false continuities' of traditional histories of ideas which tend to obliterate 'the real production of new modes of knowledge'.[125] This kind of production can only be accessed by a 'science of discursive organizations',[126] Jacques Revel explains, and speaks in conjunction with Foucault's *The Birth of the Clinic* (*Naissance de la clinique*, 1963) of a 'strictly structuralist approach'.[127] What counts at this point is neither the question whether Foucault's construction of a new history of ideas actually reveals 'the real production of new modes of knowledge', nor the complementary question whether Jean Piaget is right in considering Foucault's description of the human science *episteme* as completely arbitrary.[128]

It seems more important to realize that in works such as *Madness and Civilization*, *The Order of Things* and *The Archaeology of Knowledge*, reason and its truths are considered (with Nietzsche) 'genealogically', from the outside as it were, thereby undergoing a process of fragmentation, pluralization and particularization which reveals their relative character. In *Madness and Civilization*, for example, the relationship between madness and reason is presented as an interdependence and the exclusion of madness by a rationalist, but historically particular reason as a kind of self-limitation or even self-amputation: 'In our era, the experience of madness remains silent in the composure of a knowledge which, knowing too much about madness, forgets it.'[129]

By excluding 'blind madness' both from the institutions and from the realm of knowledge, the reason of the 'classical age', of the seventeenth century, blinds itself. Unlike the Renaissance, which tended to attribute to madness certain prophetic qualities, seventeenth-century rationalism systematically excludes madness, thus depriving reason of its Other and of its ability to think this Other. Commenting on this situation, Arlette Farge points out: 'The tragic element of madness, a source of knowledge and truth, vanishes in the dark.'[130] René Major completes this picture by referring to 'the reason of madness in Foucault'.[131] For Foucault blames classical rationalism for having halved reason by separating it from madness.

On the one hand, this criticism is reminiscent of Horkheimer's and Adorno's critique of reason in the *Dialectic of Enlightenment*, where the exclusion of artistic mimesis from a domineering rationalism comes under attack[132]; on the other hand, it bears witness to Foucault's drastic particularization of the concept of reason. What Foucault has in mind is not a universal reason in progress, whose course can be traced back to the dawn of history, but the particular reason of classicism which systematically excluded madness and which, in the nineteenth century, was superseded by a completely different type of reason: by that of the human sciences which discovered the human being as subject and object. In *The Order of Things*, he refers to a 'fundamental event that occurred in the Western *episteme* towards the end of the eighteenth century'.[133] This episteme inaugurates something entirely new: a new reason and a new set of truths. Both concepts – reason and truth – can, from Foucault's point of view, only be used in a plural or 'pluralized' form, as Paul Rabinow puts it: 'His is a constant pluralizing and decapitalizing of all the great concepts, first principles, and fundamental grounds that our tradition has produced.'[134]

This 'pluralizing', which is confirmed from one epistemic mutation to the next, is accompanied in *The Order of Things* by visual metaphors most of which tend to transform the rationalist or dialectical consciousness into a spatial perception of structures, events and objects. Like in some of Robbe-Grillet's novels (*La Jalousie, Topologie d'une cité fantôme*), an anonymous observer describes the sudden, unforeseen emergence of new constellations – without ever being able to explain it.[135] In this situation, 'man appears in his ambiguous position as an object of knowledge and as a subject that knows: enslaved sovereign, observed spectator (. . .)'.[136] A few pages later, Foucault evokes 'the recent manifestation of man'[137] which, even today, prevents us from recognizing the historical limitations and the finitude of man as subject and object of knowledge. Should the hypothesis that man might fall prey to a new kind of rationality located beyond all humanist and anthropocentric perspectives and tending to dissolve the human in a biological and genetic continuum be confirmed, then society would enter a new episteme situated beyond modernity.

In Foucault's retrospective account, modernity, viewed as an era of humanism and human science, appears as a thing of the past: 'But, more fundamentally, our culture crossed the threshold beyond which we recognize our modernity when finitude was conceived in an interminable cross-reference with itself.'[138] The postmodern age, which begins to take shape in Foucault's writings, is a constellation in which the fragmentation of history and the concomitant emergence of multiple truths are accompanied by a pluralization or fragmentation of individual subjects. It is possibly also an age of interchangeable values and orientations or an 'age of oblivion',[139] as Burghart Schmidt puts it, where fascists turn into radical democrats and yesterday's communists reappear as today's successful capitalists or advertising experts.

From Foucault's point of view, it is an age in which the unity of the subject and its knowledge is negated by an archaeology full of breaks and discontinuities: 'The authority of the creative subject, as the *raison d'être* of an *œuvre* and the principle of its unity, is quite alien to it.'[140] (Although a critique of Foucault's concepts of *episteme* and *archaeology* is not part of this chapter, it ought to be pointed out that Foucault does not even envisage the possibility of a dialectic between continuity and discontinuity. However, interruptions and breaks do not necessarily exclude continuities as the Russian revolution of 1917 shows. Essential elements of the tsarist regime – for example the centralized administration – reappeared under communist rule and have survived until the present day. Foucault's work can certainly be interpreted as a break with French rationalism; but at the same time it incorporates Canguilhem's epistemology and thus revives Bachelard's rationalism along with his theory of *epistemological breaks* [*coupures épistémologiques*]. Even a theory geared towards discontinuities has its continuities.)[141]

Gilles Deleuze is fascinated by one aspect in Foucault's work: by the Nietzschean or genealogical reduction of the universal to the particular, of truth to power and play, of the subject to the regulated corporeity of the individual and of thought to physical life. What Bianca Rosenthal has to say about Camus and Nietzsche, applies in many respects to Foucault and Deleuze: 'The thought of both thinkers is oriented towards life on earth, life for them is the supreme value.'[142] Life and body, not spirit as a selfless aspiration towards objective knowledge and supra-individual truth, are their aims.

Knowledge and truth are considered by both postmodern philosophers as instruments of domination (Foucault) or of self-realization (Deleuze). About the nexus of power and truth Deleuze writes in his book on Foucault: 'There is no model of truth that does not refer back to a kind of power, and no knowledge or even science that does not express or imply, in an act, power that is being exerted.'[143]

Deleuze, whose presentation of Foucault's work is far from 'objective', because his primary aim is a reconstruction of Foucault's thought in accordance with his own theoretical premises, also particularizes the concept of truth by linking it to power structures. Moreover, his Nietzschean notion of *play* contributes to the conception of truth as a local, personal and contingent factor. 'We can say, in fact, that there are "games of truth", or rather procedures for truth. Truth is inseparable from the procedure establishing it (. . .),'[144] he remarks commenting on Foucault's *Discipline and Punish*.

This is to a certain extent also Deleuze's point of view. He too sees truth 'from the outside', and it appears to him as pluralized and particularized. Not the Platonic or Hegelian concept of truth is at stake here, a concept encompassing and surpassing all other concepts, but a multitude of truths, produced *ad hoc* by individuals and groups. Deleuze sums up the postmodern tendency towards particularization and pluralization in a concise formula when he concludes: 'Beneath the universal there are games or transmissions of particular features, and the universal or eternal nature of man is merely the shadow of a particular and ephemeral combination carried by a historical stratum.'[145] Considered in this perspective, his thought begins to take shape.

For in this context, his early interest in David Hume's empiricism no longer appears as a personal whim, but as a prelude to a Nietzschean philosophy which later on turns against both Plato's theory of ideas and Hegel's historicist view of the Idea as evolution. His discovery that, in Hume's work, totality is 'but a collection'[146] of facts, encourages Deleuze to rebel against Hegel's notion of totality, especially against his postulate that it synthesizes all contradictions. Deleuze rules out all attempts to overcome contradiction and disparity. In *Logic of Sense* (*Logique du sens*, 1969), he pleads against Plato in favour of the cynics and Stoics and in favour of a philosophy of the surface which renounces once and for all the distinction between essence and appearance: 'There is nothing behind the curtain except unnameable mixtures, nothing above the carpet except the empty sky. Sense appears and is played out at the surface (. . .).'[147] Nietzsche expressed this idea with similar words in his well-known remarks about the role of reason in philosophy: 'The apparent world is the only one: the "true" world is nothing but an *added lie* . . .'[148]

Deleuze radicalizes this idea by relating it to empiricism, nominalism and Nietzsche's myth of Dionysos. The explosive force of this combination destroys all general concepts such as *essence, truth* or *subject* and transforms the knowable world into a disparate coexistence of individual cases, of 'nomadic singularities'.[149] In such a world, any kind of search for a supra-individual, impersonal truth becomes inconceivable, meaningless: 'Truth is not relegated to the background (. . .), but is conceived of as a multiplicity.'[150] And: 'Questions are neither encountered by the philosopher nor do they arise from gaps in our knowledge or from ignorance: they are created.'[151]

The fact is that the Nietzschean Deleuze, who adopts a polemical stance vis-à-vis Plato and Hegel, maps out an anti-objectivist, creative philosophy which is at the same time a philosophy of vitalism. Unlike in Foucault's case, where the particularization of thought is partly due to its symbiotic relationship with power, it is due in the case of Deleuze to a strong link between thought and creativity. The latter is deduced from Nietzsche's 'will to power'. Answering the question why he wrote about Hume's empiricism, Deleuze explains: 'Because empiricism is like the English novel. The idea is neither to write a philosophical novel nor to overload a novel with philosophy. The idea is to be philosophical as a novelist, to be a novelist in philosophy.'[152] This rapprochement between philosophy and literature is particularly significant within the postmodern problematic because it announces a basic scepticism vis-à-vis modern conceptual universalism and a complementary enhancement of the non-conceptual, the particular. It will be shown that this tendency can also be observed in the philosophies of Vattimo and Rorty.

How is one to understand Deleuze's metaphor 'novelist in philosophy'? Such a novelist is neither a mediator between the Platonic world of pure forms and a contingent world of appearance nor a mouthpiece of the Hegelian 'world spirit' – nor of a different kind of objectivity. He is rather the creator of his own idiosyncratic world which cannot be criticized or refuted by comparisons with other philosophical creations. 'Thought is creation, not will to truth,'[153] argues Deleuze and refers to Nietzsche. When he defines, with Guattari, the philosophical activity as 'a constructivism',[154] he means neither Maturana's and Varela's radical constructivism nor Paul Lorenzen's more moderate constructivist approach.[155] He means the creative and artistic act of philosophers, who invent their own language, thus empowering themselves to coin concepts that are *specific* enough to distinguish one philosophical writer from another. Not objective or intersubjective knowledge is the aim of such philosophers (Deleuze regards philosophical discussions with suspicion and scepticism), but the attempt to bring about an important event and turn it into an intellectual adventure: 'Philosophy does not consist in knowing and is not inspired by truth. Rather, it is categories like Interesting, Remarkable, or Important that determine success or failure.'[156]

Deleuze and Guattari compare philosophical concepts with heroes of novels who are expected to be original and unique: 'Melville said that great novelistic characters must be Originals, Unique. The same is true of conceptual personae.

They must be remarkable, even if they are antipathetic; a concept must be interesting, even if it is repulsive.'[157] These postulates are illustrated by Nietzsche's notion of 'bad conscience': certainly a disagreeable notion and an anti-hero of philosophy, but a notion without which Nietzsche's philosophy would hardly be conceivable. Thus thinkers come to be identified with their thoughts and turn into living concepts like *Hegel-World-Spirit, Marx-Proletariat* or *Heidegger-Being.* Such concepts do not differ substantially from Shakespeare's Hamlet, Cervantes's Don Quixote and Proust's Marcel. 'The philosopher is the idiosyncrasy of his conceptual personae,'[158] Deleuze and Guattari explain. Have they not themselves come to represent pleasant and less pleasant concepts such as *anti-Oedipus, rhizome* or *schizo-analysis?*

It would certainly be unjust to turn Habermas's critique of Derrida against Deleuze and Guattari and blame them for amalgamating philosophy and literature.[159] For they are quite explicit in their attempts to draw a line between philosophy and non-conceptual art: 'Art thinks no less than philosophy, but it thinks through affects and percepts.'[160] (One may ask oneself at this stage how original such delimitations are, since they do not seem to differ radically from traditional, especially Hegelian, attempts to distinguish conceptual philosophy from an art addressing senses and emotions.)

However, even without the dissolution of philosophy in literature, one of the consequences of this generic rapprochement is a drastic particularization and pluralization of conceptual thought. It is not by chance that Deleuze and Guattari are not keen on philosophical discussions.[161] For it is virtually impossible to mediate conceptually between heterogeneous 'philosophical novels' in which original 'conceptual heroes' are at the centre of the scene. Interlocutors never mean one and the same thing, Deleuze and Guattari explain, and, referring to dialogue, they add: 'It never takes place on the same plane.'[162]

The only mode of communication they can imagine is rhizomatic thought within which autonomous or even autarkical worlds of ideas are linked by subterranean passages. Each of these worlds is unique, a *unique event (événement)* resisting conceptual definitions and comparisons with other events. As an alternative to conceptual thought, which they compare to a tree, vertically structured by the dominating trunk, Deleuze and Guattari imagine a *rhizomatic thought* (from the Greek *rhiza* = root) that spreads in all directions like a fantastic root and possibly crosses other modes of thought in a completely haphazard way.

Nevertheless, a rhizome is not to be identified with a root: it resembles a subterranean network of tubers linked by bulbs and stalks.[163] In the postmodern social and linguistic context, it goes almost without saying that the rhizome-metaphor cannot be turned into a clearly defined concept. It seems none the less possible (from a late modern point of view) to bring about a conceptual approximation because the authors define and explain the rhizome (without intending it, of course) as a 'principle of connexion and heterogeneity': 'Any point of a rhizome can be connected to anything other, and must be.'[164]

The rhizome thus appears as an attempt to relate all elements of a particular context to one another – even the most distant ones. The best example of a successful rhizome (some philosophical theories are optimal illustrations of their own tenets) is probably Deleuze's and Guattari's voluminous work *Mille plateaux.* In their introduction, the authors present the following formula: 'RHI-ZOMATICS = SCHIZOANALYSIS = STRATOANALYSIS = PRAGMATICS = MICROPOLITICS'.[165] The idea is to establish rhizomatic links between language, the unconscious and politics without relying on a dominant factor (comparable to the tree-trunk) or an encompassing structure in the sense of Greimas's deep structure or Althusser's *structure à dominante.*

The rhizomatic tissue is not a conceptual hierarchy in the sense of Comte's system or Hegel's totality. This becomes clear in Deleuze's description of the *event* (*événement*) which, according to the French philosopher, can only be understood as a unique moment that lights up between the past and the future. It cannot be made present or defined (delimited) because it splits up endlessly between the past and the future.[166] Only the rhizome as a mobile tissue is capable of representing the unique event which cannot be fixed by concepts: 'The point is that science becomes more event-oriented instead of being structural. It draws lines and routes, makes jumps instead of constructing axioms. The disappearance of tree-like schemes, which yield to rhizomatic movements, is a sign of this change.'[167] The reader who would like to know which science Deleuze refers to and how the scientists in question proceed in practice, is left unsatisfied. But this seems to be the price for breaking with modernity, rationalism and dialectics.

Among the most important innovations of Deleuze's thought is undoubtedly his rejection of Platonic objectivism and of intersubjective testing of hypotheses (of philosophical discussions). Together with his attempt to introduce artistic creativity into philosophical discourse and his dissolution of hierarchical conceptuality in the rhizome, it leads to what Manfred Frank calls 'the collapse of reason's claim to universal validity'.[168]

This postmodern disintegration of the universality of reason also makes itself felt in the case of Richard Rorty who resembles Deleuze and Guattari insofar as he is equally anxious to replace Platonism, rationalism and objectivism by a rapprochement between philosophy and literature. Although it is inadmissible to pretend that the American pragmatist and the rebellious founder of schizoanalysis agree in most respects, especially since their political views are incompatible, it seems meaningful to have a closer look at the particularizing and pluralizing tendencies in Rorty's work in order to compare them (independently of all rhizomatic speculations) with corresponding tendencies in Foucault and Deleuze.

For Foucault's idea that knowledge is not universal, that is that transitions from one historical period, from one culture to another may invalidate it, because it is inextricably tied up with particular power and discourse constellations, is not only confirmed by Deleuze's anti-Platonism and anti-rationalism, but also by Rorty's critique of Platonic, rationalist and Kantian objectivism. Knowledge and truth are historical and cultural phenomena that may change in time: 'For the pragmatist, by contrast, "knowledge" is, like "truth", simply a compliment paid to the beliefs which we think so well justified that, for the moment, further justification is not needed.'[169] The expression 'for the time being' seems to be the crucial element here, for Rorty is convinced (as was shown above) that the Platonic or Kantian claim to universal principles of knowledge has become untenable. In the postmodern situation, we ought to prefer Dewey's pragmatic questions to universalism: 'Which communities' purposes shall I share? and What sort of person would I prefer to be?' These questions ought to replace Kant's questions: 'What Should I Do? What May I Hope? What is Man?'[170]

Rorty, who dismisses somewhat rashly all the provisional results yielded by discussions on anthropological constants and cultural universals,[171] confines himself to the North-American brand of bourgeois liberalism mentioned above. A self-critical ethnocentric particularization referred to as 'anti-anti-ethnocentrism' appears to him as the final insight:

> Anti-anti-ethnocentrism does not say that we are trapped within our monad or our language, but merely that the well-windowed monad we live in is no more closely linked to the nature of humanity or the demands of rationality than the relatively windowless monads which surround us.[172]

Even on a metaphorical level it is not clear why a monad with a large number of windows should not afford a better view of the (material and conceptual) world than a monad without windows. On a conceptual level, Rorty's argument turns out to be even less convincing. For it is hard to see why a group of scientists studying the ecosystem of the earth, and the clearing of rainforests in particular, should not be able to adopt a more rational point of view (i.e. one that is in the *interest* of humanity as a whole) than dictators, mafia-organizations or the members of a tribe who believe that the earth is the centre of the universe. It is quite simple to dismiss vague notions such as 'human nature', as long as one ignores the debates about universals and the question concerning the possibility of generalizing certain (human) interests.

In such a situation, the only way out seems to be a final farewell to 'universal transcultural rationality'[173] and a conversion to contingency in the Nietzschean sense:

> If, with Davidson, we drop the notion of language as fitting the world, we can see the point of Bloom's and Nietzsche's claim that the strong maker, the person who uses words as they have never before been used, is best able to appreciate her own contingency.[174]

The discovery of contingency in biological (Maturana), semiotic (Prieto) or sociological constructivism (Bourdieu) *may* enable us to treat our insights as constructions the truth or viability of which can be tested by intersubjective criticism. It does *not necessarily* entail a replacement of conceptual thought and argument by literature or 'textuality'.

However, Rorty seems to postulate a necessity when – like Deleuze – he replaces conceptual universalism by 'creation'. Unlike nineteenth century idealism, which, according to Rorty, tried to replace the natural sciences by a philosophical science, 'twentieth-century textualism wants to place literature in the center, and to treat both science and philosophy as, at best, literary genres.'[175] Rorty goes on to explain what he means by literature: 'By "literature", then, I shall mean the areas of culture which, quite self-consciously, forego agreement on an encompassing critical vocabulary, and thus forego argumentation.'[176] It is hardly possible to be more particularistic, for Deleuze and Guattari were, in spite of their virulent anti-universalism, quite serious in distinguishing *concepts* of philosophy from artistic *percepts*.

Like Geoffrey H. Hartman, a literary critic and a deconstructionist, Rorty considers Jacques Derrida's experimental text *Glas* as a model of postmodern textuality: 'It is no small feat to get this sort of thing down on paper, but what we find in *Glas* is not a new terrain. It is a realistic account of a terrain upon which we have been camping for some time.'[177] It could prove worthwhile to analyse Rorty's use of the word *we*. For it might become clear that, although this pronoun usually means 'the liberal American pragmatists', it is used in such a way as to refer – at least implicitly – to the rest of humanity.

However, not all contemporary philosophers are camping on Derrida's terrain, but only those among them who, like Rorty and some other postmodernists, draw their inspiration from Nietzsche or the romantics in order to score points in their struggle against universalist rationalism. Without much ado and without seriously consulting with William James and John Dewey, Rorty locates all of pragmatism within the romantic philosophical tradition: 'But if, as I do, one views pragmatism as a successor movement to romanticism, one will see this notion of reason as one of its principal targets.'[178] Not only Rorty's critique of reason owes a lot to Schelling and Friedrich Schlegel, but even his attempts to turn literature and art into privileged modes of knowledge in the twentieth century are of romantic origin. In his well-known article 'About Incomprehensibility' ('Über die Unverständlichkeit'), Friedrich Schlegel proclaims 'that [he] consider[s] art to be the core of humanity'.[179]

One may wonder at this point whether the semantic opposition between rationalism and romanticism would not yield a more meaningful construction than the opposition between modernity and postmodernity, as proposed above. Would it not be more plausible to consider the philosophies commented on here as postmodern revivals of romantic theories? Would the romanticism-hypothesis not have the advantage of introducing rationalism as the true rival of postmodern romanticism, instead of relying on a heterogeneous and increasingly self-critical modernity (overarching Enlightenment, Kantianism, Hegelianism and Marxism) as described by Toulmin?[180]

This hypothesis is not unproblematical because philosophers such as Foucault, Deleuze, Lyotard and Derrida can more easily be understood as Nietzscheans than as romantics in the philosophical or aesthetic sense. This even applies to sociologists such as Bauman (cf. Chapter 2). However, the hypothesis shows how intricate the concept of modernity is, especially because the modern period, unlike postmodernity, spans centuries and (considered from a purely chrono-logical point of view) even includes rebellious, anti-rationalist romanticism.

It is not so much the romantic heritage that holds together the various post-modern philosophies, but a more recent and more original tendency towards particularization and pluralization which Gianni Vattimo circumscribes by the metaphor of *weak thought* (*pensiero debole*). Like Foucault, Deleuze, Lyotard and Rorty, he imagines a mode of thinking which renounces univocity and unifica-tion on all levels in order to play with the manifold. He joins together the most important aspects of postmodern philosophies when, following Nietzsche, he proclaims that the distinction between Being and Appearance is due to an illusion:

> There is no liberation beyond appearances in a so-called realm of authentic Being; there is, however, a liberty in the sense of a mobility between 'appear-ances' which, of course, are no longer called this, as Nietzsche teaches us: now that 'the true world has turned into a fable', a true Being that would degrade them to lies and falsities no longer exists.[181]

If this diagnosis is correct, it becomes difficult to assess the vast number of appearances, and the subject is committed not only to multiplicity, but also to indifference as exchangeability of ephemeral phenomena. Eventually, it finds itself in a situation comparable to that of Marcello Clerici, Alberto Moravia's post-war hero. Towards the end of Moravia's novel *Il conformista* (1951), the disillusioned fascist has to recognize that 'everything was just and unjust at the same time' ('tutto era stato al tempo stesso giusto e ingiusto') and that he might just as well have opted for another ideology ('che avrebbe potuto fare cose tutte diverse').[182]

It goes without saying that Vattimo and other postmodernists adopt a com-pletely different stance, presenting the fragmentation and pluralization of the subject (*schizo-sujet, soggetto debole*) as a liberation. To Vattimo, 'postmodern man' ('uomo post-moderno') appears as an individual (*sic*) capable of accepting his own plurality: 'individuality as multiplicity' ('individualità come molteplicità').[183] The question a postmodern ethic cannot possibly avoid is: how a 'divided sub-ject' ('soggetto scisso') can be made responsible for actions of any kind.

The complementary question that imposes itself in this context is: whether the 'weak thought' of postmodernity is actually the best response to an instru-mental reason tied up with domination over nature, as Vattimo would make us believe. Wolfgang Welsch tries to make Vattimo's and Rovatti's theses sound plausible when he explains:

> Hence Vattimo and Rovatti neither deny the existence of pluralization nor the conclusion that it has led to a weakening of reason; however, they remind

us that all this should no longer be assessed with reference to an ideal of strength [i.e. of strong reason], but within the new perspective of weakness.[184]

Weak, particularizing and pluralizing thought may look attractive because it favours minorities and marginal groups; it loses some of its appeal as soon as it becomes clear that it turns its back on the social sciences, thus condemning itself to the kind of marginal position it sympathizes with. In the following section, the anti-conceptual and anti-theoretical bias of this thought will be dealt with in more detail and criticized.

As an alternative to 'weak thought' one can also imagine a dialogical theory emerging from contemporary discussions between philosophy and the social sciences.[185] 'Weak thought' is an ambivalent notion in the sense that it may not only further reciprocity and pluralism but also discredit conceptualization and condone ideological prejudice.

## 3.4  Epistemology II: Language, Concept, Particularity – From Deleuze and Derrida to Vattimo

A critical discussion of postmodern epistemology would be incomplete if it did not take into account the 'linguistic turn' which contributed decisively to the strengthening of neo-romantic and especially Nietzschean tendencies towards particularization and pluralization. Two works by Gilles Deleuze, *Différence et répétition* (1968) and *Logique du sens* (1969), came out almost simultaneously and can be considered as complementary insofar as the first presents the linguistic problematic of the second in concrete terms. At the same time, it evokes Derrida's notion of *différance* (a neologism) which came about in the same social and linguistic situation as Deleuze's *différence*.

One of the fundamental ideas of *The Logic of Sense* is that an event cannot be conceptually defined because it is endlessly being split into past and future, to the extent that a presence of meaning becomes impossible. In a complementary way, the author of *Difference and Repetition* explains why repetition (of a word, a concept, an event) can never be repetition of the *same*: because the repeated elements are never held together by a common conceptual denominator functioning as their origin and guaranteeing a presence of meaning amidst variation and change.

In order to illustrate this thesis, Deleuze distinguishes two types of repetition: the Platonic and the Nietzschean. Unlike the Platonic repetition, which is based on the idea of an unchanging original, the Nietzschean idea of repetition aims at pure difference: not difference in relation to an invariable original matrix, but movement, departure, divergence as such.

Deleuze questions the Platonic distinction of original and copy and proposes an 'inversion of Platonism': 'The task of modern philosophy has been defined: to overturn Platonism.'[186] In this case, *renversement* does not only mean 'inversion', but also implies a subversive movement, because 'the Heraclitan world still growls in Platonism'.[187] At this point, one could go even further in the sense of Deleuze and add: the Nietzschean world is inherent in Plato's system of ideas and always ready to break it up.

Like Derrida in *La Dissémination* (1972), Deleuze believes that a certain Anti-Platonism is contained in Platonism:

> Among the most extraordinary pages in Plato, demonstrating the anti-Platonism at the heart of Platonism, are those which suggest that the different, the dissimilar, the unequal – in short, becoming – may well be not merely defects which affect copies like a ransom paid for their secondary character or a counterpart to their resemblance, but rather models themselves, terrifying models of the *pseudos* in which unfolds the power of the false.[188]

In other words: some remarks in Plato's works make us doubt the existence of an original identical with itself or of a constant concept, from which all differing or similar units can be derived as more or less faithful copies. The Platonic relationship between essence and appearance, original and copy is not actually inverted by Deleuze in order to turn essence into a derivate of appearance, but simply dissolved in a Nietzschean manner. In the end, the world of 'appearance' coincides with reality, and the contrast between *phenomenon* and *noumenon* disappears. At the same time, the complementary distinction between *original* and *copy* (*simulacrum*) loses its function, and the world of *simulacra* turns out to be – as with Nietzsche and Baudrillard – the only possible one. The differing *simulacra* cannot be reduced to a common source or original; they can only be related to the differences that separate them: 'Systems in which different relates to different through difference itself are systems of simulacra.'[189] In other words: only the differences manifest themselves, not a common denominator underlying all the diverging *simulacra* which would enable us to subsume them under a conceptually definable unit functioning as the presence of meaning.

Both in *Difference and Repetition* and in *The Logic of Sense*, Deleuze turns against the Platonic and Hegelian tendency towards unification and identity. As in all postmodern philosophies, the 'bad guys' in Deleuze's thought are 'the categories of representation'[190] incarnated in the One, the Identical or the Same. Repetition as repetition of the non-identical and the multiple evokes Nietzsche's 'eternal return' as imagined by Deleuze: 'The eternal return does not cause the same and the similar to return, but is itself derived from a world of pure difference.'[191]

It goes almost without saying that only a multiple subject in the sense of Lyotard and Vattimo can correspond to a world of pure differences. As with Vattimo, the world of appearance is, in the case of Deleuze, a world of multiplicity, divergence and contingence: 'The subject of eternal return is not the same but the different, not the similar but the dissimilar, not the one but the many, not necessity but chance.'[192] The Nietzschean and Anti-Platonic or Anti-Hegelian aspect of this passage is not only the rhetoric of multiplicity, but also the emphasis on chance vis-à-vis necessity: a tendency inaugurated by the Young Hegelians, some of whom can be considered as precursors of Nietzsche.[193]

Deleuze, who proclaims in *The Logic of Sense* that the multiple is approved of and that the different is enjoyable,[194] is interpreted by Wolfgang Welsch in the sense that he does not postulate the absolute character of otherness (like Lyotard), but instead pleads in favour of a transversal linking of heterogeneous elements: 'The idea is to understand types of otherness which do not differ radically because they contain moments of identity.'[195] However, the answer to the question how the rhizome is to fulfil a mediating function between heterogeneous units, remains the big secret of Deleuze, Guattari and Welsch. For in *Thousand Plateaus*, the rhizome is described somewhat vaguely as 'an a-centered, nonhierarchical, nonsignifying system without a General'. It is 'defined solely by a circulation of states'.[196] Not a word is said about a mediating function, that is about mediation between heterogeneous elements or types of thought.

Although there are attempts in Deleuze's work to reunite the disparate units of the celebrated multiplicity (especially when the author mentions a '*discordant harmony* [*accord par la discordance*]'[197] in Kant's theory of the sublime), there can be no misunderstanding as far as the general intention underlying his argument goes. It is meant to contest the universal validity of concepts and even tends to doubt the latter's existence. The initial aim is to think difference without a concept. The other aim is to show how the different and multiple breaks up conceptual structures.[198]

Distinguishing the *concept* from the *idea*, Deleuze writes about the latter that it delivers the different in 'positive systems in which different is related to different, making divergence, disparity and decentring so many objects of affirmation which rupture the framework of conceptual representation'.[199] In view of this anti-conceptual bias inspired by the mythical notion of *différence* and a radical particularization of thought, which is incompatible with the conceptual interests of theory, it is hard to see the 'moments of identity' mentioned by Wolfgang Welsch in conjunction with Deleuze's philosophy. For the 'identical' and the 'similar', both of which are dismissed as illusions by Deleuze (as was shown above), are only conceivable in conceptual terms.

Unlike Adorno, who would like 'to transcend the concept', but only 'by way of the concept',[200] that is without sacrificing ratio to mimesis, some postmodern authors have no qualms about sacrificing the conceptual to the literary, philosophy to the rhetoric of tropes. This does not only apply to Deleuze, Rorty and especially Lyotard, who dismisses all kinds of theory in *Libidinal Economy*,[201] but to a certain degree also to Derrida, who considers the concept as a necessary evil used by the deconstructionist in his attempts to decompose the metaphysical machinery. Considered in a postmodern perspective, the concept does not further knowledge, but obstructs it because it is an illusion: because it disintegrates as soon as it is treated as a definable 'presence of meaning'.

In very much the same way as in Deleuze's work, where Nietzschean repetition never yields the Same, but only something Else, that is a diverging, differing *simulacrum*, in Derrida's work repetition is only conceivable as *iterability* (*itérabilité*), that is as an endless shift or postponement of meaning. In contrast to Anglo-American speech act theory as developed by Austin and Searle, in contrast to Greimas's rationalist semiotics, both geared towards the idea of meaningful *iterativity* (Greimas), that is a repetition that illustrates and consolidates meaning, Derrida believes that repetition leads to the disintegration of meaning. The repetition of one and the same word or semantic unit in a text does not contribute to its better definition, but entails a *postponement of the presence of meaning* which never ends, since – as with Deleuze – it merely reveals differences and not a determinate conceptual meaning (cf. Section 4.5).

The poststructuralist authors put in question Saussure's idea of a *transcendental signified* which can only be conceived of as *presence of meaning* (*présence du sens*, Derrida). The approach that presupposes a presence of meaning and underlies Saussure's synchronic linguistics is seen by Derrida as originating in the rationalist illusion that it is possible to determine the meaning of an individual element within the context of the totality of language. But the system of language undergoes historical change and is permanently open, and the rationalist Saussure is perfectly right in assuming that the meaning of a word like *literature, writing* or *text* does not exist in itself, because it can only be defined negatively in relation to 'neighbouring' or semantically similar (i.e. differing) words. He nevertheless overlooks the fact that this difference in similarity is not a divergence from a *stable signified* (an original concept in the sense of Saussure), but an endless 'shift', an endless postponement of meaning.

Derrida calls this postponement *différance*, using a neologism based on the French verb *différer* (to differ, diverge, postpone), in order to remind us of the fact that the differentiation of literature and writing, literature and text cannot be fixed in relation to a metaphysical presence of one or several *signifieds*, because it leads to an endless postponement of meaning. He describes the latter as a never-ending movement leading from one *signifier* (*signifiant*) to the next:

> But is it by chance that the book is, first and foremost, volume? And that the meaning of meaning (in the general sense of meaning and not in the sense of signalization) is infinite implication, the indefinite referral of signifier to signifier? And that its force is a certain pure and infinite equivocality which gives signified meaning no respite, no rest, but engages it in its own *economy* so that it always signifies again and differs? Except in the *Livre irréalisé* by Mallarmé, that which is written is never identical to itself.[202]

At this point the argument returns to Deleuze: there is only difference in the sense of divergence or shift, and it cannot be explained with reference to an all-time identical signified functioning as origin or original. Like Deleuze, Derrida continues Nietzsche's train of thought when he asserts that there is no Platonic essence in the sense of an unchangeable concept or signified, but only the unending collusion of polysemic signifiers in the realm of appearance. At the same time, he refers to Heidegger who, dealing with the difference between Being and Existence,[203] suggests that Being can only be extrapolated 'from the difference'[204] as such.

Both Derrida and Deleuze set out to renew Nietzsche's and Heidegger's critique of European metaphysics and turn their backs on a mode of conceptual thought that is inextricably intertwined with the principle of domination. Both philosophers challenge this kind of thought by insisting on the particular and non-conceptual which is at the same time the multiple. The collusion of signifiers, so vividly described by Derrida, is not only oriented towards the particular as signifier, as a unique phonetic unit, but also towards the polysemy of the text which invites the reader to activate its semantic potential and the corresponding multiplicity of interpretations.

At first sight, this particularistic attitude towards language and text could be regarded as late modern or modernist in the sense of Adorno: a philosopher who always tried to resist 'the brutal untruth of a subsuming form forced on from above'.[205] However, it goes well beyond late modernity and beyond Adorno's critical intentions whenever it turns the concept into an instrument for subverting the conceptual discourse of theory. For in Adorno's philosophy, mimesis, concept, theory, subject and truth – that is the particular and the general – are inseparable. Adorno's modernist stance makes itself felt in *Negative Dialectics* when the author proclaims: 'In sharp contrast to the usual ideal of science, the objectivity of dialectical cognition needs not less subjectivity, but more.'[206] Based on the refusal to abandon theory, subjectivity and the concept, this attitude is not only repudiated by Deleuze and Derrida, but also by Vattimo.

In *Le avventure della differenza* (1980), he writes about Deleuze and Derrida: 'From the very outset, difference has the same meaning for Deleuze and for Derrida. It means in fact that each apparent immediacy is the double of an original that does not exist.'[207] In the postmodern and deconstructionist context, where repetition necessarily involves shifts in meaning, Vattimo's assumption that the notion of *difference* (*differenza*) has the *same meaning* in Deleuze and Derrida is surprisingly naïve. But it shows that no argument aiming at coherence can renounce generalization and unification.

In contrast to Adorno, whose dialectics of particularity[208] he frequently refers to, but in full agreement with Deleuze and Derrida, Vattimo fails to see the necessity, the inevitability of this generalization (inherent in his own discourse). He only sees the shifts in meaning and the destruction of the presence of meaning when he mentions the 'de-stitution of the definitiveness of presence' ('de-stituzione della definitività della presenza'),[209] trying to understand difference exclusively as 'breaking in' or 'staving in' ('sfondamento').[210]

In Vattimo's case, the disintegration of the individual subject is complementary to the disintegration of meaning and the negation of its presence (*présence du sens*, Derrida). It was mentioned in the previous section and is commented on by Peter Caravetta who speaks, in conjunction with Vattimo, of a 'decline and eventual disappearance of subject and subjectivity'.[211] Vattimo himself invokes Nietzsche's critique of the subject and reminds us of the latter's 'destruction in the development of 20th century analytic psychology'.[212] In a complementary way, avant-garde art appears to him as a 'destructuring' power ('la portata destrutturante dell'arte')[213] which calls the unity and the identity of the subject into question.

In this context, he considers the disintegration of the subject as a liberation from its own fundamental subjection and describes this process within the framework of a *radical hermeneutic* (*ermeneutica radicale*) in conjunction with the disintegration of metaphysical meaning:

> The world of symbolic forms – philosophy, art, culture as a whole – retains a certain autonomy vis-à-vis technological rationality, insofar as it is the place where the subject as a subjected subject (soggetto-assoggettato), as the last incarnation of the structures of domination and empowered by technique to dominate the world, is un-done, dislocated, destructured.[214]

In other words: philosophy resists the technical and technological domination of the subject over the object by pursuing a systematic deconstruction of subjectivity.

It ought to have become clear that this decomposition of the subject in the theories of Vattimo, Derrida and Deleuze runs parallel to a decomposition of the concept by *difference* (Deleuze, Vattimo) or by *différance* (Derrida). Both processes of decomposition or deconstruction are considered by the postmodern philosophers as subversions of political, technical and technological domination in which Heidegger had already recognized a crucial aspect of metaphysics.

Postmodern deconstructionists seem oblivious of the fact that the disintegration of the concept and the subject may eventually coincide with a tacit submission to the powers that be. For without conceptuality and subjectivity, the kind of social criticism most brands of deconstruction continue to adhere to, becomes impossible. Whoever decomposes the subject along with the concept, is bound to acquiesce in the intermedial fragmentation of the individual subject in late capitalist society, thus depriving it of its experience, its continuity and its critical capacities.

> Without concepts, argues Adorno, that experience would lack continuity. By definition, the part it takes in the discursive medium makes it always more than purely individual. (. . .) Because it is general in itself, and to the extent to which it is general, individual experience goes as far as the universal.[215]

Without this *universality inherent in the particular experience of the individual,* critique and resistance collapse. This is why an attempt will be made in the next section to describe the dialectical relationship between the particular and the general in the critical debates between Lyotard and Habermas.

## 3.5  Epistemology III: Lyotard vs Habermas

What follows can be summed up in a few words: Lyotard's particularizing and Habermas's universalizing reactions to the postmodern problematic will be criticized within the context mapped out here and related dialectically to one another. It will be shown that Lyotard's model of radical particularization overlaps with Habermas's universal pragmatics by negating social subjectivity. In both cases the argument brings about a situation both thinkers try to avoid: a situation of indifference where ideological or theoretical positions, social roles and even individuals appear as interchangeable.

At this stage, it seems to make sense to return to the starting point of the second section: to the critique of metanarratives in postmodernity. Unlike Lyotard and other postmodern thinkers, who consider the metanarratives of Christianity, the Enlightenment and Marxism–Leninism with incredulity, tacitly assuming that mutual understanding cannot be reached between these narratives, Habermas speaks of 'the unfinished project of modernity'. This expression is not meant to plead in favour of a naïve continuation of Enlightenment rationalism which Adorno and Horkheimer have linked to the subject's domination over nature. Rather, it is meant to reinforce the other component of the Enlightenment tradition: its drive towards emancipation inherent in all of Adorno's and Horkheimer's works.

Nevertheless, Habermas criticizes Adorno's orientation towards artistic mimesis, the essay, the model and paratactic writing, arguing that it is bound to end in some kind of poststructuralism.[216] As an alternative, he proposes a communicative renewal of reason:

> The motivating idea is the reconciliation of a modernity alienated from itself, i.e. the idea that, without giving up the differentiations which have made modernity possible in the social, the cultural and the economic sphere, one will find forms of social life in which autonomy and dependence peacefully coexist; that one will be able to go upright within a community of shared values that is not tainted by the dubious nature of archaic communitarianism.[217]

The path to reconciliation is laid open by universal pragmatics, a hermeneutic approach aiming at the emancipating potential of the social sciences, rather than at Adorno's artistic mimesis.

Some of Lyotard's reactions to the postmodern problematic show striking similarities to Adorno's brand of Critical Theory (cf. Section 3.7), but they are diametrically opposed to Habermas's project. Unlike Habermas, who expects universal pragmatics, defined as a theory of communicative action, to bring about mutual understanding and consensus and to overcome postmodern fragmentation, Lyotard explains why social and linguistic consensus is impossible in contemporary society.

In the final phase of his intellectual development, he no longer starts from Nietzschean, but from Kantian premises and, more specifically, from Kant's *Critique of Judgement*. This is a work based on the idea that the different types of reason (the pure, the practical and the aesthetic) are heterogeneous, but can nevertheless be related to one another. In *Instructions païennes*, Lyotard answers the question whether he has become a Kantian:

> If you like, but only in the sense of the third Critique. I do not mean the Kant of the concept or the moral law, but the Kant of imagination, who has recovered from the illness of knowledge (maladie du savoir) and rule, having discovered the paganism of art and nature.[218]

It becomes clear at this point that Lyotard's Kantianism is permeated by a latent Nietzscheanism which is reminiscent of Camus's pagan philosophy. The idea is to defend the unique human creature against the abstract universality of rules and laws by relying on the non-conceptual character of art and nature.

It goes almost without saying that we are dealing here with a strongly particularizing interpretation of Kant's philosophy which accentuates the differences between the various types of reason, neglecting the affinities and transitions between them. Wolfgang Welsch warns that this way of looking at things should not be confused with Kant's own perspective: 'Against Kant's emphasis, Lyotard insists on the modern "decomposition of language into families of heteronomous language games".'[219] He adds: 'Lyotard believes that this view is borne out by the state of the contemporary world. Links are established, but only by the "blindly calculating reason" of "capital".'[220]

This is the real problem that can only by grasped in a sociological and philosophical context (cf. Section 3.2). Unlike Habermas, who has internalized the disastrous ideological battles of the Weimar Republic, and therefore envisages a consensus, the Paris intellectual rejects everything that smacks of a reconciliation with bourgeois state reason. His adversary is a global capitalism held responsible for levelling out all differences and propagating a universalism based on the exchange value: 'Thus, the economic genre of capital in no way requires the deliberative political concatenation, which admits the heterogeneity of genres of discourse. To the contrary, it requires the suppression of that heterogeneity.'[221] The tendency towards particularization and pluralization in Lyotard's discourse is primarily a reaction to the abstract universality of market laws (of the 'world market'). At the same time, and more specifically, it is a revolt against the centralized French state which Jean-Marie Vincent describes in 1979, the year when *La Condition postmoderne* is published: 'The contemporary state is certainly a Moloch instrumentalized by a capital which crushes and models human matter.'[222] In a society where intellectual life is dominated by this kind of language, the search for meaningful communication and consensus appears as futile.

This is one of the reasons why, in *La Condition postmoderne*, that is two years after the discussions in *Instructions païennes* (1977), Lyotard replaces his particularizing Kantianism by Wittgenstein's notion of *language game* in order to illustrate the irreducible heterogeneity of language which he compares to the islands of an archipelago. Starting from Wittgenstein's premise that each language game is autonomous, because it obeys specific rules, Lyotard argues 'that there is no possibility that language games can be unified or totalized in any metadiscourse'.[223]

At this stage, it should already be pointed out that Lyotard does not really apply this thesis to himself, because he has no qualms about combining Kant's and Wittgenstein's heterogeneous and partly incompatible languages. Moreover, he develops a totalizing meta-discourse in order to show why extremely heterogeneous metanarratives such as Christianity, Enlightenment and Marxism, which he tacitly subsumes under *one* linguistic genre, lose their credibility.

Lyotard, who believes (cf. Section 3.2) that the heteronomous application of linguistic rules to different discourse genres causes an *injustice* (*tort*), because the relations between idiosyncratic types of language are marked by a *différend* that cannot be solved by *lawsuits* (*litiges*), commits an injustice on a large scale when he subsumes Christian, rationalist and Marxist discourses under the common denominator 'metanarrative'. His early attempts to combine a Marxist terminology with the languages of Freud and W. Reich do not bear witness to a high regard for linguistic particularities such as language games or paralogies. The latter are not really defined by Lyotard: 'An accurate definition of "paralogy" is not offered by Lyotard in *The Postmodern Condition*. He describes it roughly as an "open systematic", the "local", the "anti-method".'[224]

Lyotard's definitions of particular languages, which he believes to be heterogeneous or even incommensurate, may be more concrete than his notion of paralogy; but they are not much clearer. While the author of *The Postmodern Condition* refers to heterogeneous *language games* in the sense of Wittgenstein, this concept is replaced in *Le Différend* (1983) and in later publications by concepts such as *phrase, phrase regimen, discourse* and *discourse genre*. It is not made clear how these concepts are related to Wittgenstein's *language game*. It is obvious, however, that Lyotard's rather unorthodox combination of Kant's and Wittgenstein's terminologies aims at particularization:

The analysis of the language games confirms and corroborates, like the critique of judgement, the dissociation of language from itself. Language is without unity, there are only language islands, each of them is governed by a different order, none of them can be translated into another.[225]

It is not simple to defend such an extreme position against criticism, especially since in everyday language economic discourses are frequently translated into political and legal ones and the latter commented on in ethical or educational terms. Moreover, Lyotard himself keeps combining extremely heterogeneous languages without worrying too much about their compatibility.

However, criticism presupposes a clear and precise definition of the object in question. In Lyotard's case, a definition in this sense is not readily available. For he does not really explain how a *language game* differs from a *genre of discourse* and how the latter can be distinguished from a *phrase regimen* (*régime de phrase*). A comparison between Wolfgang Welsch's plausible presentation and Lyotard's own explanations will highlight some of the difficulties. Commenting on the difference between phrase regimens and discourse genres, Welsch remarks:

> Phrase regimens are for example: to argue, to recognize, to describe, to narrate, to ask, to show. They prescribe rules for sentences and speech acts. (. . .) Examples illustrating genres of discourse are: to engage in a dialogue, teach, dispense justice, advertise. They are more complex than phrase regimens. They contain sentences originating in different phrase regimens. Moreover, genres of discourse have a final structure.[226]

Apart from the fact that even arguments and narrations may have a final, that is teleological structure, Welsch's apparently clear summary reveals problems which are mainly due to the fact that, although he illustrates some of Lyotard's concepts by way of examples, he leaves them undefined. Would it not be possible to subsume the relatively complex discourse genres of dialogue, law administration and teaching to even more general discursive modes (i.e. general concepts) such as argumentation, cognition and narration? Greimas, for example, analyses the legal discourse as a narrative genre among many.[227]

These remarks are relevant insofar as the author of *The Differend* increases the confusion by talking about an 'economic' and an 'academic genre of discourse' ('genre du discours économique', 'genre du discours académique') and by adding the 'universalist discourses' ('discours universalistes') in order to describe the great metanarratives of progress, socialism, welfare and knowledge.[228] One need not be a fanatical rationalist or logician in order to object that 'dialogue' or 'teaching' belong to a *class* completely different from the 'economic genre of discourse', the rhetoric of progress or of socialism.

Conceptual ambiguities of this kind make it even more difficult to understand Lyotard, since it is not always clear what his thesis concerning incompatibilities or 'differends' actually means. Most of us will readily agree that argumentation and narration are subject to different rules and that the languages of law and advertising are heterogeneous spheres – although advertising does have legal components. However, it seems difficult to follow Lyotard when, as a radical Kantian, he objects to 'one genre being invaded by another, in particular (. . .) ethics and law by the cognitive'.[229] But how are law and jurisprudence supposed to function without a conceptual or cognitive metalanguage?

One thing seems to be clear: a sentence or phrase belonging to a particular genre of discourse and obeying particular *rules of concatenation* (*règles d'enchaînement*) cannot be linked to a sentence of heterogeneous origin:

Wherever somebody chooses to continue a discussion involving a move from one discourse genre to another, a conflict erupts concerning the legitimacy of such a move. Such a conflict, it is argued, cannot be settled, precisely because rules of concatenation are missing.[230]

We are thus dealing with a linguistic *differend* that cannot be settled like a lawsuit because an encompassing metalanguage is not available (or not recognized by all parties concerned).

This postmodern particularization of language and communication seems reasonable because it is problematical, both from an epistemological and an historical point of view, to apply the criteria of one discourse to the functioning of another. Thus a reasonable and rational advocate of Critical Theory will hesitate to reject Karl Popper's and Hans Albert's Critical Rationalism for being 'undialectical'; at the same time, reasonable exponents of Critical Rationalism will hesitate to reject Adorno's or Habermas's Critical Theory because it fails to meet the criterion of 'refutability'.

However, this does not mean, as Lyotard might assume, that the discourses of Critical Theory and Critical Rationalism are incommensurate and that their relationship can only be conceived of as a 'differend'. For in some crucial points these discourses overlap; but in other points they diverge. It would be important to follow this dialectic of congruence and divergence, instead of imagining a global incompatibility or a 'differend'.

Lyotard carries particularization to extremes whenever he assumes that the 'differend' is inherent in the discourse genres because each of these combines heterogeneous sentences belonging to different phrase regimens:

Genres of discourse determine stakes, they submit phrases from different regimens to a single finality: the question, the example, the argument, the narration, the exclamation are in forensic rhetoric the heterogeneous means of persuading. It does not follow that differends between phrases should be eliminated.[231]

However, this is an assumption Lyotard fails to make clear. Why should different aspects of legal rhetoric – the question, the argument, the exclamation, the narration – clash in a contradiction or a 'differend'? Would the literary text, often mentioned by Lyotard, not be the incarnation of injustice because it tends to combine all sorts of heterogeneous languages from everyday life in narrations, quotations, parodies and dialogues?

On the one hand, Lyotard's assumption of incompatibility is due to his emphasis on the particular, on the other hand, it is due to his rejection of the concept of subject. This makes him overlook the fact that each discourse structure is based on a subjective intention and the corresponding teleology, both of which are linked to individual or collective action. Lyotard adopts quite a different perspective when he argues that the heterogeneity of language, of its discourses and phrase regimens, leads to the dissolution of subjectivity and of the concept of subject: '(. . .) Each so-called individual is divisible and plausibly divided into a number of partners (. . .).'[232]

Unfortunately, this thesis is contradicted by Lyotard's own work which not only combines discourse genres and phrase regimens by an underlying subjective intentionality, but also integrates heterogeneous discourses (Marx and Freud, Kant and Wittgenstein) into highly questionable teleological schemes. A symptomatic text from *Postmodern Fables* illustrates this point: 'The contemporary world offers a picture of liberal, imperialist capitalism after its triumph over its last two challengers, fascism and communism: so Marxism would say, were it not defunct.'[233] Even if one assumes that the first sentence could originate in a Neo-Marxist discourse, one will object – with Lyotard – to the second sentence: it constitutes an *injustice*, a *tort*, because it belongs to a discourse genre very different from the first.

The problem is due to the fact that virtually all of Lyotard's texts manipulate, combine and synthesize heterogeneous discourses on a meta-textual level. It may very well be that this is inevitable if one sets out to explain and criticize theories in a historical and social context; but in view of this situation, Lyotard should not insist on an extreme particularism that is disavowed by his own discursive practice.

The fact that his attempts at particularization and pluralization are contradictory is emphasized by Manfred Frank who aptly points out that even the discovery of a *differend* presupposes a point of view situated above the conflicting positions and relating them to one another: 'As soon as we speak of a "tort", we presuppose the validity of the judgement concerning the antagonistic nature of the conflict.'[234] He adds:

> Like identification which, if it is not to be trivial, presupposes difference in at least one respect (. . .), so, conversely, a contradiction cannot be ascertained if the opposites differ in all respects. Hence, no 'differend' can be total. But considering that the complete and total incompatibility underlying the conflict is crucial to the 'differend', one has to go one step further and say: the 'differend' as defined by Lyotard is logically impossible.[235]

One could radicalize Manfred Frank's objection and argue that a conflict is more likely to erupt between discourses which are genetically (socially, linguistically) related than between completely unrelated discourses. Lyotard's example of a 'differend between labor-power and capital'[236] takes place between discourses with related terminologies and oriented in particular towards their common denominator of the 'public or private ownership of the means of production'. It is not by distant Buddhism that the Catholic Church feels challenged, but by the Old Catholic orthodoxy and by the reformist Protestants who speak virtually the same language.

However, Lyotard also refers to what is completely strange to Western universal reason: for example to the colonized African or native American cultures which are tacitly subsumed under the 1789 Declaration of Human Rights. Naturally, this 'differend' is hardly comparable to that between labour power and capital, because, in this particular case, the heterogeneous cultures involved lack a common language. (At this stage, it becomes clear that Lyotard's attempts to illustrate the *differend* tend to deconstruct the latter.)

It is nevertheless true that an injustice is committed whenever an alien culture or a foreign legal system are subordinated to one's own culture or law. In spite of this insight, one should not assume that a radical heterogeneity or incommensurability is at stake. For a contradiction or a conflict between cultures is only conceivable if the latter – like labour power and capital – emit mutually comprehensible but incompatible messages leading to conflicts: for example, messages ordering or prohibiting human sacrifice for religious ends. Although the word 'human' may assume different meanings and connotations in different cultures, it is not untranslatable, because it denotes the same referent in all cases: namely the person who is meant to be sacrificed.[237] In this respect, Mafred Frank is right in arguing that no 'differend' can be total, and Lyotard's answer that Frank's notion of language is far too general, while he himself refers exclusively to *natural language* (*langue naturelle*),[238] is beside the point. For it is well known that natural languages can be translated into one another, while myths and ideologies resist translations into other myths or ideologies.

By defending his idea of heterogeneous and incommensurate languages, Lyotard conveys the impression of an extremely fragmented and pluralized social context in which the isolated, monadic cultural particularities allow for only two attitudes: complete indifference or violence expressing a radical negation of incomprehensible otherness. *Both attitudes are beyond communication.* This situation corresponds to a capitalist order governed by Lyotard's *genre économique:* an order the post-Marxist philosopher rejects whenever he contests the abstract and levelling rule of the global exchange value by mobilizing 'the heterogeneity of phrase regimens and of genres of discourse'[239] against it. *Thus extreme particularization turns into indifference, defined here as interchangeability of incompatible norms and values.* In what follows, it will appear that Habermas's universal pragmatics are also marked by a tendency towards indifference, although they are based on completely different premises. Only a consistent dialectic between the particular and the universal can avoid this postmodern tendency.

Lyotard is quite lucid when it comes to assessing the problems underlying Habermas's theory of communicative consensus: '(. . .) But his conception is based on the validity of the narrative of emancipation.'[240] In other words: Habermas's universalistic approach can only be validated within his grand metanarrative oriented towards the goal of an emancipated humanity. As was pointed out earlier on, Lyotard also thinks within the framework of a metanarrative which he tacitly assumes to be universally valid: a metanarrative aiming at heterogeneity and particularization. This seems to be his fundamental contradiction.

What exactly does Habermas's narrative of human emancipation look like? A concise summary can be found in his well-known article 'Modernity – An Unfinished Project' (1980):

> As always, people disagree on the question whether to hold on to the intentions of Enlightenment, albeit indirectly, or whether to abandon the project of modernity altogether and limit the cognitive potentials which point beyond technical progress, economic growth and rational administration to such a degree that a life practice geared to extinct traditions remains untouched by them.[241]

This passage contains in a nutshell all of Habermas's later thoughts, the different phases of which cannot be dealt with here. Habermas is one of those thinkers who have decided to adhere to a self-critical concept of Enlightenment in order to realize the cognitive and emancipatory potential of this current of thought in contemporary society. For Habermas, Enlightenment becomes a metonymy of modernity as a whole. Nevertheless, the passage quoted above can also be read as a criticism of modernity as social differentiation and rationalization: a criticism inspired by Durkheim, M. Weber and Simmel (cf. Chapter 2).

Like these sociologists of 'crisis', Habermas considers modern social evolution as a functional process of differentiation[242] leading to a situation where societies are no longer based on the lineage principles of archaic or feudal cultures, because they are increasingly being structured by *systems* such as *politics, economics, finance* and *strategy*. Although Habermas does appreciate modern rationalization as differentiation, because it tends to free individuals from traditional constraints, he also sheds light on its dark sides. There is a danger, he believes, that the systems will rely exclusively on 'rational, goal-oriented action' in the sense of Max Weber and on 'instrumental reason' in the sense of Max Horkheimer, in order to boost technical progress, economic growth and rational administration, thereby neglecting communicative reason and action.

In the case of Habermas, 'Capital' does not appear as the universal evildoer as in the case of Lyotard, since it contributes to the liberation of individuals from feudal and traditional bonds. However, it is a danger, because it tends to replace human communication and mutual understanding by the reified media of *power* and *money*, thus bringing about a 'colonization of the life world'.

Habermas reacts to this late modern and postmodern challenge by introducing two key concepts: *life world* and *communicative action*. What matters here are neither these concepts as such nor the controversies they provoked in the past, but their meaning within the *postmodern problematic* and their importance for Habermas's *claim to universality*.

Starting from Husserl's phenomenology and his transcendental, transhistoric concept of *life world*, which refers to the intersubjectively shared premises of social reality, Habermas proposes a sociological concept which contains 'the *structural components of culture* (cultural knowledge), *society* (legitimate order) and *personality* (personal competence) (. . .)'.[243] The fact that this concept is based on the will to communicate and to reach a consensus is confirmed by Habermas himself: 'The life world, then, offers both an intuitively preunderstood *context* for an action situation and *resources* for the interpretive process in which participants in communication engage as they strive to meet the need for agreement in the action situation.'[244] Commenting on the concept of life world, Antje Linkenbach considers it quite rightly as 'a concept of society viewed in the *perspective of mutual understanding*'.[245]

It is amusing to observe how Habermas inverts Lyotard's social theory and epistemology. In contrast to the French postmodernist, who views society and language as fragmented worlds marked by incompatible values and norms, Habermas deduces his theory of communicative action from a notion of society based on consensus: 'I prefer to introduce the concept of *life world* as a concept complementary to communicative action and take communicative action to be a *medium* facilitating the *reproduction* of the symbolic life world structures.'[246] The concept of life world thus becomes a guarantee not only of successful communication, but also of generalization and universalization: of the universal validity of norms and orientations common to all inhabitants of a life world.

In order to understand the *link between communication and life world* in Habermas's work, one should take into account the fact that he uses *two concepts of life world* (*Lebenswelt*): a *formal concept*, which is an idealization in a transcendental and phenomenological sense, and a *sociological concept*, which takes into account a social reality marked by conflict. To critics blaming him for excluding social conflict from his life world communication and for reducing social life to an idyllic ideal, he responds with a clear distinction between the formal and the sociological concept:

> The misunderstanding according to which I am obliged, for categorical reasons, to exclude phenomena such as dissent and power from the life world, is once again due, I suppose, to the confusion of the formal-pragmatic with the sociological concept of life world. (. . .) But from a sociological point of view, it goes without saying that strategic interaction is part and parcel of society considered as life world.[247]

At this stage, the question is not whether it is legitimate to introduce a separation that boils down to a dichotomy between an ideal linguistic community and a conflict-ridden social reality.[248] At the moment, it seems more urgent to find out what function such a separation fulfils in Habermas's discourse.

It enables him to deduce the concept of ideal speech situation from the formal concept of life world: that is from a life world unhampered by conflicts, contradictory interests and the quest for power. The ideal speech situation is implicitly *presupposed* by interlocutors because Habermas believes that each communication situation ideally *presupposes* a common will to reach a consensus and 'that in each discussion we *assume* the existence of an ideal speech situation'.[249]

But what exactly is to be presupposed? What does the ideal speech situation look like?

1. It is qualitatively different from communication situations in everyday life. 2. It is free from the constraints of domination or power structures and implies the equality of all participants on the level of argumentation. 3. It presupposes that the communicative roles involved are interchangeable. 4. It is (implicitly) presupposed by the participants in every real communication.

It is difficult not to notice the universalistic approach underlying these criteria: an approach made possible by an *idealist abstraction*. On the one hand, this abstraction is based on the formal notion of an idealized life world, on the other hand, on 'four universal categories of speech acts'.[250] Following Searle and other American speech act theorists, Habermas presents these speech acts as underlying an ideal speech situation that is embedded in a formally defined life world: the *communicatives* aiming at mutual understanding, the *constatives* aiming at truth, the *expressives* aiming at truthfulness and the *regulatives* aiming at correctness.

What matters in the present context is the fact that, in the case of Habermas as in the case of Searle, all of these speech acts are *sentences*. Following Searle, Habermas defines the speech act as a kind of sentence: 'A speech act brings about the conditions allowing a sentence to be used in an utterance; but at the same time it has the form of a sentence.'[251] In other words: a speech act is a *sentence* fulfilling a *communicative* or *pragmatic* function.

Although many sentences can easily be attributed to scientific or ideological languages (e.g. the sentence: 'The party is the avant-garde of the proletariat'), because they fulfil concrete functions in particular discourses, most sentences are neutral – as long as they are isolated from contexts. Sentences such as 'Habermas uses the expression *ideal speech situation*' or 'In 1917, another revolution broke out in Russia', are ideologically neutral (unlike the sentence: 'In 1917, the October Revolution put an end to capitalist exploitation'), because they can be integrated into most discourses – defined as *semantic and narrative structures*[252] – without the use of quotation marks. However, they lose their neutrality as soon as they are integrated into a Marxist, feminist, liberal or deconstructivist discourse and endowed with a particular meaning by semantic and narrative mechanisms specific to that discourse. They signify and function within a particular discourse in accordance with the intentions of a collective (party, trade union, firm) or an individual subject which constructs its identity in a discourse defined as a *narrative programme*.[253]

Habermas, who defines discourse as a meta-communicative *discussion*[254] and ignores discourse as a transphrastic, semantic and *narrative structure*, is obliged to view communication as an exchange of *neutral and universally functioning sentences which he divides into the four speech act categories mentioned above*. This means, however, that discourse as a semantic and narrative structure integrating sentences and forming subjectivity is ignored: 'The production of sentences in accordance with rules of grammar is after all something else than using sentences in accordance with pragmatic rules which constitute the infrastructure of speech situations in general.'[255] This description overlooks that 'using sentences in accordance with pragmatic rules' is not only geared towards the criteria of natural languages and the conventions of particular communications, but also obeys the norms of *group languages* and their discourses in the sense of teleologically functioning semantic and narrative structures.

In short, the 'infrastructure of speech situations' is not merely based on the pragmatic rules of everyday language, but also on the rules of sociolects and discourses which articulate *particular* (theoretical, ideological or religious) interests. This means that each communication that takes place in society and raises questions concerning correctness, truth, truthfulness and mutual understanding, *presupposes the existence of discursive structures articulating subjective interests*. These cannot be neutralized within a universal language. This also means that a non-conflictual, undistorted communication *cannot be presupposed*: for it is impossible to eliminate *subjectivity as discourse*.

In one respect Lyotard is certainly right: discourses originate in heterogeneous phrase regimens, and it is not always possible to overcome their heterogeneity. But this is precisely what Habermas attempts when he claims that in the ideal speech situation the 'chance to put forward arguments', the 'exchangeability of communicative roles' and the 'compulsion of the better argument' prevail: 'The consensus theory of truth claims to explain the curiously non-compulsive compulsion of the better argument by referring to the formal qualities of discourse (...).'[256] But given the fact that discourse as a meta-communicative discussion in the sense of Habermas invariably brings together heterogeneous discourses as semantic and narrative structures, the question 'who decides' imposes itself. Which discourse is to decide – as meta-discourse – that a particular argument is to be preferred to another, and according to what criteria?

It is because Habermas ignores the semiotic concept of discourse as a semantic and narrative structure that he can overlook the *differend*, thereby imposing on the interlocutors a universal language based not only on exchangeable social and linguistic roles,[257] but also on a rigorous *monosemy*: 'Different speakers may not use the same expression with different meanings.'[258] Who or, rather, which dominant discourse is supposed to prevent them from doing so – and on what grounds? If I am not allowed to use my concept of discourse, I cannot freely express my opinions and discuss with Habermas his concept of discourse. By imposing an abstract universalism, Habermas negates the *discursive subjectivity* of his interlocutors (of speakers in general), thus sacrificing social particularity to indifference as exchangeability of roles and speech acts.

His notion of an ideal speech situation is at best applicable to a homogeneous community or group the character of which is comparable to that of an archaic culture, but quite remote from a highly differentiated and ideologically

fragmented postmodern society: 'The communicated meanings are identical to
all members of a linguistic community.'[259] This might be a realistic description
of a Polynesian tribe in the eighteenth or nineteenth century – but not of
European or American politicians, journalists or scientists who are bound
to attribute different meanings to concepts such as 'democracy', 'equality', 'science' and 'ideology'. For this reason, one can only agree with John B. Thompson
when he points out that Habermas's approach 'bypasses the most pressing
problems'.[260]

Among these problems we again find Lyotard's *différend* and the always
imminent *tort* that comes about as soon as ideological, cultural or psychological
idiosyncrasies are disqualified by Habermas as pathologies and discarded in
the name of an abstract universalism.[261] Whoever has systematically compared
Lyotard's and Habermas's arguments will feel like a traveller who arrives from
cosmopolitan, Babylonian Paris in a small German town where a common language can still be presupposed. 'Here nobody steps out of line,'[262] as Jürgen
Becker puts it. This may be a caricature of the 'ideal speech situation', but the
fictive journey reveals that postmodern particularism and modern universalism
are miles apart. They do have one aspect in common, however: the *interchangeability* of contingent particularities (Lyotard) and of individuals conforming to
a universal law or language (Habermas).

In the last chapter, an attempt will be made to relate the particular to the
universal dialectically: not by a *rhizome* or by Wolfgang Welsch's *transversal
reason*,[263] but in an *interdiscursive dialogue* based on the idea that, although discourses, which turn individuals and groups into subjects, may be ideologically
heterogeneous, they are comparable and linked by linguistic universals. The
aim of this argument will be a sociological and semiotic *concept of dialogue* allowing for a dialectical link-up between the particular and the universal, between
consensus and dissent. It will appear that this kind of dialogue also has political
components.

## 3.6  Ethics: From Lyotard and Bauman to Rorty

Ethical problems have been dealt with indirectly, both in the previous section
and in conjunction with social philosophy. As in social philosophy and epistemology, the hand of the postmodern clock does oscillate between the particular
and the universal, but tends to stop at the particular. 'However, one need not
go beyond discursive reason in order to think in terms of a "coherence" located
outside the constraints of the system, a form of individuation situated beyond
the constraints of identification,'[264] writes Albrecht Wellmer. One need not, but
one can; and postmodern thinkers such as Lyotard, Bauman and Rorty tend to
believe that an ethic relying on discursive reason is bound to sacrifice the individual to a conceptual system.

What is at stake here, is once more the systematic constraint inherent in the great metaphysical narratives of Christianity, Enlightenment and Marxism. More often than not, it leads to the sacrifice of individual interests and idiosyncrasies to those of a real or mythical generality. The question underlying Lyotard's ethics is: How can responsibility be defined after the decline of the universal idea? His answer is not very original. For it simply pleads in favour of tolerance vis-à-vis postmodern multiplicity and heterogeneity: 'The multiplicity of responsibilities, and their independence (their incompatibility), oblige and will oblige those who take on those responsibilities, small or great, to be flexible, tolerant, and svelte.'[265]

These and similar arguments have a particularizing effect because they presuppose heterogeneity and dissent, excluding at the same time general maxims in the sense of Kant. In *Postmodern Fables*, where he objects to the invasion of ethics by cognitive principles (cf. Section 3.5), Lyotard pleads in favour of an autonomy of the ethical realm and against the rationalist and Kantian idea that general ethical principles are to be deduced from practical reason: 'If a law were knowable, ethics could be resolved into a procedure of cognition.'[266] At the same time, the particular, which Lyotard's ethics and notion of justice are based on, would be sacrificed. The question remains, however, whether a concept of justice aiming at the particular is conceivable.

For justice has always – not since Kant, but from Plato to John Rawls – been defined as a *principle open to generalization*. Thus John Rawls, for example, considers a social order as just which any potential citizen could agree with without knowing what her or his position within this order would be.[267] Hence the agreement ought to be independent of the individual's social, cultural, psychic or linguistic idiosyncrasies. A similar universalistic approach can be detected in Habermas's (and Thomas McCarthy's) transformation of Kant's categorical imperative:

> From this viewpoint, the categorical imperative needs to be reformulated as follows: 'Rather than ascribing as valid to all others any maxim that I can will to be universal law, I must submit my maxim to all others for purposes of discursively testing its claims to universality. The emphasis shifts from what each can will without contradiction to be a general law, to what all can will in agreement to be a universal norm.'[268]

Such a norm is inconceivable in Lyotard's discourse because the latter postulates a radical heterogeneity of linguistic, social and legal norms.

Unlike Kant, Rawls and Habermas, Lyotard is unable and unwilling to envisage the application of a universal norm, but proposes instead a defensive notion of justice aiming primarily at 'testifying in favour of the differend' ('témoigner du différend').[269] He pleads in favour of a 'defensive practice'[270] whose goal is not a new social order, but the revelation of injustice. Responsible action in contemporary society means 'discovering the differends and drawing attention to them'.[271]

This principle (if it is one) is not only related to the linguistic differend between discourses and 'phrase regimens', situated at the centre of *The Differend*,[272] for it also involves the defence of minority interests in a society threatened by the streamlining and unifying tendencies of global capitalism. 'We must constantly reaffirm the rights of minorities, women, children, gays, the South, the Third World, the poor, the rights of citizenship, the right to culture and education, the rights of animals and the environment, and I'll skip over the rest.'[273] But in whose name does Lyotard pretend to speak, whenever he rejects general principles in the sense of Rawls or Habermas? What exactly does he mean by 'we must', 'il nous faut'?

Should it become clear that he only speaks in his own name because he can no longer recognize the emancipating narratives of Enlightenment, Marxism and Critical Theory, then it is difficult to see why one should refuse to support other disadvantaged groups: the farmers, the miners, the fishermen or the rural nobility – all of whom can be considered as marginalized minorities in contemporary French society. In a post-Marxist discourse, which has renounced Marx's notion of *Lumpenproletariat*, it may seem meaningful to side with Lyotard's more recent marginal groupings. For they are not arbitrarily selected particularities, but appear as victims of repression within a critical metanarrative pleading for human emancipation in general.

In Adorno's discourse, the universal human interest is also represented by a marginalized particularity symbolized by the artist: 'The artist who is the bearer of the work of art is not the individual who produces it; rather, through his work, through passive activity, he becomes the representative of the total social subject.'[274] In this perspective, the process of particularization has reached a point where the general social subject can only be represented by a critical artist like Valéry who exceeds his particularity by evoking universal emancipation.

But in Lyotard's case, notions such as 'general subject' (*Gesamtsubjekt*, Adorno) have become inconceivable, and Jacob Rogozinski quite aptly remarks: 'The idea is no longer to legitimate what is just, but to verbalize the unjust.'[275] However, even this minimalist programme of ethics is bound to fail: for it is hardly possible to verbalize the unjust without implicitly founding a metanarrative, that is without committing a new injustice. 'Our hypothesis is', Rogozinski continues, 'that the emergence of the ethical question introduces the differend in *Le Différend* – that it separates the latter from itself, thus making it explode.'[276] In other words: the epistemological aporia described in the previous section, where it was shown that differends and cases of injustice can only be articulated in a metanarrative committing a new kind of injustice, is now repeated on an ethical level. For Lyotard is obliged to assemble and generalize contradictory interests of heterogeneous minorities in order to define the injustice they suffer *together*.

A remark from his preface to *Des dispositifs pulsionnels* (1979) shows to what extent his hostility to generalization yields arbitrariness and indifference: 'Is everything permitted then? All the smart tricks are.'[277] He hastens to add that no trick can be considered smart if it threatens the individuals concerned with death. In this case, a trick could still be considered smart if it deprived people of their property or of their right to vote. At the end of the day, everything seems permitted in a situation where general principles yield to particularization and indifference. What some people consider to be a clever trick may be experienced by others as an irresponsible act or a crime.

The dissolution of the universal entails the dissolution of the subject. In a situation where there is neither a general law nor a homogeneous subject manifesting itself in discourse and action, there can be no responsibility (cf. Section 3.2).

Zygmunt Bauman's *Postmodern Ethics* (1993), a work strongly influenced by Lyotard, reveals to what extent the refusal of generalization leads to a lack of conceptual clarity. Following Lyotard, Bauman starts from a critique of the metanarrative of human emancipation and radicalizes this critique (as was shown in the previous chapter, Section 2.1) by asserting that the metanarratives of Enlightenment and Marxism are indirectly responsible for the National-Socialist and Stalinist camps because they aim at universality and unification. Millions, he argues, were sacrificed to the modern idea of human emancipation: 'One should sacrifice a thousand lives to save ten thousand. It is the future goodness that is but disguised as the present cruelty.'[278] Rationalists, fascists and Marxists-Leninists, he believes, acted according to this maxim.

This rather one-sided critique of the major discourses of emancipation completely disregards the importance of Enlightenment and Marxist thought for the liberal and socialist democratization of societies (e.g. through the trade union movements) and overlooks the self-criticism of modernity so thoroughly reconstructed by Toulmin.[279] It is hardly surprising therefore that Bauman views all kinds of universalism with distrust or hostility and even tries to deconstruct the conceptual foundations of theoretical generalization. He imagines a non-conceptual ethic based on pre-social moral impulses:

> (. . .) The idea of universal morality, if it is to survive at all, may only fall back on the innate pre-social moral impulses common to humankind (. . .), or on equally common elementary structures of human-being-in-the world, similarly antedating all societal interference (. . .).[280]

Such speculations are reminiscent of Rousseau's image of uncorrupted individuals in the state of nature and presuppose 'pre-social moral impulses' without raising the question whether morals and moral impulses are conceivable outside social contexts. Even if 'pre-social moral impulses' did actually exist, it is by no means certain that they would aim at global humanitarian values (they might very well be *spontaneously* tribal or sectarian: the postmodernist who is so fond of the particular should realize this).

Bauman agrees with Lyotard whenever he tries to map out an ethic located beyond the conceptually defined rule and goes to great lengths to avoid conceptual generalization and formalization: 'The morality of the moral subject does not, therefore, have the character of a rule. One may say that the moral is what *resists* codification, formalization, socialization, universalization.'[281]

In view of this particularistic refusal of conceptual generalization, it is hardly surprising that Bauman's ethic is an ethic of uncertainty and discontent with its own premises: '*The moral self is a self always haunted by the suspicion that it is not moral enough.*'[282] He goes on to quote Wladyslaw Bartoszewski who says about the responsibility of the individual during the National-Socialist occupation: 'Only those who died bringing help can say that they have done enough.'[283] The truth content of this paradoxical sentence consists in the exclusion of all kinds of premature complacency. However, it can hardly be deduced from pre-social impulses which are ambivalent and aim at self-preservation, not at morals. It seems to be much closer to Kantian and Christian imperatives: 'Act in such a way that your neighbour is treated as an end in itself, not as a means.' Or: 'In extreme situations you have to risk your life in order to make sure that your neighbours are also treated as God's children.' Bauman's own paradox seems to consists in the fact that, on the one hand, he defends general postulates (e.g. the readiness to risk or sacrifice one's own life in certain situations) but, on the other hand, denies their social and conceptual foundation. The only foundation he is prepared to admit is emotional.

Even his arguments in favour of an ethic of alterity, inspired by Emmanuel Lévinas's theory of the Other,[284] is based on emotions. Bauman considers it as the postmodern ethic par excellence when he explains: 'If postmodernity is a retreat from the blind alleys into which radically pursued ambitions of modernity have led, a postmodern ethics would be one that readmits the Other as a neighbour (. . .).'[285] But there is no need, as Bakhtin has shown,[286] to renounce conceptualization and generalization in order to admit alterity.

On the contrary, the last chapter will reveal that the orientation towards the Other can be founded rationally and politically, because only in this form can it guarantee a survival of humanity as a whole. The *rational, universal* maxim is based on the idea that I can only survive if I am prepared to consider the Other as an end with whose help I can solve the most pressing economic, political and ecological problems of humanity.

Like Lyotard, Bauman is aware of the fact that the indifference of market laws represents an acute threat to an ethic based on emotions and warns against a 'ban on emotional engagement, indifference to qualitative difference'.[287] An example of emotional atrophy is the tourist who appears to him as 'dissolved in numbers, interchangeable, depersonalized'.[288] In view of this – probably correct – diagnosis, it does not seem to make sense to base ethics on pre-social emotions and impulses. For it is precisely such emotions which are unscrupulously manipulated by the tourist industry. In this situation, the remedy might be a political and ethical theory of alterity and dialogue which projects both concepts onto a social and institutional level. It will be mapped out in the last chapter.

In the second section, it was shown that, although Richard Rorty starts from liberal premises, thereby reacting very differently to the postmodern problematic from Lyotard, he does agree with the French philosopher when it comes to defending particularization and pluralism.[289] He also agrees with Bauman whenever he refuses to found ethics by rational and conceptual means. Instead of appealing to reason, he relies on an intuitive sensitivity common to all human beings and reminiscent of Bauman's 'pre-social moral impulses' and of Lyotard's 'defensive practice' (cf. supra).

He writes about the liberal ironist who has learned to accept her ethnocentrism with a certain amount of self-irony: 'She thinks that what unites her with the rest of the species is not a common language but *just* susceptibility to pain and in particular to that special sort of pain which the brutes do not share with the humans – humiliation.'[290] She does not believe in a truth accepted as self-evident by all, but only in 'a common selfish hope (. . .) that one's world – the little things around (. . .) – will not be destroyed'.[291]

It seems worthwhile to have a closer look at this passage which brings together salient features of the postmodern problematic. To begin with, one is struck by the fact that all kinds of conceptuality in the sense of a 'common language', a 'common truth' or a 'common goal' are avoided and replaced by affective reactions: by sensitivity to pain, humiliation, hope. It is by no means certain, however, that such reactions are anthropological constants (rejected by Rorty himself: cf. Section 3.2) that can be taken to have the same meaning everywhere, at all times. European feudal lords, Touareg and Bedouins may have quite different ideas about pain and humiliation from those of an American businessman. Massive financial losses, which might prompt him to commit suicide, leave them unimpressed. They might feel threatened or offended by an attack on their faith or their honour.[292] To modern revolutionaries, Rorty's egocentric hope to preserve the world of small things around him would appear as a symptom of petty bourgeois hysteria. In short: the emotions which – unlike concepts – he considers to be universal or 'human' in character are those of a liberal, postmodern society. Emotions, like concepts, are socially and culturally determined. The avowed ethnocentric could have anticipated this argument.

It should be remembered in this context that Rorty considers Habermas's consensus concerning 'the universally human'[293] to be a superfluous metaphysical relic and that he rejects the idea of goals common to humanity as a whole as an illusion. Rorty concludes that we should simply abandon the search for such common factors.[294]

It is not as simple as that. The comments on social philosophy in this chapter have shown that there are common factors and goals: for example the protection of the environment, the struggle against infections and epidemics, the prevention of wars and nuclear disasters, etc. One could add the process of democratization which, as Habermas points out, is also a process of rationalization. It may not be attractive to dictators and oligarchs, but it is in the interest of majorities (as recent events in Burma/Myanmar show).

Rorty's entire approach reveals how questionable the postmodern tendency towards particularization is. It discredits the struggle for emancipation which is bound to fail if the philosophical and sociological question concerning the global interests of humanity is discarded as irrelevant or deconstructed by a one-sided emphasis on particularities, contradictions and disagreements. If it weren't dead, as Lyotard puts it, Marxism would criticize Rorty's philosophy as reactionary. However, the deficits of this kind of philosophy might also prompt the sudden resurrection of Marxism.

To conclude, a fundamental contradiction within postmodern ethics should be pointed out here. It cannot avoid questions concerning general principles, but at the same time refuses to answer these questions by defining such principles and retreats into the realm of affects and emotions. The contradiction consists in the fact that thinkers such as Bauman and Rorty do focus on the general (the moral impulse, Bauman; the sensitivity to pain, Rorty), but at the same time reject a conceptualization which could express the general as principle or collective interest. By opting for the particular, they opt for the arbitrary: for the exchangeable, the in-different. This contradiction is analogous to the dilemma of postmodern epistemologies: that is the attempt to formulate general explanations and principles in a discourse focusing on the particular.

## 3.7 Aesthetics: Heterotopy and the Sublime, Allegory and Aporia

Postmodern aesthetics is complementary to postmodern ethics, epistemology and social philosophy insofar as it foregrounds the manifold and the heterogeneous. One should nevertheless avoid the simplifying assumption that there is such as thing as a homogeneous postmodern aesthetic theory. Its existence is as chimerical as that of postmodern ethics, epistemology or social theory. It should nevertheless be possible to detect *common tendencies* and goals in the aesthetics of Vattimo, Lyotard and de Man and to relate them to the corresponding tendencies in the other domains discussed above.

Although Vattimo agrees with Lyotard when it comes to rejecting aesthetic utopia as a unification of humanity in the Kantian or Neo-Kantian sense, he differs radically from him whenever he welcomes the aesthetic pluralism of mass and consumer society, the *heterotopy* of which he opposes to the totalizing utopias of modernity.

Vattimo's conception of heterotopy is to be considered in conjunction with his Lyotardian critique of modern metanarratives and his Heideggerian notion of *Verwindung*.[295] As was pointed out in the second section, Vattimo starts from Nietzsche's notion of 'eternal return' and from the thesis that the utopian projects of rationalism, Marxism, the avant-gardes and, most recently, the 1968-movements, were not realized, but dissolved in a *postmodern heterotopy*. From an historical point of view, this development can be construed as a *Verwindung* or 'grudging acceptance' of things as they are and opposed to the originally intended *overcoming* (*Überwindung, dépassement*) of bourgeois-capitalist society: 'Precisely this difference between *Verwindung* and *Überwindung* can help us to define in philosophical terms the "post-" in "post-modernism."'[296] In what sense? Insofar as the modern and modernist (also avant-garde) hope that bourgeois society would be replaced by a different and fundamentally better social order was vitiated. This may be the main reason why to some contemporary observers modernity not only appears as an *unfinished* (Habermas), but also as an *undesirable* project.

This does not mean, as Welsch aptly points out,[297] that Vattimo opposes modernity and suggests that we should break with it. It should be taken to mean that he considers modern utopias, especially the utopia of *overcoming* (*Überwindung*), as illusory or as outright dangerous. Modernity did not realize the totalitarian utopias of the rationalists, the Marxists or the Futurists, who were aiming at unity or uniformity, says Vattimo, but it did fulfil the modern promise to respect plurality and particularity: 'With the demise of the idea of a central rationality of history, the world of generalized communication explodes like a multiplicity of "local" rationalities – ethnic, sexual, religious, cultural or aesthetic minorities – that finally speak up for themselves.'[298] Vattimo speaks of a 'liberation of diversity'.[299]

In the aesthetic realm, this process of differentiation takes on the form of heterotopy which now replaces the utopian hopes of aestheticism, the avant-garde and the 1968-movements. This is why we are not facing 'a pure and simple realization of utopia, but (. . .) a realization that has been distorted and transformed'.[300] This heterotopy is *aesthetic plurality*: a radical pluralization of society, which does not recognize just one notion of the beautiful, but many such notions anchored in competing aesthetic communities held together by different criteria, norms and values.

European mass culture is partly responsible for this kind of heterotopy, and Vattimo even considers it as its historical origin. From his point of view, it does not appear as an agent of superficial levelling, but as a source of aesthetic inventiveness and multiplicity. By mixing cultures and subcultures, mass society has crucially contributed to the rise of the manifold and to the development of aesthetic pluralism.[301]

The idea that commercial mass culture does not entail an atrophy of aesthetic judgement may sound encouraging, but it is by no means certain that it is true. Instead of putting forward apodictic arguments, the advocate of postmodernity should have had a closer look at the infantile and regressive character of popular music[302] as analysed by Adorno. Moreover, he could have asked himself whether Umberto Eco's subtly constructed, but nonetheless highly marketable novel *The Name of the Rose* was not reduced to commercial stereotypes by 'its' film version. In the end, it was made to coincide with the media-sponsored image of the Middle Ages, relied on and exploited by profit-minded managers of culture.

In this case, it seems appropriate to take into account the literary and media context, because Vattimo (like Baudrillard) quite rightly assumes that, in the present situation, the aesthetic sphere does not coincide with that of art. Not only the frequently observed 'marginality of literature'[303] seems to be a *fait accompli*, but the marginality of art as a whole: in a society where happenings, body art, cyberpunk and advertising have become part and parcel of aesthetics. In this society, art can only claim to be an aspect of the aesthetic realm – and possibly not even the central one any more.

Aesthetic experience is no longer confined to the artistic sphere: it expands well beyond art in the traditional meaning of this word into the sphere of mass media, advertising and cosmetics. The 'aesthetic object' is no longer a synonym of 'artwork', and the latter has ceased to represent the forces of human emancipation linked to artistic production in the sense of Adorno and Marcuse.[304]

In Vattimo's case, the aesthetic sphere appears as a multitude of heterogeneous communities, some of which may continue to revere art, while others may worship cyberpunk or treat rock concerts as substitutes for religious rites. One can welcome this heterotopy as a democratic liberation from prescriptive aesthetics and canonized artistic forms. However, one can also recognize in this sort of commercialized pluralism a funfair of art or of sensations in the sense of Karel Teige[305] – the kind of culture industry Adorno and Horkheimer kept warning us against. The ambivalence of this setup probably consists in the fact that competent observers are capable of sorting out the items which agree with their taste, while incompetent consumers fall prey to the 'psychotechnical manipulation'[306] by the media.

This is where Lyotard's – in many respects Adornian – critique of consumerist postmodernism sets in, which the French philosopher associates with the 'trans-avant-garde' of the Italian architect Achille Bonito Oliva and of American architects and artists such as Charles Jencks. In his book on *The Inhuman*, he asks the reader not to confuse trans-avant-garde postmodernism with his own 'postmodern condition' and explains that 'trans-avant-garde' activities 'are a pretext for squandering'[307] the heritage of the historical avant-gardes:

> To the extent that this postmodernism, via critics, museum and gallery directors and collectors, puts strong pressure on the artists, it consists in aligning research in painting with a *de facto* state of 'culture' and in deresponsibilizing the artists with respect to the question of the unpresentable. Now in my view this question is the only one worthy of what is at stake in life and thought in the coming century.[308]

For about a century, Lyotard argues elsewhere, the arts have been focusing not on the beautiful, but on the sublime.[309] In this situation, one might assume that, as an alternative to Vattimo's, Eco's and Jencks's consumer-oriented aesthetics, Lyotard would be tempted to propose a *modernist* aesthetic of the unpresentable. This, however, turns out to be an erroneous assessment of his stance within the postmodern problematic.

In Germany, Peter Bürger falls prey to this error when he starts from the idea that, by opposing Oliva's and Jencks's 'militant anti-modernism', Lyotard has to 'break with postmodern aesthetics'.[310] This error is due to three factors: to the simplifying assumption that there is only one postmodern aesthetic represented by the works of Oliva, Jencks et al.; to the complementary assumption that someone who rejects this aesthetic is an adversary of postmodern aesthetics – that is a modernist; finally, to the ignorance of Lyotard's fundamental aesthetic work *Discours, figure* (1971) and of his *Leçons sur l'Analytique du sublime* (1991), the key arguments of which are announced by *L'Enthousiasme* (1986) and *L'Inhumain* (1988).[311]

However, we are not dealing with just one postmodern aesthetic, but with different postmodern (and late modern) reactions to the contemporary problematic. Although Lyotard distances himself from the grand metanarratives and, like Vattimo, emphasizes the heterogeneous, the particular and the non-conceptual, he rejects a heterotopy which, according to his theory, amounts to an integration of the entire aesthetic sphere into the culture industry of late capitalism. This is why he asks the reader not to confuse his 'postmodern condition' with the aesthetics of Oliva and Jencks (and, one might add, with those of Eco and Vattimo). (Cf. Eco in Section 4.2.) One should consider this gesture of critical dissociation in conjunction with some late modern or modernist controversies and bear in mind that some of the most prominent modernists, such as Adorno, Brecht and Sartre, strongly disagreed on crucial points. Their aesthetics and poetics are certainly not compatible with those of T. S. Eliot – who can nevertheless be said to deal with some of their basic *problems*.

Lyotard's and Vattimo's approaches to postmodern aesthetics are complementary insofar as Lyotard is not only aware of the heterogeneity of the social and aesthetic spheres, but translates this heterogeneity into his key philosophical concepts of *aporia* and *differend*. Both concepts are relevant to his aesthetic theory. The differend is not only a particularizing and pluralizing concept of postmodernity; it is at the same time a basic concept of Lyotard's first major work on art: of *Discours, figure* (1971).

In this early work, he deals with the aesthetic problems of art which confront philosophers with a dilemma: the necessity to verbalize the non-verbal, to translate figures and colours into speech. Starting from a postmodern idea *avant la lettre*, from the Nietzschean idea that 'Western rationality kills art together with the dream,'[312] Lyotard remarks: 'The painting should not be read, as contemporary semiologists would have it; Klee thought it should be grazed on (qu'il est à brouter) (. . .).'[313] Following Emmanuel Lévinas's philosophy of alterity, Lyotard tries to bring out the untranslatable alterity of colours and figures that resists language and conceptualization: 'We expect the words to express the pre-eminence of the figure (que les mots *disent* la pré-éminence de la figure), we wish to *denote* the Other of denotation (*signifier* l'autre de la signification).'[314]

In this sentence, a tension makes itself felt which Lyotard circumscribed later by the word *differend*: between colour and word, figure and concept, no definable transitions seem to exist. 'He has poised the visible figure against discourse itself',[315] writes John McGowan about the author of *Discours, figure*. Whoever tries with Hegel[316] to grasp the picture by conceptual means commits an injustice, a *tort* in the sense of *Le Différend* and *Discours, figure*, a doctoral thesis which anticipates, in an aesthetic context, some of the key problems addressed by Lyotard in his later life. Thus a discourse about painting can only be a self-deconstructing discourse that renounces the notion of a homogeneous and unifying subject.

By re-interpreting Kant's concept of the sublime in the 1980s, Lyotard seems to return to his early work: to its problematic of the Other and the Incommensurate. The idea is to develop an aesthetic of heterogeneity and contradiction, an aesthetic indebted to modernism and the avant-garde, but geared towards the postmodern problematic. Lyotard insists on the links between the latter and modernism, arguing that postmodernism is a permanent re-naissance of the modern, not its end. Freud, Duchamp, Bohr, Gertrude Stein, but also Rabelais, Sterne and several others appear to him as protagonists of a postmodern spirit, because they insist on the paradox and the incommensurate.[317]

This kind of projection of a contemporary problematic and its questions into the (remote) past is also to be found in Russian Formalism. The formalists, especially Shklovsky, recognized in Lawrence Sterne a precursor of the futurist avant-garde and of the principle of estrangement. Derrida and de Man adopt a similar attitude when they attempt to show that Rousseau's text deconstructs itself. In none of these cases is Sterne presented as a postmodern or futurist author, Rousseau as a deconstructionist; what matters to all of the contemporary thinkers is a justification and exemplification of the modernist or postmodernist problematic by a somewhat desultory recourse to traditions.

Projected into a postmodern and neo-avant-garde context, the sublime appears to Lyotard as an *aesthetic expression of the differend*. 'The differend cannot be resolved. But it can be felt as such, as differend. This is the sublime feeling.'[318] How exactly is the sublime as differend to be understood? '*Sublime* is what, by its resistance to the interest of the senses, we like directly',[319] writes Kant and explains: 'The beautiful prepares us for loving something, even nature, without interest; the sublime, for esteeming it even against our interest (of sense).'[320] In other words: the sublime is contradictory because it elicits admiration and at the same time inspires fear and terror by its sheer greatness or power. Kant speaks of 'threatening rocks, thunderclouds piling up in the sky (. . .), volcanoes with all their destructive power, hurricanes with all the devastation they leave behind, the boundless ocean heaved up (. . .)'.[321] Lyotard develops this train of thought when he redefines the sublime as differend, that is as a *contradiction between that which reason can conceive and that which can be imagined within a form.*

The antagonism between a reason capable of conceiving the sublime as an absolute or endless entity, that is as an Idea, and an understanding linked to imagination, is turned by Lyotard into an allegory: 'Reason thus enters "the scene" in the place of understanding. It challenges the thought that imagines: "make the absolute that I conceive present with your forms". Yet form is limitation. (. . .) It cannot present the absolute.'[322] The differend between reason and imagination consists in the fact that the infinite in the mathematical sense and the tremendous in the dynamic sense can be thought by reason, but not imagined. The billions of light years which lie between us and the most distant galaxies can be expressed in mathematical terms, but they defy imagination.

This is why Lyotard speaks of a 'differend of the finite and the infinite'[323] that cannot be resolved insofar as reason and imagination are two heterogeneous modes of perception. They cannot be reduced to a common denominator or to a homogeneous set of criteria because the rules of the one are not those of the other.[324] Thus the postmodern character of the sublime is also to be found in the contradictory or aporetic structure which excludes all kinds of unification in the structuralist sense or in the sense of Hegel's *Aufhebung* and at the same time casts doubts upon the subject as a unified and unifying instance.

While the beautiful contributes, by virtue of its harmony and its universal validity, to the constitution of the subject, the sublime threatens the very foundations of subjectivity. About the subject (set in quotation marks) Lyotard writes: 'Taste promised him a beautiful life; the sublime threatens to make him disappear.'[325] For the sublime does not only combine two heterogeneous modes of perception (reason and imagination); it also amalgamates contradictory emotions: joy and awe, admiration and fear. The subject appears as torn between these incompatible emotions. Lyotard goes on to explain: 'The sublime feeling is an emotion, a violent emotion, close to unreason, which forces thought to the extremes of pleasure and displeasure, from joyous exaltation to terror (. . .).'[326] In *L'Enthousiasme*, where he relies heavily on Kant in an attempt to relate enthusiasm to the sublime, the historical, revolutionary enthusiasm appears both as an 'extreme mode of the sublime'[327] and as 'located on the brink of madness'.[328] The oscillation between pleasure and pain, joy and terror, enthusiasm and madness eventually leads to a dissolution of the subject which frequently accompanies social upheavals and revolutions.

It becomes clear at the same time – and here the analysis returns to the beginning of the chapter – how closely related are reason and unreason, reason and madness. Reason's demand that the sublime be represented by imagination, by the senses, turns into madness. The postmodern attempt to relate reason and madness to one another, instead of separating them in a rationalist manner, is inspired by the idea that a seemingly rational reality is imbued with madness and that only a thought aware of the contradictions and aporias of the sublime is capable of understanding late capitalism. Lyotard speaks of a 'connivance' between capitalism and the avant-garde in the realm of innovation and concludes: 'There is something of the sublime in capitalist economy.'[329]

In this situation, late modern and postmodern art and literature take on the well-nigh impossible task of presenting the unpresentable: 'The sublime is perhaps the only mode of artistic sensibility to characterize the modern.'[330] Elsewhere, Lyotard remarks about capitalism that its aesthetics are inspired by the sublime, not by the beautiful.[331] If this hypothesis is correct, then art and aesthetics in late capitalism, considered as the basis of postmodernism by Fredric Jameson,[332] can only be structured by the contradictions and aporias of the sublime. In this perspective, postmodern art does not appear as a consumer-friendly revision of the avant-gardes in the sense of Eco, but as their continuation and radicalization.

This fact is overlooked by Peter Bürger who believes that Lyotard distances himself from 'postmodern aesthetics' in general (cf. supra). However, Lyotard merely rejects postmodern aesthetics in the sense of Jencks, Oliva and Eco and at the same time maps out an aesthetic of postmodernism which radicalizes modernism and the avant-gardes without acknowledging their political, utopian orientations. For such orientations are only conceivable within modern metanarratives. The assumption that Lyotard's aesthetic of the sublime is considered as postmodern by its author is borne out by its dependence on the key concept of *differend*, announced by various notions of *La Condition postmoderne* such as *paralogie, agonistique langagière* and *hétéromorphie des jeux de langage*. (Assuming that the key concept of Lyotard's postmodernity, the *differend*, is also inherent in his aesthetic, one cannot possibly consider the latter as modern. For in this case one of the major thinkers of postmodernity would not be postmodern . . .)

In the literary sphere, this aesthetic is reminiscent of the experimental texts of the neo-avant-gardes which will be commented on in more detail in Chapter 5: the postmodern experiments of authors such as Pynchon, Ransmayr, Azúa, Robbe-Grillet and Wiener. On the one hand, they all agree in rejecting the political or aesthetic utopias in the sense of Brecht or Proust; on the other hand, they try to reveal to what extent traditional notions of reality and subjectivity have lost their validity.

'Centuries have been waiting for the event to materialize, and one day it is there, and one can admire it, it has arrived.'[333] As far as Oswald Wiener is concerned, this is the end of the metanarrative. The subject follows: 'I want to say something, but I cannot find the words, the reason, moreover, I don't really know what to say.'[334] Of course, Lyotard's and Wiener's reactions to the postmodern problematic do not exclude other, contrasting reactions – for example those of Jencks, Vattimo or Eco – because they are complementary, as the brief comparison of Lyotard's and Vattimo's approaches shows.

Postmodern aesthetics of the sublime are confirmed and completed by Paul de Man's theory of literature which focuses on the key concepts of *allegory* and *aporia*. Since 'aporia' will be discussed in some detail towards the end of the next chapter (Section 4.4), allegory as a negation of the symbol will be dealt with in what follows. It should be made clear at the outset that de Man's concepts of aporia and allegory point towards Lyotard's problem of the sublime because they also imply *an unresolvable aesthetic contradiction which undermines the foundations of subjectivity*. When Lyotard writes: 'The elements are heterogeneous, but their union is necessary: one cannot think one without the other,'[335] he sums up some of Paul de Man's allegorical, 'aporetic' readings of literature and the contradictions underlying this aporia.

Lyotard's Kantian contrast between the unifying beautiful and a sublime which destroys unity is analogous to de Man's opposition between symbol and allegory. De Man views the symbol as a unifying figure that synthesizes the ideal and the material, idea and world in a harmonious totality. The aesthetic model he has in mind is obviously Hegel's classicist totality as expressed in the syntheses of matter and mind brought about by ancient Greek sculpture. Without commenting on Hegel's concept of symbol, which refers to pre-classical phenomena such as ancient Egyptian architecture, marked (according to Hegel) by a *discrepancy* between mind and matter, meaning and form,[336] de Man defines Hegel's aesthetic as an aesthetic of the symbol. 'Hegel, then, is a theoretician of the symbol,'[337] he points out in order to underline the fact that, quite apart from his concept of symbol, Hegel's aesthetic is a theory of unification, totalization and harmonization inspired by the classical ideal.

To de Man, this ideal appears as imbued with ideology. It is a key element of European (Platonic and Hegelian) metaphysics and has decisively contributed to the representation of meaning and to the construction of a meaningful totality. Hegel is considered by Paul de Man as *the* author of the modern metanarrative:

> We are Hegelian when we try to systematize the relationships between the various art forms or genres according to different modes of representation or when we try to conceive of historical periodization as a development, progressive or regressive, of a collective or individual consciousness.[338]

It goes without saying that, as a staunch supporter of deconstruction, Paul de Man is not a Hegelian, but one of the most intransigent critics of Hegelianism: of its metanarratives and its 'symbolist' aesthetics.

The latter functions as an ideology insofar as it turns art and literature into monuments of national history, thus exposing them to abuse. In his introduction to de Man's writings (1953–1978), Lindsay Waters presents a concise definition of 'aesthetic ideology': 'It is an ideology that requires that literature be dominated by the knowing subject who ascribes meaning and moral to the text. It is an ideology that monumentalises literature by setting it up as a symbol of civilization.'[339] Here too, the symbol is seen as a unifying figure fulfilling an ideological function.

Within the problematic of postmodernity and deconstruction, it is hardly surprising that de Man opposes *allegory* as a figure of subversion and disintegration to the *symbol*, which has a certain affinity to other unifying concepts (e.g. Derrida's *presence of meaning*, Deleuze's *original* and Lyotard's notion of the *beautiful*). Comparing Walter Benjamin's and Paul de Man's concepts of allegory, Romano Luperini points out that 'the symbol is defined as a unity of appearance and essence, while allegory reveals their dissociation (. . .).'[340] In a situation where appearance is no longer hiding an essence, the subject cannot hope to tackle the world of appearance (the only one, according to Nietzsche) by relying on abstract concepts.

After Benjamin, another theoretician of a semantically subversive allegory, de Man points to the discrepancy between subject and object. Reality cannot be grasped by the subject, he argues, because an unbridgeable gap between the idea and the world of things, between subject and object, comes to light. On this level of argument, a Kantian, anti-Hegelian element can be observed in de Man's thought. The subject constructs its objects in space and time and cannot assume with Hegel that the concept is inherent in reality in such a way that the latter can be identified with the subject's intentions. But at the same time, a specifically deconstructionist element surfaces: the constructions of the subject no longer correspond to reality, to the object; moreover, they contradict each other because neither reality nor subjectivity can be regarded as coherent entities. This is the actual reason why de Man believes that all literary texts are to be read as contradictory, aporetic structures: *as allegories of their own unreadability*.

To him, this unreadability appears as a symptom of the unbridgeable gap between subject and object, between theoretical discourse and poetic figure. In his comments,[341] the description of this gap and of the contrast between symbol and allegory turns imperceptibly into an allegory. By negating all types of coherence and all attempts of the subject to identify with the real, allegory emphasizes alterity: that which is different and for ever resists identification in the sense of a subjective, Hegelian appropriation of the world. It becomes clear, at this stage, that de Man's notion of allegory has little to do with 'allegory as a pictorial representation of a concept or an event' – or with the *Concise Oxford* definition: 'a story, play, poem, picture, etc., in which the meaning or message is represented symbolically'. (This is virtually an inversion of what de Man means.)

De Man's idiosyncratic definition can best be explained within the postmodern problematic as mapped out above. Like Deleuze, Derrida and especially Lyotard, de Man goes to great lengths in order to discredit the rationalist and Hegelian thesis according to which humanity, history and text are meaningful totalities. Thus literary texts appear to him as aporetic de-constructs which tell the story of their own semantic disintegration. In this respect, de Man's allegory is comparable to Lyotard's notion of the sublime which also evokes the disintegration of meaning amidst contradictions and aporias.

Lyotard's comments on Hildegard Brenner's study of National-Socialist cultural policy and on Hans-Jürgen Syberberg's films reveal to what extent his notion of symbol as an ideological figure coincides with that of Paul de Man.

According to Lyotard, Brenner's and Syberberg's works explain how neo-romantic, neo-classical and symbolic forms imposed by the cultural commissars and collaborationist artists – painters and musicians especially – had to block the negative dialectic of the *Is it happening?*, by translating and betraying the question as a waiting for some fabulous subject or identity: 'Is the pure people coming?', 'Is the Führer coming?' 'Is Siegfried coming?'[342]

Thus the negativity of utopian expectation was vitiated by the ideological expectation of the 'people', the 'Führer' or 'Siegfried'. At the same time, Lyotard concludes, the aesthetic of the sublime was neutralized and turned into myth. Instead of speaking of a 'politics of myth',[343] he could also have said 'aesthetic ideology'.

It becomes clear at this point that what Lyotard and de Man have in mind is not simply an inversion of rationalist or Hegelian theses about the constitution of meaningful totalities, but a specific critique of ideology. This critique differs in some crucial points from the negativity underlying the critical theories of Adorno and Horkheimer. While these theories are based on the concepts of truth, subjectivity and social emancipation, the destructive negativity of postmodern theories tends to dismantle the key concepts of Critical Theory and abandon its utopian hopes.

Their emphasis on heterogeneity and particularity, along with their rejection of conceptualization, turn Adorno's (conceptualized) particularity into an absurdity. In a situation where the concept is no longer available as an analytical and critical instrument, the subject, defined as an autonomous critical instance, can only abdicate. Albrecht Wellmer quite rightly points out that, for Adorno and Horkheimer, 'the disintegration of the subject in late industrial society' implied 'a movement of *regression*'.[344] The negative character of allegory and the sublime would only be meaningful if it could be used by a critical subject as a starting point of social emancipation. In its postmodern form, this negativity turns into an empty negation of meaning and subjectivity. It thus tends to coincide with indifference as interchangeability of values (cf. Section 4.4).

In this context, it is hardly surprising to find that Paul de Man does not consider modernity and modernism as historical processes of emancipation, but as movements of 'eternal return' in Nietzsche's sense:

(. . .) Paul de Man's discussion of 'Modernism' shows it to be a concept by no means unique to a single period but a recurrent ever-repeated self-subverting move in each period's sense of itself in relation to previous periods. If de Man is right the term 'post-Modern' is a tautology or an oxymoron, since no writer or critic ever reaches the modern, in the sense of the authentically self-born, much less goes beyond it.[315]

However, de Man need not be right, and in the next chapter – as in the first and second – the question concerning the transition from a modern and modernist to a postmodern form of society and literature will be at the centre of the scene. For it seems unlikely, from the point of view of the social sciences, that social and literary evolutions can be understood as 'eternal returns of the same' in the Nietzschean sense. The rise of the European Union, for example, could hardly be explained in this perspective – unless it was interpreted as a renaissance of the Roman Empire or the Holy Roman Empire. But there is hardly any room for such speculations in any of the social sciences. In the last chapter, an attempt will be made to defend social science against various brands of postmodern Nietzschean rhetoric.

# Chapter 4

# Modernism and Postmodernism:
# Literary Criticism

The title of this chapter suggests that there is a shift in the problematic on the literary level, as the philosophical and sociological contrast between modernity and postmodernity fades into the background and is eclipsed by the literary contrast between *modernism* and *postmodernism*. Unlike most philosophers and sociologists, who feel challenged by the crisis of modernity as modernization, rationalization and Enlightenment, literary theoreticians deal with the question how modernism (as late modernity: cf. Chapter 1) is related to a postmodernism defined predominantly as an aesthetic phenomenon.

Insofar as modernism is considered as a self-reflection and self-criticism of modernity in the works of Baudelaire, Dostoevsky, Joyce, D. H. Lawrence, Thomas Mann, Hermann Hesse, Kafka, Pirandello or Camus, it cannot be treated as an equivalent of modernity in the philosophical or sociological sense. For the latter was inaugurated by the processes of rationalization in the sixteenth and seventeenth century. This argument is also to be found in Matei Calinescu's *Faces of Modernity*, where 'modernity as an aesthetic concept' (i.e. modernism)[1] is distinguished from modernity as Enlightenment and rationalization. Starting from this distinction of modernity and modernism (as late modern self-criticism of modernity), it seems to make sense to proceed symmetrically and to speak of 'postmodernism' in the literary context. Although this term has the advantage of being more concrete because it takes into account the specific character of literary and artistic problems, it does have the disadvantage of suggesting that postmodern literature and literary criticism cannot be understood as reactions to modernity as rationalization and Enlightenment. It insinuates that postmodernism is to be viewed exclusively as a reaction to modernism or aesthetic modernity.

This, however, amounts to a distortion of the perspective and eliminates crucial aspects of postmodern literature. One thus overlooks the fact that it continues and radicalizes the modernist critique of rationalism and Hegelianism, of reason, truth and subjectivity. Proust's and Musil's critiques of rationalism, Camus's critique of metaphysical narratives and Pirandello's extreme constructivism reappear in postmodern writing which often presents itself as a radicalized modernism and a renewed attack on modernity. Once again, this attack starts from Nietzsche's and Heidegger's subversion of metaphysics (of the subject, of conceptualization and truth) and the corresponding literary critiques of Musil, Lawrence and Gide which are carried to extremes by postmodern writers. This is the reason why the term *postmodernity* will continue to be used in this chapter; but 'modernity' will be replaced by *modernism* (late modernity) in the literary context.

At this stage, one could propose a preliminary definition of postmodernity in the context of literary criticism, suggesting that *postmodern literature revolts against the metaphysical residues of modernity in modernism.* This view is confirmed by the fact that postmodern authors keep distancing themselves from modernist notions such as *truth, form, utopia, autonomy* (of the individual, of art) and *the subject.* Postmodern *nouveaux romanciers* like Alain Robbe-Grillet or Jean Ricardou tend to view Malraux's, Sartre's or Camus's existential problems with an indulgent smile.

Similarly, postmodern authors like Maurice Roche have no qualms about discarding unsolved metaphysical problems of modernity and modernism, and they do not seem to show any concern for the persistent trends towards modernization and rationalization underlying postmodernity. Novelists such as Eco or Robbe-Grillet are not afraid of symbioses between literature and the culture industry, and a former *nouveau romancier* like Robbe-Grillet returns to readable prose and produces *ciné-romans*,[2] scanning the market for new prospects and outlets. Although this orientation towards new technologies, markets and hybrid forms is not to be found in all postmodern works, it heralds a trend which was less pronounced in modernism: the artist's will to succeed in the 'art fair',[3] as Teige puts it.

Should this trend prevail, then one of the modernist nightmares of Mallarmé, Huysmans, Hesse and Adorno would become reality: a modernization without modern and modernist critique, a modernization amidst indifference. Where the last remnants of metaphysics are thrown overboard, a scenario of this kind becomes conceivable, because a rejection of the concept of truth entails a rejection of social criticism. This is why Adorno, who was well aware of this danger, concludes his *Negative Dialectics* with a paradox: 'There is solidarity between such thinking and metaphysics at the time of its fall.'[4]

Considering the *continuity of technical modernization*, which seems to link early modernity with postmodernity, once again the sociological, philosophical and aesthetic question crops up whether it would make sense to consider postmodernity as yet another thrust towards modernization *within* modernity. It is difficult to answer it as long as one does not go beyond the literary realm. Ihab Hassan may have a point when he reacts with a counter-question: 'In short, can we understand postmodernism in literature without some attempt to perceive the lineaments of a postmodern society (. . .)?'[5]

Precisely because it is precarious to attempt a definition of modernity, modernism and postmodernity in purely literary terms, it seemed to make sense to place a sociological chapter at the beginning of this book in order to grasp the social problematic on which everything else is based. In that chapter,

Wolfgang Welsch's thesis about the realization of pluralism in postmodernity turned out to be plausible; but at the same time it became clear that the reverse of the pluralist coin is social indifference as predicted by Simmel and commented on by Touraine, Etzioni and Jameson.

Along with the metaphysical concept of truth, this indifference discredits critical theories of society and the very possibility of criticism which is bound to fail without a quest for truth. If this sketch of the social and epistemological situation is correct, then a crucial dimension of modernity is irretrievably lost, and we are witnessing a 'qualitative leap' in social and artistic development. It is not by chance that the decline of modern critical intellectuals has been diagnosed by such different authors as Lyotard, Wolf Lepenies and Frank Furedi.[6] Their gradual disappearance from the postmodern scene is a sign of the times.

On a complementary level, Jameson speaks of a disappearance of critical distance,[7] and Jochen C. Schütze develops this idea when he describes the dissolution of Kant's and Gadamer's critical projects within the postmodern problematic: 'Instead of a "critique of life" art is supposed to promote the "sensorial expansion of life". It is not responsible for a critique of culture, but rather invites a complicity with the dominant icons of consumer society.'[8] In a somewhat different context, Jochen K. Schütze confirms that 'indifference is the salient feature of postmodern experience,'[9] and, commenting on Baudrillard's work, he shows that, along with art, theory loses its critical dimension:

> Nowadays it would be naïve (. . .) to expect theory to treat its objects otherwise than in an opportunistic and playful manner. The era of rational projects countering the irrational course of world affairs, the era of revolutionary or messianic interventions, is gone.[10]

This diagnosis suggests that something new has cropped up in society and art, something that calls the idea of a continuous development from modernity and modernism to postmodernity into question.

In what follows, the reactions of literary criticism to the postmodern problematic will be dealt with in conjunction with the sociological and philosophical problems discussed in Chapters 2 and 3. It will be argued that most of these reactions can be understood in relation to the *problem of ambivalence* which structures modernism (late modernity), distinguishing it from a postmodernity structured by *indifference* and complementary phenomena such as pluralism and particularization. This construction underlies both the fourth and the fifth chapter.

## 4.1 Construction Attempts

Countless attempts have been made to distinguish literary and artistic modernism from postmodernity (or postmodernism). However, they are so heterogeneous that it is well-nigh impossible to relate them to one another within a systematic classification. Nevertheless, at least three types of construction can be distinguished on a metatheoretical level:

1. Some authors have submitted contrastive stylistic analyses permitting modernist texts to be distinguished from postmodern(ist) texts (Fokkema, Hassan).
2. Others (Hutcheon, Zurbrugg) follow the political impulse and oppose a popular and democratic postmodernism to an elitist and conservative modernism. Their stance is contested, as might be expected, by advocates of modernism (Eagleton, Jameson) whose discourses are structurally similar to those of the postmodernists (for or against), although their aims are quite different.
3. A third group of authors is more cautious, trying to understand modernism and postmodernity as complexes of questions and answers, that is as paradigms in the sense of Kuhn (Quinones, McHale).

The fact is that the first two groups think within the postmodern problematic and react to its developments without actually reflecting their own positions within this problematic, while the third group does adopt a reflexive attitude, trying to take into account its own social and linguistic situation. While Fokkema, Hassan, Hutcheon and Zurbrugg tend to regard modernism and postmodernism as relatively homogenous poetics or aesthetic and political ideologies, McHale looks into the heterogeneity and polyphony of the two historical complexes. Since 'pluralism' and 'heterogeneity' belong to the most frequently used and abused buzz words of postmodernity, it seems appropriate to explain their function in the modern-postmodern discussion.

Malcolm Bradbury may have a point when he says that the word 'modernism' 'gives coherence to a collage of different tendencies and movements, often epistemologically at odds with or in revolt against others, arising from a variety of different traditions and lineages, different political and cultural situations',[11] that it means different things in different countries ('one country's modern was not another's')[12] and that we ought to speak of 'modernisms' and 'postmodernisms'.

This somewhat complacent nominalism is endorsed by Matei Calinescu, who regards Jameson as a vulgar Marxist, accusing him of trying to delete differences in an essentialist manner. Like Welsch, Calinescu is convinced of having found in pluralism the philosopher's stone: 'A pluralistic methodology, beyond its obvious merits in dealing with a plural phenomenon such as literature, could also turn out to be the best defense against the ghost of totality which haunts all great theatrical-ideological schemes.'[13] This polemic against the 'ghost of totality' is itself postmodern and can only be concretely understood within the problematic as a whole.

Calinescu's plea for plurality, which should not turn into an ideology of pluralism, is justified in the sense that it would hardly be meaningful, after the collapse of European communism and of socialist realism, to follow Lukács and other Marxists in condemning modernism and postmodernity as aspects of 'artistic decadence'.[14] Not only in sociology and philosophy, but also in literary criticism, the plural character of the late modern and the postmodern problematics ought to be reckoned with. However, this should not be taken to mean that literary theory will fall prey to a postmodern randomness, solely held together by Bradbury's idea that modern and postmodern literature is extremely heterogeneous. In the next section, the dialectic between heterogeneity and homogeneity will be described in relation to the *concept of problematic.*

It can certainly be shown, following Bradbury, that modernity, late modernity (modernism) and postmodernity not only differ from culture to culture, but are constructed differently even *within* national contexts. In their book *Modernism 1890–1930*, for example, Malcolm Bradbury and James McFarlane construct this period very differently from David Lodge whose postmodernity begins in 1916.[15] Adorno's aesthetic modernity (since 1850) has little to do with Habermas's 'project of modernity' (chronologically it coincides with some Anglo-American constructions of modernism), and even the Spanish *modernismo* is torn by contradictory definitions – as was shown in the first chapter.

In view of this heterogeneity, Douwe W. Fokkema's attempt to construct modernism and postmodernism by contrasting them with romanticism, realism and symbolism as literary periods seems quite plausible. 'One of the crucial phenomena in literary history', he argues, 'is the change of norm systems: the replacement of Romanticism by Realism, of Realism by Symbolism and Modernism, and of Modernism by Postmodernism are major events in literary history.'[16] It seems reasonable to go along with this kind of historical narrative, especially since modernism will be considered here (in the next section) as a reaction to realism and romanticism. Fokkema's problem consists in his attempt to construct modernism and postmodernism (postmodernity) as systems of aesthetic norms and as social codes (he refers to a 'sociocode of modernism'),[17] because he tends to obliterate the heterogeneity of the modernist and postmodern problematics.

Whenever he tries to describe the 'modernist code' of representative authors like Thomas Mann, Gide, Proust, Larbaud, Joyce, Aldous Huxley, Virginia Woolf and Pirandello, using expressions such as 'epistemological doubt', 'metalingual comment', 'openness of texts' or 'respect for the idiosyncrasies of the reader', he reveals essential aspects of literary modernity. But at the same time he glosses over crucial contrasts between Gide, Proust and Joyce: contrasts due to the implementation of contradictory aesthetic norms. The obliteration of these aesthetic and ideological incompatibilities is not due to chance, but to the fact that – in spite of using the term 'sociocode' – Fokkema neglects the nexus between text and society.

For the social, political contrasts between Proust and Joyce explain why the two authors adhered to different aesthetic and stylistic norms. At the same time, political controversies account for the aesthetic and philosophical divergences between modern existentialists, such as Sartre and Camus, which eventually led to a personal conflict. How are we to understand Proust's, Sartre's, Hesse's and Kafka's aesthetic positions if we ignore their respective views on nature, the subject, reason and human domination over nature?

Similarly, the differences between postmodern authors like John Fowles, Umberto Eco, Jürgen Becker and Alain Robbe-Grillet cannot be considered independently of the *political heterogeneity of the postmodern problematic*. Unlike Becker, who plays with language and continues avant-garde experiments, Eco writes the readable, consumer- and film-oriented text. At the other end of the postmodern spectrum, Werner Schwab's punk theatre sets the stage for a desperate revolt against a one-dimensional market society. Like modernism, postmodern literature cannot be confined to a static and homogeneous system of values and norms: to a 'code'. In short, Fokkema overlooks the social heterogeneity brought about by antagonistic groups, schools, movements and ideologies which together are responsible for a late modern or postmodern dynamic.

In this respect, Ihab Hassan quite rightly stresses the importance of the social context of postmodernism (cf. above). Unfortunately, he does not analyse it, and his well-known attempt to assemble the salient features of postmodern literature suffers, like Fokkema's, from a lack of sociological reflection, both on the historical and on the literary level.

In *The Dismemberment of Orpheus* (1971), he sets out from the plausible idea that, in the course of literary evolution, all forms and genres are increasingly questioned, so that literature approaches a situation where its language is silenced by self-consciousness and self-criticism. Hassan speaks of a 'literature of silence'[18] which has its origin in modernism and reaches its climax at the beginning of the postmodern era. He is probably right in locating the emerging silence in the transition from literary existentialism to the Nouveau Roman. About existentialism he remarks that the (late) modern Subject oscillates between nihilism and holiness, searching for the meaning of life.[19] It seems to him that in the Nouveau Roman this oscillation ceases together with the metaphysical search for meaning: 'In Sartre, humanism still persists at the edge of reason; in Robbe-Grillet, *chosisme*, denying the relevance of reason, silences the ordinary voice.'[20]

Revolving around the problem of silence in literature, a thematic reconstruction of this kind may have its *raison d'être*, especially since it overlaps with the constructions of other authors and some of the findings presented in this chapter. Its flaws are mainly due to the fact that it glosses over the social heterogeneity of modernism and postmodernism, presenting both periods as relatively homogeneous aesthetic systems.

Hassan sees modernism as a formalistic and hypotactic whole, while postmodernism appears to him as a playful, paratactic and deconstructionist paradigm: 'But if much of modernism appears as hieratic, hypotactical, and formalist, postmodernism strikes us by contrast as playful, paratactical, and deconstructionist.'[21] The result of such reasoning is a dualistic scheme in which negatively connotated aspects of modernism are opposed to positively connotated aspects of postmodernism: *form/anti-form, purpose/play, design/chance, hierarchy/anarchy, mastery-logos/exhaustion-silence, distance/participation, creation-totalization/decreation-deconstruction, synthesis/antithesis, presence/absence, centering/ dispersal, hypotaxis/parataxis, root-depth/rhizome-surface, signified/signifier, metaphysics/ irony, etc.*[22]

Although it is not reproduced here integrally, this catalogue of salient traits reveals its fundamental flaws. Thus Musil, whom Hassan considers as a modernist author in the sense of D. H. Lawrence, Rilke, Thomas Mann, Pound and Eliot, would have to be defined as postmodern within the framework of Hassan's scheme, because his style is marked by antithesis, absence, deconstruction, dissemination, parataxis and irony. What applies to Musil also applies to other modernists such as Svevo, Pirandello, Hesse, Döblin, Broch and Céline.[23]

Hassan's scheme leads to the question which he raises in *Paracriticism* in a political context: whether modernists such as Yeats, Pound, Rilke, Eliot, Claudel, Lawrence, Proust, Faulkner and Wyndham Lewis were not actually conservatives or even crypto-fascists. He cautiously adds that Thomas Mann, Hemingway and Gide are exceptions and that authors like Brecht, Camus, Grass and Mailer were made possible by the Second World War. He does not even mention Bernanos, who was ostracized by official Catholicism, Malraux in his Marxist phase, Hermann Hesse, Heinrich Mann, Alfred Döblin, Lorca, Kafka, Hašek, Krleža, Svevo, the early Joyce and Auden. Once again, it becomes clear that modernism and postmodernity cannot be viewed as homogeneous aesthetics or ideologies because they combine contradictory literary and political positions.

Like Hassan, Linda Hutcheon seems to ignore this fact, although she differs from both Hassan and Fokkema by insisting on the social and political components of modernist and postmodern fiction. More than Hassan, she constructs literary modernism and postmodernism as two incompatible ideological systems: '(. . .) Postmodern fiction has come to contest the modernist ideology of artistic autonomy, individual expression, and the deliberate separation of art from mass culture and everyday life.'[24] Although this may be a fair assessment of the contrast between a conservative modernist like T. S. Eliot and a popular postmodernist like Eco, it sounds nonsensical as soon as it is repeated in conjunction with politically committed writers such as the early Dos Passos, Brecht, Hesse, Krleža and Hašek who could be opposed to politically abstinent postmodernists such as Claude Simon, Jürgen Becker and the Italo Calvino of the 1970s. Becker, for instance, whose work Hassan also locates within the postmodern constellation, was accused of being apolitical or even conservative.[25]

This kind of comparative approach, which goes well beyond the Anglo-American realm in defining modernism and postmodernity, is completely absent from the work of Linda Hutcheon who identifies modernism with a 'hermetic ahistoric formalism and aestheticism'.[26] She speaks of a 'romantic and modernist heritage of non-engagement',[27] as if Sartre, Lorca, Brecht, Virginia Woolf, Hašek or Hemingway had never existed. Moreover, she tends to identify modernism as a whole with T. S. Eliot's conservative and elitist stance, adding the names of Pound, Céline and Yeats in order to increase the plausibility of her approach. At times it is amusing to observe how, in Hutcheon's analyses, Thomas Mann is portrayed as the guardian of a conservative aesthetic, while the name of his highly critical and socially committed brother Heinrich is never mentioned. And it is quite surprising to see how Brecht, who simply does not fit into Hutcheon's model of a conservative modernism, is eventually treated as the precursor of a popular postmodernism.[28] Hutcheon's dualistic approach is implicitly disavowed by more recent work: for example by *The Modernism Handbook* (ed. P. Tew, A. Murray, 2009), where critical writers like W. H. Auden, D. H. Lawrence and James Joyce are at the centre of the modernist scene.[29]

A similar dualism underlies Nicholas Zurbrugg's *The Parameters of Postmodernism*, where the American composer John Cage is presented as the true exponent of postmodern aesthetics which are subdivided into various *C-effects* (thus named after Cage). This lonely postmodern hero is opposed by various anti-heroes of the *B-effects*: European apocalyptic thinkers, who, having lost all mental flexibility, can read the signs of postmodern times exclusively as symptoms of historical decline: 'European theorists such as Benjamin, Barthes, Bürger, Baudrillard, Bonito Oliva, and Bourdieu.'[30] A European intellectual may find it difficult to discern a common denominator linking the works of these authors (except for the letter B) – but this is probably due to the apocalyptic blindness imputed to him by Zurbrugg.

Zurbrugg's train of thought, which overlaps with Hutcheon's in some crucial points, is epitomized by the end of his book:

> The B-effect thinkers of postmodern culture may well convince themselves that innovation, individuality, and independent creativity are logically impossible. Again, that's their problem. Living and thinking in the nineties, it seems more productive to follow the positive contemporaneity of C-effect thinkers such as Cage (. . .).[31]

Like Hutcheon, Zurbrugg confronts conservative modernists with progressive and creative postmodernists without ever dealing with the problem of a conservative postmodernity and a revolutionary modernism (cf. Section 2.3).

Nevertheless, his attempts at relating postmodern art to electronic technologies have their merits because they reveal the presence of modern (i.e. pre-modernist) rationalization and organization within postmodern creativity. Postmodernity may also be construed as a synthesis of new technologies and archaic rites: '(. . .) Postmodern modes of collective art vary from high-tech, multimedia experiments to semishamanistic ritual.'[32] There is no need for the apocalyptic thinkers to worry about the subject: 'Briefly, the subject is alive and well in postmodern culture, if often a little more fragmented than hitherto and frequently rather more *electronic* in character than its modernist precursors.'[33] Postmodernity thus appears as progress – and not only as a critique of the modern ideology of progress in the sense of Bauman.

Unfortunately, apocalyptic thinkers, especially the Marxists among them, are unlikely to feel reassured by Zurbrugg's remarks, since they tend to argue, like Hutcheon and Zurbrugg himself, within dualistic structures. In Jameson's case, the aesthetic verdict on postmodernity turns out to be relatively mild because, as a Marxist reader of Brecht, he tends to welcome the popular orientation of contemporary art and style:

> (. . .) Culturally I write as a relatively enthusiastic consumer of postmodernism, at least of some parts of it: I like the architecture and a lot of the newer visual work, in particular the newer photography. The music is not bad to listen to, or the poetry to read (. . .).[34]

However, examples or analyses confirming the plausibility of these judgements are missing. Nevertheless, Jameson is well aware of the fact that postmodern art is almost entirely determined by marketing and market laws. About the various postmodernisms he writes that 'all at least share a resonant affirmation, when not an outright celebration, of the market as such'.[35]

Although this global assessment is correct in its general form and will be taken seriously in this chapter, especially since it is confirmed by contemporary economic analyses of culture,[36] it is inapplicable to key postmodern works such as Robbe-Grillet's *Dans le labyrinthe*, Italo Calvino's *Città invisibili* and Thomas Bernhard's novels.[37] For these works are more likely to be understood as critical reactions to postmodern commercialization than as expressions of it.

Within the Marxist camp, Terry Eagleton's critical analyses of the postmodern problematic are far more radical and polemical than Jameson's. What makes modernism valuable in Eagleton's eyes, is its search for meaning and truth. He believes that in postmodernism this search is replaced by a one-dimensional desire for power and money which eclipses all social alternatives: 'The depthless, styleless, dehistoricized, decathected surfaces of postmodernist culture are not meant to signify an alienation, for the very concept of alienation must secretly posit a dream of authenticity which postmodernism finds quite unintelligible.'[38]

Although it is true that social criticism is inconceivable without a concept of truth, without a search for meaning, this does not imply that postmodern art and literature have to be 'styleless' and a-historical, especially since some postmodern artworks turn out to be revolts against the 'postmodern condition'. But it could well be that all of postmodern art bears witness to the contemporary difficulty or impossibility to postulate norms and values. It should not be blamed for this.

Unlike Hutcheon, Zurbrugg and the Marxists, who write *within* the postmodern problematic and argue in favour or against certain aspects of this problematic, authors such as Ricardo J. Quinones and Brian McHale try to consider modernism and postmodernity from the outside as it were, that is as noetic systems or paradigms which allow for certain questions and answers, but not for others. The perspectives of these authors are similar to those of Thomas S. Kuhn and Michel Foucault who would also like to know what can be experienced, thought and said within certain systems in a particular historical period.

This systemic approach seems preferable to the more ideological and dualistic approaches of Hutcheon, Zurburgg, Jameson and Eagleton, insofar as it makes it easier to think of modernism and postmodernity as complex and relatively heterogeneous systems of norms and values – and not as ideologies, aesthetics or stylistic totalities. In some respects, it corresponds to the notion of problematic proposed here. However, the problematic, as defined in the last part of this chapter and specified in the fifth in a literary context, also includes philosophical and especially sociological aspects neglected by Quinones and McHale.

Nevertheless, Quinones attempts to explain the rise of modernism, which, he believes, was anticipated by Nietzsche and Dostoevsky, in conjunction with a shift in the social systems of Europe and North America: '(. . .) Literary Modernism was part of a significant shift in values (. . .).'[39] This shift was caused, among other things, by the crisis of bourgeois-humanist and liberal values: a crisis analysed by modernists such as D. H. Lawrence and Thomas Mann. One possible reaction to this crisis is a cosmopolitan attitude sympathetic to 'diversity' and 'fragmentation'.[40] (One should remember at this point that Hassan tries to explain modernism using concepts such as *hierarchy, totalization* and *synthesis.*) In short, Quinones sees modernism partly as a self-criticism of modernity (e.g. of European and American individualism as it developed since the Renaissance), partly as a new constellation of problems, questions and answers.

A similar pattern of thought is to be found in the works of Brian McHale who views modernism and postmodernism – more consistently than Quinones – as *noetic systems*. Unlike modernism, which is dominated by *epistemological* questions, postmodernism, according to McHale, should be conceived as a predominantly *ontological* system. 'The dominant of modernist fiction is *epistemological*',[41] he argues. The characteristic questions of epistemologically structured modernism are: 'How can I interpret this world I belong to?' – 'What can I know?' – 'Who knows it and how reliable is his knowledge?' – 'Where are the limits of the knowable?' Postmodernism, on the other hand, raises ontological questions: 'What kind of world is this?' – 'What should I do in this world?' – 'Which of my selves should do it?' – 'What is a world?' – 'What worlds are there, how are they made, and how do they differ?', etc.[42]

Unlike in Proust's *Sodome et Gomorrhe*, where the narrator asks mainly epistemological questions – for example in conjunction with Monsieur de Charlus's and Jupien's homosexuality –, in Alain Robbe-Grillet's *La Maison de rendez-vous*, questions concerning the constitution of the fictional world(s) are in the foreground. McHale believes that the extreme epistemological uncertainty, which makes itself felt especially in late modernism, eventually turns into ontological instability and pluralism: 'Push epistemological questions far enough and they "tip over" into ontological questions.'[43]

The question is, however, whether McHale's undoubtedly useful, but somewhat abstract model is applicable in all cases: 'What kind of world is this?' – 'What should be done in this world?' – Are these not ontological questions which frequently crop up in Kafka's novels and in some of his short stories – for example in *The Metamorphosis*? Should Kafka – the modernist *par excellence* – be considered as a postmodern author?

Whatever the answers to this question – and to similar questions concerning Joyce[44] – may be, the authors quoted here agree that modernism and postmodernism are international and intercultural phenomena which cannot be satisfactorily dealt with by a single national philology. The argument that Linda Hutcheon tends to identify modernism with T. S. Eliot's work and the aesthetics of the conservative New Critics has already been put forward; it is even more appropriate in the case of David Lodge whose analyses are almost exclusively oriented towards British and North American writers.

This reductionist treatment of an international text corpus inevitably leads to one-sided definitions of modernism as a pessimistic reaction to the 'death of God' and to the idea 'that the world was a wasteland, a place of meaningless suffering, unsuccessful communication and shattered illusions'.[45] This description, which is obviously inspired by Eliot's *Wasteland*, may very well be applicable to various works of modernism, but becomes irrelevant in the case of Gide's *Nourritures terrestres*, Virginia Woolf's *Orlando*, Brecht's Epic Theatre and the revolutionary manifestos of the avant-garde movements – which are considered here as components of the modernist (late modern) problematic.

What Lodge has to say about modernism is to be considered with scepticism for another reason. His idea that a viable definition of modernism 'must be sought beyond boundaries of the arts'[46] is undoubtedly sound. But one should bear in mind that postmodern architecture, for example, which is often mentioned as a model reaction to functionalist modernism, shows to what extent 'modernity', 'modernism' and 'postmodernity' mean very different things in different arts. Le Corbusier's utilitarian and rationalist modernity of the interwar period turns out to be the very opposite of literary modernism. For it is the kind of modernity modernist writers from Baudelaire and Kafka to Döblin and Hermann Hesse rebelled against – along with some founding fathers of sociology such as Georg Simmel, Emile Durkheim and Alfred Weber[47] (cf. Chapter 1).

Some difficulties resulting from the attempt to subsume literature, architecture and other arts under a single notion of modernity or modernism are illustrated by David Harvey's – otherwise informative – study *The Condition of Postmodernity* which puts architecture at the centre of the scene. It may be true that, after 1848, modernism was essentially an 'urban phenomenon',[48] as Harvey would have it, but it is precisely this phenomenon that some of the most influential modernist writers – from Hamsun and Kafka to Döblin – called into question: not by projecting rural utopias, but by analysing urban alienation. Therefore it does not seem to make a lot of sense to assimilate the literary experiment to the technical and architectural one. However, this is precisely what Harvey does when he speaks in general terms of 'the experience of space and time in Western capitalism',[49] referring to the technical ideology of the Italian Futurists and to Ezra Pound's 'thirst for machine efficiency'[50] (both of which are completely absent from French Surrealism, from Kafka's or Hesse's works). They are only *one* aspect of modernism, only *one* of its answers.

In short, it is not possible to assimilate the literary problematic to the heterogeneous problematic of architecture or of other arts. Although a construction of modernism and postmodernity, which encompasses all forms of art, may be desirable and even feasible, it seems more meaningful in the present situation, especially in view of the heterogeneity of artistic genres, aesthetic perspectives and terminological intricacies, to limit the construction to the realm of verbal communication. As discursive forms, literature, philosophy and the cultural sciences interact within language and thus constitute a semiotic whole. Non-verbal arts such as painting, music and architecture are subject to different laws and rhythms of development (as Lyotard, Pierre Francastel and Otto Pächt have shown)[51]: especially architecture which has to respond to the changing needs of urbanization and is generally more exposed to economic pressures.

## 4.2 The Problematics of Modernism and Postmodernism: Ambiguity, Ambivalence and Indifference

At present, the literary and aesthetic debates tend to acquire an exemplary status, because one of the (derogatory) meanings of the word 'postmodernism' cropped up between 1959 and 1960, when the American critics Irving Howe and Harry Levin[52] dismissed post-war literature as 'postmodern' – that is inferior. In their eyes, it was no match for the works of modernist masters such as T. S. Eliot, Thomas Mann, Joyce or Proust. 'It remained for Leslie Fiedler and myself, among others', Ihab Hassan remembers, 'to employ the term during the sixties with premature approbation, and even with a touch of bravado'.[53] It will be shown that Leslie Fiedler in particular considers postmodern writing as a decisive attempt to bridge the gap between highbrow and popular literature.

In the literary world, John Barth also turns the tables on advocates of high modernism such as Howe and Levin when, in his well-known articles 'The Literature of Exhaustion' (1967) and 'The Literature of Replenishment: Postmodernist Fiction' (1980), he criticizes modernism for being anaemic and maps out postmodern alternatives. He believes that the global dismissal by the modernists of realist narrative, fictional illusion, bourgeois rationality and middle class moral values is far too one-sided. 'Disjunction, simultaneity, irrationalism, anti-illusionism, self-reflexiveness, medium-as-message, political olympianism, and a moral pluralism approaching moral entropy – these are not the whole story either.'[54]

The postmodern programme envisaged by Barth is meant to bridge the gap between literature and everyday life and pleads in favour of a synthesis between the narrative conventions of the nineteenth and the experiments of the twentieth century: 'My ideal postmodernist author neither merely repudiates nor merely imitates either his twentieth-century modernist parents or his nineteenth-century premodernist grandparents.'[55] Without radically breaking with the modernist tradition, Barth ponders on the values of pre-modernist aesthetics and poetics 'whose historical roots are famously and honorably in middle-class popular culture'.[56]

This plea in favour of a literary renovation based on a recourse to old narrative techniques may sound conservative; however, it anticipates Umberto Eco's critique of modernism and the avant-garde 3 years later:

But the moment comes when the avant-garde (the modern) can go no further, because it has produced a metalanguage that speaks of its impossible texts (conceptual art). The postmodern reply to the modern consists of recognizing that the past, since it cannot be really destroyed, because its destruction leads to silence, must be revisited: but with irony, not innocently.[57]

Here, as in other cases, the alternative to modernism appears to be a renewal of traditional narrative.

In this social and linguistic situation, where some critics turn their back on a sterile or conformist literature, while others celebrate a postmodernity which reinvents middle-class aesthetic norms and accepts some patterns of the culture industry, one feels tempted to side with one or the other party and to mount a Marxist or Adornian attack against postmodern windmills. This is exactly what Terry Eagleton does whenever he associates all of postmodern literature with reification and an affirmative ideology. Linda Hutcheon's counter-attack ('Postmodernism does not, as Terry Eagleton asserts . . .')[58] is not long in coming, and the modernist dialogue of the deaf that took place between Lukács, Brecht and Anna Seghers is reproduced in a postmodern setting.

On the whole, it is more likely that 'modernism' and 'postmodernity' do not 'do' anything because they are complex and relatively heterogeneous systems or problematics, which gradually emerge from the problematics of romanticism and realism, as shifts in society, culture and literature occur. This is roughly what Rolf Günter Renner means when he explains:

The question concerning the relationship between the concepts *modern* and *postmodern* cannot aim at a classification of periods in the usual literary-historical sense, but instead has to describe a constellation of discourses and

modes of experience, which emerge in modernity, but at the same time mark
its boundaries.[59]

Two remarks seem appropriate here. Constructing modernism and postmodernity as constellations of discourses and forms of experience does look more
promising than reducing them to ideologies, aesthetics or stylistics. What is
called 'problematic' here overlaps in some respects with Renner's (Mallarmé's,
Adorno's) notion of constellation. One should add, however, that modernism
and postmodernity can be considered chronologically or historically as periods
or epochs, especially if certain social transformations are taken into account:
provided, of course, that periods such as romanticism or realism are also
constructed as *problematics* instead of being viewed as aesthetics or ideologies.
Thus romanticism, which Quinones and Gillespie[60] consider as the actual pred-
ecessor of modernism, appears, on closer scrutiny, as a complex system of ideological and aesthetic positions wherein Shelley's anarchism and Chateaubriand's
or Novalis's conservatism compete and collide. In this respect, Renner could
have adopted a bolder stance by arguing that even older literary periods ought
to be viewed as constellations.

Realism, which, in many literary theories, is presented as the premodernist
stage of development,[61] can be defined as a socially-minded, critical and even
revolutionary movement. Stephan Kohl hardly exaggerates when he points to
the 'close link which was made in those days between democracy, the revolution
of 1848 and realism'.[62] European realism was nonetheless accused of conservatism: not only because of Balzac's legitimistic propensities, but also in view of
C. F. Meyer's historical flight from modernity which, in the German-speaking
world, stood in stark contrast to Spielhagen's radical liberalism. So all things
considered, not even realism can be construed as a homogeneous ideological
or aesthetic bloc.

Nevertheless, most realists seem to share the assumption that it is possible to
reproduce reality by mimetic means and to overcome ambiguity whenever it
stands in the way of cognitive or aesthetic attempts to grasp the real. In this
respect, the realists are Hegelians, and Hegel himself is quite rightly defined as
a philosophical realist by John E. Smith: 'Hegel was, in this regard, a thorough-
going realist: what we know is the things themselves, their properties, unities
and relations. For Hegel, the real is not "behind" or "beyond", but actually
*present* in what we apprehend.'[63] Like the realist writer, although in a different
context, Hegel believes in the possibility of eliminating ambiguities and contradictions encountered in our thought by relying on a synthesizing dialectic.

In a complementary fashion, Balzac would like to be 'a more or less faithful
painter' ('peintre plus ou moins fidèle')[64] of his society and presents his novel
*Les Paysans* as a scientific study of his age: 'I study the movement of my time,
and I publish this work.' ('J'étudie la marche de mon époque, et je publie
cet ouvrage.')[65] The idea to paint one's age mimetically by narrative means
presupposes the possibility of defining situations, characters and actions more

or less univocally. In Balzac's work, this possibility still exists because author and narrator both believe that cognitive, ethical and psychic ambiguities can be resolved to such a degree that truth emerges at the end of the day (Hegel would say: that essence appears behind the appearances).

At the very beginning of *Illusions perdues*, the narrator tries to define Mme de Bargeton, 'one of the most important characters of this story' ('un des person-nages les plus importants de cette histoire').[66] A few pages later, this narrative project is brought to an end: Mme de Bargeton's essence is summed up by a clear-sighted observer as 'love without a lover' ('l'amour sans l'amant').[67] In order to banish all doubts, the narrator confirms this diagnosis: 'And it was true' ('Et c'était vrai').[68]

Very much like Balzac, who intended to be a faithful painter of his society, George Eliot believed in the ideal of representation which, in the famous seventeenth chapter of *Adam Bede*, she illustrates by the metaphors of reflection and the mirror:

> The mirror is doubtless defective; the outlines will sometimes be disturbed; the reflection faint or confused; but I feel as much bound to tell you, as precisely as I can, what that reflection is, as if I were in the witness-box narrating my experience on oath.[69]

In the world of modernist and postmodern narrators, this kind of realistic confidence is inconceivable.

Most realists start from the assumption that their narrators are capable of presenting things as they are and that reflections about the contingency of the narrator's position are to be avoided. 'Only an advancing epic account which completely excludes the narrator as such is permitted,'[70] explains Stephan Kohl in his analysis of Spielhagen's novels. This realist perspective is also to be found in the works of the Italian verist (realist-naturalist) Giovanni Verga who, in his introduction to the novella *L'amante di Gramigna*, pleads in favour of a truthful description of objects and events that makes us forget the presence of the narra-tor. The work of art 'will bear the imprint of the real event' ('avrà l'impronta dell'avvenimento reale'), and it will seem to us 'that it *made itself*' ('sembrerà *essersi fatta da sé*').[71] Along with the question concerning the contingency of the narra-tor's discourse, the question concerning the construction of reality is deleted.

This ontological confidence or naïveté is lost in later realism:

> Within 19th century German realism, the work of Raabe shows in an exemplary way to what extent the conviction that a knowable harmony of the universe exists is increasingly threatened by doubt and to what extent the description of a general 'coherence of things' only succeeds as a subjective act.[72]

In this commentary by Stephan Kohl, the contours of the newly emerging modernist problematic become discernible. From now on, the epistemological and aesthetic *ambiguity*, which was still considered to be surmountable by Hegel and most realist writers, turns into *ambivalence* which can no longer be over-come by logical, phenomenological or dialectical syntheses. At the same time, it becomes increasingly obvious that reality is invariably a philosophical, poetic or narrative construction, that is a subjective creation or invention: a contin-gent conjecture in the sense of Popper that is exposed to refutation by events and competing conjectures.

The most prominent thinker of extreme ambivalence is, as was shown in the third chapter, Friedrich Nietzsche, whose anti-Hegelianism and anti-realism have lastingly influenced modernist writers. His re-evaluation of all values leads to an *ambivalence as coincidentia oppositorum* that makes itself felt not only in eth-ics and aesthetics, but also in epistemology: 'Cannot *all* values be overturned? And is Good perhaps Evil? And God only an invention, a nicety of the devil? Is everything perhaps ultimately false?'[73]

Nietzsche casts a modernist doubt upon Hegelianism's and realism's Holy of Holies, upon the concept of truth: 'That the world is *not* the abstract essence of an eternal reasonableness is sufficiently proved by the fact that that *bit of the world* which we know – I mean our human reason – is none too reasonable.'[74] This kind of self-knowledge, which can only consider 'the final demonstration' ironically and negatively, also has an impact on our logical competence:

> How did logic come into existence in man's head? Certainly out of illogic, whose realm originally must have been immense. Innumerable beings who made inferences in a way different from ours perished; for all that, their ways might have been truer. Those, for example, who did not know how to find often enough what is 'equal' as regards both nourishment and hostile animals – those, in other words, who subsumed things too slowly and cautiously – were favored with a lesser probability of survival than those who guessed immedi-ately upon encountering similar instances that they must be equal.[75]

(In this case, the German word *gleich* should have been translated by *identical*, not by *equal*.)

This passage is not only important because it exposes logic to the doubt aris-ing from extreme ambivalence (logic as non-logic), but also because it reveals the link between ambivalence, contingency and particularization which is at the centre of the modernist problematic (cf. Chapter 3). According to Nietzsche, logic was invented by those who, plagued by fear or hunger, subsumed too hastily, classified too perfunctorily. If this argument, which is bound to turn into a nightmare in the eyes of every Cartesian or Hegelian, is correct, then our logic is contingent and dependent on chance: it ceases to be universally valid.

Nietzsche's reasoning is completed by Baudelaire's critical comments on reli-gion which link religion and prostitution, the holy and the profane, Christianity and paganism, truth and superstition within a discourse inspired by sacrilege:

(. . .) Paganism and Christianity prove each other mutually.
(. . .) Superstition is the reservoir of all truths.[76]

It is striking how, relying on Benjamin Constant[77] and long before Nietzsche, Baudelaire introduces extreme ambivalence as *coincidentia oppositorum* into the French context. By linking superstition and truth, he announces Nietzsche's well-known text about truth as metaphor[78] in which the philosopher explains the rhetorical origins of the notion of truth. In the works of both authors, 'truth' falls prey to the coincidence of opposites, also mentioned by Walter Benjamin in conjunction with Baudelaire,[79] and to the process of particularization which results from this coincidence. In a situation where truth appears sometimes as a product of superstition, sometimes as a result of interacting rhetorical figures, its contingent character can no longer be concealed, and its universal status is challenged. But what does ambivalence, so thoroughly analysed by Bakhtin in conjunction with Dostoevsky's work, look like as a structuring principle of modernist literature? Before the modernist problematic is reconstructed here in order to serve as a theoretical model for the fifth chapter, some of its key concepts such as ambivalence, irony, contingency and the crisis of the subject will be commented on in the light of Virginia Woolf's novel *Orlando*. What Alan Wilde writes about the unity of opposites, about paradox and irony can be applied to this novel which may be regarded as a model of the modernist paradigm: 'The confusions of the world are shaped into an equal poise of opposites: the form of an unresolvable paradox.'[80]

Like the works of Musil or Proust, Virginia Woolf's novel *Orlando* (1928) is structured by a basic ambivalence that makes itself felt on virtually all levels of the text. To begin with, there is Orlando's androgyny: 'His form combined in one the strength of a man and a woman's grace.'[81] Although the myth of the androgynous being is very old and to be found in antiquity (e.g. in Plato's *Symposion*), it moves to the centre of the modernist scene, where it becomes an aspect of ambivalence defined as the irreducible unity of opposites.

This post-Hegelian unity of opposites calls into question Hegel's synthesizing dialectic and his key concept of *Aufhebung*. Referring to Woolf's 'utopian concept of androgyny', Makiko Minow-Pinkney quite rightly points out: 'It is not, at any rate, a Hegelian *Aufhebung* of opposed terms.'[82] Far from being instrumental in consolidating meaning, like Hegel's system, modernist, Nietzschean ambivalence subverts it in such a way that the hero-heroine finds it hard to find his or her bearings: 'Thus it was in a highly ambiguous condition, uncertain whether she was alive or dead, man or woman, Duke or nonentity, that she posted down to her country seat (. . .).'[83]

At the same time, ambivalence invades the human subject itself, undermining its unity and its sense of identity. In this context, Virginia Woolf's hero-heroine anticipates some of the contemporary debates on the female subject and especially on deconstructionist feminism:

And here it would seem from some ambiguity in her terms that she was cen-
suring both sexes equally, as if she belonged to neither; and indeed, for the
time being, she seemed to vacillate; she was man; she was woman; she knew
the secrets, shared the weaknesses of each. It was a most bewildering and
whirligig state of mind to be in.[84]

This confused, vacillating subject is the subject of modernism: the subject
that also appears in the novels and plays of Musil, Pirandello, Svevo, Kafka and
Joyce. However, one should beware of disregarding the other side of the coin
and of considering exclusively the subject's crisis without acknowledging the
increase in its capacities, an increase due precisely to its multiplicity. For the
narrator adds later on that 'the pleasures of life were increased and its experiences multiplied.'[85]

Nevertheless, one of the consequences of the 'multiplicity of the I', the 'mul-
tiplicité du moi',[86] as the French modernist Paul Bourget puts it, is an inability
to act which characterizes many modernist heroes. One may think of Musil's
Ulrich, Svevo's Zeno Cosini or Proust's protagonists Jean Santeuil or Marcel.
In this respect, Virginia Woolf's Orlando is no exception. The narrator enumer-
ates all sorts of heroic deeds and adventures frequently encountered by readers
of traditional novels and then asks whether Orlando did any of these things.
Her answer hardly comes as a surprise: 'Alas, – a thousand times, alas, Orlando
did none of them.'[87] Like other modernist characters, Woolf's hero 'will neither
love nor kill, but will only think and imagine',[88] thus revealing her- or himself as
a kindred spirit of other modernist anti-heroes from Joyce's Stephen to Sartre's
Roquentin.

It is easy to perceive the link between ambivalence, a subjectivity in crisis and
the lack of action in the novel. In a context where social values have become
uncertain because incompatible value judgements are simultaneously valid,
subjectivity falls prey to this uncertainty, and the subject is incapable of mapping out a 'narrative programme' (Greimas) made up of acts and events.

However, this should not be taken to mean that a hero, who 'will only think
and imagine', has abandoned all value judgements and said farewell to all political, aesthetic or moral values. On the contrary: the modernist novel is a pro-
tracted search for such values, and in *Orlando*, one of the central values is
literature itself. Finally, the protagonist's poem *The Oak Tree* appears as the only
thing that really matters and that eclipses money, fame and witty talk: 'She had
thought then, of the oak tree here on its hill, and what has that got to do with
this, she had wondered? What has praise and fame to do with poetry?'[89] This
conclusion is reminiscent of Marcel Proust's *Time Regained* where we read: 'Real
life, life at last laid bare and illuminated – the only life in consequence which
can be said to be really lived – is literature (. . .).' ('La vraie vie, la vie enfin
découverte et éclaircie, la seule vie par conséquent *pleinement vécue, c'est la
littérature* [. . .].')[90] This belief in art, which relates Proust to Virginia Woolf, is
one of the fundamental aspects of the modernist literary and philosophical

problematic the works of which are marked by a tenacious metaphysical quest for truth. In this respect, the postmodern problematic differs radically from the modern and the modernist: *its thinkers and writers have abandoned the quest and its utopias.*

Some of the basic components of modernist literature (and even philosophy) are to be found in Virginia Woolf's *Orlando* and can be related to Brian McHale's construction and its epistemological or ontological questions. The model that follows ought to make it clear that modernism is not an ideologically or aesthetically homogeneous whole, but a *set of problems* to which different authors react in very different ways: confirming, contradicting or ignoring each other. However, it is the *affinity of the problems* that constitutes the relative homogeneity of the problematic which is nevertheless an open and changing historical system.

It is the awareness of the contradictory character of values, norms, actions and statements most of which are marked by an intrinsic **ambivalence**. Some **key stylistic concepts** can be deduced from the latter: *the paradox* (Kafka, Wilde), *parataxis* (Proust, Adorno), *constructivism* (Pirandello, Unamuno), *an agnostic narrator* (Joyce, Kafka), *carnevalization* (Céline, Sartre), *estrangement* (Brecht, Khlebnikov), *essayism* (Musil, Joyce), *irony and self-irony* (Woolf, Musil), *extreme polysemy* (Kafka, Faulkner). **Problems**: *unity of opposites* (resulting questions: What is good? What is evil? What is right, what is wrong?); *the complementary critique of the concept of truth* (resulting questions: What is true? What is truth?); *a doubt concerning the (Comtian, Hegelian) system and the possibility of representing the development of humanity within the framework of a grand metanarrative* (resulting questions: Who speaks? Who narrates? With what intention, with what kind of competence?); *a critique of the narrative syntax: of the anecdotal narration in modernist prose or of 'action' in drama* (resulting questions: Who narrates? What claims to power does the narration involve?); *the awareness of a crisis of individual and collective subjectivity* (resulting questions: Who are we? Who am I? Who is he/she?); *the stress on contingency and chance and an increasing scepticism towards the notion of necessity* (resulting questions: What is given and what is constructed? To what extent is the construction necessary or true?); *the discrepancy between subject and object and the discontent in civilization and society* (resulting questions: Can reality and its objects be known? What kind of reality do we live in? Can nature be known? Is an alternative reality conceivable on an aesthetic, oneiric or political [revolutionary] level?); *the conception of nature as a liberation of the subject (D. H. Lawrence, Hesse, Camus) or as a threat to it (Kafka, Sartre)* (resulting questions: Is nature a liberation from culture and from the cultural super-ego? Is nature a threat to culture and to the subject as its product?)

It seems essential to bear in mind that this constellation of problems and questions allows for very different reactions and answers ranging from Brecht's avant-garde realism and Auden's political engagement to T. S. Eliot's conservatism and Wyndham Lewis's or Marinetti's fascism. One thus avoids the kind of one-sided reductionism underlying a work like Leon Surette's *The Birth of*

*Modernism*: in many respects a stimulating study which nevertheless reduces modernist aesthetics and stylistics to those of Ezra Pound, T. S. Eliot and W. B. Yeats. Considering this text corpus, it is not surprising that the author can conclude: 'Modernism was committed to stylistic severity and tolerated metaphysical and epistemological absolutism.'[91] He adds: 'Modernism was classically severe (. . .), occult or mystical.'[92] This definition may very well apply to Eliot, Pound und Yeats; however, it ceases to be valid in the case of Céline, Brecht, Svevo, Pirandello, Döblin, Krleža and Hašek. In order to avoid this kind of one-sidedness, the problematic of postmodernity will now be defined in contrast with that of modernism (late modernity).

It is the spreading consciousness of the interchangeability or **indifference** of values, emotions, actions and statements. The following **stylistic concepts** can be deduced from this: *pluralism, de-differentiation of styles* (Pynchon), *radical constructivism* (J. Ricardou), *extreme forms of intertextuality and polyphony* (Cl. Simon), *the combination of heterogeneous codes* (Pynchon, Süskind), *an anachronistic narrative making events from different historical periods coincide* (L. Goytisolo, Ransmayr), *competing narrative perspectives* (Barth, Butor), *the dissolution of genres* (Jürgen Becker), *carnevalization* (Th. Bernhard), *estrangement* (W. Schwab), *extreme polysemy and polyphony* (Jürgen Becker, Robbe-Grillet), *a return to linear narrative and traditional forms of the novel* (Eco, Fowles), *a systematic foregrounding of the fictive reader* (Calvino). **Problems**: *interchangeability of values* (resulting questions: Why is something considered good by some people and bad by others? Why do some call 'wrong' what is called 'right' by others?); *rejection of the metaphysical notion of truth by radical particularization* (resulting questions: How do concepts of truth come about? What is true for whom?); *rejection of the historical metanarratives* (resulting questions: What function do these narrative structures fulfil? What interests do they articulate?); *a playful attitude towards narrative and dramatic action* (resulting questions: Who narrates? What effects does the narration have?); *a playful attitude towards subjectivity* (resulting questions: Are we not they? Am I not the other?); *contingency and construction are dissociated from the quest for truth and from aesthetic, metaphysical and political values* (resulting questions: How does the construction affect readers or spectators?); *doubts concerning the subject-object-dialectic and a tendency to give up the critique of society and culture (the concomitant decline of the critical intellectual)* (resulting questions: What is a critical attitude towards society good for? Is such an attitude possible without metaphysical premises? What is utopia good for? Is it not dangerous?); *an ecological attitude towards nature* (resulting questions: Who will save nature and the environment? What does domination over nature mean?)

If one compares the two (inevitably sketchy) models of modernism and postmodernity, then the following consequences seem to ensue:

1. It is not meaningful to define modernism and postmodernism or postmodernity exclusively on a stylistic level because stylistic features only assume a concrete meaning within the global contexts of ambivalence or indifference.

While *estrangement* expresses a metaphysical or critical attitude in modernism (e.g. in the case of Kafka or Brecht), it fulfils a predominantly aesthetic function in postmodern works (e.g. in Eco's *The Name of the Rose*: 'Naturally, a manuscript') or is meant to provoke without aiming at major social changes (e.g. in W. Schwab's theatre).

2. Both modernism and postmodernity are stylistically heterogeneous. However, modernism is held together by the revolt of most of its authors (from Auden and Brecht to Huysmans, Céline, Breton and Marinetti) against bourgeois society, and this revolt is partly inspired by Marx, partly by Nietzsche. Its critical impulses, which account for its affinity with Adorno's and Horkheimer's Critical Theory, are dampened and its utopian projects discarded in postmodernity. (Social criticism is defined here in the sense of Critical Theory as a truth-searching discourse aiming at alternatives and not as a purely destructive negation.)

3. The linguistic and stylistic heterogeneity of postmodern literature is to be explained in conjunction with the related concepts of *indifference* and *pluralism*. Both are possible: the radical avant-garde experiment (the early Barth, Becker, Schwab) and the conventional narrative, which it is increasingly difficult to debunk, because the ideologies in whose name it could be debunked have lost most of their credibility.

As far as the – constructed – transition from modernism to postmodernity goes, 'shifts in sensibility, practices and discourse formations',[93] as Huyssen puts it, can be observed and related to corresponding shifts in the sociological and philosophical problematic (cf. Chapters 2 and 3). Within the context of indifference, questions concerning truth and social emancipation lose their meaning. The contemporary observer tends to consider them from the outside, as it were, and to argue – with the cultural anthropologist – that they depend on a particular sort of culture.

Proust's search for authentic art and Kafka's search for 'the Law' are replaced in Alain Robbe-Grillet's *Dans le labyrinthe* by a search without an object, without a goal. The grand metaphysical narratives are neither exposed to doubt nor to criticism – as with Musil or Broch – but finally rejected and replaced by playful experiments with traditional (Eco, Fowles) or innovative (Barth, Robbe-Grillet) narrative forms. Like the modernists, postmodern writers ponder on their fictional constructions, but unlike Mallarmé, the Proust of the *Recherche* or the Sartre of *La Nausée*, they do not attribute a truth content to these constructions, the particularity and contingency of which they readily admit.

Postmodern texts are not primarily intended to be critiques of society. Instead they are meant to be 1. radical experiments *without utopian goals* in the sense of the old European avant-gardes (Barth, Calvino, Robbe-Grillet, Butor, Pynchon); 2. they may also be readable narratives combining popular tradition with modernist experiment (Eco, Fowles, Süskind, the recent Barth); 3. sometimes they are ideological (ecological, feminist or conservative) reactions to the problematic

of indifference (Marge Piercy, Ernest Callenbach) which – as was shown above –
tends to invite dualistic responses; 4. finally, they may also be aesthetic and
political revolts against a society many authors experience as meaningless and
nihilistic – without, however, proposing revolutionary or utopian alternatives
(Félix de Azúa, Thomas Bernhard, Christoph Ransmayr).

These four text models will be discussed in some detail in the fifth chapter.
In what follows, John Barth's experimental short story *Lost in the Funhouse* will
be presented as a possible postmodern answer to Virginia Woolf's *Orlando*.
Unlike this novel, which is a reaction to modernist ambivalence, Barth's text
reacts to postmodern indifference. It should be remembered that, in the
present context, indifference does not mean emotional indifference or non-
commitment, but the interchangeable character of social values.

The central modernist value that falls prey to postmodern pluralism and relativism is *art*. Placed at the top of the cultural hierarchy by Virginia Woolf and
Proust, it is considered by an author like Barth as just one possibility of filling
one's life with meaning. In many respects, *Lost in the Funhouse* can be read as
a parody of the artist novel in the sense of Joyce's *A Portrait of the Artist as a Young
Man* or of Thomas Mann's *Tonio Kröger* (a novella) and *Doctor Faustus*. To Barth's
narrator, art appears as a contingent social practice without any special aesthetic, moral or political authority.

Ambrose, the hero of the story, is a neurotic youth, psychologically comparable to Mann's Tonio Kröger or Joyce's Stephen. However, he differs from these
modernist characters and from Woolf's Orlando by his postmodern lack of
perspective, 'the unadventurous story of his life'[94] and the absence of modernist
religious, political or aesthetic utopias. The only perspective open to him is literature as a funhouse:

> He wishes he had never entered the funhouse. But he has. Then he wishes he
> were dead. But he's not. Therefore he will construct funhouses for others
> and be their secret operator – though he would rather be among the lovers
> for whom funhouses are designed.[95]

At the end of Barth's short story, literature no longer appears, as in Woolf's
*Orlando* or in Proust's *Recherche*, as the authentic value and the real life. It is a
game among others, comparable to tennis, ping-pong or football; it has ceased
to be a vocation in the religious, Proustian sense. Its norms and values cannot in
any way pretend to be superior to those of other social systems or subsystems.

Time and again, indifference becomes manifest in Barth's prose: 'Everything's finished. Name eight. Story, novel, literature, art, humanism, humanity,
the self itself.' The narrator adds: 'Wait, the story's not finished.'[96] However,
the story is just a game taking place between the reader and the author, the art-
ful constructor of postmodern funhouses, who knows all the ins and outs and
reacts to the stereotypes of literary history: 'The brown hair on Ambrose's
mother's forearms gleamed in the sun like. (. . .) The smell of Uncle Karl's cigar

smoke reminded one of.'[97] The comparisons and associations, which took up a lot of space in romanticism, realism and modernism, have become indifferent, interchangeable.

The author signals, not without irony, that even narrative events and sequences no longer matter because they have become interchangeable: 'Naturally he didn't have nerve enough to ask Magda to go through the funhouse with him. With incredible nerve and to everyone's surprise he invited Magda, quietly and politely, to go through the funhouse with him.'[98] What matters here, is not truth in the sense of realism or modernism,[99] but a self-reflecting, playful use of literary forms. This is what makes Barth's *Lost in the Funhouse* postmodern in the sense of the first type of text commented on above.

The involvement of this kind of postmodern literature in commercial culture is commented on by Joseph Tabbi in *Postmodern Sublime*:

There is no more pointed fictional meditation on commercial culture's cooptation of high postmodernism than Wallace's brilliant story 'Westward the Course of Empire Takes Its Way', which has John Barth (named 'Ambrose' after his most famous fictional persona) collaborating with the advertising director of McDonald's restaurants on a nationwide chain of 'Funhouse' discotheques.[100]

Unlike ambivalence, which, as an open dialectic, had a great critical potential, indifference tends towards social integration – in spite of its irony and its playful, anti-ideological stance.

## 4.3 Avant-garde, Popular Culture and Postmodern 'De-differentiation'

In order to understand the relationship between the avant-garde movements and postmodernity, it seems meaningful to start from two hypotheses: postmodern literary revolts (Félix de Azúa, Thomas Bernhard, Christoph Ransmayr) are neither modernist nor avant-garde because they lack revolutionary or utopian goals. In this respect, they differ from Brecht's Epic Theatre and from historical avant-garde movements such as surrealism, futurism (Marinetti *and* Khlebnikov) or Czech Poetism, all of which sought to bring about a cultural revolution in the wake of the political one. The second hypothesis aims at the heterogeneity of the modernist problematic. Only if one reduces modernism to one of its aspects – for example conservatism, formalism or autonomy aesthetics – can one postulate a contradiction between it and the avant-garde.

This is exactly what Douwe Fokkema does when, following Matei Calinescu, he argues that the 'modernist code (. . .) differs sharply from the coexisting code of Surrealism'.[101] It will be shown that, on closer examination, this contrast fades away because surrealism is part and parcel of the modernist problematic – in very much the same way as poetism and the futurist movements. (More recent work reveals to what extent modernism and the avant-garde movements form a coherent problematic.)[102]

Like Fokkema, but in a theoretical context inspired by the Frankfurt School, Peter Bürger believes that the avant-garde is a critique of the aesthetics of autonomy underlying modernist art. By sealing itself off from late capitalist communication, this kind of art condemns itself to silence and social irrelevance: 'The avant-garde protest, whose aim it is to reunite art with the practice of life, reveals the link between autonomy and a lack of social impact.'[103] The avant-garde can be considered as a self-criticism of art insofar as it is an attempt to make art return to daily life, where it was in the Middle Ages and even in the Renaissance when its autonomy was born. In some of its forms, modernist art carries this autonomy to extremes and produces works which break with society by formal hermeticism and a refusal of meaning and communication.

Avant-garde movements attempt to break out of this isolation by viewing art functionally as a social institution, from the outside as it were, and by trying to give it a revolutionary turn. At the same time, they perpetuate the hostility of aestheticism towards the bourgeois order.[104] Bürger goes one step further by linking the practical orientation of avant-garde art to referentiality: 'In the avant-garde work, the individual sign does not primarily refer to the work as a whole, but to reality.'[105] This semiotically naïve appraisal is primarily due to the fact that Bürger deals with art in general, considering Duchamps's *ready mades*, Breton's *Nadja* and Magritte's paintings within a single perspective. However, the idea that the oneirically organized text of *Nadja* is not a *secondary modelling system* in the sense of Lotman, but a message referring directly to the real world, is hardly plausible. At this point, Bürger's sociological explanation is called into question, especially since literature and painting are different semiotic systems which – as the Czech Structuralists and the Russian Formalists knew – ought to be dealt with by separate methods.

Developing his research on the avant-garde, Bürger interprets postmodern attempts to close the gap between highbrow and popular art as an 'irruption of the avant-garde problematic into the art of modernism'.[106] 'The taboos', he explains, 'which work-centred modernism established, are again called into question: unlike the modernism of the 1950s and 1960s, which was marked by aspirations towards the purity of the artistic medium, contemporary art is dominated by a drive towards impurity'.[107] On the whole, Bürger tends to identify literary modernism with 'purist modernism' which 'excludes the semantic component as an element incompatible with the purity of the aesthetic'.[108] Unfortunately, this definition seems more appropriate in the case of Dadaism or the 'transmental language' of Russian Futurism than in the case of 'classical' modernism as it appears in Thomas Mann's *Doctor Faustus* or in Proust's *Recherche* . . .

Here again, we are dealing with a one-sided and reductionist definition of modernism. This may be one reason why Bürger feels obliged to distinguish 'two modernities': 'However, this work-centred modernity could only become culturally dominant by accepting the repression of the other modernity that opposes it: the historical avant-garde movements.'[109] Could it not be that there is only one heterogeneous modernist problematic and that Bürger separates what ought to dialectically related? An answer to this question will be provided at the end of this discussion (cf. also Section 5.3).

At this stage, it should be remembered that Andreas Huyssen tries to develop some of Bürger's theses about the avant-garde by applying them to the North-American literary context. He shows to what extent literary modernism, which was institutionalized and canonized in post-war America, turned into a cultural hegemony of highbrow literature that was subsequently challenged by post-war avant-garde movements. He holds the view 'that American postmodernism of the Sixties can be read as a late but autonomous phase of those historical avant-garde movements which, in Europe, came to be suppressed in the age of Hitler and Stalin'.[110] He adds: 'Only in the United States could a recourse to the historical avant-gardes of Europe serve as a weapon against classical modernism as defined in the Anglo-Saxon world (. . .).'[111] What matters is the end of this sentence, for it shows that the new American avant-garde did not rebel against modernism as such, a fact confirmed by Huyssens himself,[112] but against one of its conservative strains which occupied the centre of the American literary scene in the 1960s. In order to round off the picture, Huyssens could have pointed out that it was precisely in the 1960s that one of the most prominent writers of critical modernism enjoyed immense popularity among American youth: Hermann Hesse.

Here again, it becomes clear that Bürger tends to confound a conservative brand of aesthetic modernism with the problematic as a whole and to deduce it from aestheticism, as Astradur Eysteinsson noticed in his lucid study:

> It may well be that Bürger can classify a great deal of aestheticist or symbolist literature under his concept of the 'organic' or 'classicist' work, but he gives us no good reasons to place the works of Joyce, Kafka, Pound, or other representative modernists within an aestheticist trajectory.[113]

It is a fact that the works of authors such as Hesse, Auden, Sartre, Lorca, Moravia, Céline and Heinrich Mann cannot possibly be subsumed under Bürger's concept of aesthetic (aestheticist?) modernism. For the Zola-reader Heinrich Mann, whose works nobody would wish to remove from the modernist library, wrote: 'The writers of France, who, from Rousseau to Zola, fought the powers that be, had an easy task: they had a people to rely on.'[114]

Whoever considers modernism, like Eysteinsson, Lethen and the author of this book, as a heterogeneous whole, will tend to present the relationship between modernism and the avant-garde in the following terms:

> In that case, 'modernism' is necessarily the broader term, while the concept of the 'avant-garde' has proven to enjoy a good deal of 'free play' *within* the

overall reach of modernism. At the same time, nothing that is modernist can escape the touch of the avant-garde.[115]

The avant-gardes appear in this context as 'more radical, norm-breaking aspects of modernism'[116] which will be discussed later in some detail.

A completely different theoretical stance is adopted by Scott Lash in conjunction with Bürger's thesis concerning the 'irruption of the avant-garde problematic into modern art'. He radicalizes this thesis by defining the avant-garde movements as postmodernist: 'I take the avant-garde of the 1920s to be postmodernist.'[117] The critique addressed to Bürger by Eysteinsson, namely that he does not analyse the manifestos and other key texts of the avant-gardes (of surrealism, futurism) could be repeated in the case of Scott Lash. 'Surrealist spokesperson André Breton'[118] is quoted once or twice after a certain Donald Kuspit; Marinetti, Khlebnikov and Nezval are missing altogether.

Nevertheless, Lash's way of looking at matters is stimulating because it casts light on three crucial aspects of the postmodernity-debate: the idea that, unlike modernist art, which obeys the law of differentiation, postmodern art is governed by the principle of de-differentiation; the complementary idea that, due to certain social changes, the postmodern public is also de-differentiated in the sense that the homogeneity of the late modern cultural scene (dominated by a cultivated bourgeoisie) is replaced by heterogeneity; finally, the idea that postmodern de-differentiation was first announced by avant-garde artists and Walter Benjamin, all of whom Lash subsumes under the concept of postmodernism. Let us begin with the last of these three ideas and return to the first and the second when the relationship between the avant-garde and popular culture becomes relevant.

Starting from Bürger's questionable premise that Adorno's aesthetic of artistic autonomy is hostile to the avant-garde (as if French Surrealists and Russian Futurists had not defended their aesthetic autonomy against the Marxists),[119] Scott Lash tries to explain the controversy between Adorno and Benjamin by referring to Adorno's modernism and Benjamin's 'break with a high modernist and auratic aesthetic'.[120] Apart from the fact that it does not make sense to call the aesthetics of Auden, Joyce, Svevo or Sartre 'auratic', Scott Lash seems to have overlooked the crucial point: the fact that Benjamin considers the 'destruction of the aura' as a late modern or modernist phenomenon to be found in Baudelaire's poetry: 'He [Baudelaire] named the price to be paid for the sensation of modernity: the destruction of the aura in the choc. He had to pay dearly for going along with this destruction. However, it is the law of his poetry.'[121]

In this situation, Lash could choose two ways of saving his argument. He could argue that Baudelaire was already a postmodern poet, thus fulfilling Eco's prophecy that an ever more generous definition of postmodernism might soon arrive at Homer. Fortunately, Lash does not do this, but instead opts for the plausible thesis according to which Baudelaire is a precursor of modernism: 'Baudelaire, arguably the godfather of aesthetic modernism (. . .)'.[122] He also avoids the second possibility of saving his argument by retreating to high modernism: he could argue that, although modernism owed its vigour to an urban and anti-auratic impulse, which tended towards the technical reproduction of art, it nevertheless embraced auratic autonomy – albeit at the beginning of the twentieth century. This argument would also be difficult to sustain because Scott Lash could not explain a modernist return to auratic art and because many authors of high modernism – Joyce, Svevo, Hesse, Céline, Sartre – cannot be understood within the framework of an auratic aesthetic of autonomy. In short, Lash's attempt to present Benjamin as a forerunner of postmodernism is ill-founded.

One should add that Benjamin cannot really be understood in this role: not only because he views the disappearance of the aura with 'nostalgia', as Adorno puts it, but also because his messianic perspective, his revolutionary attitude and his plea in favour of a proletarian theatre for children do not fit a one-dimensional postmodernity within which revolutionary consciousness appears as an anachronism.

However, it becomes clear at this stage why Scott Lash links Benjamin and the avant-garde to postmodernism: 'My point here is that the surrealists and Benjamin spoke of the destruction of the (modernist and auratic) distinction between art and life.'[123] Lash, who has a penchant for Marxism and a de-differentiated popular culture, needs precursors – *within the postmodern problematic* – who justify his rejection of an allegedly autonomist and elitist art in a Marxist and avant-garde context. Once again, modernism is thus one-sidedly pinned to an autonomist aesthetic and an elitist point of view.

Lash's alternative to this (somewhat fictive) modernism is: a de-differentiation of forms and styles and an orientation towards society and its popular culture. Again, Benjamin appears as his favourite point of reference: 'Benjamin's valuation of popular cultural products, which can envisage critique from an aesthetic dimension that is integral to the social, is consistent with a *post*modernist aesthetic.'[124] This kind of postmodernist aesthetic thrives, as was pointed out above, on the de-differentiation of the public and of the works of art: a social change welcomed by the Marxists of the 1960s and 1970s.

Lash starts from the idea that one of the reasons why the historical avant-garde failed was the homogeneity and the specialization of the art public in the interwar period. The 'post-industrial middle classes',[125] however, appear to him as culturally heterogeneous groupings which might appreciate the postmodern mixture of styles and postmodern intertextuality. But these groupings are all middle class and belong to what Lash himself calls the ' "Yuppified" post-industrial bourgeoisie'[126] which is notoriously indifferent to social criticism and averse to revolution.

Thanks to its ambivalence and its drive towards de-differentiation, postmodern art could also elicit a favourable response from the working-class and motivate its members to accept pluralism and tolerance: '(. . .) Then tolerance for other racial, ethnic, gender, and sexual identities on the part of working-class individuals is more likely, as well as perhaps willingness to work within an inevitably pluralist – if it is to prosper – left political culture.'[127] The question how this growing tolerance is to be related to Marx's and Benjamin's revolutionary project, which was not pluralist in nature, is not quite clear. However, Marx and Benjamin were not obliged to struggle with postmodern issues that seem to absorb all the energies of the British sociologist.

He probably has a point when, at the end of his sociological analyses, he distinguishes a conservative from a progressive postmodernity, associating the progressive brand with tolerance and pluralism (this idea would have been very useful in his critique of modernism which could also be divided into conservative and revolutionary strains). One will certainly agree with him whenever he emphasizes the domination of the exchange value and the omnipresence of reification in postmodern culture: 'Similarly postmodernization in a large measure represents the triumph of commodification not just in mass culture but in the previously auratic, and potentially critical, culture of elites.'[128]

Apologists of a postmodern popular culture do not consider reification and commodification when they deploy a pseudo-democractic rhetoric aiming at a reconciliation between elite and mass culture. Thus Leslie A. Fiedler exuberantly praises the marketing of art when he writes about American popular novelists: 'It is not compromise by the market place they fear; on the contrary, they choose the genre most associated with exploitation by the mass media: notably, the Western, Science Fiction, and Pornography.'[129] The fact that commercial publishers decide what is marketable and what isn't, that they dictate to their authors the approach to adopt and a market-oriented style based on stereotypes, does not seem to bother Fiedler.[130]

He stresses the subversive character of pop-art which he considers as 'a threat to all hierarchies'.[131] Unfortunately, he omits to tell us which social hierarchies have so far been broken up by pop-art in the USA: certainly not the hierarchies within the conformist trade unions; possibly some university hierarchies mocked by Fiedler because they had to accept that nowadays popular novels and pornography are being dealt with in seminars along with Mallarmé and Faulkner.

Jim Collins resumes Fiedler's argument when he defines postmodern art and literature as an experiment which does not aim at originality, but synthesizes incompatible aesthetics and styles: 'incorporates the heterogeneity of those conflicting styles'.[132] This heterogeneity of styles and texts corresponds to a de-differentiated postmodern public, and Collins seems to join Lash when he speaks of the 'fragmentation of a unitary public sphere into multiple reading publics'.[133]

It does not occur to Collins that this aesthetic and cultural plurality might merely be an *apparent plurality* organized by a versatile culture industry which endlessly varies ideological and commercial stereotypes. Following Fiedler, he stresses the critical and subversive character of mass culture: 'The desire to see mass culture texts and their decodings as expressions of contradiction, ambivalence, and all-purpose discontent marks a significant move away from the elitist denunciations of the Frankfurt School.'[134] Eventually, this rhetoric reveals its own theoretical flaws: for if mass-culture articulates an all-purpose discontent, it does not bring about any substantial change, neither in the consciousness of individuals nor within social institutions. On the contrary, it merely functions as a social emergency outlet (*Ventilsitte*, Simmel) and contributes to the stabilization of the social system as a whole. Nowhere does Collins show *what kind* of critical or subversive impact popular genres have – and on what groups.

Modernism and the avant-garde, which were opposed to each other by some of the authors commented on here, form a heterogeneous unit – described by A. Eysteinsson – because they are held together by their critical and utopian stance. As Aleksandar Flaker shows in *Poetika osporavanja* (*Poetics of Contradiction*),[135] their revolutionary project is partly rooted in romanticism to which the avant-garde movements owe some decisive impulses. Whenever Marcel Proust criticizes the rhetoric of conversation cultivated by the Faubourg Saint-Germain in Paris, he follows the same anti-bourgeois romantic impulse that makes itself felt in André Breton's manifestos of surrealism. The surrealist in turn joins the modernist whenever he invokes the romantics Nerval and E. T. H. Hoffmann, analyses the unconscious (Proust's *mémoire involontaire*) and defines man as an incorrigible dreamer : 'l'homme, ce rêveur définitif.'[136]

One such dreamer is Harry Haller in Hermann Hesse's *Steppenwolf*, and his dreams are – as was pointed out in the 1970s[137] – surrealist in character. This is amply illustrated by the 'Jolly Hunting. Great Automobile Hunt', an oneiric scene from the Magic Theatre, in which the 'simplest surrealist act' as described by André Breton (walking down the street and shooting aimlessly into the crowd) is practised on cars.

But Hesse, who in his novel experiments with a rapprochement between popular and highbrow culture, is not so much interested in spectacular gags and tricks, because he focuses on a critique of capitalist society quite similar to that of Critical Theory.

Right at the beginning of the novel, he mentions the depressing days of inner 'emptiness and despair, when, on this ravaged earth, sucked dry by the vampires of finance, the world of men and of so-called culture grins back at us with the lying, vulgar, brazen glamour of a Fair and dogs us with the persistence of an emetic (. . .)'. ('. . . jene argen Tage der inneren Leere und Verzweiflung, an denen uns, inmitten der zerstörten und von Aktiengesellschaften ausgesogenen Erde, die Menschenwelt und sogenannte Kultur in ihrem verlogenen und gemeinen blechernen Jahrmarktsglanz auf Schritt und Tritt wie ein Brechmittel entgegengrinst [. . .]'.)[138]

Whoever brackets out this modernist critique of a failing project of modernization, can only produce caricatures of modernism. The common goal of modernism, avant-garde and Critical Theory, which will be commented on in the next chapter, was to overcome the existing order. In some cases, it assumed aesthetic (Mallarmé, Proust, Breton), in other cases political (Auden, Spender, Aragon, Breton) or religious (Auden, Bernanos) dimensions.[139] In the last section of this chapter, it will be shown that this critical and utopian impulse, which cannot survive without a persistent search for meaning, disappears in postmodern literature and in the corresponding poststructuralist literary theories.

## 4.4  Postmodernism as Poststructuralism: Iterability, Aporia and Intertextuality

If the prefix 'post' were the only common denominator of postmodernity and poststructuralism, there would be no need to discuss this topic. However, a commentary seems to make sense because the prefix suggests in both cases that the metaphysical, religious, aesthetic or political search for meaning is a thing of the past. Following John Barth, who dismisses the metaphysical search embarked on by Virginia Woolf and other modernists, poststructuralist theoreticians such as Roland Barthes, Jacques Derrida or Paul de Man declare the hermeneutic and structuralist search for coherence and meaning to be an illusion. For them it is a logocentric prejudice that can only survive within rationalist and Hegelian metaphysical systems. At present, these systems appear as products of modernity whose foundations were shaken by modernist critiques and which have lost all credibility in the postmodern age.

In this context, Walter Benjamin indicates to what extent he adheres to the modern and modernist problematics when he remarks in an essay on Nikolai Lesskov: 'The "meaning of life" is in fact the centre around which the novel revolves.'[140] This statement may be applicable to Proust and possibly to Sartre, but it has no validity whatsoever in the case of Alain Robbe-Grillet. In a review of Robbe-Grillet's novels, Roland Barthes points out that in these texts, objects and individuals are described as 'being there' without questions being asked concerning their meaning, their *raison d'être*.[141] The Barthes of the late 1970s, a Nietzschean critic, who replaces the conceptual logos by playful associations of signifiers, is a kindred spirit of the *nouveau romancier* in the sense that he bids farewell to structuralist concepts such as 'system', 'meaning' and 'the signi-fied'[142] in order to replace them by a polysemic collusion of signifiers. He thus confirms the postmodern trend towards particularization that runs parallel to pluralization, de-differentiation and indifference.

In what follows, it will be shown how this postmodern trend manifests itself in Barthes's and Derrida's *signifiant*, Derrida's *itérabilité* and *différance*, J. Hillis Miller's *repetition* and G. H. Hartman's *intertextuality*, where it supersedes the structuralist question concerning a conceptually definable meaning. Completing the picture, Paul de Man's and J. Hillis Miller's notion of aporia will illustrate the link between particularity, pluralism and indifference. In all of these cases, Nietzsche appears as the philosopher who initiated the tendency towards particularization.

Commenting on Georges Bataille, Barthes remarks that the rhetoric of some-body like Ignatius of Loyola obeys rules that substantially differ from those of ordinary conceptual logic. He concludes: 'Whenever it is the body which writes, and not ideology, there's a chance the text will join us in our modernity.'[143] Starting from Nietzsche's idea that metaphysical truth, as defined and conse-crated by traditional philosophy, is in fact a camouflage of rhetoric, a 'mobile army of metaphors, metonymies, anthropomorphisms',[144] Barthes tries to take a look behind the conceptual scenes in order to find out what happens if one stops ignoring the uniqueness of phenomena, if one refrains from subsuming them under general concepts. He takes seriously Nietzsche's dictum: 'Each concept is due to our equating what is not equal. (. . .) Overlooking the indi-vidual and real yields the concept (. . .).'[145]

The result, at least in literary criticism, is a drastic revaluation of the signifier and the entire expression plane in the sense of Louis Hjelmslev.[146] It is not the conceptual message, defined as a structure of signifieds, that matters in the literary or even philosophical text, but the interaction of its signifiers which cannot be defined in conceptual terms. About Balzac's short novel *Sarrazine* Barthes writes in *S/Z* that it is '*a galaxy of signifiers*'[147] – and not a conceptual structure. This focus on the signifier and the 'expression plane' implies a radical particularization of literary theory insofar as the text as a universally perceptible, communicable and translatable conceptual structure is negated. Barthes is not interested in the structuralist question common to Jakobson and Greimas[148] how signifiers are to be related to signifieds, expressions to contents; instead he chooses to consider the phonetic level of the signifiers as the only 'truth' (or 'non-truth') of the text.

It is a 'non-truth' in the sense that Barthes deliberately brackets out Adorno's question concerning the *truth content* (*Wahrheitsgehalt*) of art and literature: 'The instance of the text is not signification but the signifier, in the semiotic and the psychoanalytic acceptation of that term (. . .).'[149] For Barthes, the psy-choanalytic aspect is crucial because the ambiguous and open text arouses aesthetic desire by its endless *significance*.

What matters in the present context, is the relationship between the particu-larity of the signifiers and the openness and plurality of the text. Unlike a rationalist structuralist such as Greimas, who investigates the hierarchy of semantic structures (isotopies)[150] within texts, unlike a Hegelian structuralist such as Goldmann, who believes that literary works are meaningful totalities based on collective visions of the world,[151] Barthes would like to know how the text functions as an *irreducible plurality of meanings*.[152] His pluralist approach contrasts with Greimas's semiotic analysis, especially since Greimas considers the plurality of meanings and interpretations prompted by some literary texts as an illusion.[153] He believes that this *apparent plurality* is due to superficial or partial reading. Contesting this point of view, Barthes insists on plurality as an intrinsic quality of art and literature: '(. . .) The work holds several meanings simultaneously, by its very structure, and not as a result of some infirmity in those who read it.'[154]

It becomes clear at this point why Manfred Frank believes that poststructuralism is in fact a neostructuralism[155]: because authors such as Barthes do not simply drop the concept of structure, but change it by a radical *particularization* and *pluralization*. In both cases, they continue and reinforce modernist tendencies, which can be observed in New Criticism and Russian Formalism, but which take on extreme forms in the postmodern problematic.

One might add that Barthes, who, in *Le Plaisir du texte*, stresses the erotic aspects of reading, not only develops a Dionysian aesthetic in the Nietzschean sense, but also extols the body as rediscovered by Foucault (cf. Chapter 3). 'The text is thus understood as a body which playfully interacts with the bodies of readers and writers alike,'[156] explains Ottmar Ette. In short: the orientation towards the human and the linguistic body, towards the phonetic unit, towards the desire and the pleasure of reading, contributes both to a better grasp of uniqueness and alterity and to a drastic particularization of the notions of language and text.

This particularization is even more pronounced in the case of Jacques Derrida, who can hardly be understood as a 'neostructuralist', because his approach leads to a dissolution of the concept of structure. Derrida's position between modernism and postmodernity, which was discussed at some length in the third chapter,[157] will not be commented on here. At this stage, it seems more important to say something about his two key concepts of *itérabilité* (*iterability*) and *différance* (*differance*) in conjunction with structuralism and the theory of literature. It will be shown that Derrida radicalizes Barthes's point of view by particularizing the notion of sign – thus deconstructing the very idea of structure.

What does Derrida's *general strategy of deconstruction* actually mean? To begin with, it means, as was pointed out in the third chapter, a systematic subversion of European metaphysics in the sense of Nietzsche and Heidegger – and especially a subversion of the concept of truth defined as *presence of meaning*. It means, more specifically: a decomposition of the semantic concept of structure by a particularization of the criteria used for the definition of this concept.

The problem can be illustrated by confronting Greimas's rationalist concept of *iterativity* (*itérativité*) with Derrida's concept of *iterability* (*itérabilité*). The semiotician starts from hermeneutic premises when he holds that different elements of a text are linked by common semantic markers and that it makes sense to analyse the repetition or recurrence of these markers. He calls these recurring markers, which guarantee textual coherence, *contextual semes* or *classemes* and demonstrates in various text analyses – for example in his book on Maupassant's short story *Deux Amis*[158] – how the recurrence of classemes brings about semantic structures or isotopies, that is *coherence*.

Greimas's disciples (e.g. Joseph Courtés and Jean-Claude Coquet) later applied the concept of *isotopy* systematically to fairy tales, poems and prose in order to show to what extent complementary concepts such as *classeme* could be used for constructing the coherence of texts. In his 'Systématique des isotopies', a thorough analysis of Mallarmé's short poem *Salut,* François Rastier presents a hierarchical outline of the poem's semantic structures and arrives at the conclusion that the text is dominated by the encompassing isotopy *écriture* or *writing* (that is its main topic is 'poetic writing' itself).[159]

One realizes how important *iterativity* (repetition) is for the concept of isotopy while reading the definition proposed by Greimas and Courtés: '*Iterativity (recurrence) on a syntagmatic level of classemes which guarantee the homogeneity of a discourse as utterance*'.[160] Thus iterativity as repeated occurrence of semantic markers or classemes guarantees textual coherence.

Derrida's post-structuralist attack aims at this central concept of repetition or iterativity. However, it is not in a critique of Greimasian structural semiotics, which he never commented on, but in a critical analysis of Austin's speech act theory and the ensuing controversy with John Searle that Derrida puts forward his thesis according to which *the repetition of a text element does not consolidate meaning, but leads to its disintegration.* He thus casts doubts on the basic principle of structural semiotics and of speech act theory which both agree on the postulate that the repetition or iterativity of a sign contributes to coherence and the constitution of meaning. Variation of meaning does not lead to its disintegration, but to its development.

It is on this idea that Derrida concentrates his criticism by defining (symmetrically to iterativity) semantic repetition as *iterability*: *as a permanent deviation from previous meanings, i.e. as a semantic shift leading to semantic disintegration.* In 'Signature, event, context', where Austin's theory of meaning is deconstructed, Derrida speaks of 'unities of iterability', of 'unities separable from their internal or external context, and separable from themselves, to the extent that the very iterability which constitutes their identity never permits them to be a unity of self-identity'.[161] In this passage, two crucial ideas come to the fore: the paradoxical idea that iterability, which is responsible for the destruction of meaning and identity, forms the very identity of the semantic units; the implicitly nominalist idea that repetition as iterability does not, as Austin and Greimas would have it, confirm the general, universal meaning of the text, but, on the contrary, leads to its particularization and pluralization, because the process of semantic shifting disavows the initial meaning.

In a critique of Jean-Pierre Richard's thematic approach (*thématologie*), Derrida sets out to prove that, in Mallarmé's poetry, the word *pli* (*fold*) does not constitute a coherent theme or topic, in spite of its numerous repetitions, because it assumes contradictory meanings which lack a common denominator.[162] What remains, at the end of the day, is the irreducible particularity of the signifier: 'the indefinite referral of signifier to signifier'[163] – or *différance*, as described in the third chapter.

The latter is an aspect of iterability insofar as it decomposes conceptual thought, leaving behind an open constellation of signifiers called *signifiance* by

Roland Barthes. Like Barthes, Derrida adheres to Nietzsche's already quoted maxim whenever he describes iterability: 'Overlooking the individual produces the concept.' The post-structuralists (as nominalists)[164] never overlook the individual and particular, but they might far too often neglect the concept.

In his numerous comments on British and American literature, the American deconstructionist J. Hillis Miller shows what the emphasis on the particular at the expense of the universal and the concept means in literary theory. Following Derrida and Deleuze, he starts from the assumption that the repetition of signs leads to the disintegration, not to the consolidation of meaning and coherence.

Very much like Gilles Deleuze (cf. Chapter 3), he distinguishes two sorts of repetition: Platonic and Nietzschean. Unlike Platonic repetition, which is akin to Greimas's rationalist principle of iterativity, because the reproduction of a sign or text element is viewed as a copy of the original, Nietzschean repetition is a radical particularization:

> The other, Nietzschean mode of repetition posits a world based on difference. Each thing, this other theory would assume, is unique, intrinsically different from every other thing. Similarity arises against the background of this 'disparité du fond'. It is a world not of copies but of what Deleuze calls 'simulacra' or 'phantasms'.[165]

Theory turns into a Sisyphean project if it yields to this extreme particularism and nominalism which implies that each object 'is unique'. How could physicists, chemists and biologists classify natural phenomena if this were the case? Or do Miller's statements apply exclusively to literature?

In Miller's own analyses, the following contradiction comes to light: on the one hand, he assembles, classifies texts and text elements, but, on the other hand, he tries to prove that what we witness are pseudo-classifications because difference is the dominant factor – and not identity. Unlike natural scientists, who can rely on empirical tests in order to exclude an element as a pseudo-element from a particular class of phenomena, literary critics depend on interpretations whenever the question of similarity or disparity crops up. Miller invariably opts for disparity, in spite of choosing examples which, in the eyes of many readers, illustrate iterativity in the sense of structural semiotics. (The question remains: What are his *criteria* of classification?)

In a long analysis of Thomas Hardy's novel *Tess of the d'Urbervilles*, he lists a vast array of red elements that appear in the course of the narrative and contain *classemes* (Greimas) such as violence, sexuality and literary writing:

> the red ribbon in Tess's hair; her mouth (. . .); those red lips with which she says the characteristic 'ur' sound of her dialect; the strawberry that Alec forces her to eat; the rose that Alec gives her, with which she pricks her chin (. . .); the 'piece of blood-stained paper' (. . .).[166]

Miller mentions quite a number of other semantic units, which cannot be quoted here, and even suggests that Nietzschean and Platonic repetitions are intertwined in Hardy's novel. He nevertheless rejects the structuralist notion of semantic coherence because he believes that, in the case of Hardy, repetition is always accompanied by difference and because 'the difference is as important as the repetition'.[167] However, this is neither new nor revolutionary from a structuralist point of view. A structuralist would simply argue that the text is polysemic (i.e. combines heterogeneous isotopies, Greimas) – or that Miller is a partial or superficial reader.

Miller, however, is not interested in discovering polysemies or contradictions any semiotician is aware of, but in the deconstructionist idea that literary and non-literary texts, apart from being contradictory, are aporetic: 'Each reading culminates in an experience of the unreadability of the text at hand. The text hovers between two or more logically incompatible readings.'[168] This 'aporetic' view of the text was first presented by the Belgian-American deconstructionist Paul de Man, whose work – as was shown in Chapter 3 – not only aims at a rhetorical particularization of theoretical concepts, but in addition to that confirms postmodern indifference by foregrounding aesthetic aporias as negations of meaning.

As a Nietzschean, de Man is a thinker of extreme ambivalence which tends towards 'indifference' as '*Wesensgleichheit*' (cf. Chapter 1). If one makes truth depend on error, as de Man (following Nietzsche and Baudelaire) does, arguing that the essence of truth is error, one turns the word 'truth' into a meaningless signifier: '(. . .) If truth is the recognition of the systematic character of a certain kind of error, then it would be fully dependent on the prior existence of this error.'[169] This implies that, from a deconstructionist point of view, all efforts to distinguish truth from error – genetically or logically – are based on metaphysical illusions.

In one respect, Paul de Man's analyses of philosophical and literary texts are quite clear. Time and again, they explain to the reader why aesthetic truth in the sense of Adorno's *truth content* (*Wahrheitsgehalt*) does not exist: if in every text two equally valid, but incompatible meanings compete for recognition by the reader, meaning as coherence in the hermeneutic or structuralist sense becomes null and void.

In *Allegories of Reading*, de Man comments on a poem by Yeats (*Among Schoolchildren*), interpreting it as an allegory of its own unreadability. The questions at the end of the poem, he argues, cannot be answered because they are undecidable:

O chestnut tree, great rooted blossomer,
Are you the leaf, the blossom or the bole?
O body swayed to music, O brightening glance,
How can we know the dancer from the dance?

De Man asserts that these final questions can be answered both rhetorically (it is impossible to decide) and literally (it is necessary to decide). The meaning is undecidable, aporetic, and the poem, which is not considered by de Man in its entirety, turns out to be unreadable:

> The two readings have to engage each other in direct confrontation, for the one reading is precisely the error denounced by the other and has to be undone by it. Nor can we in any way make a valid decision as to which of the readings can be given priority over the other; none can exist in the other's absence.[170]

The indifference underlying this strategy of aporia is due to the fact that the two incompatible meanings are equally valid, equally 'true', thereby turning the question concerning the truth content of the poem into an absurdity.

However, this is not de Man's worry because he sees theory not as a conceptual discourse furthering knowledge, but as literature about literature, as rhetoric: 'Literature as well as criticism – the difference between them being delusive – is condemned (or privileged) to be forever the most rigorous and, consequently, the most unreliable language in terms of which man names and transforms himself.'[171] The apparently paradoxical expression 'the most rigorous and (. . .) the most unreliable language' is not empty rhetoric, but hints at the extreme particularization which leads, both in Derrida and de Man, to a nominalistic hyper-precision of language and terminology. Unlike in analytic philosophy, whose proximity to deconstruction is a topic of discussion,[172] this tendency towards precision induces Derrida and de Man to seek refuge in rhetoric. It is hardly surprising, therefore, that de Man, Hartman and other deconstructionists efface the difference between theory and literature.

Geoffrey H. Hartman in particular does not hesitate to assimilate theoretical discourse to the literary in an intertextual experiment that is reminiscent of Derrida's *Glas*. He favours a 'playful poetics'[173] inspired by Barthes's Nietzschean approach to the text. 'Is criticism finding its own style at last?'[174] – he asks and suggests that criticism, which should not be confused with literary theory, ought to regain the kind of creativity it knew in the romantic era when the critic was defined as the author's double. 'Make criticism creative'[175] is a fair summary of his programme. This mimetic assimilation of theory to literary discourse is – as with Barthes and de Man – an aspect of postmodern particularization and a negation of modern and modernist conceptual universalism.

Unlike late modern thinkers such as Lukács, Adorno or Goldmann, who linked truth-oriented theories to the struggle for a better society and a better future, the poststructuralists deploy a playful or tragic (aporetic) rhetoric in which the search for meaning and truth appears as an anachronism. It falls prey to the ambivalent nexus of particularism, pluralism, tolerance and indifference also observed by Peter Tepe: 'In this respect, radical pluralism shows a tendency towards indifference.'[176]

However, the penchant of the post-structuralists for particularization, pluralism and indifference as interchangeability of meanings cannot be found in the texts of Proust, Rilke, Dickens or George Eliot the post-structuralists comment on. For it is not difficult to show that what mattered most to these authors was meaning and truthfulness. The penchant in question can best be understood as a reaction to the postmodern problematic in which the values that inspired the realist and modernist search for truth and utopia lose their attraction. Many postmodern works bear witness to this process of devaluation by rejecting the metaphysical search for meaning or by parodying it.

Chapter 5

# From Modern to Postmodern Literature: Ambivalence, Indifference and Ideology

This very title announces a 'metanarrative' which is bound to irritate not only readers of Lyotard, but also French, Italian and Spanish readers, who are used to other constructions of 'modernity', 'modernism' (*modernismo*) and 'postmodernity'.* While the concept of modernity, as defined by Walter Benjamin, Theodor W. Adorno (*Moderne*) and in current German debates, overlaps in many respects with British and North-American concepts, as Eysteinsson already pointed out,[1] the word *modernismo* takes on somewhat different meanings in Spanish and South American discussions. It refers to literary innovations by authors such as Rubén Darío, José Martí or Juan Ramón Jiménez around 1900 (cf. Chapter 1).[2] In the Italian context, it was, until recently, used to describe religious innovations within Catholicism.[3] As *modernisme*, it seems to be virtually absent from French literary debates, where even the word 'post-modernism' rarely crops up. While new publications about 'postmodernism' and 'postmodernity' keep Anglo-American debates going, most French contri-butions to the discussion (at least in the 1980s and 90s) originated in Quebec – and not in France.[4] Compared with the avalanche of Anglo-American publications, even Italian comments on postmodernism appear as a *quantité négligeable*, espe-cially since relatively few of them refer to literature.[5]

This does not mean, of course, that there is no Spanish, Italian or French literary style which could be called 'postmodern' within the construction pro-posed here. But it does seem to confirm the hypothesis that all constructions of the social and cultural sciences are co-determined by ideologies and cultures.[6] The construction underlying the fourth chapter, for example, is partly a prod-uct of Critical Theory, partly a result of Anglo-American and German debates about modernity, modernism (late modernity) and postmodernity. In this respect, it is culturally specific and hence cannot be applied universally, that is across cultures, like physical concepts or Avogadro's theses about changes in the volumes of gases (1811). In China and Korea, for example, it may be valid only insofar as European and North-American terminology was taken over by

---

* All quotations from foreign *literary* texts are given both in translation and in the original version (in brackets). Whenever official translations are not quoted, the author has translated the text himself.

some intellectuals in these countries and applied to aesthetic phenomena in their respective cultures.[7]

These considerations justify neither a general distrust of concepts or constructions such as 'modernism', 'postmodernity', 'ambivalence' and 'indifference' nor a surrender to relativism. For even Freud's concept of the 'unconscious', Karl Popper's construction of the 'three worlds'[8] and literary terms like 'romanticism', 'naturalism', 'aestheticism' or 'Vorticism' are neither objective nor applicable across cultures. Nevertheless, we should not want to miss them – especially since we suspect that their elimination would entail an impoverishment of our debates.

The thesis of the fourth chapter, according to which *the transition from modernism to postmodernity brings about a concomitant shift from ambivalence to indifference*, implies that the latter becomes the dominant feature of the new problematic. Yet it should not be taken to mean that all contemporary works are exclusively structured by indifference and that the *ambiguity of realism* and the *ambivalence of modernism* disappear without trace.

Nor should it be interpreted as a value judgement in the sense of literary criticism. The idea that novels such as Pynchon's *Gravity's Rainbow*, Robbe-Grillet's *Dans le labyrinthe* or Ransmayr's *Die letzte Welt* are structured by the principle of indifference does not mean that they are less valuable than novels of modernism or realism such as Thomas Mann's *Königliche Hoheit* or Dickens's *Hard Times*.

However, it is not literary criticism that is at stake here, but a critical theory of literature which has abandoned the illusions of positivist objectivism and of value-freedom (M. Weber).[9] In spite of its social engagement, it will focus on its descriptive and explicatory tasks. It will not follow George Lukács, Leo Kofler, Terry Eagleton and other Marxists who tend to condemn avant-garde and postmodern literary experiments in the name of prescriptive aesthetics or – in the case of Lukács and Kofler – of a dogmatic theory of realism.

In a first step, one should follow Croce and Adorno and try to understand each work as a unique phenomenon and an experiment that cannot be repeated. For writers do not struggle with language and style in order to illustrate realism or postmodernity, but in order to answer a possibly timeless question: 'How can I write in the present social, linguistic and literary situation?' It is obvious that the answers of experimental writers such as Thomas Pynchon, Alain Robbe-Grillet or Jürgen Becker will differ substantially from those of Umberto Eco or John Fowles who aim at a readable style. It is nevertheless true that a literary theory, which gives up general historical or sociological concepts and the corresponding explanations, falls prey to a blind nominalism. This is amply illustrated by some critiques of Croce's aesthetics.[10] A critical theory will continue to explain collective, historical phenomena and to answer questions related to the evolution of literary genres.

Even if such questions do not focus on the aesthetic value of individual works, because the theoretician is primarily concerned with understanding and explaining literary facts, they are not devoid of value judgements. For such judgements and critiques of society are inherent in the semantic, syntactic and narrative structures of theoretical discourse which differ from theory to theory: from Marxism to psychoanalysis, from Critical Rationalism to deconstruction. The history of literature 'from ambiguity to ambivalence and from ambivalence to indifference' is based on the narrative structure of Adorno's and Horkheimer's Critical Theory according to which late capitalist society is gradually trans- formed into an economic society in which the survival of culture, art and even theory is becoming increasingly uncertain.

This means that postmodernity is criticized in the perspective of modernism or late modernity and not the other way round, as in the case of Zygmunt Bauman (cf. Section 2.1). For Critical Theory is, in all its forms, a late modern critique of modernity which cannot be assimilated to deconstruction or to Lyotard's postmodern thought – in spite of certain postmodern elements in Adorno's negative dialectic. Hence the theoretical narrative 'from ambiguity to indifference' ought to be read as a late modern critique of postmodernity. But insofar as Critical Theory is a radical and particularizing critique of modernity and an anticipation of some fundamental postmodern arguments advanced by Derrida and Lyotard, it favours a dialogical approach in which a term like 'indifference' expresses scepticism rather than outright rejection. It will appear that very different postmodern writers such as Christoph Ransmayr, Thomas Bernhard and Félix de Azúa tend to confirm this scepticism by their revolts against the contemporary social order.

## 5.1 Modernist Literature and Ambivalence: Between Nietzsche and Freud

It could probably be shown that ambivalence as a dialectical unity of opposites without (Hegelian) synthesis, as a coincidence of incompatible values (*ambo-valor*) and as an interaction of incompatible emotions (*ambi-valentia*) in the psycho- analytic sense, is the principle underlying both Nietzsche's philosophy and Freud's psychology. In the third and the fourth chapter, it was argued that Nietzsche was highly critical of Hegelianism and developed a discourse struc- tured by a coincidence of opposites which negates Hegel's synthesizing *Aufhebung* and at the same time subverts all established epistemological, ethical and aesthetic contrasts 'beyond good and evil'.

The subversive force of Nietzschean discourse makes itself felt whenever two extremes that are kept apart by common sense coincide. Walter Benjamin's remarks about the 'idea' are reminiscent of Nietzsche's way of thinking: 'The representation of an idea cannot be considered a success as long as the circle of its possible extremes has not been marked out.'[11] This is a Young Hegelian and modernist argument *par excellence* because it is based on the ambivalent principle according to which good and evil, reason and madness, hedonism and asceticism are inseparable. Only rationalists and metaphysicians continue to adhere to rigid separations based on the assumption that rationalism and irrationalism, love and hatred, restraint and dissipation are quite unrelated.

In Nietzsche's thought, not only contrasting concepts, but the corresponding semantic compounds, which conventional thought keeps apart, are interlinked: growth and decline, truth and lie, misanthropy and love, pleasure and pain are for ever interwoven. Thus times of social ascendancy appear at the same time as times of decline: 'The fact is that each period of growth involves an immense *disintegration* and *decline*: the suffering and the symptoms of degeneration *belong* to periods of tremendous progress (. . .).'[12] Truth and lie merge in Nietzsche's discourse and turn into an ambivalent unit when Nietzsche points out with an anti-Platonic and anti-Hegelian undertone: 'The "apparent" world is the only one: the "true" world is an *added lie* (. . .).'[13] Like the truth-seeking philosopher, who is unmasked as a liar, the misanthropist is discovered to be a secret lover of humanity: 'Misanthropy is the consequence of an exaggerated love of humans, of "loving cannibalism" (. . .).'[14] Such considerations are to be found in virtually all of Nietzsche's works. They announce the emerging world of psychoanalysis, in which love and hatred, Eros and Thanatos, sadism and masochism form ambivalent totalities.

Even the relationship between patient and analyst is ambivalent because the transfer involves love and hatred simultaneously: 'Transfer is ambivalent, it encompasses positive, tender and negative, hostile attitudes towards the analyst, who usually occupies the position of a parent, the father or the mother.'[15] What analysis reveals is also marked by ambivalence. Thus it can be shown that children's love of their parents is contaminated by hatred as soon as a child begins to compete in sexual matters with the father or the mother. Freud speaks of 'emotional ambivalence'.[16]

He defines the latter in conjunction with Eugen Bleuler's research[17] as an affective oscillation between love and hatred and takes the somewhat unusual view that the emotional double-bind that marks all of childhood keeps reappearing later on, especially in the libidinal economy of the neurotic. Moreover, Freud believes that ambivalence is a transcultural and transhistorical factor that cuts across phases of social and cultural development and can also be found in archaic societies.[18]

This train of thought casts light on the structural role of ambivalence in Freud's own discourse. For Freud does not only apply this concept to archaic myths and totemistic societies,[19] but also to the development of major world religions: for example when he argues that originally God and Devil formed a whole.[20]

It is not so much the anthropological or theological question whether this hypothesis is correct that matters here, but the idea that Freud – like Nietzsche – writes within the modernist problematic in which, as Marx puts it, money reconciles the opposites and links the extremes (cf. Chapter 1).

In the eighteenth century, and even in the first half of the 19th, when Jane Austen and Honoré de Balzac succeeded in revealing the true character of their often ambiguous protagonists, thus making the Hegelian essence appear behind the appearance,[21] *ambiguity*, not ambivalence was the key problem. Gradually, the latter moved to the centre of philosophical, sociological and literary debates, when it became increasingly difficult, in a highly developed market society, to define quality and to tell real value from exchange value.

This problem is located in a social context by Thomas Mann who makes his narrator Felix Krull, temporarily a waiter in a classy hotel, point out that the culturally sanctioned contrast between servant and lord is due to chance and that an exchange of roles is always conceivable. While observing the fashionable society of the hotel restaurant, Mann's hero suddenly realizes that social roles are interchangeable:

> With a change of clothes and make-up, the servitors might often just as well have been the masters, and many of those who lounged in the deep wicker chairs, smoking their cigarettes, might have played the waiter. It was pure accident that the reverse was the fact, an accident of wealth; for an aristocracy of money is an accidental and interchangeable aristocracy. (Den Anzug, die Aufmachung gewechselt, hätten sehr vielfach die Bedienenden ebensogut Herrschaft sein und hätte so mancher von denen, welche, die Zigarre im Mundwinkel, in den tiefen Korbstühlen sich rekelten – den Kellner abgeben können. Es war der reine Zufall, daß es sich umgekehrt verhielt – der Zufall des Reichtums; denn eine Aristokratie des Geldes ist eine vertauschbare Zufallsaristokratie.)[22]

The difference between servants and lords can be deconstructed because the idea of 'interchangeability' subjects the two apparently incompatible classes of individuals to ambivalence. Within this setup, the lord no longer owes his identity to unalterable cultural qualities, but to the exchange value and the market. Following Nietzsche, one could go one step further and consider the two social roles as being identical, indifferent or *wesensgleich*.

Mikhail Bakhtin was the first to relate ambivalence to the subversion of values and value hierarchies in carnival and carnival-inspired literature from Rabelais and Cervantes to Dostoevsky. In his book on Dostoevsky, he refers to the 'carnival ambivalence'[23] of Mann's *Felix Krull* and, in conjunction with Dostoevsky's work, he speaks of 'the profound ambiguity, even multiple ambiguity, of every phenomenon'.[24] He deduces all of these aspects of the novel from the popular tradition of carnival which reaches its climax in the late Middle Ages or in early Renaissance and later on reappears as 'carnivalization' (as subversion of hierarchies, re-evaluation of values, ambivalence, masquerade and polyphony) in modern literature. Dostoevsky's novels are interpreted in this context as products of a subversive aesthetic which is incompatible with political domination and monologue: 'By *relativizing* all that was externally stable, set and ready-made, carnivalization with its pathos of change and renewal permitted Dostoevsky to penetrate into the deepest layers of man and human relationships.'[25]

It seems nevertheless difficult to establish a direct link between carnival as a popular feast of the late Middle Ages and Dostoevsky's or Thomas Mann's modernist novels. This difficulty may account for the fact that Bakhtin explains carnivalesque elements in Mann's novels by hinting at 'the powerful influence of Dostoevsky'.[26] However, it seems hardly possible to make the Russian novelist's influence responsible for all carnivalesque aspects of modernism, for its ambivalence and polyphony. For all of these are collective cultural phenomena which cannot be reduced to the influence of an individual writer. Considering what has been said so far, especially in conjunction with the passage from Thomas Mann's *Felix Krull* quoted above, Bakhtin's 'carnival' should be read as a *metaphor for the exchange value and for market laws*. In this perspective, the subversion of hierarchies appears – together with ambivalence and the mask – as a consequence of the kind of interchangeability evoked by Mann's narrator.

Bakhtin's descriptions of ambivalence in Dostoevsky's novels are completed by Freud's remarks on the Russian writer's bisexual character: 'A strongly bisexual disposition thus becomes one of the conditions or confirmations of neurosis. It can certainly be presupposed in Dostoevsky's case (. . .).'[27] It is not Freud's psychoanalytic interpretation of Dostoevsky's life and work that matters here (Freud's tendency towards biographical reductionism should be criticized), but ambivalence as an almost omnipresent semantic element which also structures the modernist, Nietzschean discourse of psychoanalysis.

This structural element is at the same time one of the salient features of modernist novels, dramas and novellas (cf. Chapter 4). The modernist novel could be read as a text in which Nietzsche's and Freud's discoveries concerning the latent links between incompatible values and apparently irreconcilable emotions are dealt with ironically and projected into the fictional context.

Musil seems to continue Nietzsche's train of thought when he describes modern literature as a world dominated by the *coincidence of opposites*: 'This conviction that human phenomena are linked and that moral opposites are closely related can very well be considered as a distinctive trait of contemporary literature in contrast with the literatures of earlier ages.'[28] The fact that the modernist writer himself considers the literature of his time as a universe structured by ambivalence and that his assessment confirms the hypotheses underlying this book, does not prove anything conclusively, but it is an important point of reference which reappears in some works on Nietzsche and Musil.[29]

It is not by chance that in Musil's *The Man Without Qualities*, a novel structured by ambivalence on all levels, Freud's notion of bisexuality is incarnated in androgynous characters, especially in the posthumously published fragments, where Clarisse appears as the hermaphrodite: 'Clarisse whispered in a hoarse voice: "I am not a woman, Lindner! I am the Hermaphrodite!"'[30] In this context, Arthur Schnitzler's *Dream Story* (*Traumnovelle*, 1926: originally entitled *Doppelnovelle* or *Double Novella*) should also be mentioned because it is riddled with enigmatic, ambivalent characters leading a life between wake and dream, between enlightened consciousness and a nocturnal unconscious.[31]

Ambivalence in the psychological and psychoanalytic sense seizes the subject and makes its identity vacillate. This is one of the main topics of D. H. Lawrence's novels and novellas, some of which put the divisions and internal conflicts that threaten the unity of the individual subject at the centre of the scene. One is reminded of Virginia Woolf's *Orlando* when reading in Lawrence's *The Virgin and the Gipsy*: 'Man or woman is made up of many selves. With one self she loved this gipsy man. With many selves she ignored him or had a distaste for him.'[32] In the following sections, it will be shown how the unity of opposites, the crisis of the subject and the crisis of the modernist novel are intertwined.

## 5.2  Linguistic Aspects of Ambivalence

The carnivalesque coincidence, which suddenly overthrows all value hierarchies, characterizes virtually all modernist novels and modernism as a whole. One of its consequences is that the dominant values, which are usually the values of the dominant groups, are tied up with negative factors and thus discredited. Where the sublime and the ridiculous, the lofty and the trivial, the holy and the profane, the noble and the vulgar are wedded, a socially explosive mixture comes about which provokes laughter (as in Bakhtin's case) or furious reactions among the guardians of official culture. The global result can be a kind of collective disorientation leading to the subject's (the actor's, the narrator's, the reader's) incapacity to opt for or against certain sets of values, because it is unable to identify unambiguously with any one of them.

This lack of orientation, that undermines the subject's stance, is one of the salient features of Céline's novel *Journey to the End of the Night* (*Voyage au bout de la nuit*, 1932), a strongly carnivalized text in which ambivalence results from the mediation of culture by the exchange value – the negation of all values from Céline's point of view. The bank is turned into a church whose representatives proclaim the divine omnipotence of the dollar:

> When the faithful enter a bank, don't think that they can help themselves as they please. Far from it. In speaking to Dollar, they mumble words through a little grill; that's their confessional. (Quand les fidèles entrent dans leur Banque, faut pas croire qu'ils peuvent se servir comme ça selon leur caprice. Pas du tout. Ils parlent à Dollar en lui murmurant des choses à travers un petit grillage, ils se confessent quoi.)[33]

Unlike in postmodern texts, where carnivalization as an aspect of the exchange value is acknowledged with indifference or laughter, it provokes a scandal in modernism, where the search for the true religious, political or aesthetic value is still taken seriously.

This scandal erupts in all its violence in Alberto Moravia's short novel *La disubbidienza*, where the main protagonist Luca is taught to pray kneeling on a medieval prie-dieu facing the reproduction of one of Raffaelo's portraits of the Madonna. Behind the holy picture, Luca's parents have hidden their safe, their real, bourgeois sanctuary. When Luca finally discovers the camouflage, he reacts with indignation to the sacrilege: 'And you, why did you, for so many years, make me kneel and pray before your money?' ('E voi perché mi avete fatto pregare tanti anni inginocchiato davanti al vostro denaro?')[34]

The carnivalistic ambivalence of modernism is not merely destructive, but contains, like Céline's text, a critique of ideology. The latter is omnipresent in Jaroslav Hašek's work which had quite an impact on Bertold Brecht's modernist realism. Both authors make religion appear as an ideology by inserting it in a carnivalistic context, thus revealing its ambivalence and exposing it to the laughter of the reading public. In Hašek's satirical novel *The Adventures of the Good Soldier Shvejk*, the camp service, celebrated by the Jewish convert and army chaplain Katz, appears as a carnivalesque event which culminates in a somewhat unorthodox sermon inspired by alcohol rather that by evangelical zeal. It contains a lot of nonsense followed by unusual prayers and unheard of rites invented *ad hoc* by Katz among the half-suppressed laughter of his young audience.[35]

Analogous scenes can be found in Brecht's Epic Theatre, where war and religion are not so much associated with alcohol, but with the true interests of emperors, kings and popes who perpetuate the armed conflict in order to achieve their political goals. In a particularly characteristic scene, where Mother Courage complains to the army chaplain, because she fears that the end of the war could put an end to her business (she sells food to the troops), the chaplain consoles her saying that the emperor, the kings and the pope will see to it that the war continues, so that it can be expected to have 'a prosperous future' ('ein langes Leben').[36] In Hašek's case, the profane and the holy are joined together provoking shock and laughter; in Brecht's case, the apparently peace-keeping religion, represented by the pope, turns out to be a war ideology.

In some other cases, carnivalesque ambivalence is linked to an effect of estrangement used by modernist literature to break up ideology and make the public adopt a critical stance: not only in Brecht's Epic Theatre, where this effect is frequently brought about by polemical songs, critical comments and interruptions of action, but also in Kafka's novel *The Trial* (*Der Prozeß*, 1925), where the ambivalent figure of *Iustitia* appears as a goddess of hunting.[37] In the same modernist context, dying and death are linked in Rilke's *The Notebooks of Malte Laurids Brigge* (*Aufzeichnungen des Malte Laurids Brigge*, 1910) to modern methods of mass production:

This excellent hotel is very ancient; already in the time of King Clovis people were dying here, in a few beds. Now there are 559 beds to die in. Like a factory, of course. With production so enormous, each individual death is not made very carefully; but that isn't important. It's the quantity that counts. (Dieses ausgezeichnete Hôtel ist sehr alt, schon zu König Chlodwigs Zeiten starb man darin in einigen Betten. Jetzt wird in 559 Betten gestorben. Natürlich fabrik- mäßig. Bei so enormer Produktion ist der einzelne Tod nicht so gut ausge- führt, aber darauf kommt es auch nicht an. Die Masse macht es.)[38]

What matters on a theoretical level, is the idea that in modernism carnivaliza- tion and aesthetic estrangement do not lead to indifference (like in postmoder- nity), but to a critique of ideology accompanied by an often utopian search for the authentic set of values. In the case of Hašek, social criticism pursues the goal of national liberation, Brecht's critique unfolds within a Marxist metanar- rative, Musil's search is utopian in many ways, and Kafka's search is a quest for the true life, metaphorically referred to as 'the Law'. It will appear that in Proust's *Recherche* all ambivalences are set aside as soon as, in *Time Regained* (*Le Temps retrouvé*), the true contrast between art and life comes to light, elimi- nating all doubts and confirming literature as the authentic value and the real goal of life.

In other words: in modernism, carnivalization, ambivalence and polysemy are not ends in themselves, but are subordinated to an encompassing ideologi- cal and metaphysical search, which, in the case of Proust, Brecht, Hašek and the young Sartre, takes on the form of a teleology, but in other cases (Céline, Svevo or Camus) turns out to be a search without a *telos*. Most striking is the ideologi- cal heterogeneity of modernism which will be commented on later on: Kafka's 'Law' is among the utopias of modernist literature as much as Mallarmé's and Proust's 'Literature', Hašek's national liberation and Brecht's socialism.

*Ambivalence* and *polysemy* are dealt with in the modernist text by an *agnostic narrator* who is confronted by a multi-layered, contradictory and interpretable world and hence obliged to consider his narratives not as mimetic representa- tions of reality, but as constructs. Sartre's novel *La Nausée* is a model of this constructivist approach within which narration itself turns into a problem:

This is what fools people: a man is always a teller of tales, he lives surrounded by his stories and the stories of others, he sees everything that happens to him through them; and he tries to live his life as if he was recounting it. – But you have to choose: to live or to recount. (C'est ce qui dupe les gens: un homme, c'est toujours un conteur d'histoires, il vit entouré de ses histoires et des histoires d'autrui, il voit tout ce qui lui arrive à travers elles; et il cherche à vivre sa vie comme s'il la racontait. – Mais il faut choisir: vivre ou raconter.)[39]

In this context, one understands why Sartre blames the Catholic realist François Mauriac for endowing his narrator with divine omniscience and for refusing, both in *Thérèse Desqeyroux* and *La Fin de la nuit*, to *reflect* upon the contingent character of the narrator's point of view.[40]

The modernist awareness of the relativity and the contingency of the narrator is not only a critical asset, because it negates ideological claims to absolute
knowledge, but also a discursive problem, because it undermines the narrative
competence of the subject. In view of an ambivalent, multiple reality, in which
even the ego is no longer definable, so that Svevo's narrator can ask 'Am I good
or bad?' ('Ero io buono o cattivo?'),[41] authors such as Proust and Musil question the very possibility of narration. 'Should I make it into a novel, a philosophical study, am I a novelist?'[42] – asks Proust in one of his posthumously
published *Cahiers*. Musil comes up against similar problems in his notes on *Der
Mann ohne Eigenschaften*, a novel in which the crisis of narration becomes one of
the main topics: '?Paradox: to write the novel which it is impossible to write'.[43]

Elsewhere he explains why a mimetic narrative in the sense of realism has
become impossible in literary modernism:

> Of course, the problem first crops up with the rise of the novel. In the epic
> poem and even in a truly epic novel, character is a result of action. That is to
> say that characters were more firmly embedded in actions, because the latter
> were less ambiguous.[44]

In conjunction with the model proposed here, Musil might say that, in the
epic novels of realism, ambiguity could still be dissolved; ambivalence, however,
cannot be overcome, because opposites such as *good* and *evil, truth* and *lie appear*
as equally true or valid in the light of modernism. The scale of values underlying realism and its system of differentiation have fallen apart.

Proust's *Recherche*, which can be read as a long search for the authentic difference and the true value system, shows to what extent the modernist narrator
regrets the disintegration of this system. In a critique of the Paris leisure
class, which does not recognize a stable 'qualitative difference' ('la différence
qualitative'),[45] the narrator wonders where this difference might be. His search
is a metaphysical quest *par excellence* which moves towards a metaphysical goal –
in spite of the narrator's almost obsessive analyses of the innumerable ambivalences (of characters, actions, remarks) the novel is saturated with. Finally, the
author ends the search when he makes his narrator proclaim that Literature is
the only true reality and the real goal of life: 'Real life, life at last laid bare and
illuminated (. . .)' ('La vraie vie, la vie enfin découverte et éclaircie [. . .])'.[46]

But there is no reason to believe that Literature and Art are the supreme
social values and to postulate a dichotomy between aesthetic creation and
life. For as soon as we realize with Sartre and Bourdieu that highbrow and commercial art are socially linked,[47] we are tempted to turn Proust's aesthetic difference into Derrida's *différance* and the *Recherche* into a postmodern novel whose
narrator no longer resists an in-difference resulting from the disintegration of
the social value system. In retrospect, modernism thus appears as a nostalgic
attempt to contain by metaphysical means an ambivalence tending towards
indifference.

While the modernist subject as narrator tries to contain ambivalence by discursive means – for example in Sartre's *Nausea*, where the main character also decides to become a writer –, the subject as actor seeks to establish a political, aesthetic or religious scale of values. More often than not, such attempts are condemned to failure by extreme ambivalence: for example in Kafka's *The Trial*,[48] where it is virtually impossible to decide whether the women who pretend to help K., the painter Titorelli or the priest, whom K. consults, are in fact helpers or adversaries working for a highly ambivalent justice. A similar situation appears in the novels of Broch, Svevo and Musil, where the narrative structure turns out to be problematical because the narrator's efforts are thwarted by ambivalent (i.e. inexplicable) characters, actions and discourses. In this context, one of the key tenets of narrative theory, namely that 'the character trait is the cause of action' (Todorov),[49] becomes questionable.

In Hermann Broch's trilogy *The Sleepwalkers* (*Die Schlafwandler*, 1931–1932), for example, the anarchist Esch finds it difficult to act in an ambivalent world which keeps invalidating his dualistic ideology, thus vitiating all of his attempts to divide people around him into 'good' and 'evil' actors. Even a sunny spring day will not change this situation: 'Nothing was clear and simple, thought Esch in anger, nothing was clear and simple, even on a lovely spring day like this (. . .).' ('Nichts ist eindeutig, dachte Esch voll Zorn, nichts ist eindeutig, nicht einmal an solch schönem Frühlingstag [. . .].')[50] However, narrative action is meant to evolve from decision to decision and thus presupposes clearly defined values and ideological alternatives. It is hardly surprising therefore that Esch, who launches invectives against big business and its corrupt representatives, is full of anger whenever he observes an interdependence between ambivalence and finance.[51] His Platonic and Hegelian attempt to separate appearance from essence is doomed to failure by the ambivalent character of Eduard von Bertrand, considered quite rightly by K. R. Mandelkow as the novel's central figure.[52] It is a Nietzschean figure which suggests that appearance and essence might be identical.

Although complementary in many ways, the characters of Italo Svevo's novel *Confessions of Zeno* (*La coscienza di Zeno*, 1923) adopt a less dualistic approach than Esch. In the rare moments when he is about to take a decision, the main character, Zeno Cosini, is assailed by doubts concerning his motivation. The latter is often ambivalent. Zeno simultaneously loves and hates his friend Guido and helps him without actually knowing why:

I had fully made up my mind to get the money for him. It is difficult for me to say whether I was really doing it out of affection for him or for Ada, or perhaps also because I felt that a certain responsibility might attach to me for having worked in his office. (Ero ben deciso di procurargli quel denaro. Naturalmente non so dire se lo facessi per affetto a lui o ad Ada, o forse per liberarmi da quella piccola parte di responsabilità che poteva toccarmi per aver lavorato nel suo ufficio.)[53]

This passage is particularly interesting, partly because it reveals a psychic ambivalence in the psychoanalytic sense, an ambivalence linked by Paula Robinson to Zeno's homosexual disposition,[54] partly because it shows that the modernist narrator reacts to ambivalence by Musil's *sense of the possible* (*Möglichkeitssinn*): by resorting to an essayistic writing, to hypotheses and constructions.

All of these techniques are accompanied by *irony* which is among the most important stylistic devices used by authors such as Svevo, Musil and Pirandello.[55] In Musil's great novel, for example, Diotima's belief in eternal truths is viewed ironically:

Diotima could never have imagined a life without eternal truths, but now she was surprised to find that every single truth has a double or multiple existence. (Diotima hätte sich ein Leben ohne ewige Wahrheiten niemals vorzustellen vermocht, aber nun bemerkte sie zu ihrer Verwunderung, daß es jede ewige Wahrheit doppelt und mehrfach gibt.)[56]

In a complementary manner, the impossibility of action and the stagnation of the narrative, both of which are salient features of Musil's fragmentary novel with its three different beginnings,[57] are commented on with benevolence by the agnostic narrator:

Whenever Diotima had almost decided in favour of such an idea, she had to admit that it would also be great to do the opposite. (Jedesmal, wenn Diotima sich beinahe schon für eine solche Idee entschieden hätte, mußte sie bemerken, daß es auch etwas Großes wäre, das Gegenteil davon zu verwirklichen.)[58]

A similar irony is used by Pirandello in order to debunk the stereotypes of Italian society. His narrator considers the possibility that these stereotypes might be dissolved in the heat of a summer afternoon – along with all other conventions and customs. As long as they have not dissolved and released the 'original beast' ('bestia originaria') in the human mind, he grants his compatriots the right to condemn him in the name of their conventions: 'You can condemn.' ('Potete condannare.')[59] As in the case of Musil and Svevo, ambivalence and irony finally dismantle a sense of reality based on conventions and narrative stereotypes, thus releasing the *sense of the possible* (*Möglichkeitssinn*) which aims at the hypothetic, at openness, essayism and construction.

Scanning the literary horizons for alternatives to an obsolete, mimesis-oriented realism, which loses its credibility in the age of ambivalence, the modernists develop an open, essayistic and paratactic way of writing that is no longer constrained by the causal logic of traditional narrative. At the same time, they reflect on their narrative techniques, emphasizing that every kind of narrative is a construction, not a faithful reproduction of the real.

Pirandello, who in some respects takes Musil's 'sense of the possible' more seriously than Musil himself, shows that the reconstructions by the narrator of his own person are quite unrelated to the fantasies his relatives and neighbours have attached to his name. They have nothing to do with the figment of his wife's imagination lovingly called Gengè. To the hero-narrator, Gengè appears as a bogey unwittingly created by his wife Dida within her petty-bourgeois conventions. The narrator feels that he is quite unrelated to all of this: 'She had constructed him!' ('Se l'era costruito lei!'),[60] he exclaims reproachfully. The problem is that, within constructivism, it is difficult to decide which construction is the correct one, the one closest to reality: 'Because that Gengè of hers did exist, whereas I, for her, didn't exist at all, and never had'. ('Perché quel suo Gengè esisteva, mentre io per lei non esistevo affatto, non ero mai esistito'.)[61]

It is a well-known fact that a normal person who ends up in a psychiatric clinic by mistake finds it hard to convince the personnel that he or she is in the wrong place. The simple sentence 'I am not crazy' is usually interpreted by the personnel as a typical symptom ('all inmates say that') and easily integrated into the dominant construction. Similarly, dissidents, who are condemned by 'the Party' because they are 'no longer in touch with reality', are frequently obliged to wait for years in a psychiatric clinic until real events dissolve the ideological chimeras of the *Nomenklatura*. Does reality exist after all?[62] It exists, but it can only be perceived in a constructed form.[63] This, however, should not be taken to mean that all constructions (those of Galileo and the Church, of the dissidents and the Party) have an equal status.

Pirandello, at any rate, presents himself as a modernist constructivist when he makes his narrator point out ironically: 'Ah, you believe only houses are constructed? I construct myself continually and I construct you, and you do the same.' ('Ah, voi credete che si costruiscano soltanto le case? Io mi costruisco di continuo e vi costruisco, e voi fatte altrettanto.')[64] The confusions, which result from the conflicts of these competing constructions, yield Pirandello's *umorismo*.[65] The latter no longer admits reality's role of arbitrator, a role provided for by Cervantes's irony. This loss of reality as a point of reference announces postmodernity and Radical Constructivism.[66] Wladimir Krysinski quite rightly remarks: 'Pirandello's work appears to us as modernist and as open towards postmodernism (ouverte sur le postmodernisme).'[67] It will be shown that this assessment also applies to other modernist authors such as Camus, Moravia and Joyce.

Where the sense of the real is superseded by the sense of the possible, which makes reality disintegrate into a vast array of possible constructions, the question arises how constructions come about. Musil tries to answer this question in relation to an essayistic philosophy and an essayistic style. His narrator says about Ulrich, the hero of his fragmentary novel:

Roughly like in an essay, which, from section to section, considers a phenomenon from many perspectives, without ever defining its meaning, – for a perfectly defined phenomenon loses its volume and boils down to a concept, – he believed that he could deal with the world and his own life in the most satisfactory manner. (Ungefähr wie ein Essay in der Folge seiner Abschnitte ein Ding von vielen Seiten nimmt, ohne es ganz zu erfassen, – denn ein ganz erfaßtes Ding verliert mit einem Male seinen Umfang und schmilzt zu einem Begriff ein – glaubte er, Welt und eigenes Leben am richtigsten ansehen und behandeln zu können.)[68]

This passage not only bears witness to a constructivist approach, but also to a particularization tendency that reckons with the uniqueness of phenomena. It points beyond modernity: towards Musil's utopias, some of which are located beyond conceptual, universal reason, and towards postmodernity, which, as was shown above, is marked by a strong emphasis on the particular.

Not only Musil's hero Ulrich, but Musil as a writer adopts an essayistic approach, whenever he views his novel not as a narrative structure, but as a constellation of essays most of which are linked paradigmatically rather than syntagmatically. 'From which, strangely enough, nothing ensues' ('Woraus bemerkenswerter Weise nichts hervorgeht'), runs the a-syntactic, non-causal title of the first chapter which announces an essayistic style. It delays or interrupts the rudimentary action of the novel by inserting long digressions into history, science, philosophy or psychology. Like in André Breton's experimental text *Nadja*,[69] essayism, irony and a paradigmatic, a-syntactic style complement one another in Musil's novel. It echoes the innovations of the European avant-garde movements.

In Joyce's *Ulysses*, these modernist features announce postmodern aesthetics because Joyce's great novel is an intertextual experiment without utopian perspectives. Certain dialogues between Stephen and Bloom sound like mixtures of essay and protocol: 'Were their views in some points divergent? – Stephen dissented openly from Bloom's views on the importance of dietary and civic self help while Bloom dissented tacitly from Stephen's views on the eternal affirmation of the spirit of man in literature.'[70] Joyce's textual collages, composed of historical fragments, advertisements and notes ('Little Harry Hughes . . .'), are reminiscent of the postmodern textual experiments, published by Maurice Roche and Jürgen Becker in the 1960s and 70s, which ignore metaphysical utopias and concentrate on the semantic potential of the text.[71]

Essayistic, paradigmatic writing in the sense of Musil goes beyond this postmodern textual game. Both Musil and Proust consider the essayistic novel not only as an escape from syntactic constraints, but as a chance to explore the deeper layers of personality. Several remarks in Musil's diaries illustrate this exploratory spirit of modernism and its proximity to psychoanalysis:

As long as one continues to think in sentences with a full stop, certain things cannot be said – only vaguely felt. However, it might be possible to learn to express things in such a way as to open up and understand perspectives which today are still situated at the threshold of the unconscious.[72]

It is hard to overlook the affinities with André Breton's surrealism which is defined in the first *Manifesto* (1924) as a way of thinking independent of all rational, aesthetic or moral controls: as a 'psychic automatism in its pure state'.[73] In spite of all the differences that separate them, Musil and Breton agree in considering the unconscious as one of the utopian components of modernism and the avant-garde which, in surrealism, is linked to the revolutionary utopia.

> The Utopian vocation of surrealism, Fredric Jameson explains, lies in its attempt to endow the object world of a damaged and broken industrial society with the mystery and the depth, the "magical" qualities (. . .), of an Unconscious that seems to speak and vibrate through those things.[74]

He shows to what extent postmodern art has renounced metaphysical and ideological orientations of this sort,[75] embracing the kind of pluralistic 'anything goes' which an architect like Achille Bonito-Oliva stands for.[76]

## 5.3  Critique of Truth, the System and the Subject: Critique of Modernity

Like the sociological theories of Durkheim, Simmel, Max Weber and Alfred Weber, modernist literature can be read as a reflection and a critique of modernity since the Enlightenment period (cf. Chapter 2). Both sociological and literary modernism can be considered as a *late modern self-criticism of modernity* which begins to doubt some of its key concepts: *truth, reason* and *the subject*. Insofar as writers such as Musil, Kafka and especially Camus can no longer believe in the Christian, Hegelian and Marxist teleology, social progress and metaphysical truths, they appear, as Rolf Günter Renner puts it in conjunction with Musil,[77] as precursors of postmodern writers and philosophers.

The crisis of language, which – since Baudelaire and Mallarmé – casts doubts upon words like 'good', 'bad', 'evil', 'beautiful', 'scientific' or 'democratic', finally discredits the notion of truth, formerly dissected and dismissed by Nietzsche. The commercialization of all areas of language, the ideological conflicts, in which the last meaningful words are exploited for political ends, and a pseudo-scientific use of concepts make a modernist writer like Sartre wonder whether language has a future at all. He foresees a catastrophic situation in which all words are of equal value and equally meaningless, but 'in which we shall nevertheless be obliged to speak'.[78] The commentary of a cynic could be relatively short: the catastrophe is here and is called postmodernity. This is undoubtedly an oversimplification, but Pynchon's critical, language-conscious prose and the systematically distorted language of Werner Schwab's theatre show that the cynic has a point – in spite of his simplifying gesture.

In the social and linguistic situation described by Sartre, the concept of truth threatens to disintegrate. Sartre himself points out in an article on Brice Parain's theory of language that, within this theory, 'it is as impossible to tell a lie as it is impossible to commit an evil deed in Claudel's world'.[79] At this stage in the development of modernism, the tendency towards postmodern indifference begins to assert itself. Sartre's comments on Parain are completed by Kafka's and Musil's remarks on the concept of truth. Both authors consider this concept primarily on a pragmatic level, that is as truth in human communication. 'Truth and lie are the same. In order to be able to confess, one tells a lie,'[80] says Kafka. Analogous statements by Musil are almost Kafkaesque in character: 'The true truth between two human beings cannot be expressed. Every effort turns into an obstacle.'[81]

Italo Svevo's remarks on truth are reminiscent of Nietzsche because Svevo (like Sartre) reveals the tendency towards indifference inherent in late modernity, especially when he argues that 'naturally truth and lie are interchangeable', adding that 'by adhering to a statement which one holds to be true and by condemning another statement which one considers as false, one may assert one loves truth and nevertheless be mistaken'.[82] Ignoring the metaphysical tradition, Svevo sees truth as an individual, subjective chimera: as a contingent attitude the universal validity of which is hardly worth discussing.

Whatever holds in the case of truth also holds in the case of moral, political and aesthetic values. Authors like Sartre, Kafka, Svevo or Broch at times tend to believe that they are interchangeable, but in most cases they concentrate on their growing ambivalence and on the probability that their universal acceptance will diminish. Nowhere is the emphasis on the decreasing universality of values and on their late modern particularization as strong as in Broch's trilogy *The Sleepwalkers*. Social differentiation, so thoroughly dealt with by modern sociology from Simmel and Durkheim to Luhmann,[83] leads in Broch's novel to a 'disintegration of values' in the course of which individual value systems gain such a degree of autonomy or even independence that they resemble windowless monads:

> (. . .) Like strangers they exist side by side, an economic value-system of 'good business' next to an aesthetic one of *l'art pour l'art*, a military code of values side by side with a technical or an athletic, each autonomous, each 'in and for itself' (. . .). (Gleich Fremden stehen sie nebeneinander, das ökonomische Wertgebiet eines 'Geschäftemachens an sich' neben einem künstlerischen des l'art pour l'art, ein militärisches Wertgebiet neben einem technischen oder einem sportlichen, jedes autonom, jedes 'an sich' [. . .].)[84]

Between the individual value systems, indifference is the rule, and Broch's literary investigations reveal to what extent indifference not only results from the growing impact of the exchange value and the destruction of language by ideological conflicts, but also from the fragmentation of the social value system by the division of labour. The latter yields many partial systems each of which claims absolute validity.

It is a characteristic feature of modernist literature that it does not, like its postmodern counterpart, bracket out *problems of value and truth* or ignore them, but keeps returning to them. Not only Broch brings up the question of truth and value in his trilogy; Proust shows similar interests when he makes his narrator turn to art as the supreme value at the end of his long novel. Although Musil knows that individualism has 'come to an end', he would like to 'save its essence'.[85] Finally, Thomas Mann sums up the basic problems of the modernist value system when he makes his narrator present the ambivalent figure of Adrian Leverkühn as a synthesis of 'bad pupil' and 'genius':

> Belief in absolute values, illusory as it always is, seems to me a condition of life. But my friend's gifts measured themselves against values the relative character of which seemed to lie open to him, without any visible possibility of any other relation which would have detracted from them as values. Bad pupils there are in plenty. But Adrian presented the singular phenomenon of a bad pupil as the head of the form. (Der Glaube an absolute Werte, illusionär wie er immer sei, scheint mir eine Lebensbedingung. Meines Freundes Gaben dagegen maßen sich an Werten, deren Relativität ihm offen zu liegen schien, ohne daß eine Bezugsmöglichkeit sichtbar gewesen wäre, die sie als Werte herabgesetzt hätte. Schlechte Schüler gibt es genug. Adrian aber bot das singuläre Phänomen des schlechten Schülers *in Primusgestalt.*)[86]

On the one hand, 'absolute values' appear as illusions, on the other hand, their relativity is revealed by the ambivalent character of Adrian Leverkühn, who is one of the key figures of modernism and a metonymic representation of its problematic. He makes cultural values appear as ambivalent in a situation where market laws, ideological conflicts and the division of labour make them enter a destructive competition that is dramatically intensified in postmodernity.

In this situation, in which adjectives such as 'true', 'just', 'beautiful', 'democratic' or 'scientific' attract a growing number of question marks, not only the value system of the traditional novel with its heroes and anti-heroes falls apart, but also the value system underlying the great 'metanarratives' in the sense of Lyotard. For the doubt concerning the validity of narrative philosophical systems and 'metanarratives' of all kinds is by no means a postmodern invention. It is to be found in many modernist writers, who, as was shown earlier on, not only consider traditional narratives with suspicion, but also tend to believe that narration as such is a metaphysical relic.

Robert Musil's remarks about the crisis of the novel bear witness to the *modernist* scepticism towards 'metanarratives':

> This is how, viewed from the outside, the present crisis of the novel came to light. We no longer want to be told stories, because we feel that this is a pastime activity. (. . .) However, this is not quite correct. For communists

and nationalists and Catholics clearly do want to be told stories. This need crops up as soon as an ideology consolidates itself. When the object is given.[87]

This passage is of considerable interest, because it links the critique of the traditional novel and its narrative structures to the ideological and metaphysical narrative which, long before Lyotard, the modernist writer views with growing scepticism. It is also interesting because of its implicit distinction between the intellectuals of the interwar period, who tend to reject all kinds of naïve, 'realistic' narration, and a popular culture dominated by ideological narratives which contribute to the formation of individual and collective subjects. It was shown (cf. Chapter 2) that even postmodern intellectuals, who pretend to consider 'metanarratives' with incredulity, are prepared to take them seriously again in certain conditions.

Musil's remarks not only imply a critique of the realist novel and of ideological narratives, but at the same time cast doubts on the cultural heritage of modernity. In a complementary manner, Broch's idea of a disintegrating value system and his Nietzschean critique of the metaphysical concept of truth cast doubts on the ideological (dualistic) and teleological structures of modern metanarratives.

Musil's and Broch's critiques are completed by Albert Camus's late modern doubts concerning the teleologies of Christianity and Hegelian Marxism. To Camus, the Christian teleology (cf. Chapter 3) appears as an attempt to insert human existence into a pre-existing narrative: a 'récit écrit à l'avance'.[88] This criticism of the metaphysical narratives, and especially of the Marxist idea of a social development aiming at a classless society, led to a conflict between Sartre and Camus.[89] The latter's alternative to Sartre's marriage of existentialism and Marxism is described by A. Rühling as a return to ancient Greek thought, to its static view of the world and its 'respect of destiny'.[90]

This Nietzschean return to the Mediterranean thought of antiquity, to a *pensée de midi* (Camus), implies a modernist rejection of all Christian, rationalist, Marxist and fascist discourses which form the subjectivities of the individual and the group (the organization, the party) and empower the subject to dominate nature. Although this refusal of instrumental thought is by no means a feature of modernism as a whole (Sartre, Brecht and Marinetti would not go along with it for very different reasons), it is nevertheless one of its most important components (Kafka, Hesse, Musil, Breton and Baroja would endorse it), because it casts doubts on modern subjectivity and its developments.

Writers such as Camus or Hesse distance themselves from the involvement of the modern subject in technocratic forms of thought that are common to the dominant ideologies of modernity: to rationalism, Marxism and fascism. This is probably the main reason why they have always been considered with suspicion by fascists, national socialists and Marxist-Leninists.[91] Their critique of modernity not only confirms and completes certain arguments of Critical Theory (cf. Section 5.4), but also announces the postmodern critiques of modernity put forward by Lyotard, Bauman and some feminist thinkers.

The modernist criticism of the main metaphysical metanarratives and of the subject's domination over nature is marked by ambivalence in the sense that the liberation of the subject from the constraints of the religious or secular metanarratives also releases forces which the metanarratives were meant to contain for the sake of social cohesion: nature (within the individual), the non-rational, contingency, chance and the dream. Camus knew that the subject's liberation from metaphysical constraints could lead to its subjugation by nature and its contingencies, by the unconscious and chance.

This pessimistic scenario showing a vacillating subject yielding to the forces of nature and the unconscious was anticipated by the Young Hegelian Friedrich Theodor Vischer who was among the first to blame Hegel for not really having achieved the dialectical synthesis of spirit and nature he had in mind: 'He [Hegel] believes that he has succeeded in synthesizing world reason and nature, but he failed to explain their absolute discrepancy and to deduce nature's "otherness" from the idea (. . .).'[92] This failure explains why he cannot account for the natural aspects of human existence, for contingency and chance. He simply neglects these phenomena. By emphasizing 'the absolute discrepancy' between spirit and nature in Hegel's philosophy, Vischer's critique announces the disintegration of the Hegelian system in Young Hegelian thought and the dawn of the modernist era: an era of incredulity and criticism. Vischer draws our attention to the key elements of the new era which emerged from the collapse of the Hegelian system: nature, alterity, contingency and the dream.

The structural and ideological ambivalence of modernism consists in the fact that some of its authors consider these elements as symptoms of a liberated subjectivity, whereas other authors see them as a threat to the individual subject. Unlike Proust, Camus, Breton and Hesse, who react to natural contingency, to chance and dream with new aesthetic and textual experiments, Sartre, Kafka, the young Moravia and Miroslav Krleža react with scepticism and a certain hostility towards the manifestations of nature in culture.

Proust can be read as a precursor of surrealism insofar as he follows Nerval and Chateaubriand by attributing to chance a creative role in the process of the *mémoire involontaire*, of *involuntary memory*. Contingent associations seem to his narrator more authentic than the causal deductions brought about by intellect:

I had not gone in search of the two uneven paving-stones of the courtyard upon which I had stumbled. But it was precisely the fortuitous and inevitable fashion in which this and the other sensations had been encountered that proved the trueness of the past which they brought back to life (. . .). (Je n'avais pas été chercher les deux pavés inégaux de la cour où j'avais buté. Mais justement la façon fortuite, inévitable, dont la sensation avait été rencontrée, contrôlait la vérité du passé qu'elle ressuscitait, des images qu'elle déclenchait [. . .].)[93]

The truth discovered by Proust is not intellectual, rational truth, but the truth of the unconscious *mémoire involontaire* supported by the *instinct artistique*, to which the novelist subjects the intellect of everyday life.

His discovery is radicalized by the surrealists around Breton, who, influenced by Baudelaire and Apollinaire, link Freud's notion of the unconscious to the discovery of the *objet trouvé* and the oneiric associations it triggers off. Like Proust, the surrealists believe that truth as authentic experience is not to be found in everyday life or within the intellectual sphere, but only in the realm of the unconscious, the dream and *objective chance* (*hasard objectif*). What is more, Breton believes that the mechanisms of the unconscious and the contingent contribute decisively to the liberation of the individual from the constraints of everyday routine. 'The finding of the object', he writes in *L'Amour fou*, 'fulfils in this case exactly the same function as the dream in the sense that it liberates the individual.' ('La trouvaille d'objet remplit ici rigoureusement le même office que le rêve, en ce sens qu'elle libère l'individu [. . .].')[94] In conjunction with Breton's surrealism one could repeat what Karl Riha writes about Dadaism between the wars: 'To be open to chance, to open up to chance will become a literary criterion of innovation in the course of this decade (. . .).'[95] The surrealist *attente mystique* is precisely this openness to the contingent, to chance.

Other modernist authors such as Svevo, Pirandello and Hesse consider the impact of chance on the lives of their characters with irony and *umorismo*. While Svevo shows (in this respect similar to Musil, the author of *Die Schwärmer*) how chance becomes responsible for Zeno's marriage with Augusta, because Zeno, by mistake, keeps touching Augusta's foot under the table instead of touching Ada's, Pirandello's hero Vitangelo Moscarda discovers by chance that he has an uneven nose and subsequently inaugurates an endless process of self-reflection and self-construction. In a complementary manner, Hermann Hesse's Harry Haller, who suffers from a divided self, experiences in the Magic Theatre his liberation from the obsessive idea of a unitary personality:

He held a glass up to me and again I saw the unity of my personality broken up into many selves whose number seemed even to have increased. (Er hielt mir einen Spiegel vor, wieder sah ich darin die Einheit meiner Person in viele Ichs zerfallen, ihre Zahl schien noch gewachsen zu sein.)[96]

Finally, Camus shows the reader to what extent contingent natural phenomena and chance are responsible for human actions and not rational considerations or ideological principles. The first part of his novel *The Outsider* (*L'Etranger*, 1942) ends with the submission of an apparently free subject to the forces of nature. In the fatal scene, the narrator Meursault shoots an Arab while trying to escape the unbearable heat of the sun. 'It was because of the sun' ('C'était à cause du soleil'),[97] he explains to the stunned jurors during his trial.[98]

It is not altogether surprising that writers such as Camus, Hesse and Breton expect nature in its different shapes and forms – as contingency, dream and the unconscious – to deliver the subject from the constraints of culture and its logic. These writers believe that nature is the better, healthier and more human world. Similarly to Camus, who introduces characters like Meursault (*The Outsider*) and Dr Rieux (*The Pest*), whose words and deeds cast doubts upon ascetic Christianity and its ideologies, because they obey natural instincts, Hesse opposes an unspoilt nature to a culture perverted by power and money:

> As long as there were martens, the odour of the virgin world, instinct and nature, the world was still possible, still beautiful and promising for a poet. (Solang es noch Marder gab, noch Duft der Urwelt, noch Instinkt und Natur, solange war für einen Dichter die Welt noch möglich, noch schön und verheißungsvoll.)[99]

Surrealism, which shares with Hesse's work a penchant for the unconscious and the dream, is presented by Gisela Steinwachs as an attempt to transform culture into nature.[100] In this context, Jauß's idea that modernism or late modernity is hostile to nature[101] appears as a simplification.

It is partly justified, however, insofar as there are modernist writers, who follow Baudelaire and Huysmans rather than Nietzsche, the thinker of chance,[102] in order to deliver human subjectivity from natural contingency. The young Sartre is one of them. He criticizes the surrealists for sacrificing the subject to 'objective chance', to the *hasard objectif*: 'The idea is, first of all, to blur the conventional differences between unconscious and conscious life, between dream and wake. This means that subjectivity is dissolved.'[103]

In *Nausea* (*La Nausée*, 1938), the narrator reacts to the threats of nature, chance and the unconscious by adhering to a Cartesian rationalism, temporarily professed by Sartre himself. His ideal is a geometrical figure such as the circle, because it excludes all kinds of natural contingency, all kinds of natural existence. Unlike all the natural shapes surrounding the narrator, unlike human life itself, it is not absurd.[104]

One such shape is the famous root of the chestnut-tree considered by the frightened narrator as a threat to the rational subject. Confronting the inexplicable, contingent and opaque nature, he feels condemned to reification and speechlessness. 'Things have broken free from their names' ('Les choses se sont délivrées de leurs noms'),[105] he observes. His personal problematic appears to be both modernist and Young Hegelian, because, as a rational being, he discovers – after Friedrich Theodor Vischer – that nature does not correspond to its linguistic and conceptual representations in the human world. Reacting to this modernist nightmare, the rationalist philosopher Sartre tries to ban contingency: 'The culprit is contingency,'[106] he explains later on in a discussion about his first novel.

In Kafka's as in Sartre's work, nature is always full of frightening and nauseating connotations. The men, who arrest Joseph K. at the beginning of Kafka's novel *The Trial*, are mentally retarded, and the hero is struck by their infantile and animal-like behaviour. Initially, he reacts with self-confident rationalism and, confronting 'the Law', acts under the illusion 'that he was at last faced with a rational person with whom he could discuss his situation' ('endlich einem vernünftigen Menschen gegenüberzustehen und über seine Angelegenheiten mit ihm sprechen zu können').[107] However, this confidence fades away in a 'natural' world inhabited by irrational humans some of whom behave like animals and whose sexuality has an animal touch to it. In Kafka's short stories, nature is a threatening force whenever it appears.[108]

The central problem dealt with by Kafka and Sartre is summed up by the leading Croatian modernist Miroslav Krleža when he makes the main character of his novel *The Return of Filip Latinovicz* (*Povratak Filipa Latinovicza*, 1932) remark: 'To be a subject and to feel the identity of one's being-a-subject.' ('Biti subjekt i osjećati identitet subjekta.')[109] This is the real project of modernism: the subject is to be re-invented, re-constructed, if necessary by a daring act beyond the conventions of bourgeois culture.

Such an act has both a utopian and an ideological character, and most works of modernism differ radically from postmodern artworks by linking the question of the subject to the question of reality, of authentic life and a better society. The multitude of answers, which ranges from aestheticism to socialism and fascism, accounts for the heterogeneity of the modernist problematic.

Unlike Mallarmé, Stefan George, Proust and the young Sartre, who sought authentic reality in the language of the artist, which they located outside the commercial and the ideological world, Brecht and Walter Benjamin expected the Epic Theatre to waken the revolutionary consciousness of the masses. At the other end of the political spectrum, Marinetti imagined a technical utopia geared towards the politics and the aesthetics of Italian fascism.[110] In some cases, this aesthetic and ideological heterogeneity finds its expression in the work of a single author like Joris-Karl Huysmans. He began as a naturalist, then made a crucial contribution to aestheticism with his novel *A Rebours* (1884), a few years later, in *Là-bas* (1891), was attracted to Satanism and finally converted to Catholicism in *La Cathédrale* (1898) and *Les Foules de Lourdes* (1906).

The heterogeneity of modernism sketched here is also due, as was shown above, to the incompatible concepts of nature put forward by its writers and artists. This means, among other things, that all attempts to define modernism (or postmodernism) as a *Weltanschauung* in the sense of Hans Bertens[111] or as an aesthetic, are doomed to failure: a *problematic* is something quite different. This also means that each work occupies a *particular position* within the modernist coordinate system and that it can only be defined concretely in relation to other similar or dissimilar works that react to the same problems (as the concept of nature shows). However, this insight should not lead to an aesthetic nominalism in the sense of Croce. Like the – always unique – points of inter-section in the geometrical system, individual works of modernism would be incomprehensible without the system they belong to: without the problematic.

On the whole, it could be argued that the ambivalence of modernist litera-ture consists in the fact that, as a self-criticism of modernity, it criticizes Christian, Marxist, rationalist and fascist metanarratives, but at the same time continues to adhere to some of the modern utopias. It has not altogether abandoned the value systems of modernity.

A postmodernist with a strong sense for the signs of the times might suggest that we keep the critical and analytic repertoire of modernism, but get rid of its metaphysical burden. To this the modernist advocate of Critical Theory might reply: What *raison d'être* has criticism in the long run, if all metaphysical concepts, including the concept of truth, are renounced?

## 5.4  Modernism and Critical Theory: Epilogue I

Referring to the context sketched above, Adorno wrote the last sentence of his *Negative Dialectics*: 'There is solidarity between such thinking and metaphysics at the time of its fall.'[112] Whenever this solidarity disappears, as in the case of deconstruction, philosophy runs the risk of reducing dialectics to what it used to be in antiquity: sophistry. In view of this danger, Adorno notes in *Minima Moralia*: '*Warning: not to be misused.* – The dialectic stems from the sophists; it was a mode of discussion whereby dogmatic assertions were shaken and, as the public prosecutors and comic writers put it, the lesser word made the stronger.'[113] However, the lesser word need not be true.

To authors such as Musil, Kafka, Proust and Mallarmé, Adorno is linked by the metaphysical and utopian search for truth and for an authentic language capable of evoking thoughts which are systematically drowned by the commer-cial communication of media society. Like these writers, Adorno is sensitive to whatever diverges from commerce, domination and ideology. Some sentences from his lecture on poetry and society sound like paraphrases of Mallarmé's 'Divagation première' which opposes the language of literature to that of 'universal *reporting*' ('universel *reportage*').[114] Adorno shows that, like Mallarmé, Stefan George is at pains to avoid all words imbued with commerce or ideology.[115]

Adorno's critique of language sheds light on the main aspects of the modern-ist literary and philosophical problematic: its growing distance from bourgeois-capitalist society; the break between subject and object as described by Lukács in his *Theory of the Novel*; the search for truth and the utopian expectation of a new, more human society. This expectation is also expressed in the image of a language unspoilt by ideology and commerce. Adorno expects the lyrical subject to adhere to the 'idea of a pure language'.[116] This idea not only relates his approach to the aesthetics of modernist poets, but also to those of a novelist like Proust who considers literary writing as a valid alternative to the shallow conversation of the Parisian upper classes at the turn of the century.

Like Proust and Musil, Adorno turns against all modern forms of domination – from rationalism to Hegelianism and Marxism – whenever he pleads in favour of the particular and the unique, trying to approach it in a mimetic and essayistic way instead of reducing it to a concept within a philosophical treatise. He seems to describe his own idea of theory when he writes about Proust's *Recherche*: 'It is against precisely that, against the brutal untruth of a subsuming form forced on from above, that Proust revolted.'[117] An analogous statement is to be found in Musil's long novel, whose narrator criticizes the philosopher's involvement in political domination:

> He was not a philosopher, for philosophers are violent characters, who haven't got an army at their disposal and therefore try to rule the world by locking it up in a system. (Er war kein Philosoph. Philosophen sind Gewalttäter, die keine Armee zur Verfügung haben und sich deshalb die Welt in der Weise unterwerfen, daß sie sie in ein System sperren.)[118]

The philosophers Musil has in mind here are obviously Plato, Hegel, Comte or Marx – and not Pascal, Montaigne or Nietzsche. For the heirs of Plato and Hegel tend to exclaim with Hegel 'all the worse for the facts!' whenever the facts disavow their theories.

Like Musil and other critics of modern systems of thought, Adorno develops an essayistic way of writing which enables him to approach phenomena theoretically without eliminating their particularity. With Musil and Broch, he believes that the advantages of the essay consist in its refusal to reduce objects to a principle, 'in its accentuation of the partial against the total'.[119] In his *Negative Dialectics*, he envisages a 'thinking in models' and defines negative dialectics as 'an ensemble of analyses of models'.[120] He hopes that the model will take into account the specific character of phenomena.

This penchant for the particular, which, according to Steven Best and Douglas Kellner, is responsible for the 'postmodern'[121] character of Adorno's thought, is reinforced in his *Aesthetic Theory* by the paratactic turn. In several self-critical remarks, the author observes that even the model cannot do justice to the particular and goes on to explain the paratactic (non-hypotactic, non-hierarchical and non-causal) structure of his last great work. He argues 'that a book's almost ineluctable movement from antecedent to consequence proved so incompatible with the content that for this reason any organization in the traditional sense – which up until now I have continued to follow (even in *Negative Dialectics*) – proved impracticable. The book must, so to speak, be written in equally weighed, paratactical parts that are arranged around a midpoint that they express through their constellation'.[122] The word 'constellation' points back to Adorno's early theory of language in which Walter Benjamin's principle of 'configuration' was meant to safeguard a non-violent approach to phenomena. The word is also reminiscent of Mallarmé's idea of 'UNE CONSTELLATION' as expressed in his experimental poem *Un coup de dés*.[123]

Freedom from domination, so much sought after by writers such as Kafka, Musil and Proust, is also aimed at by Adorno who envisages the kind of mimetic attitude towards the object adopted by certain forms of art. As early as in Horkheimer's and Adorno's *Dialectic of Enlightenment*, art is presented, in accordance with Schelling's romantic aesthetics, as 'the prototype of science'.[124] Continuing this train of thought, the author of *Aesthetic Theory* writes: '*Ratio* without mimesis is self-negating.'[125] Only by absorbing the mimetic elements of art, can theory avoid being transformed into a technocratic mode of thought.

This critical stance adopted by Adorno clearly represents a particular brand of modernism that is at variance with the modernist positions adopted by Marxists such as Brecht and Lukács, by surrealists such as Breton or Aragon, by rationalist existentialists such as Sartre. However, with these authors Adorno shares the belief in a metaphysical concept of truth and the metaphysical hope that there is redemption in history – a hope which threatens to turn into despair in his post-war writings. He would nevertheless repeat after Kafka: 'A life without truth is impossible.'[126]

His endorsement of the concepts of truth and subjectivity is not merely a symptom of his partial solidarity with liberal individualism, but also an attempt to associate critical thought with the non-identical, dissenting individual, whose survival is one of his main concerns:

> In view of the collective powers, which in the contemporary world are usurping the world spirit, the general and rational is better looked after by the isolated individual than by the stronger battalions which have abandoned the generality of reason in a docile manner.[127]

This idea finds its aesthetic counterpart in Adorno's essay on Valéry, where the artist appears as the representative of the historical subject (of the integrated revolutionary class).[128]

In spite of all these attempts to link the universal to the particular, Adorno's overall effort to bring about a synthesis turns into an aporia. For the isolated individual, who is meant to represent critical consciousness, stands outside the historical process, and a Critical Theory aiming at integrating artistic mimesis into its discourse becomes self-contradictory, 'because it is forced to turn against theory as such'.[129] This aporia of Critical Theory bears witness to the ambivalence of late modernity which is partly due to the post-Hegelian difficulty of reconciling the particular and the universal. This difficulty reappears within the postmodern problematic where it turns into an impossibility (cf. Chapter 3).

## 5.5 Postmodern Literature and Indifference: The Critique of Metaphysics

In what follows, postmodern literature will be considered as a radicalization of modernism consisting in extreme forms of intertextuality, carnivalization, estrangement and polysemy. In spite of this continuity (as radicalization), one should not lose sight of the global break that brought about a new, postmodern problematic.

In an article on postmodernity, H.-U. Gumbrecht argues that contemporary society 'cannot understand itself as an epoch'[130] because it lacks the historical consciousness of past ages. To this one could answer that we are not obliged to adopt the historical or a-historical consciousness of our society and that not all postmodern thinkers or theoreticians of postmodernity agree with Lyotard's idea that postmodernity is not a new era. It may have become clear that authors like Jameson, Fokkema, Hassan and McHale start from the premise that post-modern literature and art do inaugurate a new way of writing and looking at things. The question is *when* exactly this innovation begins.

The general thesis underlying this chapter is that, after the Second World War, a transition from the modernist to the postmodern problematic takes place, accompanied by a shift from ambivalence to indifference which gains momentum in the 1970s and 80s. This shift is announced within modernism itself, where indifference turns into the dominant feature in the works of authors such as Camus and Moravia. However, it does not yet occupy the centre of the problematic because the existentialist writers continue to adhere to the modern concepts of truth and subjectivity. Within the existentialist search, indifference continues to be regarded as an inauthentic feature, as 'sin'. While the indifferent narrator of Camus's *The Outsider* is condemned within a Christian-humanist discourse, which defines him as a responsible and punishable subject, the indifferent anti-hero of Moravia's novel *The Time of Indifference* (*Gli indifferenti*, 1929) admits: 'This is my real crime . . . The sin of indifference . . .' ('Questo è il mio vero delitto . . . ho peccato d'indifferenza . . .')[131] Elsewhere, the author uses the expression 'nightmare of indifference' ('incubo d'indifferenza').[132]

The writers of postmodernity wake up from this nightmare. They find that it was a nightmare of modernism caused by the kind of guilty conscience psychoanalysis has been grappling with since Freud. This guilty conscience, they believe, disappears as soon as we get rid of the burden of authenticity and subjectivity. They consider as old-fashioned, even as masochistic, the arduous search of Moravia's Michele Ardengo:

One single sincere action, one act of faith would be enough to sever him from this chaos and put those values back into their habitual perspective (. . .). (Sarebbe bastato un solo atto sincero, un atto di fede, per fermare questa baraonda e riassestare questi valori nella loro abituale prospettiva [. . .].)[133]

The question concerning the scale of social values becomes irrelevant in postmodernity.

In this context, the general thesis formulated above takes on a more concrete form, as it becomes clear that the search for authenticity, truth and subjectivity, so crucial in the modernist novel, is abandoned in postmodern literature. To authors like Alain Robbe-Grillet, Umberto Eco, Thomas Pynchon or Thomas Bernhard, the entire problem of values seems meaningless because the longing for an alternative to the existing social order appears to them as utopian in the original sense of the word: as aiming at a reality that does not exist (and cannot exist).

Thomas Bernhard's novel *Extinction* (*Auslöschung*, 1986) is a case in point. Its narrator soon realizes that there is no alternative to the world he knows: 'The people in Rome are no different, they are even more hypocritical (. . .).' ('Die Leute in Rom sind auch nicht anders, noch viel verlogener [. . .].')[134] What matters here, is not the negative tone, but the interchangeable character of locations, cities, countries which makes the postmodern writer abandon the metaphysical search of his modernist predecessors. The idea that this interchangeability leads to equivalence or indifference is confirmed by Bernhard himself when he remarks in an interview: 'My point of view is the equivalence of all things.'[135]

In a social and linguistic context, where the goals of the grand metanarratives of Christianity, rationalism, Hegelianism and Marxism lose their credibility, even the search of the novelist and the novel is deprived of its goal. Quite early on, in his first novel (*Frost*, 1963), where a student of medicine is sent out by his training doctor to find his brother, the painter Strauch, in order to observe him and gather all relevant information on him, Bernhard gives up teleological narration in the modern and modernist sense. 'Neither the narrator nor the reader finds out', writes Ralf Kock, 'why and to what end (. . .) these observations are to be carried out.'[136] This short description also applies to Robbe-Grillet's *Dans le labyrinthe* (1959), a Nouveau Roman that could be read as a parody of the modern and modernist novel, because its narrator keeps following a lost soldier who errs aimlessly through the streets of a town which was abandoned to the enemy.

In other postmodern texts, for example in John Barth's *Lost in the Funhouse* or in Félix de Azúas *Historia de un idiota contada por él mismo*, both of which will play an important part in this chapter, the modernist search appears as absurd in the light of parody. In Azúa's case, the narrator discovers that all moral, political and aesthetic values have become interchangeable, indifferent and hence useless as foundations of subjectivity.

The modernist question concerning truth, authenticity, reality and the subject is silenced within the postmodern problematic. For modernist values such as art, justice, socialism or Christian love, which were invoked by authors like Proust, Sartre, Brecht or Bernanos in order to justify subjectivity, fall prey to indifference (as interchangeability of values) in a society torn by ideological strife.

Breton's remarks on words and values in *Arcane 17* (1947) show what is meant by indifference in the socio-linguistic context of post-war France: 'The words, which referred to them [the values], for example law, justice, freedom, had taken on limited, contradictory meanings. Their elasticity was exploited by both sides to such a degree that, eventually, they expressed the very opposite of their original meaning.'[137] This passage shows how indifference can emerge from ambivalence whenever the coincidence of opposites becomes a phenomenon of everyday life. At the same time, it becomes clear what Nietzsche, the author of *Beyond Good and Evil*, means by the *identity* (*Wesensgleichheit*) of the 'intertwined' good and evil values: they are genetically, historically related and in the course of time become indistinguishable.

In the context mapped out here, postmodern literature appears as a reaction to both *modernity as the modern age* and *modernism as late modernity*. Its critique of modernity is inextricably linked to its critique of modernism. By rejecting the metaphysical and ideological search of modernists such as Proust, Kafka, Moravia or Thomas Mann, postmodern writers renounce the Platonic, Christian, rationalist and Hegelian question concerning the essence behind appearance – a question common to both Marxism and psychoanalysis. In this respect too, they appear as followers of Nietzsche who turned his back on Plato's and Hegel's essence.[138]

From a postmodern point of view, Marx's and Lukács's search for essence, for the true interests obliterated by ideologies and for the typical-essential characters in literature, becomes as futile as Freud's search for unconscious motivations. The literary discourses of postmodernity can no longer be read parallel to those of Marxism (Brecht, Auden) or to those of psychoanalysis (Svevo, Hesse, Schnitzler). For Schnitzler's heroine, who 'had revealed herself through her dream for what she really was' ('die sich in ihrem Traum enthüllt hatte als die, die sie war'),[139] leaves the literary scene, followed by her mysterious companions. She is succeeded by postmodern figures whose essence is their appearance and who cannot be understood as incarnations of Marxist or psychoanalytic discourses. However, it does not follow from this that these discourses cannot be applied to postmodern texts or artworks; after all, they are also applied to the art of antiquity and the Middle Ages.

## 5.6 Linguistic Aspects of Indifference

The construction of a problematic, a period or an epoch cannot do without schematizations and exaggerations. One could say about it what Adorno said about Freud's psychoanalysis: 'In psycho-analysis nothing is true except the exaggerations.'[140] The nominalist and the deconstructionist, who inherited some nominalist theorems, will always be right whenever they point out that certain features of literature, which are considered as postmodern, are also to be found in modern or romantic literature – possibly in Sterne's parodistic novel *Tristram Shandy* or even in the ancient works of Heliodor. In view of such nominalism, one can only refer to the global literary, philosophical and socio-logical context in order to define the specific character of a phenomenon.

Thus the idea that literature, philosophy and science do not mimetically reproduce the real can be found both in modernism and postmodernity. In this respect, both problematics can be seen as critical reactions to modern realism. However, one leaves this common ground as soon as one realizes that late modern and postmodern models of constructivism fulfil two very different functions. Unlike in the works of Mallarmé and Valéry, the young Sartre, Musil and Pirandello, who linked aesthetic construction to the notion of truth, con-struction becomes in the works of postmodern authors like John Barth, John Fowles or Alain Robbe-Grillet a reflection on the author's particularity. No essence, no truth, no general law (*une loi*, Proust) can be derived from this par-ticularity. The writer's aesthetic and political project to reinterpret *and* change the world is given up, and art appears as a kind of game.

This game is related to the problematic of indifference in the sense that it has no supra-individual, social meaning, but is produced by an isolated author and consumed by each reader in a particular, individual fashion. Art becomes *Artistik* in the sense of Gottfried Benn:

> *Artistik* is the attempt of art to present itself as content amidst a general decay of contents and to derive a new style from this experience; it is the attempt to oppose a new transcendence to the general nihilism of values: the transcend-ence of creative pleasure.[141]

Commenting on Benn's thesis, Walter Falk explains that writers of the twentieth century have time and again attempted to overcome this *Artistik* or *artisticism* by 're-introducing contents into art', by availing themselves of the experience of past epochs 'in which a generally valid system of values still existed'.[142] He himself tends to agree with the modernist Hermann Hesse who, in his novel *The Glass Bead Game*, takes the view 'that the age in which authentic cultural deeds were possible is over and that such deeds have been replaced by an artistic game that re-presents the cultural values of the past – in a fascinating and uncommitted way: the glass bead game'.[143]

Advocates of postmodernity might contest this idea in two different ways. They might object to the definition of literary postmodernity as a game within global indifference by pointing to the critical dimensions of certain novels by Thomas Pynchon, Italo Calvino, Christoph Ransmayr and Michel Butor. As anti-modernists in the sense of Fiedler or Eco, they might rejoice at the idea of an art delivered from all metaphysical burdens. After all, they might argue, a playful art can only be condemned by humourless ideologues.

The reply to these objections can be relatively concise. The critical components of indifference have been inherited from modernism by authors such as Pynchon, Ransmayr or Azúa who will be discussed in some detail in this chapter. But considering the despair inherent in the works of these authors, it is hard to rejoice at the artistic game of postmodern literature, even though such a game may exist in the novels of Fowles, Eco or Süskind. Pynchon's, Ransmayr's and Azúa's fascinating descriptions of global destruction suggest that, at the moment, the postmodern game is being played amidst of T. S. Eliot's 'Wasteland'.

The idea of re-presenting the past in a 'fascinating and uncommitted way' is taken up 37 years after Hesse's *The Glass Bead Game* (*Das Glasperlenspiel*, 1943) by Umberto Eco in his well-known novel *The Name of the Rose* (*Il nome della rosa*, 1980). In his post-script to the novel, he argues that the past 'must be revisited: but with irony, not innocently'.[144] He actually practises what he preaches by reflecting on his techniques from the very beginning of the novel: 'Naturally, a manuscript' ('naturalmente, un manoscritto'). What follows is an erudite and amusing game revolving around a fictive manuscript: '*Le manuscript de Dom Adson de Melk, traduit en français d'après l'édition de Dom J. Mabillon,*'[145] whose labyrinthine narration the reader follows like the meanders of a detective story.

Eco's text can in fact be read as a detective novel (with Jorge as the villain), although the contrast between Good and Evil is reduced to a playful construction within the postmodern game. In a conversation between Guglielmo and the old Alinardo de Grottaferrata, the Antichrist appears as a negative instance within a narrative scheme the possibilities of which are explored by the narrator: 'Ah, the Antichrist . . . He is about to come, the millennium is past; we await him . . .' ('Ah, l'Anticristo . . . Egli sta per venire, il millennio è scaduto, lo attendiamo . . .')[146] Narrator and reader tacitly agree that this mythical instance has lost its religious meaning and does not even fulfil a symbolic function comparable to that of the devil in Thomas Mann's *Doctor Faustus*.

Thus the novel turns into a commercially profitable game the gist of which is reduced to its most spectacular elements: 'Seven Deaths in Seven Days and Nights of Apocalyptic Terror' (Warner Books Edition, 1984). Werner Hüllen reads the novel as 'narrated semiotics' in a 'very conventional form': 'It tells us something about the use of codes. It does not interpret a given world, but interprets interpretation itself.'[147] This could undoubtedly also be said of Kafka's novel *The Trial*: its author makes Joseph K. and the priest interpret and reinterpret the parable 'Before the Law' in many contradictory ways. However, one would misunderstand Kafka, who considered 'writing as a form of prayer',[148] if one chose to read *The Trial* as a semiotic game.

Like *The Name of the Rose,* John Fowles's novel *The French Lieutenant's Woman* (1969) shows to what extent playful constructivism and conventional narrative complement each other. Whenever Fowles's narrator reflects on his situation as narrator, he creates a critical distance between reader and narration, reader and action, thereby signalling that all is constructed: 'I risk making Sarah sound like a bigot.' And: 'I cannot say what she might have been in our age (. . .).'[149]

Answering the questions 'Who is Sarah?' and 'Out of what shadows does she come?',[150] which, at the end of the twelfth chapter, are meant to increase the carefully organized suspense, the narrator-author suddenly interrupts the action by exposing the entire construction at the beginning of chapter 13:

> I do not know. This story I am telling is all imagination. These characters I create never existed outside my own mind. If I have pretended until now to know my characters' minds and innermost thoughts, it is because I am writing in (. . .) a convention universally accepted at the time of my story: that the novelist stands next to God. He may not know all, yet he tries to pretend that he does. But I live in the age of Alain Robbe-Grillet and Roland Barthes; if this is a novel, it cannot be a novel in the modern sense of the word. – So perhaps I am writing a transposed autobiography; perhaps I now live in one of the houses I have brought into the fiction; perhaps Charles is myself disguised. Perhaps it is only a game.[151]

This passage is particularly important for the distinction between modernist and postmodern literature. First, because it follows Eco's advice to postmodern writers to adopt an ironical, a non-naïve attitude towards literary forms of the past; secondly, because it radicalizes Viktor Shklovsky's modernist, avant-garde idea of reflecting and exposing the narrative technique; thirdly, because it bids farewell to 'the novel in the modern sense of the word' and at the same time questions the established system of literary genres: 'Perhaps I am trying to pass an essay on to you', the narrator adds. Finally, the passage suggests that the postmodern text may be just a game.

'The novel lives on and on. / We don't really care' ('Der Roman lebt und lebt. / Uns ist das alles ziemlich egal'),[152] Jürgen Becker notes in his experimental text *Ränder.* Considering this sceptical diagnostic by an author, who is generally considered as postmodern, the postmodern novel has the option of either dissolving itself into experimental prose, as happens in Becker's work, or to become a game based on the traditional novel and its techniques – without naïvety, without mimesis, but with irony.

At this stage, an aesthetic affinity between the seemingly conventional narratives of Eco and Fowles and the language experiments of Jürgen Becker, Robbe-Grillet or Roland Barthes comes to light. Following Barthes, Eco and Fowles could say: 'Not truth guides my hand, but the game, the truth of the game.'[153] But the truth of the game is an indifference which excludes all kinds of metaphysical or ideological engagement. This explains why in Barthes's comments on Sade, Fourier and Loyola, sexuality, socialism and religion are secondary or even irrelevant because the three authors become playfellows in the field of classification. Barthes is interested in *the way they classify*, not in their actual topics.

In the American literary context, John Barth also tends to turn literature into a game of signs that often begins with an exposition of the narrative construction.

*Lost in the Funhouse*, for example, is the story of an unhappy outsider called Ambrose, whose family takes him to the east coast of the USA, where he actually visits a funhouse. For him it is an occasion to realize that he is different from the others and destined to become a writer. From the very outset, the text is presented by the author as a *construct*: 'A single straight underline is the manuscript mark for italic type, *which in turn* is the printed equivalent to oral emphasis of words (. . .).'[154] A few lines further on, we are reminded of Fowles's reflexive attitude towards his narrative constructions: 'The more closely an author identifies with the narrator, literally or metaphorically, the less advisable it is, as a rule, to use the first-person narrative viewpoint.'[155] The author follows his own advice and describes with distancing irony the artistic awakening of young Ambrose whom he presents to the reader ironically as 'one of Western Culture's truly great imaginations',[156] as someone, whose eloquent suffering will inspire millions. In the end, however, Ambrose's art turns out to be *Artistik* in the sense of Benn, an aesthetic game quite unrelated to Proust's literary *Jugement dernier* (cf. Chapter 4).

It would be a mistake to use Barth's text as a model illustrating the inferior or superficial character of postmodern literature. It is comparable to Thomas Mann's novella *Tonio Kröger* and, as far as the topic goes, to Proust's *Recherche*. However, it reminds us of the impossibility to revive Mann's or Proust's value judgements within a postmodern problematic where the aura of art has vanished and where the past can only be re-presented with a certain amount of irony. Hence one can only agree with Alan Lindsay, who suggests that we should read Barth's text as an auto-reflexive construct, as the author's reflection on his own postmodern situation: 'The text is at the same time about what it means to *be* a postmodern author (. . .).'[157]

In the postmodern text, the exposure of the narrative construction is completed by the *presence of a self-reflexive, self-conscious narrator* and by the *coexistence of competing narrative perspectives*. Thus Fowles imagines different endings to his novel and comments on the alternative constructions: 'But what you must not think is that this is a less plausible ending to their story.'[158] Similarly, Robbe-Grillet reflects, in his novel *In the Labyrinth* (*Dans le labyrinthe*, 1959), on the problems of literary narrative by emphasizing the fictional character of his text: 'This story is fiction, not a testimony.' ('Ce récit est une fiction, non un témoignage.')[159] At the same time, he makes his narrator construct different hypotheses about the fictive world of the novel. Right at the beginning, the narrator, who is inside a building, believes that it rains outside; a few moments later, he says that 'outside the sun is shining': 'Dehors il y a du soleil'.[160]

This contradictory technique, which also plays an important part in Robbe-Grillet's *The Voyeur* (*Le Voyeur*, 1955) and, much later, in *Topology of a Phantom City* (*Topologie d'une cité fantôme*, 1976), is radicalized in Michel Butor's *Degrees* (*Degrés*, 1960), where three different narrators compete with one another: Pierre Vernier, Pierre Eller and Henri Jouret. The teacher Vernier sets out to give a narrative account of his social environment by choosing a somewhat unconventional starting point: the genealogical relations within his form. His project fails because these relations resist all attempts at classification. He finds it impossible to define unambiguously the *degrees of relationship* (*degrés*) between his pupils. Before he dies, Vernier appoints his nephew Pierre Eller as his successor, who in turn delegates the task of narrator to his uncle Henri Jouret. However, Vernier's successors also fail: they become entangled in contradictions and polysemies which are accompanied by the polyphony of the text as a narrative in the first and the second person singular. This kind of extreme polyphony goes well beyond modernist agnosticism and could be read as a parody of structuralism.[161]

It could also be considered as a reaction to extreme polysemy (of characters, actions, facts), and it is linked to an experimental intertextuality ranging from cryptic allusions to literal quotations. It frustrates all attempts to define the postmodern text univocally as a monologue. An intertextuality generating polyphony is possibly the most prominent feature of literary postmodernity – together with radical constructivism. Authors such as Thomas Pynchon, Michel Butor and Jürgen Becker cultivate a textual polyphony that thwarts all attempts at conceptual definition.

Pynchon's *Gravity's Rainbow* (1973), a transgeneric experimental text that could be read one-dimensionally as an epic *mise en scène* of the Second World War, is a network of allusions, quotations, American army songs and German Christmas songs: '(. . .) Where are the joys? Where else but there where the Angels sing new songs and the bells ring out in the court of the King. *Eia* – strange thousand-year sigh – *eia, wärn wir da!* were we but there . . .'[162] In another part of the novel, the Marxist-Leninist metanarrative is called into question:

> But ever since it became impossible to die for death, we have had a secular version – yours. Die to help History grow to its predestined shape. Die knowing your act will bring a good end a bit closer. Revolutionary suicide, fine. But look: if History's changes *are* inevitable, why not *not* die? Vaslav? If it's going to happen anyway, what does it matter?[163]

In this case, it does not make sense to criticize the deterministic misunderstanding underlying these questions. For Pynchon's text is a polyphonic structure, an intertextual experiment without a critical and utopian dimension in the modernist sense, in the sense of Musil or Sartre.[164]

The danger that polyphony and a radical critique of political domination turn into indifferent pluralism was spotted early on by the prominent modernist Mikhail M. Bakhtin who considered the author's point of view as an ultimate safeguard against relativism. He reacted with scepticism to the postmodern tendency towards extreme polyphony and indifference which he observed in some parts of Dostoevsky's work: 'Here Bakhtin blames Dostoevsky for calling into question the encompassing exotopy, the stability and reliability of the author's consciousness which enables the reader to know the truth.'[165]

In literary postmodernity, this stability is irretrievably lost, because radical intertextuality exposes the relativity of all competing and colliding discourses without offering convincing alternatives. In Jürgen Becker's prose, all forms of rhetoric that contribute to the stultification of everyday life are discredited by irony, parody and other stylistic devices, but even in Becker's case, an 'encompassing exotopy' based on true knowledge is not in sight – and is not even deemed desirable: 'Sacrifice is necessary. Unity is our strength. Everybody has to tow the line. The nation is invaluable.' ('Opfer müssen schon mal sein. Erst einig sind wir stark. Aus der Reihe wird hier nicht getanzt. Volk ist viel.')[166] Like Pynchon, Becker earmarks the Marxist-Leninist discourse for a merciless critique: 'Where does the socialist organization of the workers and peasants really thrive: in the pure climate of the Mark Brandenburg.' ('Denn wo gedeiht die sozialistische Organisation der Arbeiter und Bauern: im klaren Klima der Mark Brandenburg.')[167] But where does the author stand when all discourses fail amidst carnivalesque laughter?

This almost metaphysical question is answered (at least partly) by Oswald Wiener in his textual experiment *The Improvement of Central Europe* (*Die Verbesserung von Mitteleuropa*, 1969): '*my ideal*. I write for the future smart asses; in order to complete the social scene of this age.' ('*mein ideal*. ich schreibe für die kommenden klugscheisser; um das milieu dieser ära komplett zu machen.')[168] This explanation is completed a few lines further on when Wiener asks the reader to attribute a meaning to his text: 'the smart-aleck reader won't find it difficult to invent a coherence – he will be responsible for it.' ('der neunmalweise leser hat wenig schwierigkeit zusammenhang zu erfinden – er tut dies auf eigene rechnung.')[169] Marked by contingency and a pluralism tending towards indifference, this text also confirms the playful, gadget-like character of postmodern literature.

The latter is alluded to by Maurice Roche in *Compact* (1966) where, in the postscript, the Nouveau Roman is presented as a reading machine and a *gadget littéraire*: 'Most new novels (*nouveaux romans*) actually appear as closed systems, which are undoubtedly treasure troves for structural analyses, but at the same time function as precise and useless machines or as real literary gadgets.'[170] Even *Compact*, a text pretending to go beyond the Nouveau Roman, but reminiscent of Jean Ricardou's experiments with this genre, is an intertextual and polyphonic gadget: a crossword puzzle for the postmodern reader.

The playful character of the postmodern novel might explain why the reader often occupies an important position within the textual game: not only in experimental texts such as Oswald Wiener's *Die Verbesserung von Mitteleuropa*, but also in more 'readable' novels like John Fowles's *The French Lieutenant's Woman* or in Italo Calvino's experimental *and* highly readable text *If on a Winter's Night a Traveler* (*Se una notte d'inverno un viaggiatore*, 1979). Unlike modernist novels, which are meant to provoke readers, solicit their political engagement or their critical reflection, Calvino's novel begins with an invitation to play. The starting point is a presentation of the gadget and its functioning in a relaxed atmosphere: 'You are about to begin reading Italo Calvino's new novel, *If on a winter's night a traveler*. Relax. Concentrate.' ('Stai per cominciare a leggere il nuovo romanzo *Se una notte d'inverno un viaggiatore* di Italo Calvino. Rilassati. Raccogliti.')[171]

In the course of the narrative, which consists of several beginnings of novels, the construction principle underlying the gadget is explained at regular intervals, and the explanations are reminiscent of those inserted by Fowles:

> I could write it all in the second person: you, Reader . . . I could also introduce a young lady, the Other Reader, and a counterfeiter-translator, and an old writer who keeps a diary like this diary . . . (Potrei scriverlo tutto in seconda persona: tu Lettore . . . Potrei anche farci entrare una Lettrice, un traduttore falsario, un vecchio scrittore che tiene un diario come questo diario . . .)[172]

This kind of analytic approach to the novel and to literature in general is partly due to the increasingly reflexive character of writing inherited from modernism, partly to the influence of French structuralism and the Nouveau Roman.[173] This not only applies to Calvino's experimental novel, but also to the more conventional novels of Eco and Fowles. In both cases, postmodern literature appears as *Artistik* in the sense of Gottfried Benn.

It is not surprising that reader response criticism became a theoretical complement to the postmodern novel in the course of the 1970s. Two elements relate this theory to the contemporary literary practice: Roland Barthes's and Michel Foucault's idea that the author as subject is 'dead', because he is no longer responsible for the constitution of meaning,[174] and the complementary idea that the literary critic's attention is no longer focused on the author as producer and the process of literary production, but on the reader and the process of reader response. The third idea is both postmodern and anchored in reader response criticism: it is the postulate that literary criticism should no longer aim at discovering the truth content of the text or its critical dimension, but should instead investigate the playful interaction between text and reader.

It is not by chance that Hans Robert Jauß, an advocate of reader response criticism, sees Calvino's novel primarily as a reading adventure:

> As a postmodern 'novel about a novel', the *Viaggiatore* is both a mirror of the reading process within the reading process and a sum total of all fashionable theories of reading, all of which are outdone by Calvino, the *poeta doctus*, in a most amusing way.[175]

In this case, it is not the critical search for meaning and truth that motivates reading, but (as in Barthes's case) the 'pleasure of the text', 'the reflected pleasure of observing the reading process, the game of rising and vanishing expectations'.[176]

It remains to be seen in what kind of historical and social context the search for the truth content of texts and for a critical subjectivity was abandoned and for what reasons. The underlying idea is not to condemn the postmodern game in an ascetic or authoritarian spirit, but to reveal the ambivalence of this game: an ambivalence that becomes indiscernible in the postmodern context of indifference.

## 5.7 Beyond Truth and the Subject: Pluralism, Particularism, Indifference and Ideology

The reverse of the postmodern coin is brutally revealed by the Spanish-Catalonian author Félix de Azúa and subtly described by the Austrian novelist Christoph Ransmayr. While Azúa's novel *The Story of an Idiot Narrated by Himself. Or the Content of Happiness* (*Historia de un idiota contada por él mismo o El contenido de la felicidad*, 1986) narrates a hopeless search for true happiness and on the way discovers the vacuity of all social values, Ransmayr's novel *The Last World* (*Die letzte Welt*, 1988) announces the last metamorphosis of humanity: its transformation into inorganic nature.

Azúa, who dedicates his first person narrative to his 'precursors' Bouvard and Pécuchet ('este libro está dedicado a mis precursores Bouvard y Pécuchet . . .'), makes his hero rush through all the phases that are commonly covered by the European novel of apprenticeship: childhood, religion, sexuality, philosophy and art. Each of these phases is marked by two experiences of a damaged life: by the interchangeable character of all emotions, individuals, ideas and objects in market society and by the destructive force of the mechanisms of domination.

After a repressive and unhappy Catholic education, the effects of which were thoroughly analysed by Spanish modernists and by the Generation of 1898,[177] the narrator takes refuge in sexuality. He discovers that – like sport – it is dominated by the quantitative criteria of the performance principle. He compares one of his partners (the wife of a notary and his uncle's lover) to some Hindu deity: 'with six or seven breasts, half a dozen bottoms and an unlimited number of vulvas' ('hasta seis o siete pechos, media docena de culos y un número ilimitado de vulvas').[178] Like tennis, which would ideally be played with four arms, sexuality appears to the narrator as a quantitative activity similar to the earning of money, 'especially since "earning money" is the great metaphysical excuse which helps us to bear the most unbearable boredom' ('ya que "ganar dinero" es la gran excusa metafísica que ayuda a soportar los más abrumadores tedios').[179] After this discovery, sex and eros cease to play an important part in the hero's search for happiness, because he discovers that there is no truth in them. The boredom he so often refers to is comparable to Alberto Moravia's *noia* and – like the latter – a symptom of indifference.[180]

This all-pervading indifference is eventually responsible for the failure of the scientific and philosophical experiments that are important phases in the hero's search. Unlike some realist and modernist disillusion novels, which presuppose an initial faith in certain social values, Azúa's novel presupposes disillusionment. This fact is confirmed by the irony of the narrator's comments:

> I had turned my back on the false happiness of love, a simulated synthesis of ownness and otherness, in order to explore philosophical happiness which actually resolves all contradictions or maintains them, as it pleases. (Había abandonado la falsa felicidad amorosa, simulación de síntesis de lo propio y lo ajeno, para penetrar en la felicidad filosófica, la que realmente resuelve todas las contradicciones o las mantiene a su gusto.)[181]

This parody of idealist, especially Hegelian philosophy suggests that the latter may not offer the answers Azúa's hero is looking for.

In the last phase of his search, he turns to literature, but eventually discovers that even the word of the poet is null and void. Whatever is experienced as significant, as conducive to happiness at the end of Proust's *Recherche* (literature as *Jugement dernier*), is considered by Azúa as trivial. He adopts Hegel's thesis about the end of art[182] by radicalizing it: 'THIS IS NOT THE RIGHT TIME FOR ART. It comes too late.' ('ÉSTE NO ES TIEMPO PARA EL ARTE. Había llegado tarde.')[183] Finally, art is dissolved in the equivalence and interchangeability of all styles: 'BECAUSE ALL STYLES ARE GOOD' ('PORQUE TODOS LOS ESTILOS SON BUENOS').[184]

Within the postmodern problematic, the following passage seems particularly significant:

> But in our century, one can build romance hermitages, gothic cathedrals, Mesopotamian ziggurats, and everybody thinks it's wonderful because everything is valuable, because EVERYTHING IS INDIFFERENT. This peculiar feature – that style is a problem, because all styles are equally valuable – is, in fact, a symptom of our habit of calling 'art' something that deserves another name. (Pero en nuestro siglo se pueden construir ermitas románicas, catedrales góticas, zigurats mesopotámicos y a todo el mundo le parece estupendo porque todo vale, porque TODO DA LO MISMO. Esa peculiaridad – que el estilo sea un problema porque todos los estilos son equivalentes – es, de hecho, un síntoma de que llamamos 'arte' a algo que merece otro nombre.)[185]

Where everything can be defined as art, from a novel to a textual collage, from a painting to painted shoes exhibited in a museum, everything tends to become aesthetically valuable, and aesthetic criteria become blurred or even superfluous, as Baudrillard points out in his *transesthétique* (cf. Section 2.6).

At the end of his search, which can be read as a parody of the modernist quest, Azúa's narrator discovers that happiness is not even to be found in works of art. They appear to him as 'changeable, superfluous, unstable and ephemeral objects that emerge from nothingness and return to it whenever the whim of a handful of individuals sends them there' ('objetos variables, prescindibles, cambiantes y efímeros que surgen de la nada y vuelven a ella por el capricho de un puñado de hombres').[186]

The dissolution of the aesthetic truth of Mallarmé, Proust or Adorno is completed by the dissolution of the narrating or acting subject. In retrospect, he recognizes that his search is an 'experience without meaning or content' ('experiencia sin sentido ni contenido')[187] and sees his 'world falling to pieces which it is impossible to recompose in the ruined theatre of my memory' ('un mundo hecho pedazos, de imposible recomposición, esparcidos sin orden en el teatro ruinoso de mi memoria').[188] It is the 'vision of an idiot' ('la visión de un idiota'),[189] who finally has to admit to himself that he writes without a definable intention, without reason: 'in order not to be alone on all those endless, empty days' ('por hacerme compañía en días inacabables y vacíos').[190] Here again, particularization and indifference appear as complementary phenomena. Literary writing is no longer related to an aesthetic or metaphysical goal; it is a particular, interchangeable activity.

The fact that Azúa considers Flaubert's heroes Bouvard and Pécuchet as his precursors is certainly not due to trivial chance, but ought to be seen as a hint at Flaubert's importance for the postmodern problematic. Occupying a position between realism and modernism, Flaubert, an older contemporary of Nietzsche, not only reacted to the spreading of modernist ambivalence, but in his later work also anticipated some aspects of postmodern indifference, which he defines as 'equality' of all phenomena: 'égalité de tout, du bien et du mal, du beau et du laid, de l'insignifiant et du caractéristique'.[191] This discovery is reminiscent of Nietzsche's idea that Good and Evil are in reality *identical, wesensgleich*.[192]

Moreover, it becomes clear that transformations within a problematic take place gradually, are sometimes announced at a very early stage, when they appear sporadically, then reappear much later in a more compact, more visible form, whereupon they can be defined as 'romanticism', 'modernism' or 'postmodernism'. Thus postmodern indifference is already latent in modernist ambivalence – as suggested by Nietzsche's and Flaubert's works.

This final phase of the transition from modernism to postmodernity can also be observed in Christoph Ransmayr's novel *The Last World*, which could be read as a counterpart of Azúa's text. The action takes place in a fantastic world brought about by a daring transposition of Augustus's ancient Rome into a contemporary Italy dominated by media, favouritism and corruption. Amidst this postmodern anachronism, Cotta, a Roman citizen and a friend of Ovid, sets out to find the author of the *Metamorphoses* who was banished by the Roman authorities to Tomi on the Black Sea coast. His hope to find also the poet's mythical *magnum opus* remains unfulfilled, but as the action progresses, Rans-mayr's novel reads like an intertextual transformation of the famous Latin text into a contemporary prophecy.

Although its intricate network of allusions and hidden quotations cannot be reduced to this prophecy, the latter is certainly part and parcel of its semantic structure, its 'semantic gesture', as Jan Mukařovský would say.[193] Echo, the nymph, who in the *Metamorphoses* falls in love with Narcissus and who, in Ransmayr's novel, becomes Cotta's mistress for one night, describes Ovid's vision of a reified humanity whose final transformation is due to its lust for power, its stupidity and its wolfish rapaciousness:

> (. . .) Naso read this future to her from the fire one winter day. Out of every pebble, a monster! Echo shouted. The exile's prophecy to the world: humans of stone. And these creatures creeping from the slime of a race that had per-ished of its own wolfish rapacity, stupidity, and thirst of power, Naso called them the true, the genuine human race, a brood of mineral-like hardness, with hearts of basalt, eyes of jade, without feelings, without a language of love, but likewise without any stirrings of hate, sympathy, or grief, as implacable, as deaf and durable as the rocks of this coast. ([. . .] Diese Zukunft habe ihr Naso an einem Wintertag aus dem Feuer gelesen, aus jedem Kiesel ein Ungeheuer! schrie Echo, Menschen aus Stein habe der Verbannte seiner Welt prophezeit. Was aber aus dem Schlick eines an seiner wölfischen Gier, seiner Blödheit und Herrschsucht zugrundegegangenen Geschlechts her-vorkriechen werde, das habe Naso die eigentliche und wahre Menschheit genannt, eine Brut von mineralischer Härte, das Herz aus Basalt, die Augen aus Serpentin, ohne Gefühle, ohne eine Sprache der Liebe, aber auch ohne jede Regung des Hasses, des Mitgefühls oder der Trauer, so unnachgiebig, so taub und dauerhaft wie die Felsen dieser Küste.)[194]

This last metamorphosis of humanity is reminiscent of some of Moravia's characters, who are incapable of human emotions, and of the indifferent world of Camus's drama *Le Malentendu* in which the sun produces 'radiant, but com-pletely empty bodies' ('des corps resplendissants, mais vidés par l'intérieur').[195]

While Moravia and Camus keep reappearing as precursors of literary post-modernity, Ransmayr's novel could also be read within the framework of the modernist problematic: as Cotta's search for the true, authentic word that is finally recomposed by the Roman traveller himself amidst the ruins of Trachilla, where Ovid is supposed to have written his last texts:

I HAVE COMPLETED A WORK / THAT WILL WITHSTAND FIRE / AND IRON / EVEN THE WRATH OF GOD AND / ALL-CONSUMING TIME / WHENEVER IT WILL / LET DEATH NOW COME / HAVING ONLY MY BODY / WITHIN ITS POWER/ AND END MY LIFE / BUT THROUGH

THIS WORK / I WILL LIVE ON AND / LIFT MYSELF AVOVE THE STARS / AND MY NAME / WILL BE INDESTRUCTIBLE. (ICH HABE EIN WERK VOLLENDET / DAS DEM FEUER STANDHALTEN WIRD / UND DEM EISEN / SELBST DEM ZORN GOTTES UND / DER ALLESVERNICH-TENDEN ZEIT / WANN IMMER ER WILL / MAG NUN DER TOD / DER NUR ÜBER MEINEN LEIB / GEWALT HAT / MEIN LEBEN BEENDEN / ABER DURCH DIESES WERK / WERDE ICH FORTDAUERN UND MICH / HOCH ÜBER DIE STERNE EMPORSCHWINGEN UND MEIN NAME / WIRD UNZERSTÖRBAR SEIN.)[196]

This modernist project, which revives previous aesthetic projects from anti-quity to romanticism, is foiled towards the end of the novel by the destructive forces of time. They put an end to humanity and to its memory that alone could guarantee a continuity of culture. Even the work of Ovidius Naso, transcribed by his Greek servant Pythagoras, falls prey to the devastations of time:

His Greek servant had written down his tales and erected a monument to every word he spoke – but that was meaningless now and at best a game for madmen. Books mildewed, burned, turned to ashes and dust. Cairns toppled back down the slopes as formless rubble, and even letters chiselled in basalt vanished under the patience of slugs. Reality, once discovered, no longer needed recording. (Daß ein griechischer Knecht seine Erzählungen auf-gezeichnet und um jedes seiner Worte ein Denkmal errichtet hatte, war nun ohne Bedeutung und bestenfalls ein Spiel für Verrückte: Bücher verschim-melten, verbrannten, zerfielen zu Asche und Staub; Steinmale kippten als formloser Schutt in die Halden zurück, und selbst in Basalt gemeißelte Zeichen verschwanden unter der Geduld von Schnecken. Die Erfindung von Wirklichkeit bedurfte keiner Aufzeichnungen mehr.)[197]

These concluding remarks of Ransmayr's artist novel could be read as refer-ring to the experiments of Azúa's narrator with art. In both cases, art, deemed by romantics and modernists to outlast millennia, turns out to be mortal. Unlike Proust's *Recherche* and Sartre's *La Nausée*, two modernist attempts to justify sub-jectivity by aesthetic means, Azúa's and Ransmayr's texts reveal the ephemeral character of artistic subjectivity. In Ransmayr's case, the aesthetic invention of reality appears as a 'game for lunatics'.

Not only does artistic subjectivity turn out to be null and void, but subjectivity as such is questioned in postmodern literature: it is reified both in Alain Robbe-Grillet's *Le Voyeur* and in Patrick Süskind's *Das Parfum*. In *Le Voyeur* (1955), the traveller Mathias, who visits a fictive island in order to sell watches to its inhabit-ants, appears to be driven by two complementary impulses: the wish to make money and a perverse sexual desire. Although these two impulses contradict each other in theory (sexual fantasies can distract from business), they comple-ment each other in practice as two quantitative principles that are indifferent to all cultural (moral, political, aesthetic, metaphysical) values. The quantitative imagination in the commercial sense that calculates the mechanical gestures leading to the sale of a watch ('opening the lock, lifting the lid, removing the note book'; 'déclic de la serrure, rotation du couvercle en arrière, déplacement de l'agenda')[198] has its counterpart in a quantitative sexual imagination that keeps conjuring up the picture of a girl with opened legs tied to the ground.

Patricia J. Johnson points out that, in this case, a text by Camus could be read as announcing Robbe-Grillet's deterministic visions. Like Camus's Renégat (one could add Meursault), Mathias is 'quite incapable of resisting the impulse that dominates him'.[199] This interpretation is also valid in the case of Patrick Süskind's novel *Perfume* (*Das Parfum*, 1985) which has time and again been defined as a postmodern text.

Unlike Mathias, Grenouille, a murderer of young girls, does not obey a sexual impulse, but follows his refined sense of smell that eventually makes him an unrivalled producer of perfumes. His urge to murder beautiful girls, whose 'irresistible'[200] odour he appropriates in order to use it for his perfume production, does not seem to bother him. Like Mathias, like the Renegate and Ransmayr's man of the future, he is not aware of any moral, aesthetic or political values: 'A murder had been the start of this splendour – if he was at all aware of the fact, it was a matter of total indifference to him.' ('Daß am Anfang dieser Herrlichkeit ein Mord gestanden hatte, war ihm, wenn überhaupt bewußt, vollkommen gleichgültig.')[201]

In the end, Grenouille succeeds in manipulating his contemporaries by the use of highly sophisticated and original essences. A few moments before his planned execution, his perfume begins to work, and the crowds, instead of cursing him, pardon his murders and eventually even adore him like a divine being:

> They were overcome by a powerful sense of goodwill, of tenderness, of crazy, childish infatuation, yes, God help them, of love for this little homicidal man, and they were unable, unwilling to do anything about it. (Es überkam sie ein mächtiges Gefühl von Zuneigung, von Zärtlichkeit, von toller kindischer Verliebtheit, ja, weiß Gott, von Liebe zu dem kleinen Mördermann, und sie konnten, sie wollten nichts dagegen tun.)[202]

Along with the main actor, all other characters are seized by this determinism. Instead of acting in accordance with moral norms, they are dominated by two complementary impulses: sexuality and the smell of the irresistible perfume:

> The result was that the scheduled execution of one of the most abominable criminals of the age degenerated into the largest orgy the world had seen since the second century before Christ. (Die Folge war, daß die geplante Hinrichtung eines der verabscheuungswürdigsten Verbrecher seiner Zeit zum

größten Bacchanal ausartete, das die Welt seit dem zweiten vorchristlichen Jahrhundert gesehen hatte.)[203]

Then follows a description of this Bacchanalia in the course of which subjectivity is entirely dissolved and superseded by determinism. Judith Ryan quite rightly points out that Süskind does not present a new form of subjectivity, but parodies its traditional literary forms.[204]

Art and the artist novel are also parodied in Süskind's text where art is assimilated to the 'art' of perfumery. Music, considered by Nietzsche as the highest form of art, is indirectly compared by Süskind's narrator with the production of perfumes. Thus the emergence of Grenouille's olfactory talent appears as analogous to the awakening of musical genius in an artistically inclined child.[205] As in Azúa's and Ransmayr's novels – and long after Hegel – the death of the subject and of art becomes a topic in Süskind's fantastic story. The 'eternal art' of romanticism and modernism is dissolved in ephemeral perfume.

Moreover, the death of the subject casts doubts on the survival of the novel which Goethe formerly defined as a 'subjective epic'.[206] For a subjective epic without a subject is bound to become aporetic and fall apart. This was recognized early on by Jürgen Becker who pleads for the dissolution of the novel as genre. Along with subjectivity and metaphysics, it is banned from the postmodern problematic: 'Only beyond the novel does writing recover its authentic meaning; it is the dissolution of the novel's categories that releases the utopian text inherent in each novel.'[207] This text is polyphonic and pluralistic, and its plurality excludes a univocal constitution of meaning and subjectivity.

In Becker's case, the 'authentic meaning' is a radical intertextuality accompanied by a fragmented, decentred subject that is as ephemeral as the writing subject in Ransmayr's mythical world. In Becker's world, 'He' and 'We' do not refer to homogeneous units, but to unstable, heterogeneous processes of language:

He splits up into multiple figures, whose roles are all presented to him. Having to rely on himself, he can hardly grasp himself, for he hears all the different voices that talk at cross purposes in his heads. Being a plural, he sees, hears and talks in a plural form. The word *we* expresses this state of things inaccurately (he therefore adopts different manners of speaking and speaks wrongly). It pretends to be an association. (Er vervielfältigt sich in die Figuren, die alle er vorgespielt findet. Auf sich selbst gestellt, übersieht er sich kaum, hört er alle die Stimmen, die durcheinanderreden in seinen Köpfen. Er in der Mehrzahl sieht, hört und spricht in der Mehrzahl. Das Wort *wir* drückt diesen Sachverhalt ungenau aus [er spricht darum oft immer anders und falsch]. Es täuscht einen Verein vor.)[208]

This kind of polyphony is incompatible with a subjective search and the form of the novel as a 'subjective epic'.

One could of course object with Peter Härtling that even Jürgen Becker's prose does not really go beyond the genre boundaries of the novel, because it can always be read *as* a novel. Within the context mapped out here, it seems more promising, however, to follow Becker and to link the decline of the traditional novel to the dissolution of subjectivity in postmodern literature. For novels built around pseudo-subjects, such as *Le Voyeur* or *Das Parfum*, owe their thrill and suspense precisely to the determinism that negates subjectivity (Mathias and Grenouille often appear in an animal-like pose). They are no longer novels, if the novel is to be defined – with Goethe, Walter Benjamin, Theodor W. Adorno and Lucien Goldmann – as a subjective search for meaning and as a genre that opposes the established social order.

Most of the novels and dramas mentioned here (e.g. Werner Schwab's play *Mesalliance*) no longer pretend to be quests for meaning and truth. Like Calvino's later novels, they admit their particularity: their status of contingent constructions, of artistic games within a problematic dominated by the overarching category of indifference. It is within this context that Jürgen Becker's remarks on the novel (quoted above) should be re-read: 'The novel lives on and on. / We don't really care.' We don't really care, because the novel no longer pretends to establish universally valid values and no longer sees itself as a search for alternatives to the contemporary social order. In this situation, Azúa's narrator may have the last word: 'I write WITHOUT REASON' ('Escribo SIN RAZÓN'.).[209]

Naturally, it would be wrong to assume that the entire postmodern problematic is devoid of critique. It would be easy to prove the opposite: not only in conjunction with Azúa's desperate polemics or with Becker's radical critique of language, but also by evoking the critique of Victorian Puritanism in Fowles's *The French Lieutenant's Woman*. However, all of these critiques are pure negations: unlike Adorno's modernist, negative dialectic which does rely on a certain number of problematical, threatened values such as subjectivity, autonomy, truth and – criticism. It is not by chance that all of these values keep coming under fire from various postmodern groupings whose members no longer consider themselves as critical intellectuals.[210]

Although Brecht differs substantially from the authors of Critical Theory, his definition of realism illustrates a notion of critique that has become *inconceivable* within the postmodern problematic. The contrastive effect of this definition is reinforced by its anachronism which reveals the loss of values and historical perspectives in postmodernity:

To be a *realist* means: to discover the causal complexity of society / to unmask the dominant viewpoints as the viewpoints of the dominant groups / to write in the perspective of the class which presents global solutions to the most pressing problems humanity grapples with / to stress the moment of development / focusing on the concrete and allowing for abstractions.[211]

Answering within the postmodern problematic of indifference and inter-changeability, Azúa might refer to the bizarre transformation of the communist leader of the working class: 'today a well-known town planner working for a Californian estate agency' ('hoy conspicuo urbanista al servicio de una inmobiliaria californiana').[212]

Considering this dizzying speed of an accelerated[213] social change that makes a former communist leader reappear as an estate agent, one could also imagine historical metamorphoses and anachronisms telescoping antiquity and moder-nity or bringing together individuals of different historical periods. In this perspective, Luis Goytisolo arranges a meeting between Marx and Lenin ('El encuentro Marx-Lenin') in his textual experiment *Investigaciones y conjeturas de Claudio Mendoza* (1985).[214] Similarly, in his novel *Ragtime* (1975), E. L. Doctorow makes Sigmund Freud appear together with the illusionist Harry Houdini, the feminist Emma Goldmann and Henry Ford in the USA around 1900.

In this situation marked by calculated anachronisms, the homogeneity of the historical subject is lost, together with the possibility of narrating history within the framework of a unifying, teleological metanarrative. From an aes-thetic and postmodern point of view, this loss may appear as a gain: as a new way of linking heterogeneous periods, situations and figures in a dialogical experiment.

It would nevertheless be risky to view literary postmodernity one-sidedly as a collective rejection of the metaphysical metanarratives, merely because countless contemporaries believe in Lyotard's *incrédulité*. The second chapter was meant to show to what extent indifference and dualistic ideologies are related in the sense that the latter can at any moment be mobilized against the former. For this reason, it would hardly make sense to rely on an 'end of ideology' (Bell in the 1960s) in the realm of literature.

This hypothesis is borne out by the ecological and feminist novels published by Ernest Callenbach and Marge Piercy, both of whom oppose indifference and the rule of the exchange value and whose works can be related to the *social movements* as described by Touraine and Etzioni (cf. Chapter 2). In Callenbach's *Ecotopia Emerging* (1981), the enemies of ecological ideology are named right at the beginning of the novel, a narrative interspersed with social reportage. They form an impressive phalanx: profit, technocratic domination over nature, nuclear power and the 'patriarchal nation-states'.[215] Callenbach's response to this formidable challenge is his ecological and utopian project aiming – very much like his *Ecotopia: A Novel about Ecology, People and Politics in 1999* (1975) – at a world reconciled with nature and human needs. At the end of the novel, Ecotopia appears as the last hope in a world ruled by trusts and threatened by economic exploitation and military conflicts: 'On the whole, destruction still reigned; surrounded by desolation, Ecotopia seemed a small, precarious island of hope. But its inhabitants had lit a beacon that might yet guide other travel-lers home.'[216] Especially the last word in this passage carries connotations of an affirmative ideology which is not altogether distinct from the ideological image of an unspoilt village in the Cotswolds.

The fact that this ideology, which is meant to prepare individuals and groups for action, is structured by semantic dualism, was observed by Heinz Tschachler in his comments on Callenbach's novel:

> In conjunction with the hypertrophic social conscience, the ecological 'paradise' inevitably reminds us of the puritan theocracies of New England and of the fact that the high-handed dogmatization of one's own position (which necessarily implies the daemonization of the Other) has always been part of political discourse in America.[217]

However, this kind of ideology is also to be found in Europe, where reactions to ambiguity, modernist ambivalence and postmodern indifference have always been *dualistic*. A dualistic structure also forms the basis of Marge Piercy's eco-feminist novel *Woman on the Edge of Time* in which a feminized life is reconciled with nature and presented as an alternative to the perverse manipulations of a psychiatric clinic. In a setting where a mythical Mattapoisett, similar to Ecotopia, appears as a domination-free, utopian alternative to the dystopia of New York, the narrator describes her heroine as torn between these two worlds. Eventually, this double life leads to her desperate revolt against the machinations of a male-dominated psychiatry. Connie kills her doctors: ' "I just killed six people", she said to the mirror, but she washed her hands because she was terrified of the poison. "I murdered them dead. Because they are the violence-prone".'[218]

Although Piercy's novel is not only an ideological reaction to the postmodern problematic of indifference, but also a critique of society and a revolt against the latter, it starts from certain ecological and feminist premises which could be considered as symptoms of ideological tensions and linked to the feminist and ecological movements.

Within the postmodern problematic, ideological reactions and revolts are increasingly likely because most people are unable to cope with the kind of emotional indifference that finds its expression in Becker's prose:

> Sleeping until September would be the best idea. – Soon it will be indifferent. – In the evening start with a few brandies / then you don't feel it so much. – The only fascinating thing will be the face of indifference and sleep will never lose its future, and soon the others will say the same thing. (Am liebsten schlafen bis September – bald wird es gleichgültig sein – abends erst wieder einige Schnäpse / dann spürt mans nicht so – und faszinierend wird nur das Gesicht der Gleichgültigkeit sein und der Schlaf wird nie seine Zukunft verlieren und bald sagen es die Anderen alles so auch.)[219]

This is by no means certain. Some others might prefer ideology to brandy and might see to it that the great metanarratives are revived or that new metanarratives are invented. It seems important to distinguish between the sceptical postmodern intellectuals – most of whom are no longer critical intellectuals in the modern sense – and the faithful ideologues.

Once again, it becomes clear that literary postmodernity is a complex and heterogeneous problematic in which ideology as dualistic discourse is more likely to oppose indifference than ambivalence (which does not disappear). In this context, at least four different textual models could be constructed which underlie the postmodern literary constellation. They were mentioned in the fourth chapter and commented on above: 1. the text as a radical language experiment offered to the reader as a contingent, particular construct within the framework of an institutionalized game (Butor, Robbe-Grillet, M. Roche, Jürgen Becker, Calvino, Wiener, Pynchon); 2. the readable – neo-realist, neo-romantic or neo-modernist – text based on a conventional narrative (Eco, Fowles, Süskind, Ransmayr, the recent Robbe-Grillet); 3. the ideological and utopian text of the new (feminist, ecological) movements (Piercy, Callenbach); 4. the text of the destructive revolt (Azúa, Th. Bernhard, Ransmayr).

This sketch of a necessarily incomplete typology is an open structure and is meant to serve as a provisional guide within the dynamic and polymorphous problematic of postmodernity. In view of what has been said so far, the following arguments can be deduced from this typology: 1. The postmodern problematic is as heterogeneous as its modernist counterpart and hence cannot be reduced to a poetic or an aesthetic: it certainly cannot be identified with the slogan of a 'readable, popular and post-avant-garde literature'. For Calvino, Azúa, Pynchon, Schwab, Becker or Ransmayr, all of whom are considered as postmodern by literary critics, are not more 'popular' than the modernists Hesse, Brecht, Thomas Mann or Moravia. One should add that our society is too heterogeneous to permit the emergence of a homogeneous popular aesthetic which may have existed in the age of Shakespeare or Lope de Vega. 2. The four textual models are not applicable to other forms of art – architecture, music, painting – for which specific models[220] have to be developed and subsequently related to the existing literary models, if postmodernity is to be reconstructed in all of its essential aspects and facets. General statements encompassing different forms of art are to be found in many works on postmodernity, but they tend to gloss over problems specific to the individual arts and their genres.[221] 3. The authors and their works cannot be entirely accounted for within the types constructed here, and the latter could easily be deconstructed – like all typologies.

Considering that it is impossible to identify former naturalists like Huysmans or Svevo with aestheticism or the modernist experiment, any attempt to identify authors like Robbe-Grillet or Calvino with only one postmodern position is also bound to fail. Within the postmodern problematic, where indifference and ideology form a dialectical unit, an oscillation between the poles is the norm, and an ideological 'conversion' in the sense of Huysmans can never be excluded. The experimental author of today can become tomorrow's ecological, feminist or socialist prophet.

The reconstruction of the two complementary problematics was also meant to show that it is not possible to distinguish modernism and postmodernity by relying on purely formal or aesthetic criteria. Those who try it nevertheless will eventually be forced to admit with Dieter Borchmeyer: 'Moreover, most of the supposedly essential features of postmodernity can be found in the history of our century's literary modernism.'[222] Borchmeyer adds plausibly that Eco's parodies and hidden quotations hardly differ from those of Thomas Mann. This may be the case; however, one crucial difference consists in the fact that Eco's novel as a whole can be read as a playful quotation of a used and abused genre, whereas in Thomas Mann's *Doctor Faustus* Europe's entire system of values is at stake:

'I don't quite understand, dear man. What will you take back?' 'The Ninth Symphony', he replied. And then no more came, though I waited for it. ('Ich verstehe dich, Lieber, nicht ganz. Was willst du zurücknehmen?' 'Die Neunte Symphonie', erwiderte er. Und dann kam nichts mehr, wie ich auch wartete.)[223]

Maurice Roche's and Oswald Wiener's intertextuality is not comparable to Thomas Mann's, because it is inseparable from a polyphonic text without subjectivity. It is in the linguistic, historical and social context that the 'essential features' mentioned by Borchmeyer can be observed. In this particular instance, one should invoke – against all contemporary trends – Hegel's famous dictum: 'The truth is the whole.'

## 5.8  Postmodern Literature, Deconstruction and Pragmatism: Epilogue II

In Adorno's *Minima Moralia*, a collection of aphorisms, Hegel's idea of revealing essence by representing the totality of a context is radically queried by the terse remark 'the whole is the false'.[224] In conjunction with this anti-Hegelianism, deconstructionists like Geoffrey H. Hartman refer to Adorno's 'negative thinking' in order accentuate the affinities between deconstruction and Critical Theory.[225] Global appraisals of this kind ignore the fact that Adorno never tried to promote contingency in philosophy or to dismiss the notion of aesthetic truth (truth content). On the contrary, in *Minima Moralia* he insists on the objectivity of truth: 'The denial of objective truth by recourse to the subject implies the negation of the latter: no measure remains for the measure of all things; lapsing into contingency, he becomes untruth.'[226] Although a Hegelian reduction of the particular to the concept is to be avoided, philosophy has to see to it that conceptual truth is not dissolved in the particularity of the contingent.

In a complementary manner, Adorno's *Aesthetic Theory* considers the negation of meaning in modernist works as meaningful from the point of view of social criticism: 'Works of the highest level of form that are meaningless or alien to meaning are therefore more than simply meaningless because they gain content (*Gehalt*) through the negation of meaning.'[227] What is at stake here, is the truth content of art, and Adorno obstinately continues the modernist search for meaning when he adds: 'Everything depends on this: whether meaning inheres in the negation of meaning in the artwork or if negation conforms to the status quo (. . .).'[228]

This is not the point of view adopted by the deconstructionists. For them, the negation of meaning is a destruction of metaphysical meaning in the Nietzschean sense. In the last section of the fourth chapter, it became clear that detailed descriptions of semantic aporias and of the disintegration of meaning are the gist of the deconstructionist game. The idea of this game is to show that meaning is an illusion that dissolves as soon as the text in question is put under the deconstructionist magnifying glass.

> The deconstructive critic, J. Hillis Miller explains, seeks to find, by this process of retracing, the element in the system studied which is alogical, the thread in the text in question which will unravel it all, or the loose stone which will pull down the whole building.[229]

Unlike modernism and Critical Theory in particular, deconstruction does not advocate a critique of ideology capable of revealing the truth content of texts, but envisages a radical negation of meaning.

Its approach is put in literary practice by the textual experiments of Robbe-Grillet, Claude Simon, Jürgen Becker and Maurice Roche, whose radical critique of ideologies and conventional literary forms avoids alternatives, truth contents or utopias. Thus Claude Simon's novel *The Flanders Road* (*La Route des Flandres*, 1960) culminates in a vision of the world marked by incoherence, fragmentation and decay: 'an abandoned, useless building, prey to the incoherent, nonchalant, impersonal and destructive work of time' ('une bâtisse abandonnée, inutilisable, livrée à l'incohérent, nonchalant, impersonnel et destructeur travail du temps').[230] This scene is completed by Ransmayr's vision of a petrified humanity and by Azúa's descriptions of the disintegration of subjectivity.

On a theoretical level, it is paralleled by Paul de Man's theory of interpretation which the Yale deconstructionist does not view as a game in the sense of Barthes, but as a process of destruction, decomposition. The aim of this decomposition, which is also meant to break up ideological dogmas, is by no means Adorno's truth content, but the kind of lethal negativity that inspires the texts of Azúa, Schwab and Ransmayr. Continuing Nietzsche's train of thought, Paul de Man remarks: 'The wisdom of the text is self-destructive (art is true but truth kills itself), but this self-destruction is infinitely displaced in a series of successive rhetorical reversals (. . .).'[231] With a slight penchant for cynicism, one could speak in this instance of a slow death: the death of truth should arrive gradually in order to prolong the deconstructionist game.

Within the problematic of indifference, the death of meaning and truth appears as mediated by the exchange value. This is also how Gianni Vattimo sees the situation in conjunction with Heidegger and Baudrillard. He concludes: 'Nihilism is thus the reduction of Being to exchange-value.'[232]

The deconstructionist negation of meaning and truth has its counterpart in the theory of contingence as propounded by certain pragmatists. The link between the two positions is made by Adorno's remarks on truth and contingence quoted above. Like postmodern literature, which revolts, destroys and deconstructs without proposing alternatives, new truths or utopias, a pragmatist like Rorty puts forward ideas and arguments in the hope that others will accept, use and develop them. He aims neither at rational generalization nor at universal validity. His philosophical and moral project consists in 'lending an ear to the specialists in particularity, permitting them to fulfill their function as agents of love (. . .)'.[233] Here again, the postmodern tendency towards particularization prevails over Critical Theory's search for truth as aesthetic truth content or as critical insight.

If one reconsiders Rorty's argument (commented on in the third chapter) that there are no problems, which would have the effect of unifying humanity in a global action, then one faces a particularistic notion of truth that is difficult to reconcile with the universally human struggle for collective survival in a world threatened by ecological disaster. However, this particularization of thought corresponds to the particularistic tendencies in a postmodern literature whose authors have renounced the modernist search for universal, utopian values.

Although Oswald Wiener's *Die Verbesserung von Mitteleuropa* cannot be read in a denotative and naïve manner as a philosophical text, some of its sentences could refer to the discourse of pragmatism which Wiener is likely to dismiss along with the notion of truth:

truth is an element of society; a trick of political anaesthesia; reality is private, the prosthesis of the individual. the paltry character of these concepts. (wahrheit ist ein element der gesellschaft, kniffe der politischen anästhesie; wirklichkeit ist privat, die prothese des individuums. die ärmlichkeit dieser beiden begriffe.)[234]

Their paltry nature is due to the fact, observed by Sartre, Camus and the surrealists, that daily life and language are torn by commercial discourses and rival ideologies each of which fights the others with a particular notion of reality or truth. The global result is that concepts of reality and truth become interchangeable within the postmodern problematic of indifference.

In this context, Joseph K.'s desperate exclamation that untruth is turned into 'a universal principle' ('Die Lüge wird zur Weltordnung gemacht'.)[235] may soon become obsolete. For in a social and linguistic situation, where a generally accepted concept of truth no longer exists, it becomes increasingly difficult to define 'lie' or 'false consciousness'.

# Chapter 6

# Dialogical Theory: Between the Universal and the Particular

Two questions resulting from the previous two chapters will be at the centre of the following discussion: What could a critical theory of society look like in postmodernity and what stance would it adopt towards other theories? What has been said so far suggests that such a theory would not start from universalistic truths and statements, but would be an open, dialogical structure linking the particular to the universal, the identical to the other. It should be able to find its way between the Scylla of a modern or modernist universalism, as expressed in Habermas's 'ideal speech situation', and the Charybdis of a postmodern particularism in the sense of Lyotard.

Habermas, who was the first to plead in favour of a dialogical turn in the case of Critical Theory, is quite right when he points out: 'The post-empiricist theory of science has named several good reasons for believing that the shaky ground of a rationally motivated consensus among discussion partners is our only foundation – in questions of physics not less than in questions of morals.'[1]

What matters in this case is the actual existence of such a foundation and of a concomitant guarantee that the problematical concept of truth, as discussed in the previous chapter, need neither be sacrificed to an indifferent pluralism nor to an extreme particularism. In what follows, it will be argued that truth should not be decreed in a monological and universalistic manner, but should take on a dialogical form that relates the universal to the particular. The dialectical interaction of these two aspects of human thought is as crucial as the insight that the universal is inseparable from the particular without being reducible to it. The fact that certain theories and theorems can be deduced from particular – liberal, conservative, Marxist or feminist – ideologies does not diminish their general validity or usefulness.

The dialectic between the general and the particular is turned into a motor of theoretical dialogue insofar as the discussion partners, who must not be subjected to general language rules, are made to recognize the particularity of their respective ideological positions and the necessity to overcome this particularity in the course of scientific communication. It is in their interest to do so if they wish to remain open to dialogue and to improve their respective discourses by sensitizing them to new problems.

Since it was shown that, within the postmodern problematic, ideologies of various origins react polemically to pluralism, tolerance and indifference, it seems meaningful at this stage to examine the position of theory between 'ideology' and 'indifference'. The position of the theoretician between these two extremes is precarious in the sense that cultural or social sciences cannot do without covert or overt ideological orientations, but at the same time have to avoid ideological dualism and dogmatism. In this situation, indifference, which implies pluralism and relativity, becomes an important point of reference as it helps theoreticians to break out of their ideological prisons and to realize that social reality can only be known in a plural form. It is constructed differently by each politician, scientist or artist. In this context, it becomes clear that both 'ideology' and 'indifference' can only be grasped as ambivalent phenomena – not as positively or negatively loaded concepts (in the sense of 'good ideology', 'bad indifference' or vice versa).

## 6.1  Theory between Ideology and Indifference – or: 'Engagement and Critical Distance'

No theory in the cultural and social sciences can entirely dissociate itself from ideology; each theory is marked by an ideological engagement. Marx's bias in favour of the proletariat and its revolution is the main driving force behind his theory; without a certain faith in the open society and an open, critical discussion, Karl R. Popper could not have developed his Critical Rationalism; without his sympathy for the minorities, the outsiders and the marginal groups of postmodern society, Lyotard could not have mapped out a new philosophy of the particular. Every philosophical, cultural or sociological theory is rooted in an ideology, if the latter is defined as *a group language or a sociolect based on a value system, a set of semantic oppositions, certain lexical units and corresponding narrative sequences (e.g. from capitalism to socialism, from modernism to postmodernism).* The demonstration that a particular theory originates in an ideology – for example, Critical Rationalism in liberal individualism – may be illuminating, but cannot be used to refute the theory in question.

Theoreticians do not jeopardize a theory and do not turn into ideologues in the negative sense by adopting a liberal, conservative, socialist or feminist viewpoint. They do destroy their theories, however, as soon as they adopt discursive mechanisms which transform the semantic difference into dualism, identify the theoretical construction with reality (the object as such) and turn theory into an ideological monologue that excludes alternative constructions presented by other discourses. In this context, ideology in a general sense, as a system of values and a group language, can be distinguished from ideology in a restrictive, negative sense: *the latter is a dualistic discourse which the speaking subject identifies monologically with the real world and its objects.*

A comparison of the two *complementary definitions* reveals to what extent ideology in the general sense is inevitable in the cultural and social sciences. Without Marxist engagement, many aspects of capitalist society would have remained in the dark, without feminist criticism, the cultural and ideological construction of gender might only have been superficially explored. At the same time, the comparison shows that ideology as false consciousness is a linguistic, discursive problem which theorists have to investigate more thoroughly.

Their own discourses will motivate them to do so whenever their tendencies towards dualism and monologue obscure the very object their authors hope to illuminate. Although critical theories also come about in order to defend certain liberal, socialist or feminist values, critical and self-critical theorists refuse to be blinded by their own ideological engagement. Their thought is ambivalent and self-ironical in the sense of Robert Musil's ambivalent project: 'Represent a cleric in such a way that a Bolshevik is hit at the same time. Represent an idiot in such a way that the author suddenly feels: this could also be me, at least to a certain degree.'[2]

It is not possible to maintain this self-ironical distance in all social situations. It is hard to imagine it in a strongly polarized political context, where a liberal philosopher is obliged to give a secret lecture underground and has to interrupt his talk after every second sentence in order to detect the steps of the secret police in time. Norbert Elias, who introduced the concepts of 'engagement' and 'critical distance' into the theoretical domain, explains:

> The crucial question is whether it is possible to make much headway towards a more detached, more adequate and autonomous manner of thinking about social events in a situation where men in groups, on many levels, constitute grave dangers for each other.[3]

It might become possible in a postmodernity marked by indifference and pluralism, where the secret police concentrate on white collar crime, corruption or money laundering and can hardly imagine what it is like when a dissident lectures to an underground public in a sparsely illuminated cellar.

In this context, indifference may appear as a powerful antidote to ideological engagement which can both motivate and ruin theoretical discourse. Indifference and pluralism enable the theoretician to consider engagement as a possible point of view among many and to look at it 'from the outside', as it were. 'La pensée du dehors',[4] Foucault, the critic of ideology, would say. In this perspective, one's own point of view appears as relative and this relativity invites a reflexive, self-critical attitude.

Reflexivity means in this case: being aware of the semantic, syntactic and narrative mechanisms of my own discourse (e.g. 'from ambivalence to indifference') which are due to certain value judgements, selections and classifications and exclude alternative mechanisms of construction (i.e. semantic and

220      *Modern/Postmodern*

contingent character of one's own discourse, which appears as a possible *construct* of reality, not as being identical with the latter. This reflexive and constructivist attitude towards discourse has at the same time a *genetic* aspect. The
reflecting subject reconstructs the genesis of its language, thereby investigating
the historical, social and linguistic contexts of its constructions.

A reflexive and genetic consciousness encourages a dialogical attitude that
excludes dualistic and monological patterns of thought. Hermeneutics and
analytical philosophy, Marxism and Critical Rationalism, modernity and postmodernity no longer appear as absolute contrasts, as enemy actors (heroes and
anti-heroes), but as ambivalent instances whose contrasting nature is relative
(a possible construction). Does Habermas not try to bring about a synthesis of
hermeneutics and analytical philosophy? Could Marxism and Critical Rationalism not both be classified as 'modern theories' whose authors share a general
belief in social progress? Has postmodernity (since romanticism) not been the
critical undercurrent, the self-criticism of modernity?

Although none of these questions need be answered in the affirmative,
because each of them merely suggests a possible construction, all three reveal
the illusory and ideological character of dualism. Dualism eliminates ambivalence in the sense of a dialectical unity of opposites and presupposes the
mutual exclusiveness of socialism and fascism, rationalism and myth, asceticism
and libertinage. At the same time, it precludes Musil's dialectical insight that
Mussolini's ambivalent personality unites the extremes in a way that is incomprehensible to ideologues: 'In conjunction with the ideological confusion
of our time and its great impact cf. the description of Mussolini's career in
D. N. R. of May 1924. He does in fact oscillate between the different poles.'[5]

All Critical Theory can do in late capitalist society is to adopt the point of
view of ironical ambivalence and to mediate dialectically between the *extremes
of ideological dualism and indifference as radical interchangeability of values.* For
the only way of escaping from ideological dualism and monologue is a *partial*
acknowledgement of indifference which helps theory to consider itself with
irony and to recognize its relativity in pluralism; but theory can only escape
from the indifference of the exchange value and from relativism by continuing
to adhere – with Adorno, Horkheimer and Habermas – to certain social values
such as subjectivity, autonomy, irony, reflexivity and dialogue.

Without this ideological *engagement* it would irretrievably fall prey to the
dominant exchange value which makes a postmodern theorist say: 'The Postmodernist may have his private views, but sees no justification for preferring
them to views held by others.'[6] If I can abandon my views and adopt those of
my neighbours at any given moment, because I have no preference for my own
thought, it makes little sense to refer to 'my views'. In this case there are merely
free-floating opinions articulated and circulated by interchangeable individuals.
(Such is of course the situation in some postmodern contexts, especially in the
media, in certain public discussions, in talk shows, etc.)

The ideological adhesion to certain insights, values and views does not prevent dialogue, but rather enables a theory, whose subject reflects upon its own particularity and contingency, to embark on a dialogue with others. This approach is an explanation of dialogue rather than an apology of subjective value judgements. For an interlocutor, who sees no reason to prefer his own views to my views, is not interesting for me as an interlocutor. My interest is aroused by somebody, who knows and admits the particularity and contingency of his discourse, who is capable of adopting an ironical stance towards this discourse, but who nevertheless adheres to his values and theoretical premises – without a priori excluding changes. Only in this case can I assume that the involvement and the interest articulated by my interlocutor are genuine.

If he happens to be a deconstructionist in the sense of Derrida, I seek a discussion with him as deconstructionist because I wish to find out how he envisages the relationship between deconstruction and Critical Theory and whether he shares Habermas's view that Adorno's post-war theory announces post-structuralism. If he is a critical rationalist in the sense of Popper or Hans Albert, I expect him to adhere to his discourse and to explain in which points Critical Rationalism and Critical Theory overlap and where they diverge.[7] In the following section, it will be asked under what conditions a dialogue between heterogeneous theories can be successful and what results it can yield.

Following Norbert Elias, one could argue that we expect both engagement and self-critical distance from our interlocutors. On the one hand, we expect them to take seriously their own value judgements and to defend them with the best possible arguments; on the other hand, we expect them to know and to acknowledge the ambivalences, exaggerations and errors of their theoretical traditions and to consider them both critically and ironically. My basic adhesion to Critical Theory will not prevent me from questioning the radical negativity of Adorno's dialectic and from criticizing (with Hans Albert)[8] Habermas's idea that we have to presuppose an 'ideal speech situation'.

In other words: the driving force behind dialogue is not only 'scientific curiosity' in a general sense, but a genuine interest for the *alterity of the Other,* an interest specific for the cultural and social sciences. It is also specific for Mikhail M. Bakhtin's theory of dialogue in which the Other becomes the main point of reference of the speaking subject. For without the Other as a contingent, historical being, the human subject cannot develop and acquire an identity.[9] I need the Other as interlocutor in order to develop my discourse; and I not only need the agreement of the kindred spirit, but also the disagreement of the theoretical stranger.

In what follows, the dialectics of agreement and disagreement will be looked at more closely in a socio-semiotic context. Alterity and disagreement are not to be treated as disruptive factors – as is sometimes the case in Habermas's theory of communication – but as vital impulses without which theories are condemned to sterility. Nothing provokes thought as much as the well-founded, clear and subtle objection of a theoretical dissident.

It becomes clear at this stage that theory not only thrives on ideological engagement, but also on the indifference of the exchange value which tends to pluralize and to reveal the relativity of all perspectives. The question is how Critical Theory, which owes its existence to market society and its individualism, can radically criticize this society, especially since it never considered East European socialism as an alternative. It would be possible, of course, to answer this question by pointing to Adorno's and Horkheimer's negativity. However, this answer is unsatisfactory in the present situation. It seems more meaningful and more honest to leave this question open for the time being.

## 6.2  Theoretical Dialogue: Language, Sociolect, Discourse

It ought to have become clear that communication within the postmodern problematic can be viewed in two contradictory ways: in a universalistic and in a particularistic perspective. The confrontation between Habermas's universal pragmatics and Lyotard's particularistic language theory has revealed the flaws of both models. While universalism tends to neglect the particularities which are responsible for the specific, singular character of subjects, particularism tends to exaggerate the uniqueness of subjects and their opacity. It ignores the universal features underlying all successful communication. In what follows, a comparison of Popper's rationalist critique of the 'framework' with Lyotard's theory of radical heterogeneity will focus on the linguistic aspects of the problem and on the possibility of an interdiscursive dialogue: *a dialogue between heterogeneous languages.*

What is at stake here is – once more – Edward Sapir's and Lee Whorf's well-known hypothesis that our view of reality is pre-determined by the collectively sanctioned norms and structures of our language.[10] In spite of its one-sidedness, which frequently provokes criticism, this thesis contains some valuable insights: 1. There is no objective reality common to all subjects. 2. What is called reality (e.g. 'the good life', 'honour', 'sin') is a construction based on the conventions and rules of a linguistic community. 3. This implies that reality in the universal sense does not exist because there are several competing realities. 4. The various language communities are not aware of this fact, refer to reality as such and are surprised to find that their neighbours mean by 'reality' something quite different.

In this context, the Sapir–Whorf-hypothesis can be taken to mean that the ideological and theoretical languages or sociolects, within which we think, speak and act, are our *pre-constructed*[11] realities inherited from our ancestors and transformed by us and our successors. At this point, Bakhtin's theory of dialogue, which sees the subject as immersed in linguistic polyphony, serves as the starting point of a socio-semiotic *theory of interdiscursivity.* We speak within a multitude of linguistic and ideological frameworks, and the question – also raised by Wolfgang Welsch in a philosophical context – is whether *transitions* between these discourses or frameworks are conceivable or not.

From Popper's rationalist point of view, the entire problematic, as mapped out here, appears as a result of hermeneutic or dialectical obscurantism. In his critique of Thomas S. Kuhn's concept of paradigm, he considers the very idea of a *paradigm* or *framework* common to the members of a group or a generation as a pseudo-problem. Kuhn, however, has a point and reveals the linguistic aspects of the framework-problem when he defines the paradigm as a relatively homogeneous *language* used by a group of scientists: 'Proponents of different theories (or different paradigms, in the broader sense of the term) speak different languages – languages expressing different cognitive commitments, suitable for different worlds.'[12] Popper, the rationalist, the universalist, is not happy with this particularizing view. To him the framework or paradigm appears as a dangerous myth: 'It is just a dogma – a dangerous dogma – that the different frameworks are like mutually untranslatable languages.'[13] In an attempt to increase the plausibility of his argument, Popper adds that very different languages such as English, Hopi and Chinese can be learned by non-native speakers and translated into one another.

At first sight, this rationalist argument is convincing enough because it confirms our daily experience and our common sense: our texts are translated into Chinese, Korean or Japanese, and we know or at least hope that, in spite of a few irritating misunderstandings and semantic shifts, the essential thoughts reappear undistorted. In spite of some translation mistakes, a literary critic such as Roland Barthes is understood in Japan – and not misunderstood as a dogmatic Marxist, a critical rationalist or a conservative philosopher. Nevertheless, it is by no means certain that a translation actually corresponds to the original, as the rationalist seems to assume. English and German translations of Derrida's works quite often depart from the original meanings. Hence the deconstructionists and postmodernists are not entirely wrong when they doubt the possibility of translation, arguing – with Derrida and de Man – that translation is at the same time necessary and impossible.[14] It is a well-known fact that translations of poems are all but accurate replicas of the originals, as Benedetto Croce points out: they yield new poems and are works of art in their own right.[15] In view of all this, the rationalist argument seems less convincing than before.

However, the key problem is that Popper refers exclusively to *natural languages* such as English, Chinese or Hopi. For each of these languages is made up of numerous religious, ideological or technical group languages or sociolects which articulate particular collective viewpoints and therefore are not mutually translatable. Within a natural language – for example, English – the specialized languages of physicists, marketing experts or sociologists are not mutually translatable. They may not even be comprehensible to outsiders. At best they can be commented on and explained with the help of a natural language (as is the case in dictionaries).

This means that ideological, philosophical and scientific sociolects and their discourses[16] cannot simply be translated into one another because they articulate *particular*, contradictory and even incompatible interests. Popper, who follows the rationalist principle according to which the individual's good will is

quite sufficient when it comes to mutual understanding, illustrates, without
realizing it, the problem whose existence he denies:

> The only course open to the social sciences is to forget all about the verbal
> fireworks and to tackle the practical problems of our time with the help of
> the theoretical methods which are fundamentally the same in *all* sciences.
> I mean the methods of trial and error, of inventing hypotheses which can be
> practically tested, and of submitting them to practical tests.[17]

Deconstructionists and postmodernists like Lyotard would appear to Popper
as pseudo-theorists, who are fascinated by the 'verbal fireworks', thereby forget-
ting the essential: the logic of argument and the critical testing of hypotheses.
However, his own discourse shows that he irrationally chooses to ignore the
fact that not all philosophical and scientific languages apply the method of
'trial and error, of inventing hypotheses which can be practically tested', etc. – but
rather rely on hermeneutic, phenomenological, ethnomethodological or dialectical patterns of thought. Popper refuses to recognize the latter as alternatives; instead he relegates them to the realm of empty rhetoric.

It is hardly surprising that Lyotard reacts to this kind of rationalism, which
irrationally deletes the particular, with extreme counter-arguments: 'Science
possesses no general metalanguage in which all other languages can be transcribed and evaluated.'[18] In view of this impossibility, Lyotard rejects the pretensions of linguistic universalism and insists on the necessity of revealing the
*différend* and all the *wrongs* (*torts*) it entails.[19]

In his perspective, the universalistic solution proposed by Popper appears as
a *wrong* or *tort par excellence.* For Popper asks all language games to submit to the
metalanguage of Critical Rationalism and to recognize its theoretical criteria:
invention of hypotheses, tests, falsification. He does so *implicitly,* since he does
not ponder upon the problem of linguistic heterogeneity and incompatibility.
In this respect, his discourse could be considered as ideological in the critical,
restrictive sense: for it presents itself monologically as the only possible solution
and excludes all dissenting discourses as 'unscientific'.

The German postmodernist Wolfgang Welsch would consider Popper's
implicit proposal to turn Critical Rationalism into a universally valid metalanguage as an attempt at *majorization* (*Majorisierung*). He calls majorization any
attempt to present a particular language as *lingua maior,* as a universally valid
system of precepts and rules. Following Lyotard, he envisages a solution that
takes into account the heterogeneity, the particularity and the logical autonomy
of competing languages: 'The rational point of view reveals the particular logic
of the argumentations involved and invites us to respect it. It opposes all
encroachments, majorizations and certainly all attempts at totalization.'[20]

In his critique of Lyotard, Welsch does, however, criticize the French philosopher's idea of absolute linguistic heterogeneity and favours a position that takes
into account the diversity of languages (forms of thought), but at the same time

discerns *transitions* (*Übergänge*) and intersections between them. 'Only the transitory action of reason', explains Welsch, 'is able to steer a steady course between the Scylla of atomization and the Charybdis of majorization. All depends on our recognizing this transitory activity of reason in its own particularity (. . .).'[21]

In some respects, Welsch's position could be defined as a dialectical, modern–postmodern synthesis of universalism and particularism: as a *transversal reason* (Welsch) that takes into account the particular character of different languages and tries to find transitions between them. This synthesis corresponds to Welsch's general, historical thesis according to which postmodernity is not a break with modernity, but its radicalization and its fulfilment.

Welsch's main problem seems to be his one-sided view of pluralism and his failure to recognize in indifference the reverse of the pluralist coin (cf. Chapter 2). Commenting on his concept of transversal reason, he explains that this reason 'has no position because of its purity and its emptiness'[22] and thus differs from all 'majorizing' types of reason (from Plato to Hegel and Popper):

> (. . .) It does not stand above other rationalities, considering them from a superior vantage point, as it were, but moves *within* the sphere of rationality, gaining insight not by overview but by transitions, by multiple movements between rationalities which never turn into a metaposition in the sense of an Archimedean system.[23]

Transversal reason thus appears as a function of radical pluralism and of interchangeable positions. In a situation, where it is impossible to decide rationally that a certain position is preferable to another, reason is reduced to a mediating function not very different from the shuttle diplomacy of UN employees. With modest means they also try to mediate between incompatible interests and languages. As *pensiero debole* or *weak thought* (Vattimo), reason is condemned by Welsch to this kind of shuttle movement without a position of its own.

It should be added, however, that this transversality is not Welsch's last word, because he demands more than just mediation: namely *criticism*. He himself not only criticizes attempts at majorization in idealism and rationalism, but also questions Lyotard's extreme particularization. However, criticism (Gr. *krinein*: to decide, to judge) presupposes a *critical point of view* which enables us to *apply* the relevance criteria of *our* discourse, its classifications and definitions,[24] to other discourses – without asking the subjects of these discourses for permission. In short: no criticism without majorization. Whenever Welsch criticizes Hegel, Lyotard or Koslowski, his discourse turns into a majorizing metadiscourse, whether he likes it or not.

It would be helpful if he clarified the relationship between transversality and criticism. If criticism implies majorization on structural, discursive grounds and transversal reason is meant to be a critical reason, it cannot be content with searching for transitions between heterogeneous languages; it has to adopt a viewpoint which need not be an all-encompassing Archimedean position.

It cannot, however, coincide with postmodern pluralism: not only because pluralism implies heterogeneity, but also because its meaning differs from discourse to discourse, as the controversy between Koslowski and Welsch shows.[25] (It does not make sense to distinguish 'false' from 'true' pluralism, since the false one tends to be invariably the one proposed by our critics.)

The question is whether an alternative to transversal reason is conceivable within or outside the postmodern problematic: an alternative which takes into account the 'majorizing' moments of criticism and does not consider plurality or pluralism to be the philosopher's stone. There are, of course, several alternatives, but one of them is *critical interdiscursive dialogue*. It is based, as was pointed out above, on Bakhtin's idea that my discourse would not exist and develop without the dialogical, intertextual moment,[26] that is without communication with others. Adopting the language of Critical Rationalism, one could say: I depend on the criticism of others if I want to avoid suffocating in my own prejudice (criticism as the oxygen of theory).

In science and politics, prejudice is both individual and collective, as the rationalist prejudice of a universally transparent language and the complementary romantic prejudice of linguistic opacity indicate.[27] More often than not, ideological prejudice originates within scientific groups and their sociolects and is sheltered from criticism for social and emotional reasons.

A case in point is the idea of the Althusser-group that there is an 'epistemological break' between Marx's early writings and his later works, especially *The Capital*: a break that separates Marx's early humanist ideology from his mature 'science of history' which can be extrapolated by thorough exegesis.[28] The fact that other philosophers and social scientists (among them numerous Marxists) strongly disagreed with this rationalist interpretation inspired by Gaston Bachelard, never seemed to bother the Althusserians. The social hermetism of their group precluded open discussions with other groups which might have broken up a dogmatic consensus based on ideology rather than science. (Critical comments on the 'epistemological' break were published in regular intervals, but made no impact on the members of the Althusser-group who rejected them as 'humanist misunderstandings'.)[29]

However, it will not be argued here – and this is a potential misunderstanding – that intersubjective criticism *within* a scientific group is trivial or irrelevant and yields no results. For both in the natural and the social sciences, this kind of criticism is the rule and is an important motor of theory formation – along with empirical research. Within Critical Theory, for example, intersubjective criticism can contribute to a better understanding of the writings of Adorno, Benjamin, Horkheimer or Habermas and thus enhance the self-awareness of this particular theory complex. At the same time, it makes its proponents more conscious of their theory's position within society and history and vis-à-vis other theories.

Nevertheless, intersubjectivity within a group of scientists (within Critical Theory or Critical Rationalism) also has its drawbacks since it tends to confirm shared values and well-established doctrines, instead of putting them into question. This kind of consensus may turn out to be fatal because it can block self-criticism and innovation. It is in this context that the advocates of Critical Theory agreed among themselves that Critical Rationalism was a brand of positivism[30] and thus overlooked Popper's critique of Viennese positivism in the 1930s.[31] Within Critical Rationalism, the principle of falsification or refutation was never exposed to radical criticism, and the doubts expressed by Otto Neurath (1935) and a vast array of more recent critics[32] were not taken seriously because they came from 'outside' the group. Hence intersubjectivity as consolidation of ideological and scientific dogmas is not only a salient feature of the Althusser-circle, but makes itself felt within most groups of scientists whose indispensable ideological engagement also generates a propensity towards dogmatism and monologue.

The prison-house of monologue can only be broken up by an *interdiscursive dialogue involving ideologically and theoretically heterogeneous group languages and their discourses*. From a dialogical point of view, both Popper's universalism and Lyotard's particularism appear as sterile. While Popper glosses over the heterogeneity of sociolects and their discourses, Lyotard considers the heterogeneity of social languages (language games, discourse genres) as philosophy's last word.

Unlike these two extreme positions, the interdiscursive dialogue is an attempt to make a virtue of necessity by *turning the obstacles inherent in frameworks into motors of criticism and knowledge*. The communication with the other sociolect can be expected to break up the individual and collective prejudice inherent in my discourse and resistant to intersubjective criticism within my group language (i.e. Critical Theory). It contributes to self-reflection and creates a critical distance without undermining social engagement.

Very different thinkers such as Durkheim's disciple Maurice Halbwachs and Karl Mannheim were aware of the fact that communication *between heterogeneous groups and perspectives* involves problems that differ substantially from those *within groups*. In an article entitled 'Psychologie collective des raisonnements', Halbwachs remarks in 1938: 'In that way many different logics developed, each of which is exclusively valid within one grouping that invokes it having once produced it.'[33] But unlike Lyotard, the late modern sociologist concedes the relativity of this particularism and subordinates it to the universal by adding: 'All of these partial logics do have one and the same origin.'[34] Unfortunately, Halbwachs does not deal with the question how and under what conditions different group languages (sociolects) can communicate.

It is a question dealt with in great detail by Karl Mannheim who was probably the first to distinguish systematically communication *within* a collective system of ideas (a *perspective*, as he puts it) from communication *between* collective systems or perspectives. It seems worth reproducing the relevant passage here because it is a concise presentation of the problem in question:

In the case of situationally conditioned thought, objectivity comes to mean something quite new and different: (a) there is first of all the fact that in so far as different observers are immersed in the same system, they will, on the basis of the identity of their conceptual and categorical apparatus and through the common universe of discourse thereby created, arrive at similar results, and be in a position to eradicate as an error everything that deviates from this unanimity; (b) and recently there is a recognition of the fact that when observers have different perspectives, 'objectivity' is attainable only in a more roundabout fashion. In such a case, what has been correctly but differently perceived by the two perspectives must be understood in the light of the differences in structure of these varied modes of perception. An effort must be made to find a formula for translating the results of one into those of the other and to discover a common denominator for these varying perspectivistic insights.[35]

Had Lyotard taken cognizance of Mannheim's text, he might have realized that linguistic heterogeneity cannot be philosophy's final insight. Had Welsch taken cognizance of it, he might have developed a more precise notion of 'transition'. For Mannheim's analysis contains at least two important and highly relevant ideas: 'what has been correctly but differently conceived' and the problem of 'translatability' (between perspectives or groups).

In a first step, the question arises *whether* and *how* heterogeneous terminologies (i.e. discourses and indirectly sociolects) can be translated into one another. The sociologist of knowledge and the hermeneutic philosopher both believe that such a translation is possible. Postmodernists such as Lyotard and a deconstructionist like Derrida are of a different opinion. Following the particularizing trend, they hold that each translation from one natural language into another, from one group language into another entails semantic shifts that make it impossible to speak of equivalents or synonyms. 'Hjelmslev's *content* is not Morris's *designatum*, and the latter is not an equivalent of Saussure's *signifié*,' they would argue. They might add that these concepts came about in very different contexts and are even contradictory in some respects. Paradoxically, some advocates of analytic philosophy would agree with them in spite of their aversion towards postmodern and deconstructionist thought.

Critical Theory should be neither blinded by the signsplitting of deconstruction nor by the nominalism of analytic philosophy, but should start from two contradictory and complementary considerations. The first was clearly formulated by the linguist Wolfgang Dressler: 'A total and unambiguous (. . .) equivalence does not exist in translation and hence no complete translatability either, for not even within one and the same language can a synonymity of linguistic expressions (of undetermined length) be achieved.'[36] This does not only apply to the natural languages commented on by Dressler, but also to sociolects. Trying to demonstrate the equivalence of *content, designatum* and *signifié* would be a meaningless rationalist game. Instead, the second, complementary consideration should be introduced into the discussion: namely that a meaningful comparison invariably involves heterogeneous, non-identical items and that it is the common conceptuality (Greimas would speak of common *semes* or *classemes*)[37] that makes a comparison of *content, designatum* and *signifié* worthwhile. In this particular case, the common denominator is the *conceptual aspect of the sign.*

It thus becomes clear that translation is always a linguistic process oscillating between the pole of equivalence and the pole of incommensurability: a process that comes to a halt whenever one of the two poles is eliminated. The common basis of all linguistic units involved is the *natural language,* defined by Yuri Lotman as the *primary modelling system.* It is within this primary system that we establish our relevance criteria, that we define and classify. With the help of the natural language we construct objects such as 'democracy', 'art', 'work', 'leisure', 'happiness' and 'misfortune'. Quite a few people are surprised to find that these objects are constructed differently in other languages, cultures and societies.

However, even within one and the same language, the transition from one sociolect to another can lead to a collision of definitions and constructions. It is a well-known fact that Marxists and Marxists–Leninists have a completely different idea of democracy from liberals. Adorno's negative construction of art is based on relevance criteria which differ substantially from those of more popular postmodern authors such as Umberto Eco, John Barth or Leslie Fiedler.

If a particular *signifier* can acquire different meanings or *signifieds* within a particular language or culture, this is mainly due to the fact that it is being used in different sociolects (Marxism, Critical Theory, Critical Rationalism, Constructivism), where it functions within different semantic fields and fields of connotation. This is why speakers of different group languages frequently confront each other with questions of the following type: 'What do you mean by democracy, art, science, freedom, discourse?' The univocity of these words is not guaranteed by natural language as a primary modelling system because, in everyday communication, such words only manifest themselves in group languages and their discourses.

These can be defined with Lotman as *secondary modelling systems.*[38] Within a secondary modelling system of the ideological, theoretical or literary type, which contributes decisively to the formation of our perception, the signs of natural language undergo transformations as they are inserted into the semantic and narrative structures of a *sociolect* or the *idiolect* of an author.

An example in point is the word 'cosmopolitism', which has acquired positive connotations in liberal group languages, where it is frequently used as an antonym of 'nationalism' or 'chauvinism'. In Marxism–Leninism, however, it has a derogatory meaning as it is linked there to late capitalist 'imperialism' and opposed to proletarian 'internationalism'. In Habermas's philosophy, the word 'discourse' has nothing to do with 'discourse' in the sense of Greimas, Benveniste or Lyotard: it refers to a clarifying dialogue, not to a semantic and narrative structure in the sense of Greimas or a form of language in the sense of Lyotard. Words such as 'law' or 'raven' in the sense of Kafka or Poe take on new meanings within the semantic worlds or idiolects of these writers and their works.[39]

In this context, the question concerning dialogical relations between soci-olects can be reformulated. From a semiotic point of view, the problem of trans-latability of concepts no longer appears as an insurmountable hurdle. For the common conceptuality, which links the words of different sociolects to one another, is based on the *natural language*. Hence it can be assumed that the theoretical sociolects are linked to one another by the *primary system of the natural language* and that they can be commented on and explained within this primary system. Although a word like 'art' has very different meanings in Luhmann's sociology, in Russian Formalism, in Marxism or in Critical Theory, it does retain its original meaning rooted in natural language: 'art' as a cultural product, as an aesthetic phenomenon, as an object not belonging to 'nature', 'politics', 'religion' or the 'economy'.

There is enough room for disagreement; what matters is the insight that sociolects as secondary modelling systems are not hermetically sealed spheres because *they are interlinked by virtue of being embedded in a natural language*. Philosophers in the hermeneutic sense like Karl-Otto Apel are right in pointing out that natural language is our final metalanguage and our last resort in communication.[40] This idea is confirmed by a glance at scientific dictionaries (sociology, psychology, semiotics) whose authors resort to natural language in order to explain scientific concepts.[41]

The fact that a natural affinity between specialized scientific languages is usually presupposed, becomes clear in Paul Lorenzen's description of the inter-discursive dialogue, of the dialogue between 'ortho-languages', as he puts it: '*Firstly*, examples and terminological definitions might prove sufficient to iden-tify a word (or a sentence) of the author as synonymous with our own ortho-language (. . .). In this case we could *translate* into our own ortho-language.'[42] This kind of translatability, based on synonyms or near synonyms, is not due to chance, but to the fact that specialized scientific languages ('ortho-languages') are secondary modelling systems embedded in the primary system of natural language.

'*Secondly*', Lorenzen continues, 'a comparison involving the ortho-language of the author and our own can make us realize that the former contains certain concepts (i.e. conceptual distinctions) which have escaped our systematic reflection. In this case, we cannot translate the text into our own language, but we can extend our language by inserting the distinctions of the text into it.'[43] In this case, as in other cases, it can be assumed that an extension of this kind is only possible within the context of natural language and its semantics. The latent presence of this language in the communicating secondary systems suggests that the radical linguistic heterogeneity presupposed by Lyotard is an exception rather than the rule.

'*Thirdly*', concludes Lorenzen, 'the attempt to translate into one's own ortho-language or to extend the latter by introducing concepts of the [other author's] text can lead to contradictions. In this case, one's own ideas and the results arrived at by the other author have to be systematically reconsidered.'[44] This is precisely what interdiscursive dialogue is about: the idea is to trace the limits of one's own sociolect and idiolect and to go beyond them whenever it seems necessary. This is also what Mannheim means in his analysis of perspectives: 'what has been correctly but differently perceived by the two perspectives must be understood in the light of the differences in structure of these varied modes of perception.'

The discussion between two ideologically heterogeneous theories is a dialectical process of agreement and disagreement in the course of which one's own theory is sometimes confirmed, sometimes extended, adjusted or (partially) refuted. Whenever I am confronted with the other's ideological and theoretical engagement (with systems theory, Critical Rationalism or deconstruction), I am permanently under pressure to test my theorems and my 'perspective' as a whole (as Mannheim would say). In this situation, my discourse, relevance criteria and classifications no longer appear to me as the only possible ones, as being identical with reality. For I am led to consider with Luhmann 'what one (. . .) would gain if, observing an observer, one raised the question, according to what distinctions he actually observes'.[45] One does gain something: namely an insight into the relevance criteria of one's own and the other's discourse. These criteria are directly responsible for what is seen and what is missed by the subject of discourse and for 'what remains latent in observation',[46] as Luhmann puts it. In other words, the dialogue with the Other makes me aware of a new reality: *of reality as a construct of the Other.*

The Other's disagreement is both a critical and a destructive element which can break up individual and collective dogmas without, however, excluding a momentary consensus in certain crucial points. The cognitive value of this interdiscursive consensus *between* heterogeneous sociolects is superior to the consensus *within* a sociolect (a group) which might be the result of prejudice, routine and a collective lack of imagination. (A case in point is Marxism–Leninism – but it is not the only orthodoxy.)

Welsch is far too absorbed in Lyotard's particularistic way of thinking when he writes: 'The disagreement is by no means the actual goal (as Lyotard exaggeratedly asserted). However, in situations of effective disagreement, not consensus but an acknowledgement of disagreement is the final goal.'[47] One might just as well argue that a controversial discussion should culminate in a question, not in an answer. A critical dialogue does not move towards a final goal because it is an open, inconclusive process in which agreement and disagreement balance each other – very much like question and answer in many everyday conversations. What matters is the fact that the *consensus* between heterogeneous sociolects is *embedded in disagreement and criticism.*

Why is it interesting? What results can it yield? It may yield common knowledge or interdiscursive theorems based on the relevance criteria ('distinctions', 'observations' in the sense of Luhmann) of heterogeneous groups of scientists.

An example would be the concept of 'ideology', constructed both in Critical Rationalism and in Critical Theory as a *dualistic discourse* which *monologically identifies with reality* and thus becomes *immune to criticism*.[48]

This definition may be unanimously confirmed within a group of dialectical thinkers who 'know' – in conjunction with previous discussions – that the only alternative to ideological dualism is dialectics. However, this idea will be queried in a discussion with critical rationalists, who do not consider 'dialectics' as a viable alternative to ideological dualism, because they oppose empirical testing, logical analysis and the criterion of refutability to the global pretensions of ideological discourse. Dialecticians need not accept this critical repertoire, especially since they can show, with the help of text analyses, how ideological dualism is dissolved by an ironical merging of the opposites.[49] They do have to recognize, however, that the common theorems, which make up the joint construction of 'ideology', are embedded in a fundamental disagreement between the two groups. As soon as they go beyond this joint construction, beyond the terrain common to both groups, 'ideology' will appear to them as a new, critical-rationalist phenomenon that provokes reflection. For it invites them to reconsider their terminology in the light of the results obtained by the other group and to extend their language by taking into account the new definitions and 'distinctions' in the sense of Lorenzen. (This also applies to the constructions of 'modernism' and 'postmodernity' which were commented on and compared in Chapters 1 and 4.)

It is crucial that the critical rationalists be willing and able to defend their point of view, albeit reflexively and – if possible – with a certain amount of self-irony. They are not expected to change roles with me (in the sense of Habermas) or to look for transitions between the group languages involved (in the sense of Welsch). Their independent stance and the alterity of their critique encourage me to think about my own position and about the limits of the achieved consensus. This consensus is not a 'transition' (in the sense of Welsch or in the sense of Vattimo's *pensiero debole*), but a joint construction of 'ideology' based on common interdiscursive theorems (*dualism, monologue, immunization*).

Interdiscursivity in this sense could be extended to other heterogeneous sociolects. In the present case, the structural analysis of 'ideology' ('ideology' as discourse) could be completed by a functional analysis of 'ideology' in contemporary society. In the process, Luhmann's thesis about the persistence of ideologies might be confirmed by Critical Theory, Critical Rationalism, Marxism and some conservative approaches. For Luhmann concludes:

> Every day ideologies demonstrate their vitality. An end of the ideological era is not in sight. It is true, of course, that the ideological zeal wanes (because it is no longer needed) and is replaced by a routine rehearsal of ideological orientations.[50]

Advocates of Critical Theory and Critical Rationalism would probably endorse this diagnosis, adding that ideological zeal decreases only temporarily in certain social situations and increases as soon as social tensions mount. Karl-Dietrich Bracher, a somewhat conservative political scientist, would agree with them: 'The need for ideological orientation, the readiness to use and abuse political ideologies makes itself felt in moments of dramatic social progress and change.'[51] In a completely different – that is Marxist – context, this view is confirmed by István Mészáros in *The Power of Ideology*, where he rejects postmodern 'supra-ideological claims'[52] hinting at 'the vital active role which ideology plays in the social reproduction process'.[53]

The question is how the theorem concerning the *vitality of ideology* can be made plausible to a neutral observer. It might be sufficient to invoke the heterogeneous origins of the arguments presented in its support: they range from Mészáros's 'class conflict' and Bracher's 'modernization' to Luhmann's systemic approach. Their origin in different scientific groups is their strength, because they are based on the *partial consensus of several heterogeneous discourses* all of which contribute to the construction of a theoretical object called the *function of ideology*. As a product of dialogue, this object is relatively independent of individual or collective prejudice.

It does not represent 'truth' in the metaphysical sense, but it does constitute a *moment of truth* in an open process of knowledge held in motion by dialogue. This is the kind of truth a theoretician is prepared to defend against fashionable trends and commercially motivated sweeping statements about the 'end of ideology' – statements revoked by Daniel Bell himself in later publications.[54] It should be remembered, however, that these statements have had an impact on the postmodern problematic and in particular on Lyotard's idea that 'meta-narratives' have lost their credibility and have been replaced by heterogeneous 'language games'. Instead of adopting Lyotard's particularizing ideology, we should ask ourselves what relevance criteria or 'distinctions' (Luhmann) he relies on in his observations and what function his discourse fulfils within the postmodern problematic.

## 6.3 Conclusion: The Particular and the Universal in Postmodernity

The question why Lyotard's discourse turns against modern universalism with epistemological, ethical and aesthetic arguments was dealt with in the third chapter. With its postmodern penchant for particularization it opposes a system which tends to level out differences and threatens to become totalitarian. However, extreme particularization and pluralization tend to strengthen the system's dominant force: the principle of exchange, of interchangeability. The isolated particularities of pluralist societies are indifferent to each other and tend to become interchangeable. In a situation where countless groupings coexist and each of them proclaims its religious, political, ethical or aesthetic 'truth', thus contradicting all the others, the different points of view become indifferent. Founded on the principle that each grouping has a right to 'its truth' (as long as it does not impose it on others), American pluralism confirms the nullity of truth claims in pluralist indifference.

The unique character of European Marxism was due – among other things – to the fact that, hoping for a spontaneous coincidence of the particular and the universal, it proclaimed 'human rights'. The proletariat as a revolutionary class was meant to break down all class barriers, overcome the very idea of class or class society and finish the human project. This historical undertaking failed not only because capitalism proved to be a lot more flexible than socialism (and than Marxists had originally imagined), but also because official Marxism–Leninism continued to apply rigidly the Hegelian principle according to which the general interest of the state was to be preferred to the particular interests of the individual. This is how Adorno sees the problem: 'The matters of true philosophical interest at this point in history are those in which Hegel, agreeing with tradition, expressed his disinterest. They are nonconceptuality, individuality, and particularity (. . .).'[55] After the collapse of communism in Europe, many Marxists and post-Marxists became aware of this problem and began to plead in favour of the particular, the individual. Lyotard was one of them.

One of the ideas underlying this book is that this postmodern *parti pris* consolidates the pluralist-capitalist status quo instead of subverting it. The alternative mapped out here is *a dialectical, late modern thought structured by ambivalence.* It relates the historically and socially particular to the process of truth-finding and generalization. In the interdiscursive dialogue, the extremes, which have been separated in the transition from universalistic modernity to particularistic postmodernity, are joined together. The alterity of the Other is no longer seen as an obstacle, but as an incentive to overcome one's limitations and as an invitation to a common search for knowledge in dialogue. In a situation where otherness is recognized without reservations, one's own perspective need not be radically qualified and sacrificed to a relativist pluralism: for the Other, whose theoretical development also depends on the encounter with alterity, expects me to defend it with the best possible arguments.

Dialogical Theory admits neither a systemic closure nor final knowledge; it nevertheless holds on to the moments of truth it comes across; firstly, because dissenting scholars also believe in them (or in some of them), secondly, because it rejects an undifferentiated pluralism in which all values, ideologies and theories tend to become interchangeable.[56] It is aware of its own historicity and of the possibility that, in a new historical and social situation, the nexus of ideology and theory may change or even disappear. At present, this situation is no more than a speculation about the distant future.

One can only hope that the thesis about the 'vitality of ideologies' – corroborated by very different groups of scientists – will not eventually be confirmed in Europe by a resurgence of nationalist particularism and chauvinism. As a privileged inhabitant of the western half of the continent, one should avoid the illusion that only states on the European periphery can become involved in nationalist conflicts. Whoever discusses this matter with a French, Flemish,

Walloon or Polish nationalist, is taught otherwise. Unlike feminist, socialist, Christian or green movements, which are well integrated into the postmodern democratic system, nationalism could become a threat to it – especially in times of crisis. (Cf. *The Economist*, February 7–13, 2009: 'The Return of Economic Nationalism').

Although most critical intellectuals in Europe are aware of this danger, they seem to be weary of the European integration process which alone can contain nationalism and defuse its ideologies. Although Marxists and advocates of Critical Theory point out from time to time that supranational capitalism is one of the driving forces of European unification, they seldom bother to analyse in detail the interaction between the late capitalist economy and the European institutions. Pierre Bourdieu is among the few who plead in favour of a European trade union movement, a 'European social state' and a 'supranational state'[57] capable of controlling the European Central Bank. Postmodern thinkers such as Lyotard or Baudrillard have never been seriously interested in the European project. Lyotard prefers to speculate about the role of outsiders, whom even a Marxist like Lucien Goldmann is prepared to take seriously as opponents of capitalism, as he loses faith in the revolutionary potential of the 'new working class' after May 1968.[58]

Unlike the 'new working class', which has always been a conglomerate of heterogeneous groups and a chimera, European integration is part of reality. Moreover, it cannot be reduced to an epiphenomenon of late capitalism, because it contains critical elements most of which are ignored even by intellectuals with critical pretensions. The multilingual and multicultural institutions of the European Union could contribute to the transition from a monolingual and monologic national identity to a polyphonic and dialogic European identity. For the construction of a European federal state presupposes multilingual and multicultural processes of institutionalization which undermine the dualistic monologues of nationalist ideologies.

This *dialogic and critical potential* of the European project is rarely recognized. Should it continue step by step, treaty by treaty, it could yield a polyphonic political union, substantially different from other large compounds such as the United States, China or Russia, all of which are marked by linguistic and cultural hegemonies. Unity in diversity would no longer be a utopian vision but a fact of everyday life – as is the case in some European regions where the coexistence of several languages is the norm. Within this kind of polyphony, not only the nationalist monologue would be condemned to atrophy, but the question concerning an alternative social system – a question raised by sociologists such as Bourdieu and Touraine – would again be heard and taken seriously within a dialogic context.

An author like Hans Magnus Enzensberger, who writes within the postmodern problematic, only seems to be aware of the vast number of particularities that coexist in Europe: *not of the critical potential inherent in a polyphonic union, in a polyphonic 'we'*. His book *Europe, Europe (Ach Europa!*, 1987), which meticulously avoids all reference to a *common future* rallying all European regions and nations, is read by Paul Michael Lützeler as postmodern fiction:

> The audacious hypothesis can be advanced that a postmodern perspective (in the sense of Matei Calinescu, Ihab Hassan, Linda Hutcheon, Jean-François Lyotard and Wolfgang Welsch) is inherent in Enzensberger's observations and reflections. In contrast to the position of the modernists, it could be described as follows: a penchant for the particular instead of an addiction to universal grandeur, a proximity to the concrete instead of a passion for abstractions, an interest in the local and regional instead of a search for totalizing perspectives, a plurality of interpretations instead of monistic deductions and dogmatic explanations, strategies of national and regional diversification instead of perspectives of European unification (. . .).[59]

Such 'strategies of diversification' are still very much en vogue – as recent events in Ireland, Belgium, former Czechoslovakia and former Yugoslavia amply demonstrate. It should be added, however, that strengthening regional (Friulan, Catalan, Welsh, Basque, Breton) identities continues to be one of the European Union's top priorities. There is nevertheless a real danger that postmodern particularism might reinforce nationalist trends. Against the real or imagined indifference of 'Brussels technocrats', nationalists tend to mobilize the 'roots' and other idiosyncrasies of European populations. In this respect, they seem to agree with Enzensberger about whom Lützeler writes: 'Enzensberger's rejection of the Europe represented by Brussels is unambiguous.'[60] But there is no other Europe, for the alternative is not a fantastic Europe conjured up by disillusioned intellectuals, but a relapse into nationalism, which is likely to perpetuate the dependence of Europe on the USA.

In this situation, critical intellectuals are by no means condemned to decide in favour or against the 'Europe of Brussels'. They should ponder on the ambivalent stance adopted towards the French Revolution by Alexis de Tocqueville and on his insight that politics are structured by ambivalence and contradiction – a fact dualistic thinkers find hard to comprehend. The first European University in Florence-Fiesole is as much a result of European politics as superfluous regulations and the waste of subsidies (mainly by national authorities). The critical potential of the European unification process ought to be developed in spite of all shortcomings, contradictions and failures – as long as there is still time. Strengthening European institutions is only part of this process, which also includes the foundation of new European universities (especially in border areas), research centres and student exchange programmes. Systematic economic and institutional help for the Ukraine, Belarus, Macedonia, Serbia and even Russia is as much part of the European project as a continuing support for less developed regions. Adorno's general statement that 'the whole is the false'[61] appears as inadequate in this context because it hides the critical impulses, which also come from the real, political world, and eventually leads to the kind of particularism criticized above.

There is still hope that intellectuals will come to terms with the fact that between the pole of revolution and the pole of resignation there is a contradictory and conflict-ridden reality most of which is permanently being formed and reformed by more or less fallible human beings. Considered in this perspective, the European project may eventually appear to them as a viable alternative to abstract utopias of the past and as a unique opportunity to bring about a synthesis of the particular and the general: of region, nation and federation. Officially begun in 1957, this project may be the only (realistic) utopia of the twentieth century which still makes sense in the twenty-first century.

# Notes

## Chapter 1

[1] Cf. B. McHale (1992), *Constructing Postmodernism*. London/New York: Routledge. McHale's book is an attempt to reconstruct postmodernism by taking into account different narratives, i.e. different possibilities of construction – chapter I: 'Telling postmodern stories'.

[2] F. Jameson (1991) *Postmodernism, or, The Cultural Logic of Late Capitalism*. Durham: Duke University Press, p. 62. Compare with: H. Bertens (1995) *The Idea of the Postmodern*. London/New York: Routledge, p. 10: 'One can indeed speak of the postmodern world, or at least argue that the world as such has become postmodern, that is, entered a new historical era, that of postmodernity.'

[3] U. Beck (2008) *Risk Society. Towards a New Modernity* (1986). London: Sage (1992), p. 10.

[4] S. Best, D. Kellner (2001) *The Postmodern Adventure. Science, Technology, and Cultural Studies at the Third Millennium*. New York/London: The Guilford Press, p. 2. Cf. also D. Kellner (2002) Postmodern War in the Age of Bush II. In *New Political Science* 1, pp. 58–60.

[5] J. O'Neill (1995) *The Poverty of Postmodernism*. London/New York: Routledge, p. 13.

[6] A. Callinicos (1989) *Against Postmodernism. A Marxist Critique*. Cambridge: Polity, p. 6.

[7] M. Kozomara (1988) Kriza opštih mesta i Postmoderna. In *Postmoderna. Nova epoha ili zabluda*. Zagreb Biblioteka Naprijed, p. 71.

[8] H. H. Klotz (1988) Moderne und Postmoderne. In W. Welsch (ed.), *Wege aus der Moderne. Schlüsseltexte der Postmoderne-Diskussion*. Weinheim: VCH-Verlag, p. 102.

[9] F. Fechner (1990) *Politik und Postmoderne. Postmodernisierung als Demokratisierung?* Vienna: Passagen, p. 20.

[10] B. McHale, *Constructing Postmodernism*, op. cit., p. 1.

[11] Cf. P. V. Zima (1989) *Ideologie und Theorie. Eine Diskurskritik*. Tübingen: Francke.

[12] Cf. Chapter 6 in this book.

[13] Cf. S. Fish (1982) *Is There a Text in This Class? The Authority of Interpretive Communities*. 2nd edn. Cambridge, MA/London: Harvard University Press.

[14] Cf. D. Bloor (1991) *Knowledge and Social Imagery*. 2nd edn. Chicago: The University of Chicago Press [1976], p. 18.

[15] M. Hennen (1990) Zur Betriebsfähigkeit postmoderner Sozialentwürfe. In G. Eifler and O. Saame (eds), *Postmoderne. Anbruch einer neuen Epoche? Eine interdisziplinäre Erörterung*. Vienna: Passagen, p. 56.

[16] N. Zurbrugg (1993) *The Parameters of Postmodernism*. Carbondale, Edwardsville: Southern Illinois University Press, p. 45.

17  L. Hutcheon (1988) *A Poetics of Postmodernism. History, Theory, Fiction*. London/ New York: Routledge, p. 30.

18  Cf. H. Lefebvre (1962) *Introduction à la modernité. Préludes*. Paris: Minuit, chapter XI.

19  Z. Bauman (1992) *Intimations of Postmodernity*. London/New York: Routledge, p. X.

20  D. Harvey (1995) *The Condition of Postmodernity. An Enquiry into the Origins of Cultural Change*. Cambridge, Oxford: Blackwell (1990), p. 10.

21  Cf. Ch. Baudelaire (1976) La Modernité. In idem, *Œuvres complètes*, vol. II, texte établi, présenté et annoté par Cl. Pichois, Paris: Gallimard, Bibl. de la Pléiade, p. 694.

22  F. T. Vischer (1922) *Kritische Gänge*, vol. IV. Munich: Meyer & Jessen-Verlag, p. 175.

23  B. Russell (1961) *History of Western Philosophy* [1946]. London: Allen and Unwin, p. 479.

24  A. Giddens (1990) *The Consequences of Modernity*. Cambridge, Oxford: Polity-Blackwell, p. 1.

25  F. H. Tenbruck (1990) *Die kulturellen Grundlagen der Gesellschaft. Der Fall der Moderne*. 2nd edn. Opladen: Westdeutscher Verlag, p. 90.

26  R. Boyne, A. Rattansi (1990) The theory and politics of postmodernism: by way of an introduction. In R. Boyne and A. Rattansi, *Postmodernism and Society*. London: Macmillan, p. 8.

27  Cf. R. Gullón (ed.) (1980) *El modernismo visto por los modernistas*. Barcelona: Editorial Labor. Here especially: J. R. Jiménez, 'El modernismo poético en España y en Hispanoamérica'; R. Darío, 'Un esteta italiano. Gabriele D'Annunzio' and: R. Darío, 'Puvis de Chavannes'.

28  Cf. G. Azam (1989) *El modernismo desde dentro*. Barcelona: Anthropos, chapter II. Compare with E. Rull Fernández (1984) *Modernismo y la generación del 98*. Madrid: Playor, chapters I–II.

29  G. Azam, *El modernismo desde dentro*, op. cit., p. 81.

30  M. Calinescu (1977) *Faces of Modernity: Avant-Garde, Decadence, Kitsch*. Bloomington/London: Indiana University Press, p. 140.

31  S. Lash (1990) *Sociology of Postmodernism*. London/New York: Routledge, p. 158.

32  C. Wright Mills (1959) *The Sociological Imagination*. Oxford: University Press; Harmondsworth: Penguin, 1980, p. 184.

33  B. McHale, *Constructing Postmodernism*, op. cit., p. 3.

34  Cf. Welsch (1991) *Unsere postmoderne Moderne*, 3rd edn. Weinheim: VCH-Verlag, pp. 12–14.

35  Ibid., p. 13.

36  G. Azam, *El modernismo desde dentro*, op. cit., p. 43.

37  The tendency towards particularization is to be found in all postmodern currents of thought: from Foucault to Lyotard and feminism.

38  Cf. P. V. Zima (2007) *What is Theory? Cultural Theory as Discourse and Dialogue*, London/New York: Continuum, chapter II.3.

39  W. Welsch, *Unsere postmoderne Moderne*, op. cit., p. 17.

40  Cf. L. Niethammer (1989) *Posthistoire. Ist die Geschichte zu Ende?*. Reinbek: Rowohlt. Commenting on Cournot's stance, Niethammer points out: 'If one considers his writings, one does not find the key concept of "posthistoire", but one does find

a related notion.' (p. 26). Cf. also: D. Kamper, Nach der Moderne. Umrisse einer Ästhetik des Posthistoire. In Welsch (ed.), *Wege aus der Moderne*, op. cit., pp. 166–168: 'The notion of "posthistoire" then appears in the work of the sociologist Bouglé in 1901.'

41  A. Gehlen (1989) Über kulturelle Kristallisation. In W. Welsch (ed.), *Wege aus der Moderne*, op. cit., p. 141.

42  Cf. D. Bell (2000) *The End of Ideology: On the Exhaustion of Political Ideas in the Fifties*, with 'The Resumption of History in the New Century.' Cambridge, MA: Harvard University Press.

43  A distinction between religion and ideology is proposed in P. V. Zima, *Ideologie und Theorie*, op. cit., pp. 29–34.

44  J.-F. Lyotard (2004) *The Postmodern Condition: A Report on Knowledge* (1979), Manchester: University Press, p. XIV.

45  Lutz Niethammer tries to elucidate the thesis concerning 'the end of history' by distinguishing 'event-oriented history' and 'structural history': 'What Cournot anticipates in his unspecified intuitions concerning the development of the human condition, is the historical transformation of event history into structural history in the course of the 20th century.' (L. Niethammer, *Posthistoire*, op. cit., p. 29.) The idea is that event and action are gradually being replaced by structural change.

46  F. H. Tenbruck, *Die kulturellen Grundlagen der Gesellschaft*, op. cit., p. 137.

47  Ibid., p. 141.

48  J.-F. Lyotard, Answering the question: what is postmodernism? In idem, *The Postmodern Condition*, op. cit., p. 79.

49  D. Kamper, Nach der Moderne. Umrisse einer Ästhetik des Posthistoire. In W. Welsch (ed.), *Wege aus der Moderne*, op. cit., p. 172.

50  For a definition of the concept of 'mythical actant' cf. P. V. Zima, *Ideologie und Theorie*, op. cit., pp. 277–284. (The 'mythical actant' is a pseudo-subject – e.g. 'the system', 'society' – endowed with human features, intentions and actions.)

51  S. Crook (2004) The end of radical social theory? Radicalism, Modernism and Postmodernism. In R. Boyne and A. Rattansi (eds), *Postmodernism and Society*, op. cit, p. 47.

52  Ibid., p. 53.

53  Ibid., p. 66.

54  Ibid., p. 68.

55  Ibid.

56  L. Hutcheon, *A Poetics of Postmodernism*, op. cit., p. 32.

57  Ibid., p. 43.

58  Cf. B. McHale, *Constructing Postmodernism*, op. cit., p. 10. Compare McHale's position with that of W. Erzgräber, James Joyce: Zwischen Moderne und Postmoderne. In J. Alber and M. Fludernik (eds), *Moderne/Postmoderne*. Trier: Wiss. Verlag Trier, p. 109.

59  Cf. G. Lukács (1972) *Taktik und Ethik*. Neuwied/Berlin: Luchterhand.

60  Cf. W. Lepenies (1992) *Aufstieg und Fall der Intellektuellen in Europa*. Frankfurt/ New York: Campus Verlag; Paris: Editions de la Maison des Sciences de l'Homme, and F. Furedi (2006) *Where Have all the Intellectuals Gone? Confronting 21st Century Philistinism*. London/New York: Continuum.

[61] The social differentiation and de-differentiation of the modern and postmodern public is discussed in detail in S. Lash, *Sociology of Postmodernism*, op. cit., pp. 250–254.

[62] The concept of sociolect is defined in a semiotic and sociological context in P. V. Zima, *Textsoziologie. Eine kritische Einführung*, Stuttgart, Metzler, 1980, chapter III and in idem, *Ideologie und Theorie*, op. cit., p. 250: The sociolect can be defined as 'a compound of real or potential discourses which have a lexical repertoire and a semantic basis in common'.

[63] Cf. U. Beck, *Risk Society*, op. cit.

[64] Cf. U. Weisstein (1973) *Comparative Literature and Literary Theory*, Bloomington/London: Indiana University Press, p. 76.

[65] Cf. S. Lash, *Sociology of Postmodernism*, op. cit., pp. 159–161, where the author speaks of 'Benjamin's postmodernist alternative'.

[66] S. Best and D. Kellner (1991) *Postmodern Theory. Critical Interrogations*. London: Macmillan, p. 225.

[67] On this level, one could also speak with R. G. Renner of a 'postmodern constellation'. Cf. R. G. Renner (1988) *Die postmoderne Konstellation. Theorie, Text und Kunst im Ausgang der Moderne*. Freiburg: Rombach.

[68] G. W. F. Hegel (1970) *Vorlesungen über die Ästhetik*, vol. I. Frankfurt: Suhrkamp (Werkausgabe), p. 22.

[69] Cf. Z. Bauman (1993) *Modernity and Ambivalence*, Oxford: Blackwell.

[70] Typological affinities between literatures in different languages are described in P. V. Zima (1992) *Komparatistik. Einführung in die Vergleichende Literaturwissenschaft*, Tübingen/Basel: Francke, chapter III.

[71] F. Nietzsche (1980) *Aus dem Nachlaß der Achtzigerjahre*. In K. Schlechta (ed.), idem., *Werke*, vol. VI. Munich: Hanser, p. 624.

[72] F. Nietzsche (1974) *The Gay Science* (1882), *With a Prelude in Rhymes and an Appendix of Songs*. New York: Random House, Vintage Books, p. 163.

[73] F. Nietzsche (1990) *Beyond Good and Evil. Prelude to a Philosophy of the Future* (1886). London: Penguin, p. 34.

[74] K. Marx (1971) In S. Landshut (ed.), *Die Frühschriften*. Stuttgart: Kröner, p. 301.

[75] The dualism of medieval symbolic thought is commented on by J. Kristeva in *Le Texte du roman*, The Hague: Mouton, 1970, p. 27.

[76] J.-F. Lyotard, *The Postmodern Condition*, op. cit., p. XXIV.

[77] R. Musil (1978) In A. Frisé (ed.), *Gesammelte Werke*, vol. VIII. Reinbek: Rowohlt, p. 1412.

# Chapter 2

[1] The relationship between *goal-oriented* (*zweckrational*) action and market society as described by K. Marx and M. Weber is discussed in G. A. Di Marco (1984) *Marx, Nietzsche, Weber*. Naples: Guida, pp. 195–211.

[2] Some aspects of these topics are dealt with in R. Münch, *Theorie des Handelns. Zur Rekonstruktion der Beiträge von Talcott Parsons, Emile Durkheim und Max Weber*, Frankfurt: Suhrkamp, 1988.

[3] M. Weber (1973) In J. Winkelmann (ed.), *Die protestantische Ethik I*, 3rd edn. Hamburg: Siebenstern-Verlag, p. 347.

[4] G. Weippert (1965) Einleitung zur Diskussion (Industrialisierung und Kapitalismus). In *Max Weber und die Soziologie heute. Verhandlungen des fünfzehnten deutschen Soziologentages*. Tübingen: Mohr, p. 183.

[5] Max Weber und das Projekt der Moderne (1988). Eine Diskussion mit Dieter Henrich, Claus Offe und Wolfgang Schluchter. In Ch. Gneuss, Kocka (ed.), *Max Weber. Ein Symposion*. Munich: DTV, p. 160.

[6] Ibid., p. 170.

[7] A. Weber (1927) *Ideen zur Staats- und Kultursoziologie*, Berlin, Junker und Dünnhaupt, p. 39.

[8] W. J. Cahnman (1981) Tönnies in Amerika. In W. Lepenies (ed.), *Geschichte der Soziologie*, vol. IV. Frankfurt: Suhrkamp, p. 94.

[9] E. Durkheim (1964) *The Division of Labor in Society* (1893), New York/London: The Free Press/Collier/Macmillan, p. 130.

[10] Cf. N. Luhmann (1995) *Gesellschaftsstruktur und Semantik. Studien zur Wissenssoziologie der modernen Gesellschaft*, vol. IV. Frankfurt: Suhrkamp, p. 174.

[11] G. Simmel (1984) *Das Individuum und die Freiheit. Essais*. Berlin: Wagenbach, p. 196.

[12] G. Simmel (1977) *Philosophie des Geldes* (1900), 6th edn. Berlin: Duncker-Humblot, p. 311.

[13] M. Horkheimer, Th. W. Adorno (1997) *Dialectic of Enlightenment* (1947). London/New York: Verso, p. XVI.

[14] Ibid., pp. 12–13.

[15] Ibid., p. 26.

[16] Ibid., p. 9.

[17] Ibid., p. 19.

[18] Th. W. Adorno (1997) In G. Adorno and R. Tiedemann (eds), *Aesthetic Theory*. London: Athlone, p. 331.

[19] Cf. W. Benjamin (1977) Über das mimetische Vermögen. In *Gesammelte Schriften*, vol. II.1. Frankfurt: Suhrkamp.

[20] Cf. P. V. Zima (1989) *Ideologie und Theorie. Eine Diskurskritik*. Tübingen: Francke, chapter 6.2: 'Essay, Modell, Parataxis'.

[21] Z. Bauman (1992) *Intimations of Postmodernity*. London/New York: Routledge, p. 217. Compare with Z. Bauman (1997) *Postmodernity and its Discontents*, Oxford, Blackwell, where postmodernity is associated with uncertainty and individual disorientation.

[22] M. Horkheimer, Th. W. Adorno, *Dialectic of Enlightenment*, op. cit., p. 26.

[23] Z. Bauman, *Intimations of Postmodernity*, op. cit., p. 12.

[24] Ibid., p. 30.

[25] Ibid., p. 35.

[26] Ibid., p. 40.

[27] Ibid., p. 52.

[28] Cf. P. P. Pasolini (1975) *Scritti corsari*, Milan: Garzanti.

[29] Cf. Z. Bauman (1993) *Modernity and Ambivalence*. Oxford: Blackwell.

[30] Z. Bauman, *Intimations of Postmodernity*, op. cit., p. 99.

[31] Ibid., p. 30.

[32] Ibid., p. 102.

33 Ibid.
34 Cf. U. Beck (2008) *Risk Society. Towards a New Modernity* (1986). London: Sage, p. 9: 'With post-modernism things begin to get blurred.'
35 A. Touraine (1992) *Critique de la modernité.* Paris: Fayard, p. 46.
36 Ibid., p. 55.
37 Ibid., p. 103.
38 Ibid., p. 105.
39 Ibid., p. 107.
40 A. Touraine (1974) *Pour la sociologie.* Paris: Seuil, p. 33.
41 Cf. A Touraine (1965) *Sociologie de l'action.* Paris: Seuil and A. Touraine (1973) *Production de la société.* Paris: Seuil, chapter II: 'Le Système d'action historique' and chapter VI: 'Les Mouvements sociaux', where the link between the movement and the revolutionary-utopian goals is at the centre of the scene (pp. 410–431), but where the Marxist-Leninist notion of party discipline is rejected.
42 A. Touraine, *Pour la sociologie*, op. cit., p. 61.
43 A. Touraine, *Critique de la modernité*, op. cit., p. 121. Cf. also: A. Touraine (1969) *La Société post-industrielle.* Paris: Denoël, chapters I–III.
44 A. Touraine, *Critique de la modernité*, op. cit., p. 126.
45 Ibid., p. 255.
46 Ibid., p. 273.
47 Ibid., p. 292.
48 Ibid., p. 331.
49 Ibid.
50 Cf. A. Gorz (1987) *Farewell to the Working Class: An Essay on Post-Industrial Socialism.* London: Pluto Press.
51 U. Beck, *Risk Society*, op. cit., p. 19.
52 F. Fechner (1990) *Politik und Postmoderne. Postmodernisierung als Demokratisierung?* Vienna: Passagen, p. 43.
53 U. Beck, *Risk Society*, op. cit., p. 59.
54 Ibid.
55 Ibid., p. 161.
56 Ibid., p. 122.
57 Cf. D. Riesman (1953) *The Lonely Crowd. A Study of the Changing American Character* (1950), 3rd edn. New Haven: Yale University Press .
58 U. Beck (1986) *Risikogesellschaft. Auf dem Weg in eine andere Moderne.* Frankfurt: Suhrkamp, p. 157. (This text is missing in the English translation.)
59 A. Giddens (1991) *Modernity and Self-Identity. Self and Society in the Late Modern Age.* Cambridge: Polity, p. 178.
60 U. Beck (2007) *Weltrisikogesellschaft. Auf der Suche nach der verlorenen Sicherheit.* Frankfurt: Suhrkamp, pp. 376–377. Compare with the complementary article by Nico Stehr: N. Stehr (2005) Noch ist nichts entschieden: Die Chancen und Risiken der möglichen Globalisierung. In E. Kiss (ed.), *Postmoderne und/oder Rationalität*, Székesfehérvár, Kodolanyi János Foiskola, p. 218.
61 U. Beck, *Risk Society*, op. cit., pp. 228–229.
62 W. Welsch (1991) *Unsere postmoderne Moderne*, 3rd edn. Weinheim: VCH, p. 36.
63 U. Beck, *Risk Society*, op. cit., p. 90.
64 A. Touraine, *Critique de la modernité*, op. cit., p. 294.

[65] U. Beck (1988) *Gegengifte. Die organisierte Unverantwortlichkeit.* Frankfurt: Suhrkamp, p. 88.

[66] A. Giddens, *Modernity and Self-Identity,* op. cit., p. 214.

[67] Ibid., p. 215.

[68] Cf. H.-J. Hinrich's review of the German translation of Giddens's book in the *Neue Zürcher Zeitung* (13th/14th of May 1995), p. 99: 'He grossly underestimates the degree of alienation and xenophobia in our society.'

[69] The parallel development of late modern sociology and the novel is discussed in some detail in P. V. Zima (1995) *Ideologie und Theorie,* op. cit., chapter X.3.

[70] F. d'Eaubonne (1974) *Le Féminisme ou la mort.* Paris: Pierre Horay.

[71] M. M. Talbot (1998) *Language and Gender. An Introduction.* Oxford, Malden: Polity-Blackwell, p. 134.

[72] S. Johnson, U. M. Meinhof (1997) *Language and Masculinity.* Oxford/Cambridge, MA: Blackwell, p. 13.

[73] N. Fraser, L. Nicholson (1988) Social criticism without philosophy: an encounter between feminism and postmodernism. *Theory, Culture and Society (Postmodernism),* vol. V, no. 2–3, pp. 380–381.

[74] Ibid., p. 390.

[75] Ibid., pp. 390–391.

[76] Cf. C. Gilligan (1982) *In a Different Voice: Psychological Theory and Women's Development.* Cambridge, MA: Harvard University Press.

[77] N. Fraser and L. Nicholson, 'Social Criticism without Philosophy', op. cit., p. 389.

[78] A. Yeatman (1994) *Postmodern Revisionings of the Political.* New York/London: Routledge, p. 7.

[79] Ibid., p. 8.

[80] S. Best (1994) Foucault, Postmodernism, and Social Theory. In D. R. Dickens, A. Fontana (eds), *Postmodernism and Social Inquiry.* London: UCL Press, p. 29.

[81] A. Yeatman, *Postmodern Revisionings of the Political,* op. cit., p. 31.

[82] Ibid.

[83] Ibid.

[84] Cf. P. V. Zima (1993) Framework ist kein Mythos. Zu Karl R. Poppers Thesen über wissenschaftliche Kommunikation. In H. Albert and K. Salamun (eds), *Mensch und Gesellschaft aus der Sicht des Kritischen Rationalismus.* Amsterdam/Atlanta: Rodopi, pp. 320–321 and Chapter 6 in this book.

[85] The role of colloquial language as last metalanguage is discussed in detail by K. O. Apel, in: *Transformation der Philosophie* (1973), vol. II. Frankfurt: Suhrkamp, pp. 341–342.

[86] A. Yeatman, *Postmodern Revisionings of the Political,* op. cit., p. 87.

[87] Cf. K. R. Popper (1976) The Myth of the Framework. In E. Freeman (ed.), *The Abdication of Philosophy. Philosophy and the Public Good. Essays in Honour of P. A. Schilpp.* Illinois: Open Court.

[88] H. Fern Haber (1994) *Beyond Postmodern Politics.* New York/London: Routledge, p. 114. To be compared with J. Dawson and S. Earnshaw (eds) (1995), *Postmodern Subjects/Postmodern Texts.* Amsterdam/Atlanta: Rodopi.

[89] H. Fern Haber, *Beyond Postmodern Politics,* op. cit., p. 115.

[90] A. Touraine A., *Critique de la modernité,* op. cit., p. 231.

[91] L. Hutcheon, *The Politics of Postmodernism.* London/New York: Routledge, p. 142.

[92] B. Smart (1992) *Modern Conditions. Postmodern Controversies*. London/New York: Routledge, p. 57.

[93] F. Jameson (1993) *Postmodernism, or, the Cultural Logic of Late Capitalism*, 4th edn. Durham: Duke University Press, p. 18.

[94] P. Koslowski (1988) Die postmoderne Kultur. Gesellschaftlich-kulturelle Konsequenzen der technischen Entwicklung. Munich: Beck, p. 104.

[95] Ibid., p. 99.

[96] Tenbruck, F. H. (1990) *Die kulturellen Grundlagen der Gesellschaft. Der Fall der Moderne*. 2nd edn. Opladen: Westdeutscher Verlag, p. 104.

[97] Ibid., p. 117.

[98] Ibid., p. 137.

[99] Ibid., p. 118.

[100] Ibid., p. 121.

[101] Ibid.

[102] Cf. H. Albert (1980) *Traktat über kritische Vernunft*. 4th edn. Tübingen: Mohr, p. 72. Albert opposes M. Weber's idea that values are immune to criticism.

[103] Cf. P. V. Zima, *Ideologie und Theorie*, op. cit., chapter XII where the question concerning the universal status of values is discussed.

[104] P. Koslowksi (1990) Supermoderne oder Postmoderne? Dekonstruktion und Mystik in den zwei Postmodernen. In G. Eifler and O. Saame (eds), *Postmoderne. Anbruch einer neuen Epoche? Eine interdisziplinäre Erörterung*. Vienna: Passagen, p. 86.

[105] Cf. F. R. de Chateaubriand (1966) *Génie du christianisme*, vol. II. Paris: Garnier-Flammarion, p. 248.

[106] P. Koslowski, *Die postmoderne Kultur*, op. cit., p. 19.

[107] Ibid., p. 20.

[108] Ibid.

[109] Ibid., p. 152.

[110] Ibid., p. 156.

[111] Ibid., p. 51.

[112] Ibid., p. 68.

[113] Ibid., pp. 54–55.

[114] Ibid., p. 155.

[115] Ibid., p. 98.

[116] Ibid., p. 104.

[117] Cf. D. Bell (1976) *The Coming of Postindustrial Society. A Venture in Social Forecasting*. New York: Basic Books (1973), p. 27.

[118] Ibid., p. 477.

[119] Ibid., pp. 477–478.

[120] J. O'Neill (1988) Religion and Postmodernism: The Durkheimian Bond in Bell and Jameson. In *Theory, Culture and Society (Postmodernism)*, vol. V, no. 2–3, p. 495.

[121] Cf. T. Veblen (1931) *The Theory of the Leisure Class* (1899). New York: The Viking Press.

[122] Compare J. O'Neill's critique of Bell in 'Religion and Postmodernism', op. cit., pp. 496–497.

[123] C. Wright Mills introduced the word 'postmodern' into the sociological discussion, not Etzioni, as W. Welsch seems to believe in *Unsere postmoderne Moderne*, op. cit., p. 26. Cf. C. Wright Mills, *The Sociological Imagination*, Oxford, Univ. Press, 1959, Harmondsworth, Penguin, 1980, p. 184: 'We are at the ending of what is

called The Modern Age. (. . .) Now The Modern Age is being succeeded by a postmodern period.'

124 A. Etzioni (1968) *The Active Society. A Theory of Societal and Political Processes.* London/New York: Collier, Macmillan, The Free Press, p. 6.
125 Ibid., p. 8.
126 Ibid., p. 14.
127 Ibid., pp. 440–441.
128 Ibid., p. 485.
129 Ibid., p. 525.
130 G. Kelly, Off-the-self sociology. In *The Times Higher*, 24 March 1995, p. 21. Compare with the anonymous commentary in *The Economist* of the 18 March 1995, p. 16: 'Mr. Etzioni and his followers appeal to a combination of popular anxieties about the future and nostalgia for a partly imaginary past.'
131 Cf. L. Goldmann (1971) *La Création culturelle dans la société moderne.* Paris: Denoël-Gonthier, chapter V: 'Pensée dialectique et sujet transindividuel'.
132 Cf. A. Etzioni (1988) *The Moral Dimension. Toward a New Economics.* New York/London: The Free Press, Macmillan, chapter I.
133 A. Etzioni (1995) *The Spirit of Community. Rights, Responsibilities and the Communitarian Agenda.* London: Fontana, p. 9.
134 Ibid., p. 18.
135 Ibid., p. 122.
136 Ibid., p. 148.
137 J. O'Neill (1995) *The Poverty of Postmodernism.* London: Routledge, p. 22.
138 Ibid., p. 95.
139 Ibid., p. 4.
140 Ibid., p. 94.
141 Cf. M. Ryan (1982) *Marxism and Deconstruction. A Critical Articulation.* Baltimore/London: The Johns Hopkins University Press, p. 21.
142 J. O'Neill, *The Poverty of Postmodernism*, op. cit., p. 160.
143 Ibid., p. 182.
144 Ibid., p. 185.
145 S. Best, D. Kellner (2001) *The Postmodern Adventure. Science, Technology, and Cultural Studies at the Third Millennium.* New York/London: The Guilford Press, p. 256.
146 Ibid.
147 F. Jameson, *Postmodernism, or, The Cultural Logic of Late Capitalism*, op. cit., pp. 35–36.
148 Ibid., p. 305.
149 Ibid., pp. 290–295.
150 Ibid., p. 18.
151 Ibid., p. 371.
152 Ibid., pp. 159–160.
153 Ibid., pp. 382–383.
154 Ibid., p. 306.
155 A. Callinicos (1994) *Against Postmodernism. A Marxist Critique.* Cambridge: Polity (1989), p. 9.
156 Cf. A. Callinicos, *Against Postmodernism*, op. cit., p. 171.
157 Cf. F. Furedi (2006) *Where Have all the Intellectuals Gone? Confronting 21st Century Philistinism*, 2nd edn. London/New York: Continuum.

[158] T. Eagleton (1996) *The Illusions of Postmodernism.* Oxford: Blackwell, p. 23.
[159] A. Callinicos, *Against Postmodernism,* op. cit., p. 22.
[160] Ibid., p. 125.
[161] R. Münch (1993) *Die Kultur der Moderne, vol. I, Ihre Grundlagen und ihre Entwicklung in England und Amerika.* Frankfurt: Suhrkamp, p. 13.
[162] Ibid.
[163] R. Münch (1992) *Die Struktur der Moderne. Grundmuster und differentielle Gestaltung des institutionellen Aufbaus der modernen Gesellschaften.* Frankfurt: Suhrkamp, p. 27.
[164] W. Welsch, *Unsere postmoderne Moderne,* op. cit., p. XV.
[165] Ibid., p. 189.
[166] Ibid., p. 322.
[167] Ibid., p. 323.
[168] P. L. Berger, B. Berger, H. Kellner (1973) *The Homeless Mind. Modernization and Consciousness.* New York: Random House-Vintage Books, p. 181.
[169] Ibid., p. 165.
[170] Cf. W. Welsch, *Unsere postmoderne Moderne,* op. cit., pp. 26–31 and pp. 189–192.
[171] M. Weber (1973) *Soziologie. Universalgeschichtliche Analysen. Politik.* Stuttgart: Kröner, p. 272.
[172] Cf. P. V. Zima (1995) Ideologie. Funktion und Struktur. In H. Bay and Ch. Hamann (eds), *Ideologie nach ihrem 'Ende'. Gesellschaftskritik zwischen Marxismus und Postmoderne.* Opladen: Westdeutscher Verlag, pp. 73–75.
[173] W. Welsch, *Unsere postmoderne Moderne,* op. cit., p. 322.
[174] J. Baudrillard (1992) *L'Illusion de la fin ou La Grève des événements.* Paris: Galilée, p. 59.
[175] Ibid., p. 112.
[176] W. Welsch, *Unsere postmoderne Moderne,* op. cit., p. 153.
[177] Ibid., p. 152.
[178] Ibid., p. 153.
[179] J. Baudrillard (1985) *La Gauche divine. Chronique des années 1977–1984.* Paris: Grasset, p. 25.
[180] J. Baudrillard (1981) *Simulacres et simulation.* Paris: Galilée, p. 64.
[181] J. Baudrillard, *La Gauche divine,* op. cit., p. 23.
[182] Ibid., p. 87.
[183] Cf. J. Baudrillard (1975) *Le Miroir de la production.* Paris: Galilée, p. 99.
[184] Ch. Norris (1990) Lost in the Funhouse. Baudrillard and the Politics of Postmodernism. In R. Boyne and A. Rattansi (eds), *Postmodernism and Society.* London: Macmillan, p. 121.
[185] G. W. F. Hegel (1970) *Vorlesungen über die Ästhetik I.* Frankfurt: Suhrkamp (Werkausgabe), p. 22.
[186] J. Baudrillard (1993) *Symbolic Exchange and Death* (1976). London: Sage, p. 89.
[187] Ibid. (F. Nietzsche [1974] *The Gay Science* [1882], *With a Prelude in Rhymes and an Appendix of Songs.* New York: Random House-Vintage Books, p. 38.)
[188] J. Baudrillard, *Simulacres et simulation,* op. cit., p. 229.
[189] Ibid., p. 230.
[190] Hegel speaks of a 'Furie des Zerstörens'. In *Grundlinien der Philosophie des Rechts, Werke,* vol. VII. Frankfurt: Suhrkamp, 1970, p. 50.

[191]  J. Baudrillard, *Le Miroir de la production*, op. cit., p. 10.

[192]  J. Baudrillard (1990) *La Transparence du mal. Essai sur les phénomènes extrêmes.*
Paris: Galilée, p. 13.

[193]  Ibid.

[194]  J. Baudrillard (1972) *Pour une critique de l'économie politique du signe.* Paris:
Gallimard, p. 94.

[195]  Ibid., p. 101.

[196]  Ibid., p. 164.

[197]  Ibid., pp. 190 and 195 and J. Baudrillard M. Guillaume (1992) *Figures de l'altérité.*
Paris: Ed. Descartes, p. 58.

[198]  J. Baudrillard (1995) *Le Crime parfait.* Paris: Galilée, p. 18.

[199]  Cf. J. Baudrillard (1979) *De la séduction.* Paris: Galilée, p. 137.

[200]  J. Baudrillard, *Symbolic Exchange and Death*, op. cit, p. 72.

[201]  J. Baudrillard, *Simulacres et simulation*, op. cit., p. 17.

[202]  Ibid.

[203]  J. Baudrillard, *Symbolic Exchange and Death*, op. cit., pp. 8–9.

[204]  Ibid., p. 9.

[205]  M. Billig (1994) Sod Baudrillard! Or Ideology Critique in Disney World. In
H. W. Simons and M. Billig (eds), *After Postmodernism. Reconstructing Ideology
Critique.* London: Sage.

[206]  J. Baudrillard, *L'Illusion de la fin*, op. cit., p. 66.

[207]  Cf. S. Best and D. Kellner who react to Baudrillard's theory of indifference
with a Marxist critique, blaming the French sociologist for his 'transpolitical
indifference': 'Baudrillard's imaginary is thus a highly abstract sign fetishism
which abstracts from social relations and political economy (. . .).' (S. Best,
D. Kellner [1991] *Postmodern Theory. Critical Interrogations.* London: Macmillan,
pp. 142 and 138.)

[208]  J. Baudrillard, *De la séduction*, op. cit., p. 78.

[209]  W. F. Haug (1976) *Kritik der Warenästhetik*, 5th edn. Frankfurt: Suhrkamp, p. 15.

[210]  Commenting on Baudrillard's dissolution of the use value, Klaus Kraemer quite
rightly points out that the latter cannot be avoided or deleted. Cf. K. Kraemer
(1994) Schwerelosigkeit der Zeichen? Die Paradoxie des selbstreferentiellen
Zeichens bei Baudrillard. In R. Bohn and D. Fuder (eds), *Baudrillard, Simulation
und Verführung.* Munich: Fink, p. 68.

[211]  Cf. J. Baudrillard (1968) *Le Système des objets. La consommation des signes.* Paris:
Gallimard, pp. 131–132.

[212]  G. Bergfleth (1982) Baudrillard und die Todesrevolte. In J. Baudrillard (ed.),
*Der symbolische Tausch und der Tod.* Munich: Matthes und Seitz, pp. 370–371.

[213]  Cf. L. Goldmann (1967) *Introduction à la philosphie de Kant.* Paris (1948):
Gallimard, pp. 303–304.

[214]  G. Bergfleth, 'Baudrillard und die Todesrevolte', op. cit., p. 376.

[215]  J. Baudrillard, *Symbolic Exchange and Death*, op. cit., p. 177.

[216]  Baudrillard's attitude towards terrorism is ambivalent: on the one hand, he considers it as a revolt against a system that is becoming totalitarian, on the other
hand, he considers it as 'an involuntary accomplice of the system as a whole':
*Simulacres et simulation*, op. cit., pp. 233–234.

[217]  Cf. J.-P. Sartre (1979) L'Engagement de Mallarmé. In *Obliques Sartre*, p. 194.

[218]  J. Baudrillard (1999) *L'Echange impossible.* Paris : Galilée, p. 72.

[219] J. Baudrillard, *Simulacres et simulation*, op. cit., p. 57.

[220] J. Baudrillard *L'Illusion de la fin*, p. 103.

[221] Ibid., p. 47. Cf. also: ibid., p. 162: '(. . .) history as such has become endless'.

[222] J. Baudrillard, *La Transparence du Mal*, op. cit., p. 49.

[223] J. Baudrillard, *L'Illusion de la fin*, op. cit., p. 72.

[224] J. Baudrillard, *La Transparence du Mal*, op. cit., p. 44.

[225] J. Baudrillard, *L'Illusion de la fin*, op. cit., p. 23.

[226] J. Baudrillard, *Le Crime parfait*, op. cit., p. 96.

[227] J. Baudrillard (1986) *Amérique*. Paris: Grasset-Fasquelle, p. 82.

[228] J. Baudrillard, *Le Crime parfait*, op. cit., p. 187.

# Chapter 3

[1] Cf. J.-F. Lyotard (1992) *The Postmodern Explained to Children. Correspondence 1982–1985* (1986). London: Turnaround, pp. 21–25.

[2] Cf. W. Welsch (1991) *Unsere postmoderne Moderne*, 3rd edn. Weinheim: VCH-Verlag, pp. 82–85: 'This is why my basic thesis postulates that postmodernity is actually the radical modernity of our age (. . .).'

[3] J.-F. Lyotard (2004) *The Postmodern Condition: A Report on Knowledge* (1979). Manchester: Manchester University Press, p. XXIV.

[4] J.-F. Lyotard, *The Postmodern Explained to Children*, op. cit., p. 31.

[5] Ibid., p. 32.

[6] Cf. H.-G. Gadamer (1975) *Wahrheit und Methode*, 4th edn. Tübingen: Mohr-Siebeck, p. 115.

[7] U. Beck (1992) *Risk Society. Towards a New Modernity* (1986). London: Sage, pp. 14–15.

[8] A. Giddens (1990) *The Consequences of Modernity*. Cambridge: Polity Press, p. 5.

[9] Th. W. Adorno (2000) *Negative Dialectics* (1966). London/New York: Routledge, p. 179.

[10] Ibid., p. 178.

[11] M. Foucault (1994) La Mort du père (1975). In idem, *Dits et écrits II*. Paris: Gallimard, p. 734.

[12] Cf. A. Touraine (1973) *Production de la société*. Paris: Seuil, p. 486.

[13] A. von Schelting was among the first to comment on Mannheim's epistemological problem: how are the different world views or 'perspectives' to be criticized, if a universal truth common to all critics is not available? Cf. A. von Schelting (1982) 'Die Grenzen der Soziologie des Wissens'. In: V. Meja and N. Stehr (eds) *Der Streit um die Wissenssoziologie*, vol. II. Frankfurt: Suhrkamp, pp. 843–848.

[14] R. Musil (1978) In A. Frisé (ed.), *Der Mann ohne Eigenschaften, Gesammelte Werke*, vol. I. Reinbek: Rowohlt, p. 229.

[15] R. Rorty (1999) *Philosophy and Social Hope*. London: Penguin, p. 236.

[16] W. Welsch (1995) *Vernunft. Die zeitgenössische Vernunftkritik und das Konzept der transversalen Vernunft*. Frankfurt: Suhrkamp, p. 362.

[17] The idea of an 'interdiscursive dialogue' is discussed in detail in P. V. Zima (2007) *What is Theory? Cultural Theory as Discourse and Dialogue*. London/New York: Continuum, Part Three.

[18] 'Actantial models' in the sense of A. J. Greimas, J. Courtés (1979) *Sémiotique. Dictionnaire raisonné de la théorie du langage.* Paris: Hachette, pp. 3–4.

[19] F. Nietzsche, (1980) In K. Schlechta (ed.), *Werke*, vol. VI. Munich: Hanser, p. 702.

[20] G. Vattimo (1991) *The End of Modernity. Nihilism and Hermeneutics in Postmodern Culture* (1985). Baltimore: The Johns Hopkins Univ. Press, p. 164.

[21] J.-F. Lyotard (2003) *Postmodern Fables* (1993). Minneapolis/London: University of Minnesota Press, p. 71.

[22] Cf. D. Bell (2000) *The End of Ideology. On the Exhaustion of Political Ideas in the Fifties* (1960), with 'The Resumption of History in the New Century'. Cambridge, MA: Harvard University Press.

[23] Cf. P. V. Zima, *Ideologie und Theorie*, op. cit., chapter I.

[24] F. Nietzsche, *Werke*, vol. V, op. cit., p. 323.

[25] G. Deleuze (2006) *Nietzsche and Philosophy* (1962). London/New York: Continuum, p. 24.

[26] G. Deleuze (1992) *Nietzsche*, 9th edn. Paris: PUF (1965), p. 36.

[27] J.-F. Lyotard (1994) *Des dispositifs pulsionnels*, Paris, Galilée (1973), p. 218.

[28] Ibid., p. 219.

[29] G. Vattimo, *The End of Modernity*, op. cit., p. 7.

[30] H. Fink-Eitel (1992) *Foucault zur Einführung*, 2nd edn. Hamburg: Junius, p. 89.

[31] M. Foucault (1984) Nietzsche, Genealogy, History. In P. Rabinow (ed.), *The Foucault Reader*. New York: Pantheon Books, p. 95.

[32] Ibid., p. 94.

[33] G. Vattimo (1991) *Al di là del soggetto. Nietzsche, Heidegger e l'ermeneutica*, 4th edn. Milan: Feltrinelli (1981), p. 111.

[34] J.-G. Merquior (1986) *Foucault ou le nihilisme de la chaire*. Paris: PUF, p. 118.

[35] Ibid.

[36] Ibid., p. 117.

[37] F. Nietzsche, *Werke*, vol. III, op. cit., p. 73.

[38] M. Foucault, Débat sur la poésie. In idem, *Dits et écrits I*, op. cit., p. 400.

[39] G. Vattimo, *Al di là del soggetto*, op. cit., p. 11.

[40] G. Deleuze, *Nietzsche and Philosophy*, op. cit., p. 96.

[41] Ibid., p. 102.

[42] R. Rorty (1991) *Objectivity, Relativism, and Truth. Philosophical Papers*, vol. I. Cambridge: Cambridge University Press, p. 32.

[43] F. Nietzsche, *Werke*, vol. III, op. cit., p. 113.

[44] R. Rorty (1994) *Consequences of Pragmatism*. 6th edn. Minneapolis: University of Minnesota Press [1982], p. 141.

[45] G. Deleuze, *Nietzsche and Philosophy*, op. cit., p. 16.

[46] Ibid.

[47] Ibid., p. 225.

[48] Ibid., p. 224.

[49] Ibid.

[50] Ibid., p. 223.

[51] Cf. S. Best, D. Kellner (1991) *Postmodern Theory. Critical Interrogations*. London: Macmillan, p. 82.

[52] G. Vattimo, *The End of Modernity*, op. cit., p. 10.

[53] T. W. Adorno, *Negative Dialectics*, op. cit., p. 10.

[51] A. Camus (1963) *The Rebel*. Harmondsworth: Penguin, p. 60. (*L'Homme révolté*. In idem, *Essais*. Paris: Gallimard, Bibl. de la Pléiade, 1965, p. 478.)

[55] A. Camus, *The Rebel*, op. cit., p. 207.

[56] M. Foucault (2007) *The Order of Things. An Archaeology of the Human Sciences* (1966). London/New York: Routledge, p. 396.

[57] M. Foucault (2006) *Madness and Civilization. A History of Insanity in the Age of Reason* (1961). London/New York: Routledge, p. 263.

[58] R. Reid (1992) Corps clinique, corps génétique. In L. Giard (ed), *Michel Foucault. Lire l'œuvre*. Grenoble: J. Millon, p. 126.

[59] Habermas, J. (2005) *The Philosophical Discourse of Modernity. Twelve Lectures* (1985). Cambridge/Maldon: Polity, pp. 242–243.

[60] Cf. Foucault, M., Lettre à quelques leaders de la gauche (1977). In idem, *Dits et écrits III*, op. cit., p. 398, where he rejects the entire socialist tradition.

[61] S. Best, D. Kellner, *Postmodern Theory*, op. cit., p. 56.

[62] M. Foucault (1994) Les Intellectuels et le pouvoir (entretien avec G. Deleuze; 4 mars 1972). In idem, *Dits et écrits* II (1954–1988). Paris: Gallimard, p. 313.

[63] Ibid.

[64] Ibid., p. 315.

[65] Ibid.

[66] Ibid.

[67] Ibid., p. 307.

[68] J.-F. Lyotard, *The Postmodern Condition*, op. cit, p. 15.

[69] M. Foucault (1994) Why the ancient world was not a golden age, but what we can learn from it anyway. In P. Rabinow (ed), *The Foucault Reader*, op. cit., p. 363.

[70] Ch. Norris (1993) *The Truth about Postmodernism*. Oxford: Blackwell, p. 70.

[71] Cf. A. Barry, T. Osborne and N. Rose (eds) (1996) *Foucault and Political Reason. Liberalism, Neo-Liberalism and Rationalities of Government*. London: UCL Press, p. 8: 'The task, according to Foucault, was not to denounce the idea of liberty as a fiction, but to analyze the conditions within which the practice of freedom has been possible.'

[72] G. Deleuze (2006) *Foucault* (1986). London/New York: Continuum, p. 77.

[73] Cf. J. Lacan (1971) *Ecrits II*. Paris: Seuil, pp. 162–163.

[74] G. Deleuze, F. Guattari (1977) *Anti-Oedipus: Capitalism and Schizophrenia* (1972/73). New York: The Viking Press, p. 302.

[75] The relationship between sexuality, ideology and the family in the works of W. Reich is commented on in detail by: Y. Buin (1972) *L'œuvre européenne de Reich*. Paris: Editions Universitaires, chapter II.

[76] G. Deleuze, F. Guattari, *Anti-Oedipus*, op. cit., p. 332.

[77] G. Deleuze, F. Guattari (1987) *A Thousand Plateaus. Capitalism and Schizophrenia*. Minneapolis: University of Minnesota Press, p. 379.

[78] S. Best, D. Kellner, *Postmodern Theory*, op. cit., p. 97.

[79] G. Deleuze, In M. Foucault and G. Deleuze (eds), 'Les Intellectuels et le pouvoir', op. cit., p. 312.

[80] J.-F. Lyotard, *Postmodern Fables*, op. cit., p. 199.

[81] Jean-Marie Benoist's book *Marx est mort*. Paris: Gallimard, 1970 bears witness to this fact.

[82] J.-F. Lyotard (1994) *Dérive à partir de Marx et Freud*. Paris (1973): Galilée, p. 21.

[83] J.-F. Lyotard (2004) *Libidinal Economy* (1974). London/New York: Continuum, p. 100.

[84] Ch. Bürger seems to have overlooked this collectively subversive element in Lyotard's approach, since she believes that his 'anarchism' is geared towards the individual. Cf. Ch. Bürger and P. Bürger (eds) (1987) *Postmoderne: Alltag, Allegorie und Avantgarde*. Frankfurt: Suhrkamp, pp. 131–132.

[85] J.-F. Lyotard, *Libidinal Economy*, op. cit., p. 100.

[86] J.-F. Lyotard, *Dérive à partir de Marx et Freud*, op. cit., p. 17.

[87] J.-F. Lyotard, *The Postmodern Condition*, op. cit., p. 60.

[88] G. Warmer, K. Gloy (1995) *Lyotard. Darstellung und Kritik seines Sprachbegriffs.* Aachen: Ein-Fach-Verlag, p. 27.

[89] J. Rogozinski (1989) Lyotard: le différend, la présence. In *Témoigner du différend. Quand phraser ne se peut. Autour de Jean-François Lyotard*. Paris: Osiris, p. 64.

[90] Cf. C. Douzinas, P. Goodrich, Y. Hachamovitch (1994) *Politics, Postmodernity and Critical Legal Studies. The Legality of the Contingent.* London/New York: Routledge, p. 24: 'The law is necessarily committed to the form of universality and abstract equality, but a just decision must also respect the requests of the contingent incarnate and concrete other, it must pass through the ethics of alterity in order to respond to its own embeddedness in justice.'

[91] The concepts of 'logocentrism' and 'phallogocentrism' are discussed in some detail in P. V. Zima, *Deconstruction and Critical Theory* (2002). London: Turnshare, chapter II.

[92] J.-F. Lyotard (1999) *The Differend. Phrases in Dispute* (1983). Minneapolis: University of Minnesota Press, p. 141.

[93] The anarchistic tradition in French thought is analysed in detail in P. Ansart (1970) *Naissance de l'anarchisme. Essai d'une explication sociologique du proudhonisme.* Paris: PUF.

[94] J.-F. Lyotard, *Des dispositifs pulsionnels*, op. cit., pp. 226–227.

[95] G. Vattimo (1992) *The Transparent Society* (1989). Baltimore: The Johns Hopkins University Press, p. 68.

[96] Ibid.

[97] Cf. ibid., p. 69.

[98] Ibid., p. 69.

[99] Ibid., pp. 69–70.

[100] Cf. R. Rorty (1999) *Philosophy and Social Hope*. London: Penguin, pp. 202–209.

[101] R. Rorty, *Objectivity, Relativism, and Truth*, op. cit., pp. 31–32.

[102] Commenting on Rorty's pseudo-Hegelianism, Allen Hance quite rightly remarks: 'With Hegel, the transcendental turn does not result in insouciant pragmatism with its conception of truth as what society lets us say. It results, rather, in the elaboration of a phenomenological ontology.' (A. Hance [1995] 'Pragmatism as Naturalized Hegelianism: Overcoming Transcendental Philosophy?' In H. J. Saatkamp (ed.) *Rorty and Pragmatism. The Philosopher Responds to his Critics.* Nashville/London: Vanderbilt University Press, p. 108.)

[103] R. Rorty, *Objectivism, Relativism, and Truth*, op. cit., p. 177.

[104] Ibid., p. 199.

[105] Ibid., p. 214.

[106] R. Rorty (2007) *Contingency, Irony, and Solidarity*. Cambridge: Cambridge University Press (1989), p. 20.

107 R. Rorty, *Consequences of Pragmatism*, op. cit., p. 207.

108 Ibid.

109 R. Rorty, *Objectivity, Relativism, and Truth*, op. cit., p. 190.

110 R. Rorty, *Contingency, Irony, and Solidarity*, op. cit., p. 61.

111 H. Fern Haber (1994) *Beyond Postmodern Politics. Lyotard, Rorty, Foucault.* London/ New York: Routledge, p. 44.

112 Cf. the lucid critique of Rorty in N. Geras (ed.) (1995) *Solidarity in the Conversation of Humankind: The Ungroundable Liberalism of Richard Rorty.* London: Verso, especially chapter I. Geras shows that Rorty has to start from universalistic premises.

113 The relationship between interests and values in view of their potentially universal status is discussed in P. V. Zima, *Ideologie und Theorie*, op. cit., chapter XII.3.

114 R. Rorty, *Contingency, Irony, and Solidarity*, op. cit., p. 65.

115 Ibid., p. 120.

116 Cf. R. Rorty, Solidarity or Objectivity? In idem, *Objectivity, Relativism, and Truth*, op. cit.

117 M. Foucault, Structuralisme et poststructuralisme (1983). In idem, *Dits et écrits IV*, op. cit, p. 446.

118 Ibid., p. 438.

119 Ibid., p. 440. In this interview, Foucault links his concept of reason to that of Critical Theory: 'Or il est certain que si j'avais pu connaître l'école de Francfort, si je l'avais connue à temps, bien du travail m'aurait été épargné (. . .).'

120 Ibid., p. 435.

121 Cf. J. Piaget (1974) *Le Structuralisme.* Paris: PUF, chapter VII and G. Schiwy (1970) *Der französische Strukturalismus.* 4th edn. Reinbek: Rowohlt , chapter II.

122 M. Foucault (1984) The Order of Discourse. In M. J. Shapiro (ed.), *Language and Politics.* Oxford: Blackwell, p. 129.

123 M. Foucault (1986) *La Pensée du dehors.* Paris: Fata Morgana, p. 23.

124 Time and again, the link between particularization and Foucault's Nietzschean heritage comes to the fore.

125 Ch. Sinding (1986) La Méthode de la clinique. In L. Giard (ed.), *Michel Foucault. Lire l'œuvre*, op. cit., p. 63.

126 J. Revel (1986) Le Moment historiographique. In L. Giard (ed.), *Michel Foucault. Lire l'œuvre*, op. cit., p. 94.

127 Ibid.

128 J. Piaget, *Le Structuralisme*, op. cit., pp. 112–113.

129 M. Foucault, *Madness and Civilization*, op. cit., p. XIV.

130 A. Farge (1992) Michel Foucault et les archives de l'exclusion (La vie des homes infâmes). In *Penser la folie. Essais sur Michel Foucault.* Paris: Galilée, p. 66.

131 R. Major (1992) Crises de la raison, crises de la folie ou 'la folie' de Foucault. In *Penser la folie*, op. cit., p. 125.

132 The affinity between Foucault's critique of reason and Critical Theory is analysed in P. V. Zima (2007) *Theorie des Subjekts. Subjektivität und Identität zwischen Moderne und Postmoderne.* 2nd edn. Tübingen/Basel: Francke, p. 236.

133 M. Foucault, *The Order of Things*, op. cit., p. 270.

134 P. Rabinow, Introduction. In P. Rabinow (ed.), *The Foucault Reader*, op. cit., p. 14.

135 In this respect, L. Goldmann is not entirely wrong when he blames the structuralists for describing structures without explaining them functionally: Cf. L. Goldmann, T. W. Adorno (1973) Discussion extraite des actes du second colloque international sur la sociologie de la littérature tenu à Royaumont. In *Revue de l'Institut de Sociologie* 3–4, p. 541.

136 M. Foucault, *The Order of Things*, op. cit., p. 340.

137 Ibid., p. 351.

138 Ibid., p. 346.

139 Cf. B. Schmidt (1994) *Postmoderne – Strategien des Vergessens*. 2nd edn. Frankfurt: Suhrkamp. What disappears, according to the author, is also the ability to distinguish past and present.

140 M. Foucault (2002) *The Archaeology of Knowledge* (1969). London/New York: Routledge, p. 156.

141 Cf. G. Bachelard (1983) *La Philosophie du non*. 9th edn. Paris: PUF, pp. 32–33. The relationship between continuity and discontinuity in Foucault is discussed in P. V. Zima (2006) Anwesenheit und Abwesenheit des Werks: Zu Foucaults Subjekt- und Werkbegriff. In K.-M. Bogdal and A. Geisenhanslüke (eds), *Die Abwesenheit des Werkes. Nach Foucault*. Heidelberg: Synchron, pp. 189–190.

142 B. Rosenthal (1977) *Die Idee des Absurden. Friedrich Nietzsche und Albert Camus*. Bonn: Bouvier, p. 16.

143 G. Deleuze, *Foucault*, op. cit., pp. 33–34.

144 Ibid., p. 53.

145 Ibid., p. 75.

146 G. Deleuze (1993) *Empirisme et subjectivité*. 5th edn. Paris: PUF (1953), p. 21.

147 G. Deleuze (2001) *The Logic of Sense* (1969). London/New York: Continuum, p. 150.

148 F. Nietzsche, *Werke*, vol. IV, op. cit., p. 958.

149 G. Deleuze, *The Logic of Sense*, op. cit., p. 122.

150 F. Zourabichvili (1994) *Deleuze. Une philosophie de l'événement*. Paris: PUF, p. 26.

151 Ibid.

152 G. Deleuze, C. Parnet (1977) *Dialogues*. Paris: Flammarion, p. 68.

153 G. Deleuze, F. Guattari (1994) *What is Philosophy?* London/New York: Verso, p. 54.

154 Ibid., p. 35.

155 Cf. P. Lorenzen (1974) *Konstruktive Wissenschaftstheorie*. Frankfurt: Suhrkamp.

156 G. Deleuze, F. Guattari, *What is Philosophy?*, op. cit., p. 82.

157 Ibid., p. 83.

158 Ibid., p. 64.

159 Cf. J. Habermas, *The Philosophical Discourse of Modernity*, op. cit., pp. 185–210.

160 G. Deleuze, F. Guattari, *What is Philosophy?*, op. cit., p. 66.

161 Cf. ibid., p. 28.

162 Ibid., p. 28.

163 G. Deleuze, F. Guattari, *Thousand Plateaus*, op. cit., p. 7.

164 Ibid.

165 Ibid., p. 22.

166 Cf. G. Deleuze, *The Logic of Meaning*, op. cit., pp. 178–179.

167 G. Deleuze, C. Parent, *Dialogues*, op. cit., p. 82.

168 M. Frank (1984) *Was ist Neostrukturalismus?* Frankfurt: Suhrkamp, p. 14.

169  R. Rorty, *Obvjectivity, Relativism, and Truth*, op. cit., p. 24.
170  R. Rorty, Dewey between Hegel and Darwin. In H. J. Saatkamp (ed.), *Rorty and Pragmatism*, op. cit., p. 15.
171  An illuminating account of cultural universals can be found in E. Holenstein (1985) *Menschliches Selbstverständnis*. Frankfurt: Suhrkamp, p. 125.
172  R. Rorty, *Objectivity, Relativism, and Truth*, op. cit., p. 204.
173  Ibid., p. 26.
174  R. Rorty, *Contingency, Irony, and Solidarity*, op. cit., p. 28.
175  R. Rorty, *Consequences of Pragmatism*, op. cit., p. 141.
176  Ibid., p. 142.
177  R. Rorty (1984) Deconstruction and Circumvention. In *Critical Inquiry* 11, p. 15.
178  R. Rorty, *Objectivity, Relativism, and Truth*, op. cit., pp. 61–62.
179  F. Schlegel (1967) Über die Unverständlichkeit. In idem, *Kritische Ausgabe*, vol. III. Paderborn: Schöningh, p. 364.
180  Cf. S. E. Toulmin (1992) *Cosmopolis: Hidden Agenda of Modernity*. Chicago: Chicago University Press.
181  G. Vattimo, *Al di là del soggetto*, op. cit., p. 11.
182  A. Moravia, *Il Conformista*. Milan: Bompiani (1951), p. 266.
183  G. Vattimo, *Al di là del soggetto*, op. cit., p. 49.
184  W. Welsch, *Vernunft*, op. cit., p. 195.
185  Cf. P. V. Zima, *What is Theory?*, op. cit., Part Three.
186  G. Deleuze (2004) *Difference and Repetition* (1968). London/New York: Continuum, p. 71.
187  Ibid.
188  Ibid., p. 156.
189  Ibid., p. 347.
190  Ibid., p. 153.
191  Ibid.
192  Ibid., pp. 164–165.
193  The Young Hegelian F. T. Vischer, for example, blames Hegel for neglecting chance, the particular and the dream. Cf. F. T. Vischer (1922) Der Traum. In idem, *Kritische Gänge*, vol. IV. Munich: Meyer und Jessen, pp. 482–483.
194  Cf. G. Deleuze, *The Logic of Sense*, op. cit., p. 315.
195  W. Welsch, *Vernunft*, op. cit., p. 356.
196  G. Deleuze, F. Guattari, *Thousand Plateaus*, op. cit., p. 21.
197  G. Deleuze, *Difference and Repetition*, op. cit, p. 183.
198  Cf. ibid., p. 335.
199  Ibid., p. 360.
200  T. W. Adorno, *Negative Dialectics*, op. cit., p. 15.
201  Cf. J.-F. Lyotard, *Libidinal Economy*, op. cit., pp. 248–249.
202  J. Derrida (1978) *Writing and Difference* (1967). London/Henley: Routledge and Kegan Paul, p. 29.
203  M. Heidegger (1990) *Identität und Differenz.* 9th edn. Pfullingen: Neske (1957), p. 57.
204  Ibid.
205  T. W. Adorno (1991) Short Commentaries on Proust. In R. Tiedemann (ed.), idem, *Notes to Literature*, vol. I (1961). New York: Columbia University Press, p. 174.
206  T. W. Adorno, *Negative Dialectics*, op. cit., p. 40.

207  G. Vattimo (1980) *Le avventure della differenza. Che cosa significa pensare dopo Nietzsche e Heidegger.* Milan: Garzanti, p. 159.

208  Cf. P. V. Zima (2005) *L'Ecole de Francfort. Dialectique de la particularité.* Paris (1974): L'Harmattan (augmented ed.), where the tendency towards particularization is at the centre of the discussion.

209  G. Vattimo, *Le avventure della differenza,* op. cit., p. 8.

210  Ibid., p. 9.

211  P. Caravetta (2–3 June 1988) On Gianni Vattimo's Postmodern Hermeneutics. In *Theory, Culture, and Society,* , p. 395.

212  G. Vattimo, *Le avventure della differenza,* op. cit., p. 54.

213  Ibid., p. 109.

214  Ibid., p. 121.

215  T. W. Adorno, *Negative Dialectics,* op. cit., p. 46.

216  J. Habermas (1985) Dialektik der Rationalisierung. In idem, *Die neue Unübersichtlichkeit.* Frankfurt: Suhrkamp, p. 172: 'If one takes seriously Adorno's *Negative Dialectics* and his *Aesthetic Theory* and at the same time attempts to leave this scenario inspired by Beckett, one has to become something like a post-structuralist.'

217  Ibid., p. 202.

218  J.-F. Lyotard (1977) *Instructions païennes.* Paris: Galilée, p. 36.

219  W. Welsch, *Vernunft,* op. cit., p. 333.

220  Ibid., p. 334.

221  J.-F. Lyotard (1988) *The Differend. Phrases in dispute* (1983). Minneapolis: University of Minnesota Press, p. 178.

222  J.-M. Vincent (1979) *Les Mensonges de l'Etat.* Paris: Le Sycomore, p. 130.

223  J.-F. Lyotard, *The Postmodern Condition,* op. cit., p. 36.

224  G. Warmer, K. Gloy, *Lyotard,* op. cit., pp. 21–22.

225  J.-F. Lyotard (1984) *Tombeau de l'intellectuel et autres papiers.* Paris: Galilée, p. 61.

226  W. Welsch, *Vernunft,* op. cit., pp. 314–315.

227  Cf. A. J. Greimas (1976) Analyse sémiotique d'un discours juridique. In idem, *Sémiotique et sciences sociales.* Paris: Seuil, p. 84.

228  J.-F. Lyotard, *The Differend,* op. cit., pp. VIII, 178.

229  J.-F. Lyotard, *Postmodern Fables,* op. cit., p. 135.

230  G. Warmer, K. Gloy, *Lyotard,* op. cit., pp. 97–98.

231  J.-F. Lyotard, *The Differend,* op. cit., p. 29.

232  J.-F. Lyotard, *Postmodern Fables,* op. cit., p. 140.

233  Ibid., p. 199.

234  M. Frank (1988) *Die Grenzen der Verständigung. Ein Geistergespräch zwischen Lyotard und Habermas.* Frankfurt: Suhrkamp, p. 61.

235  Ibid., p. 79.

236  J.-F. Lyotard, *The Differend,* op. cit., p. 10.

237  The relationship between translatability and intranslatability is discussed in: P. V. Zima (1996) Der Unfaßbare Rest. Übersetzung zwischen Dekonstruktion und Semiotik. In J. Strutz and P. V. Zima (eds), *Literarische Polyphonie. Übersetzung und Mehrsprachigkeit in der Literatur.* Tübingen: Narr, pp. 30–32.

238  J.-F. Lyotard, *Postmodern Fables,* op. cit., p. 132.

239  J.-F. Lyotard, *The Differend,* op. cit., p. 181.

240  J.-F. Lyotard, *The Postmodern Condition,* op. cit., p. 60.

[241] J. Habermas (1990) *Die Moderne – ein unvollendetes Projekt. Philosophisch-politische Aufsätze 1977–1990*. Leipzig: Reclam, p. 42.

[242] Cf. for example G. Simmel (1890) *Über sociale Differenzierung*. Leipzig: Duncker und Humblot.

[243] A. Linkenbach (1986) *Opake Gestalten des Denkens. Jürgen Habermas und die Rationalität fremder Lebensformen*. Munich: Fink, p. 253.

[244] J. Habermas (2003) *Moral Consciousness and Communicative Action* (1983). Cambridge/Oxford: Polity/Blackwell, p. 136.

[245] A. Linkenbach, *Opake Gestalten des Denkens*, op. cit., p. 253.

[246] J. Habermas (1986) *Vorstudien und Ergänzungen zur Theorie des kommunikativen Handelns*. 2nd edn. Frankfurt: Suhrkamp, p. 546.

[247] J. Habermas (1986) Entgegnung. In A. Honneth and J. Joas (eds), *Kommunikatives Handeln. Beiträge zu Jürgen Habermas 'Theorie des kommunikativen Handelns'*. Frankfurt: Suhrkamp, pp. 372–373.

[248] Habermas, whose theory is partly inspired by Kant, rarely invokes the dialectical concept of *mediation*. However, the ideal speech situation is inconceivable without the real (material, ideological) *subjectivity* of the interlocutors, if these are not to be sublimated into pure spirits. At the same time, the real communication situation consists of ideological, strategic *and* communicative elements. Without a will to communicate there is no common strategy.

[249] J. Habermas (1971) Vorbereitende Bemerkungen zu einer Theorie der kommunikativen Kompetenz. In J. Habermas and N. Luhmann (eds), *Theorie der Gesellschaft oder Sozialtechnologie – Was leistet die Systemforschung?* Frankfurt: Suhrkamp, p. 136.

[250] H. Gripp (1984) *Jürgen Habermas*. Paderborn: Schöningh, p. 49.

[251] J. Habermas, Vorbereitende Bemerkungen zu einer Theorie der kommunikativen Kompetenz, op. cit., p. 103.

[252] 'Discourse' is defined here in conjunction with Greimasian semiotics as a transphrastic, semantic and narrative structure produced by an individual or collective *subject of enunciation* (*sujet d'énonciation*) and based on the interaction of *actants* as *sujets d'énoncé*.

[253] The *relative coherence* of a legal, political or scientific discourse bears witness to the presence of a collective or individual subject acting in accordance with a particular intention.

[254] Cf. J. Habermas, *Moral Consciousness and Communicative Action*, op. cit., p. 66.

[255] J. Habermas, *Vorstudien und Ergänzungen zur Theorie des kommunikativen Handelns*, op. cit., p. 387.

[256] Ibid., p. 161.

[257] Ibid., p. 532.

[258] J. Habermas, *Moral Consciousness and Communicative Action*, op. cit., p. 87.

[259] J. Habermas (1973) Der Universalanspruch der Hermeneutik. In idem, *Kultur und Kritik*. Frankfurt: Suhrkamp, p. 283.

[260] J. B. Thompson (1982) Universal Pragmatics. In J. B. Thompson and D. Held (eds), *Habermas. Critical Debates*. London: Macmillan, p. 297.

[261] Habermas's ideas about linguistic 'deformations' and 'pathologies' are repressive in the sense of Foucault and Lyotard. Cf. J. Habermas (1982) Der Universalanspruch

der Hermeneutik, op. cit., pp. 287–293. Cf. also: S. Ashenden and D. Owen (eds) (1999) *Foucault contra Habermas*. London: Sage, pp. 196–197.

[262] J. Becker (1970) *Felder, Ränder, Umgebungen*. Frankfurt: Suhrkamp, p. 63.

[263] Cf. W. Welsch, *Vernunft*, op. cit., chapters VII and VIII.

[264] A. Wellmer (1993) *Zur Dialektik von Moderne und Postmoderne*. 5th edn. Frankfurt: Suhrkamp, p. 96.

[265] J.-F. Lyotard (1993) *Political Writings*. London: UCL, p. 7.

[266] J.-F. Lyotard, *Postmodern Fables*, op. cit., p. 136.

[267] Cf. J. Rawls (1999) *A Theory of Justice* (1971). Cambridge, MA: Harvard University Press.

[268] J. Habermas, *Moral Consciousness and Communicative Action*, op. cit., p. 67. (Habermas quotes Thomas McCarthy.)

[269] J.-F. Lyotard, Débat. In *Témoigner du différend*, op. cit., p. 119.

[270] J.-F. Lyotard, *Postmodern Fables*, op. cit., p. 68.

[271] J.-F. Lyotard (1986) *L'Enthousiasme. La critique kantienne de l'histoire*. Paris: Galilée, p. 114.

[272] The fact that *Le Différend* is not simply a work on linguistic philosophy, but also a work on justice is confirmed in a discussion between Lyotard, van Reijen and Veerman: '*Le Différend* re-establishes what is at stake in justice as *Au juste* had summarily but not (. . .) falsely indicated.' (W. van Reijen, D. Veerman (1988) An Interview with Jean-François Lyotard. In *Theory, Culture, and Society* 2–3, p. 301.)

[273] J.-F. Lyotard, *Postmodern Fables*, op. cit., p. 68.

[274] T. W. Adorno (1991) The Artist as Deputy. In R. Tiedemann (ed.), idem, *Notes to Literature*, vol. I (1958). New York: Columbia University Press, p. 107.

[275] J. Rogozinski, Lyotard: le différend, la présence. In *Témoigner du différend*, op. cit., p. 64.

[276] Ibid., p. 65.

[277] J.-F. Lyotard, *Des dispositifs pulsionnels*, op. cit., p. 19.

[278] Z. Bauman (1993) *Postmodern Ethics*. Oxford: Blackwell, p. 225.

[279] Cf. S. Toulmin, *Cosmopolis*, op. cit.

[280] Z. Bauman, *Postmodern Ethics*, op. cit., p. 43.

[281] Ibid., p. 54.

[282] Ibid., p. 80.

[283] Ibid.

[284] Cf. E. Lévinas (2006) *Entre Nous*. London/New York: Continuum.

[285] Z. Bauman, *Postmodern Ethics*, op. cit., p. 84.

[286] Cf. M. M. Bakhtin (1979) 'K metodologii gumanitarnych nauk' ('On the Methodology of the Human Sciences'). In idem, *Estetika slovesnogo tvorčestva*. Moscow: Iskusstvo and T. Todorov, Bakhtine et l'altérité. In *Poétique* 40, 1979.

[287] Z. Bauman, *Postmodern Ethics*, op. cit., p. 159.

[288] Ibid., p. 242.

[289] Cf. R. Rorty (1985) Le Cosmopolitisme sans émancipation (en réponse à Jean-François Lyotard). In *Critique* 456, where particularism appears as the common cause of the two philosophers.

[290] R. Rorty, *Contingency, Irony, and Solidarity*, op. cit., p. 92.

[291] Ibid.

[292] Different forms of honour are discussed in an historical perspective in: L. Vogt and A. Zingerle (eds) (1994) *Ehre. Archaische Momente in der Moderne*. Frankfurt: Suhrkamp.

293 R. Rorty, *Contingency, Irony, and Solidarity*, op. cit., p. 84 – Rorty's critique of Habermas and Lyotard is specified in: R. Rorty (1984) Habermas and Lyotard on Postmodernity. In *Praxis International* 4/I, pp. 32–44.

294 Cf. R. Rorty, *Contingency, Irony, and Solidarity*, op. cit., pp. 85–89. But compare with his remarks in: R. Rorty, *Philosophy and Social Hope*, op. cit., pp. 229–239.

295 Cf. M. G. Weiß (2006) *Gianni Vattimo. Einführung.* 2nd edn. Vienna: Passagen, chapter II where Heidegger's and Vattimo's notion of *Verwindung* is discussed in detail.

296 G. Vattimo, *The End of Modernity*, op. cit., p. 164.

297 Cf. W. Welsch, *Unsere postmoderne Moderne*, op. cit., p. 138.

298 G. Vattimo, *The Transparent Society*, op. cit., pp. 8–9.

299 Ibid., p. 9.

300 Ibid., p. 69.

301 Cf. ibid., p. 67.

302 Cf. T. W. Adorno (1968) *Einleitung in die Musiksoziologie. Zwölf theoretische Vorlesungen.* Reinbek: Rowohlt, p. 28.

303 Cf. H. Gamper (1991) 'Keiner wagt mehr seine Person daran.' Zur Situation der Literaturwissenschaft nach vollendeter Marginalisierung der Literatur. In F. Griesheimer and A. Prinz (eds), *Wozu Literaturwissenschaft?* Tübingen: Francke. Cf. also: T. Todorov (2007) *La Littérature en péril.* Paris: Flammarion.

304 G. Vattimo, *The Transparent Society*, op. cit., pp. 62–64.

305 Cf. K. Teige (1964) In J. Brabec, O. Hilmerová and K. Chvatík (eds), *Jarmark umění.* Prague: Československý Spisovatel.

306 The expression 'psycho-technical manipulation' was coined by Adorno: cf. T. W. Adorno, *Notes to Literature*, vol. I, op. cit., p. 107.

307 J.-F. Lyotard (1993) *The Inhuman. Reflections on Time* (1988). Cambridge/Oxford: Polity/Blackwell, p. 127.

308 Ibid.

309 Ibid., p. 135.

310 P. Bürger (1987) Eine Ästhetik des Erhabenen. In Ch. Bürger, Moderne als Postmoderne: Jean-François Lyotard. In Ch. Bürger and P. Bürger (eds), *Postmoderne: Alltag, Allegorie und Avantgarde.* Frankfurt: Suhrkamp, p. 138.

311 Naturally, Bürger, whose text was published in 1987, could not know *L'Inhumain* (1988) and *Leçons sur l'Analytique du sublime* (1991), but *Discours, figure* (1971) would have shown him to what extent Lyotard's postmodern theory of the differend is announced by his early aesthetic.

312 J.-F. Lyotard (1971) *Discours, figure.* Paris: Klincksieck, p. 14.

313 Ibid.

314 Ibid., p. 18.

315 J. Mc Gowan (1991) *Postmodernism and its Critics.* Ithaca/London: Cornell University Press, p. 182.

316 Cf. G. W. F., (1970) *Vorlesungen über die Ästhetik*, vol. III. Frankfurt: Suhrkamp, p. 43 and pp. 94–95.

317 Cf. J.-F. Lyotard, *Tombeau de l'intellectuel et autres papiers*, op. cit., pp. 84–85.

318 J.-F. Lyotard (1994) *Lessons on the Analytic of the Sublime (Kant's 'Critique of Judgment', §§ 23–29)* (1991). Stanford: Stanford University Press, p. 234.

319 I. Kant (1987) *Critique of Judgment* (1790). Indianapolis/Cambridge: Hackett Publishing Company, p. 127.

320   Ibid.

321   Ibid., p. 120.

322   J.-F. Lyotard, *Lessons on the Analytic of the Sublime*, op. cit., p. 123.

323   Ibid., p. 151.

324   In this context, Ch. Pries speaks of a 'failure of imagination': cf. Ch. Pries (1991) 'Königsberger Avantgarde', oder: Wie modern war Immanuel Kant?. In W. Welsch and Ch. Pries (eds), *Ästhetik im Widerstreit. Interventionen zum Werk von Jean-François Lyotard*. Weinheim: VCH-Verlag, p. 156.

325   J.-F. Lyotard, *Lessons on the Analytic of the Sublime*, op. cit., p. 144.

326   Ibid., p. 228.

327   J.-F. Lyotard, *L'Enthousiasme*, op. cit., p. 61.

328   Ibid., p. 63.

329   J.-F. Lyotard, *The Inhuman*, op. cit., p. 105.

330   Ibid., p. 93.

331   J.-F. Lyotard, *Tombeau de l'intellectuel et autres papiers*, op. cit., p. 79.

332   Cf. F. Jameson, *Postmodernism, or, the Cultural Logic of Late Capitalism*. Durham: Duke University Press.

333   O. Wiener (1985) *Die Verbesserung von Mitteleuropa*. Reinbek: Rowohlt (1969), p. XIX.

334   Ibid., p. XIII.

335   J.-F. Lyotard, *Lessons on the Analytic of the Sublime*, op. cit., p. 95.

336   G. W. F. Hegel, *Vorlesungen über die Ästhetik*, vol. I, op. cit., p. 546.

337   P. de Man (1982) Sign and Symbol in Hegel's Aesthetics. In *Critical Inquiry* 8, p. 765.

338   Ibid., p. 763.

339   L. Waters (1989) In P. de Man (ed.), *Critical Writings. 1953–1978*. Minneapolis: University of Minnesota Press, p. LVIII.

340   R. Luperini (1995) Per una rivalutazione dell'allegoria: da Benjamin a de Man. In M. D'Ambrosio (ed.), *Il testo, l'analisi, l'interpretazione*. Naples: Liguori, p. 70.

341   P. de Man (1996) In A. Warminski (ed.), *Aesthetic Ideology*. Minneapolis: University of Minnesota Press.

342   J.-F. Lyotard, *The Inhuman*, op. cit., p. 104.

343   Ibid., p. 104.

344   A. Wellmer, *Zur Dialektik von Moderne und Postmoderne*, op. cit., pp. 74–75.

345   J. H. Miller (1991) *Theory now and then*. New York/London: Harvester, Wheatsheaf, p. 210.

# Chapter 4

1   M. Calinescu (1977) *Faces of Modernity: Avant-Garde, Decadence, Kitsch, Postmodernism*. Bloomington, IN/London: Indiana University Press, chapter I.

2   Cf. A. Robbe-Grillet (1994) *Le Miroir qui revient*, Paris: Minuit (1984) and idem, *Les Derniers jours de Corinthe*. Paris: Minuit. (Both texts have an autobiographic character.)

3   Cf. K. Teige (1964) In J. Brabec, O. Hilmerová and K. Chvatík (eds), *Jarmark umění*. Prague: Československý Spisovatel. Teige believes that, apart from commercial and academic art, there is an authentic avant-garde art which he derives from the revolts of European Romanticism.

[4] T. W. Adorno (2000) *Negative Dialectics* (1966). London/New York: Routledge, p. 408.
[5] I. Hassan (1987) *The Postmodern Turn. Essays in Postmodern Theory and Culture.* Ohio: State University Press, p. 90.
[6] Cf. F. Furedi (2006) *Where have all the Intellectuals gone? Confronting 21st Century Philistinism.* 2nd edn. London/New York: Continuum.
[7] Cf. F. Jameson (1991) *Postmodernism, or, the Cultural Logic of Late Capitalism.* Durham: Duke University Press, pp. 204–207.
[8] J. C. Schütze (1986) Aporien der Kulturkritik – Aspekte der postmodernen Theoriebildung. In A. Huyssen and K. R. Scherpe (eds), *Postmoderne. Zeichen eines kulturellen Wandels.* Reinbek: Rowohlt, p. 94.
[9] J. K. Schütze, (1994) Von der mangelnden Fremdheit des Anderen. In A. Berger and G. E. Moser (eds), *Jenseits des Diskurses. Literatur und Sprache in der Postmoderne.* Vienna: Passagen, p. 59.
[10] Ibid., pp. 58–59.
[11] M. Bradbury (1983) Modernisms/Postmodernisms. In I. Hassan and S. Hassan (eds), *Innovation/Renovation. New Perspectives on the Humanities.* Madison/London: University of Wisconsin Press, p. 316.
[12] Ibid., p. 315.
[13] M. Calinescu (1987) Introductory remarks: postmodernism, the mimetic and theatrical fallacies. In M. Calinescu and D. W. Fokkema (eds), *Exploring Postmodernism.* Amsterdam/Philadelphia: J. Benjamins, p. 14.
[14] Cf. G. Lukács (1971) Franz Kafka oder Thomas Mann? In G. Lukács, *Die Gegenwartsbedeutung des kritischen Realismus, Werke,* vol. IV. Neuwied/Berlin: Luchterhand, p. 550.
[15] Cf. M. Bradbury and J. McFarlane (eds), (1978) *Modernism 1890–1930.* Sussex, New Jersey: Harvester Press, Humanities Press, p. 31: 'Although (. . .) it is impossible to fix on any one particular time as the start of the Modern movement, 1880 is taken as the point where the Enlightenment's "critical intelligence" had combined with Romanticism's "exploring sensibility" to stimulate the work of the first generation of truly modern writers, all owing something to Flaubert and Baudelaire (. . .).'
[16] D. W. Fokkema (1984) *Literary History, Modernism, and Postmodernism* (The Harvard University Ersamus Lectures, Spring 1983). Amsterdam/Philadelphia: J. Benjamins, p. 5.
[17] Ibid., p. 12.
[18] I. Hassan (1961) *The Dismemberment of Orpheus. Toward a Postmodern Literature.* New York: Oxford University Press, p. 19.
[19] I. Hassan (1961) *Radical Innocence: Studies in the Contemporary American Novel.* Princeton: University Press, p. 19.
[20] I. Hassan, *The Dismemberment of Orpheus,* op. cit., p. 23.
[21] I. Hassan, *The Postmodern Turn,* op. cit., p. 91.
[22] Ibid., pp. 91–92.
[23] The confusion of modernist and postmodernist features is discussed in U. Schulz-Buschhaus (1995) Critica e recupero dei generi – Considerazioni sul 'Moderno' e sul 'Postmoderno'. In *Problemi* 101, p. 5.
[24] L. Hutcheon (1989) *The Politics of Postmodernism.* London/New York: Routledge, p. 15.

[25] Cf. for example L. Kreutzer (ed.) (1972) *Über Jürgen Becker.* Frankfurt: Suhrkamp, especially the discussions with M. Leier, K. Schöning and Ch. Linder.

[26] L. Hutcheon (1988) *A Poetics of Postmodernism.* London/New York: Routledge, p. 88.

[27] Ibid., p. 179.

[28] Ibid., pp. 218–221. 'Brecht's theatre and postmodernist art' are lumped together.

[29] Cf. P. Tew and A. Murray (eds) (2009) *The Modernism Handbook.* London/New York: Continuum, pp. 44–58.

[30] N. Zurbrugg (1993) *The Parameters of Postmodernism.* Carbondale, Edwardsville: Southern Illinois University Press, p. XI.

[31] Ibid., pp. 166–167.

[32] Ibid., p. 39.

[33] Ibid., p. 40.

[34] F. Jameson, *Postmodernism, or, The Cultural Logic of Late Capitalism,* op. cit., p. 298.

[35] Ibid., p. 305.

[36] Cf. K. Drummond (2006) The migration of art from museum to market: consuming Caravaggio. In *Marketing Theory,* vol. VI (1), p. 96.

[37] Cf. P. V. Zima (2008) *Der europäische Künstlerroman. Von der romantischen Utopie zur postmodernen Parodie.* Tübingen: Francke, chapters VI and VII.

[38] T. Eagleton (1986) *Against the Grain. Selected Essays.* London/New York: Verso, p. 132. The fact that Eagleton's perspective is 'socialist' is confirmed in his more recent book *The Illusions of Postmodernism,* Oxford, Blackwell, 1996, p. IX: 'Throughout this study, I have judged postmodernism from a broadly socialist perspective (. . .).'

[39] R. J. Quinones (1985) *Mapping Literary Modernism. Time and Development.* Princeton: Princeton University Press, p. 23.

[40] Quinones speaks of the 'Modernist capacity to exploit and develop the virtues of cosmopolitanism, diversity and fragmentation'. (p. 27) He thereby disavows Hassan's scheme which defines these features as postmodern.

[41] B. McHale (1987) *Postmodernist Fiction.* London/New York: Routledge, p. 9.

[42] Ibid.

[43] Ibid., p. 11 (Cf. ibid.: 'In postmodernist texts, in other words, epistemology *is backgrounded,* as the price for foregrounding ontology.').

[44] While Hassan considers Joyce's *A Portrait of the Artist as a Young Man* as modernist and *Finnegans Wake* as postmodern (*The Postmodern Turn,* op. cit., p. 88), McHale sees *Ulysses* as divided between modernism and postmodernism: 'Split roughly down the middle, its first half has long served as a norm for "High Modernist" poetics, while only recently have we begun to regard its second half as normatively postmodernist.' (*Constructing Postmodernism,* op. cit., p. 10.)

[45] D. Lodge (1977) *The Modes of Modern Writing: Metaphor, Metonymy, and the Typology of Modern Literature.* London: Edward Arnold, p. 157.

[46] Ibid., pp. 74–75.

[47] Cf. for example Le Corbusier's *Quand les cathédrales étaient blanches.* Paris: Plon, 1937; Denoël-Gonthier, 1971, which could be read as a manifesto of the modern, rationalist architect.

[48] D. Harvey (1990) *The Condition of Postmodernity.* Oxford: Blackwell, p. 25.

⁴⁹ Ibid., p. 29.

⁵⁰ Ibid., p. 33.

⁵¹ Cf. J.-F. Lyotard (1971) *Discours, figure.* Paris: Klincksieck; P. Francastel (1970) *Etudes de sociologie de l'art.* Paris: Denoël-Gonthier, p. 12; O. Pächt (1986) *Methodisches zur kunsttheoretischen Praxis. Ausgewählte Schriften.* 2nd edn. Munich: Prestel, p. 249.

⁵² Cf. I. Howe (1959) Mass society and post-modern fiction. In *Partisan Review* 26, pp. 420–436 and H. Levin (1966) What was Modernism. In idem, *Refractions. Essays in Comparative Literature.* New York: Columbia University Press.

⁵³ I. Hassan, *The Postmodern Turn*, op. cit., p. 86.

⁵⁴ J. Barth (January 1980) The literature of replenishment. postmodern fiction. In *Atlantic Monthly*, p. 70. For a discussion of John Barth's position between modernism and postmodernism, cf. U. Arlart (1984) *'Exhaustion' und 'Replenishment'. Die Fiktion in der Fiktion bei John Barth.* Heidelberg: Winter.

⁵⁵ J. Barth, 'The literature of replenishment', op. cit., p. 70.

⁵⁶ Ibid.

⁵⁷ U. Eco (1984) *Reflections on the Name of the Rose.* London: Secker and Warburg, p. 67.

⁵⁸ L. Hutcheon, *A Poetics of Postmodernism*, op. cit., p. 159.

⁵⁹ R. G. Renner (1988) *Die postmoderne Konstellation. Theorie, Text und Kunst im Ausgang der Moderne.* Freiburg: Rombach, p. 25.

⁶⁰ Cf. G. Gillespie (2006) *Echoland. Readings from Humanism to Postmodernism.* Brussels/Berne/Berlin: Peter Lang, p. 17.

⁶¹ Cf. A. Eysteinsson (1990) *The Concept of Modernism.* Ithaca/London: Cornell University Press, p. 5: 'Realism is therefore a key term that in various ways highlights the social background against which modernism receives its significance as a "negative practice, or as a poetics of the nonorganic text".'

⁶² S. Kohl (1977) *Realismus: Theorie und Geschichte.* Munich: Fink, p. 84.

⁶³ J. E. Smith (1974) Hegel's Critique of Kant. In J. J. O'Malley et al. (eds), *Hegel and the History of Philosophy.* The Hague: Nijhoff, p. 118.

⁶⁴ H. de Balzac (1965) *La Comédie humaine*, vol. I. Paris: Seuil, p. 52.

⁶⁵ H. de Balzac (1968) *Les Paysans* (1844). Paris: Gallimard (Livre de poche), p. 19.

⁶⁶ H. de Balzac (1962) *Illusions perdues* (1837–1839). Paris: Gallimard (Livre de poche), p. 39.

⁶⁷ Ibid., p. 48.

⁶⁸ Ibid.

⁶⁹ G. Eliot (1980) *Adam Bede* (1859). London: Penguin, p. 221.

⁷⁰ S. Kohl, *Realismus*, op. cit., p. 107.

⁷¹ G. Verga (1973) Introduzione a *L'amante di Gramigna*. In P. Pullega (ed.), *Leggere Verga. Antologia della critica verghiana.* Bologna: Zanichelli, p. 361.

⁷² S. Kohl, *Realismus*, op. cit., p. 111.

⁷³ F. Nietzsche (2008) *Human, All-Too-Human. Parts 1 and 2* (1878–1879). *Beyond Good and Evil* (1886). Ware: Wordsworth Editions, p. 6.

⁷⁴ Ibid., p. 389.

⁷⁵ F. Nietzsche (1974) *The Gay Science. With a Prelude in Rhymes and an Appendix of Songs.* New York: Random House/Vintage Books, p. 171.

⁷⁶ Ch. Baudelaire (1975) Mon cœur mis à nu. In Cl. Pichois (ed.), idem, *Œuvres complètes*, vol. I. Paris: Gallimard, Bibl. de la Pléiade, p. 678.

[77] Cf. B. Constant (1824) *De la religion considérée dans ses sources, ses formes et ses développements.* Paris: Tallandier, vol. I, p. 350.

[78] F. Nietzsche, Über Wahrheit und Lüge im außermoralischen Sinne. In idem, *Werke*, vol. V, op. cit., p. 319.

[79] Cf. W. Benjamin (1974) *Charles Baudelaire. Ein Lyriker im Zeitalter des Hochkapitalismus.* Frankfurt: Suhrkamp, p. 99.

[80] A. Wilde (1981) *Horizons of Assent: Modernism, Postmodernism, and the Ironic Imagination.* Baltimore/London: The Johns Hopkins University Press, p. 10.

[81] V. Woolf (1992) *Orlando* (1928). Oxford: Oxford University Press, pp. 132–133.

[82] M. Minow-Pinkney (1987) *Virginia Woolf and the Problem of the Subject.* Brighton: The Harvester Press, p. 10.

[83] Woolf, V., *Orlando*, op. cit., p. 161.

[84] Ibid., p. 152.

[85] Ibid., p. 211.

[86] Cf. M. Mansuy (1968) *Un moderne. Paul Bourget. De l'enfance au Disciple.* Paris: Les Belles Lettres (nouvelle édition), p. 391.

[87] V. Woolf, *Orlando*, op. cit., p. 256.

[88] Ibid., p. 257.

[89] Ibid., pp. 309–310.

[90] M. Proust (1970) *Time Regained.* Part Two. In idem, *Remembrance of Things Past* (1913–1927), vol. XII. London: Chatto and Windus, p. 262. (J.-Y. Tadié [éd.] *A la recherche du temps perdu*, vol. IV, Paris: Gallimard, Bibl. de la Pléiade, 1989, p. 474.)

[91] Surette, L. (1993) *The Birth of Modernism. Ezra Pound, T. S. Eliot, W. B. Yeats, and the Occult.* Montreal/Kingston: McGill-Queen's University Press, p. 286. Compare with W. Crooke (2008) *Mysticism and Modernity. Nationalism and the Irrational in Hermann Hesse, Robert Musil and Max Frisch.* Oxford/Berne/Berlin: Peter Lang. Using a different text corpus, the author dissociates modernist mysticism from occultism.

[92] L. Surette, *The Birth of Modernism*, op. cit., p. 286.

[93] A. Huyssens, In D. Harvey, *The Condition of Postmodernity*, op. cit., p. 39.

[94] J. Barth (1988) *Lost in the Funhouse. Fiction for Print, Tape, Live Voice* (1968). New York/London/Toronto: Doubleday-Anchor, p. 96.

[95] Ibid., p. 97.

[96] Ibid., pp. 107–108.

[97] Ibid., p. 74.

[98] Ibid., p. 90.

[99] Bo Petterson may be right in emphasizing the role of realist elements in postmodernism; however, such elements are usually embedded in a playful constructivism. Cf. B. Petterson (Spring 2007) The real in the unreal. Mimesis and postmodern American fiction. In *The European English Messenger* 16.1, p. 38.

[100] J. Tabbi (1996) *Postmodern Sublime. Technology and American Writing from Mailer to Cyberpunk.* Ithaca/London: Cornell University Press, pp. 77–78.

[101] D. W. Fokkema, *Literary History, Modernism, and Postmodernism*, op. cit., p. 33. Compare with M. Calinescu, *Faces of Modernity. Avant-Garde, Decadence, Kitsch*, op. cit., p. 140.

[102] Cf. J. Murphet (2009) *Multimedia Modernism. Literature and the Anglo-American Avant-garde.* Cambridge: Cambridge University Press, pp. 8–9.

[103] P. Bürger (1974) *Theorie der Avantgarde*. Frankfurt: Suhrkamp, p. 29.

[104] Cf. ibid., p. 67.

[105] Ibid., p. 126.

[106] P. Bürger (1987) Vorbemerkung. In Ch. Bürger and P. Bürger (eds), *Postmoderne: Alltag, Allegorie und Avantgarde*. Frankfurt: Suhrkamp, p. 11.

[107] Ibid.

[108] Ibid.

[109] P. Bürger (1988) Das Verschwinden der Bedeutung. Versuch einer postmodernen Lektüre von Michel Tournier, Botho Strauß und Peter Handke. In P. Kemper (ed.), *"Postmoderne" oder der Kampf um die Zukunft*. Frankfurt: Fischer, p. 297.

[110] A. Huyssen, Postmoderne – eine amerikanische Internationale? In A. Huyssen and K. R. Scherpe (eds), *Postmoderne*, op. cit., p. 18.

[111] Ibid.

[112] Cf. ibid., pp. 18–19.

[113] A. Eysteinsson, *The Concept of Modernism*, op. cit., p. 176.

[114] H. Mann (1963) *Geist und Tat*. Munich: DTV, pp. 8–9.

[115] A. Eysteinsson, *The Concept of Modernism*, op. cit., p. 177. Compare with H. Lethen (1986), Modernism cut in half: the exclusion of the Avant-Garde and the debate on postmodernism. In D. W. Fokkema and H. Bertens (eds), *Approaching Postmodernism*. Amsterdam/Philadelphia: J. Benjamins, pp. 233–238.

[116] A. Eysteinsson, *The Concept of Modernism*, op. cit., p. 177.

[117] S. Lash (1990) *Sociology of Postmodernism*. London/New York: Routledge, p. 158.

[118] Ibid., p. 168.

[119] Cf. Y. Janin (November 1966) Préliminaires à une étude sociologique du surréalisme. In *Cahiers de philosophie*.

[120] S. Lash, *Sociology of Postmodernism*, op. cit., p. 169.

[121] W. Benjamin, *Charles Baudelaire*, op. cit., p. 149.

[122] S. Lash, *Sociology of Postmodernism*, op. cit., p. 172.

[123] Ibid., p. 167.

[124] Ibid., p. 156.

[125] Ibid., p. 20.

[126] Ibid., p. 21.

[127] Ibid., p. 30.

[128] Ibid., p. 52.

[129] L. A. Fiedler (1971) *Cross the Border – Close the Gap*. New York: Stein and Day, p. 69.

[130] Cf. for example: F. Ruloff-Häny (1976) *Liebe und Geld. Der moderne Trivialroman und seine Struktur*. Stuttgart: Artemis.

[131] L. A. Fiedler, *Cross the Border – Close the Gap*, op. cit., p. 78.

[132] J. Collins (1989) *Uncommon Cultures. Popular Culture and Post-Modernism*. New York/London: Routledge, p. 115.

[133] Ibid., p. 7.

[134] Ibid., p. 19.

[135] A. Flaker (1982) *Poetika osporavanja. Avangarda i književna ljevica*. Zagreb: Školska knjiga, pp. 50–51. Flaker emphasizes the romantic elements in the Slovenian avant-garde and in particular in the work of the futurist writer Srečko Kosovel. He points out that two different Kosovel-receptions are conceivable: a romantic and an avant-garde one.

[136]  A. Breton (1969) *Manifestes du surréalisme*. Paris: Gallimard, p. 11.

[137]  Cf. P. V. Zima (1978) Krise des Subjekts als Krise des Romans. Überlegungen zur 'Kritischen Theorie' und den Romantexten Prousts, Musils, Kafkas und Hesses. In *Romanistische Zeitschrift für Literaturgeschichte* 1, pp. 71–75.

[138]  H. Hesse (1963) *Steppenwolf*. London: Penguin, p. 34. (*Der Steppenwolf* [1927], Frankfurt: Suhrkamp, 1972, p. 30.)

[139]  The social engagement of the Auden Generation is dealt with in detail in S. Hynes (1976) *The Auden Generation. Literature and Politics in England in the 1930s*. London/Boston: Faber and Faber. Hynes sheds light on the kind of left-wing modernism authors like Linda Hutcheon ignore.

[140]  W. Benjamin (1969) *Über Literatur*. Frankfurt: Suhrkamp, p. 50.

[141]  Cf. R. Barthes (1964) *Essais critiques*. Paris: Seuil, p. 31.

[142]  Cf. R. Barthes (1986) *The Rustle of Language*. Oxford: Blackwell, p. 233.

[143]  R. Barthes (1985) *The Grain of the Voice. Interviews 1962–1980*. London: Jonathan Cape, p. 191.

[144]  F. Nietzsche, Über Wahrheit und Lüge im außermoralischen Sinn. In idem, *Werke*, vol. V, op. cit., p. 314.

[145]  Ibid., p. 313.

[146]  L. Hjelmslev defines the *expression plane* as the sum total of signifiers: L. Hjelmslev (1969) *Prolegomena to a Theory of Language*. Madison/Milwaukee/London: The University of Wisconsin Press, pp. 47–60.

[147]  R. Barthes (1975) *S/Z*. London: Jonathan Cape, p. 5.

[148]  Cf. A. J. Greimas (1972) Pour une théorie du discours poétique. In A. J. Greimas (ed.), *Essais de sémiotique poétique*. Paris: Larousse, chapter III.1: 'L'isomorphisme de l'expression et du contenu'.

[149]  R. Barthes (1988) *The Semiotic Challenge*. Oxford: Blackwell, p. 7.

[150]  Cf. A. J. Greimas (1983) *Structural Semantics. An Attempt at Method*. Lincoln/London: University of Nebraska Press, chapter VI.

[151]  Cf. L. Goldmann (1964) *The Hidden God. A Study of the Tragic Vision in the Pensées of Pascal and the Tragedies of Racine*. London: Routledge, p. 19.

[152]  R. Barthes, *S/Z*, op. cit, pp. 8–9.

[153]  A. J. Greimas (1988) *Maupassant. The Semiotics of Text. Practical Exercises*. Amsterdam/Philadelphia: J. Benjamins, chapter I.

[154]  R. Barthes (1998) *Criticism and Truth* (1966). London: The Athlone Press (1987), p. 67.

[155]  Cf. M. Frank (1984) *Was ist Neostrukturalismus?* Frankfurt: Suhrkamp.

[156]  O. Ette (1998) *Roland Barthes. Eine intellektuelle Biographie*. Frankfurt: Suhrkamp, p. 329.

[157]  Cf. also Ch. Norris (2000) *Deconstruction and the 'Unfinished Project of Modernity'*. London: Athlone.

[158]  Cf. A. J. Greimas, *Maupassant*, op. cit., p. chapter I.

[159]  F. Rastier, Systématique des isotopies. In A. J. Greimas (ed.), *Essais de sémiotique poétique*, op. cit., pp. 92–93.

[160]  A. J. Greimas, J. Courtés (1982) *Semiotics of Language. An Analytical Dictionary*. Bloomington: Indiana University Press: 'isotopy'.

[161]  J. Derrida (1982) *Margins of Philosophy*. London: Routledge and Kegan Paul, p. 318.

[162] Cf. J. Derrida (1981) *Dissemination.* Chicago: University of Chicago Press.

[163] J. Derrida (1978) *Writing and Difference.* London: Routledge and Kegan Paul, p. 25.

[164] On the role of nominalism in Derrida's philosophy, Cf. Ch. Norris (1989) *The Deconstructive Turn. Essays in the Rhetoric of Philosophy.* London/New York: Routledge, p. 10. Cf. also Ch. Norris (2003) Why Derrida is not a postmodernist. In K. Stierstorfer (ed.), *Beyond Postmodernism. Reassessments in Literature, Theory, and Culture.* Berlin/New York: de Gruyter, pp. 144–145. Norris deals neither with the problem of indifference nor with the complementary problem of particularization – which is a postmodern aspect of Derrida's discourse.

[165] J. H. Miller (1982) *Fiction and Repetition. Seven English Novels.* Cambridge, MA: Harvard University Press, p. 6.

[166] Ibid., p. 123.

[167] Ibid., p. 128.

[168] J. H. Miller (1992) *Ariadne's Thread. Story Lines.* New Haven/London: Yale University Press, p. 224.

[169] P. de Man (1979) *Allegories of Reading. Figural Language in Rousseau, Nietzsche, Rilke, and Proust.* New Haven/London: Yale University Press, p. 17.

[170] Ibid., p. 12.

[171] Ibid., p. 19.

[172] Cf. S. C. Wheeler (2000) *Deconstruction and Analytic Philosophy.* Stanford: Stanford University Press.

[173] G. H. Hartman (1970) *Beyond Formalism. Critical Essays 1958–1970.* New Haven/London: Yale University Press, p. 339.

[174] G. H. Hartman (1985) *Easy Pieces.* New York: Columbia University Press, p. 44.

[175] Ibid.

[176] P. Tepe (1992) *Postmoderne/Poststrukturalismus.* Vienna: Passagen, p. 38. The relationship between indifference and pluralism is also discussed in J. Moreno (1988) Indiferente posmodernidad. In *Revista Muface* 94.

# Chapter 5

[1] Cf. A. Eysteinsson (1990) *The Concept of Modernism.* Ithaca/London: Cornell University Press, p. 40.

[2] Cf. A. Ruiz Abreu (1984) *Modernismo y generación del 98.* Mexico: Ed. Trillas; E. Rull Fernández (1984) *Modernismo y la generación del 98.* Madrid: Playor; E. Marini Palmieri (1989) *Modernismo literario hispanoamericano. Carácteres esotéricos en las obras de Darío y Lugones.* Buenos Aires: García Cambeiro – and in particular M. C. A. Vidal (1989) *¿Qué es el posmodernismo?* Alicante: Univ. de Alicante, pp. 35–37: 'Modernismo ¿versus? Posmodernismo'.

[3] Cf. G. Gentile (1962) Modernismo e i rapporti fra religione e filosofia, Opere complete, vol. XXXV; C. Marcora and G. Rigamonti (eds) (1979) *Aspetti religiosi e culturali della società lombarda negli anni della crisi modernista (1898–1914).* Milan: Cairoli. More recently G. Ferroni (1996) *Dopo la fine. Sulla condizione postuma della letteratura.* Turin: Einaudi: chapter III: 'Moderno, postumo e postmoderno'.

[4] In this context, the bibliography published by B. Hovercroft and S. Söderlind is particularly informative. It was included in a special issue (39) of *Tangence* published under the title *La fiction postmoderne*. Most of the titles listed are from the English-speaking world, most of the French titles from Quebec. An important exception is (apart from works by Foucault, Derrida and Lyotard): J. Zylberberg (ed.) (1986) *Masses et postmodernité*. Paris: Klincksieck.

[5] Cf. for example G. Mazzoni (1988) *Postmoderne e la critica*. Rome: Guerini e Associati.

[6] Cf. Zima, P. V. (2007) *What is Theory? Cultural Theory as Discourse and Dialogue*. London/New York: Continuum, chapter I: 'The Cultural Character of Theory'.

[7] The Chinese view of postmodernity is presented in Wang Ning, Constructing Postmodernism: The Chinese Case and its Different Versions. In *Canadian Review of Comparative Literature/Revue Canadienne de Littérature Comparée*, March–June 1993. Wang Ning's analysis shows that postmodernity is primarily a West European and American phenomenon: 'a cultural phenomenon in the highly developed capitalist countries or postindustrial societies'. (p. 50) Compare with Choi Moon-gyoo (1996) *(Tal) Hjondaesong gua Munhag ui Ihae ([Post]Modernity and Literature)*. Seoul: Minumsa, who concentrates on the European discussions of modernity and postmodernity.

[8] Cf. K. R. Popper (1981) *Objective Knowledge. An Evolutionary Approach*. Oxford: The Clarendon Press (revised ed.), chapter III: 'Epistemology without a Knowing Subject'.

[9] Cf. P. V. Zima (1989) *Ideologie und Theorie. Eine Diskurskritik*. Tübingen: Francke, chapter IV: 'Ideologie und Wertfreiheit: Von Max Weber zum Kritischen Rationalismus'.

[10] Cf. P. V. Zima (2005) *The Philosophy of Modern Literary Theory*. London/New York: Athlone/Continuum (1999), chapter II.

[11] W. Benjamin (1972) *Ursprung des deutschen Trauerspiels*. Frankfurt: Suhrkamp, p. 31.

[12] F. Nietzsche (1980) In K. Schlechta (ed.), *Werke*, vol. VI. Munich: Hanser, p. 625.

[13] F. Nietzsche, *Werke*, vol. IV, op. cit., p. 958.

[14] F. Nietzsche, *Werke*, vol. III, op. cit., p. 142.

[15] S. Freud (1982) *Studienausgabe, Ergänzungsband*. Frankfurt: Fischer, p. 413.

[16] S. Freud, *Studienausgabe*, vol. III, op. cit., p. 95.

[17] Cf. S. Freud, *Studienausgabe*, vol. III, op. cit., p. 94: 'The term "ambivalence" was coined by Bleuler who distinguishes three sorts of ambivalence: affective, intellectual and of the will.'

[18] S. Freud, *Studienausgabe*, vol. V, op. cit., p. 284.

[19] Cf. S. Freud, *Studienausgabe*, vol. X, op. cit., p. 191.

[20] S. Freud, *Studienausgabe*, vol. VII, op. cit., p. 301.

[21] The problem of ambiguity in J. Austen and H. de Balzac is commented on in P. V. Zima (1999) *Roman und Ideologie. Zur Sozialgeschichte des modernen Romans*. Munich: Fink (1986), pp. 22–25.

[22] T. Mann (1958) *Confessions of Felix Krull, Confidence Man*. Harmondsworth: Penguin, p. 199. (*Bekenntnisse des Hochstaplers Felix Krull*. Frankfurt: Fischer [1954], 1974, pp. 224–225.)

[23] M. M. Bakhtin (1984) *Problems of Dostoevsky's Poetics* ([1928]). Minneapolis/London: University of Minnesota Press, p. 180.

[24] Ibid., p. 30.

[25] Ibid., p. 166.

[26] Ibid., p. 179 (note 26).

[27] S. Freud (1984) *Studienausgabe*, vol. X, op. cit., pp. 277–278.

[28] R. Musil (1978) *Gesammelte Werke*, vol. IX. Reinbek: Rowohlt, p. 1682. Cf. also Estela Cédola's analysis of ambivalence in Borges: *Borges o la coincidencia de los opuestos*. Buenos Aires, Editorial Universitaria, 1987.

[29] Cf. Ch. Dresler-Brumme (1987) *Nietzsches Philosophie in Musils Roman 'Der Mann ohne Eigenschaften'. Eine vergleichende Betrachtung als Beitrag zum Verständnis*. Frankfurt: Athenäum, pp. 91, 97.

[30] R. Musil, *Gesammelte Werke*, vol. V, op. cit., p. 1538.

[31] Cf. A. Schnitzler (1999) *Dream Story*. Harmondsworth: Penguin. (*Die Braut. Traum-novelle* [1926], Stuttgart: Reclam, 1976.)

[32] D. H. Lawrence (1982) The Virgin and the Gipsy. In idem, *The Complete Short Novels*. Harmondsworth: Penguin, p. 541.

[33] L.-F. Céline (1988) *Journey to the End of the Night*. London: John Calder, p. 177. (*Voyage au bout de la nuit*, Paris [1932], Gallimard, 1952, p. 248.)

[34] A. Moravia (1975) *La disubbidienza*. Milan: Bompiani (1945), p. 35.

[35] J. Hašek (1987) *Osudy dobrého vojáka Švejka* (1920–1923), vol. I/2. Prague: Československý Spisovatel, p. 104.

[36] B. Brecht (1991) *Mother Courage and her Children*. New York: Grove Press, p. 75. (*Mutter Courage und ihre Kinder* [1941]. Frankfurt: Suhrkamp, 1966, p. 66.)

[37] F. Kafka (2008) *The Trial*. Ware, London: Wordsworth Editions, pp. 110–111. (*Der Prozeß* [1925], Frankfurt: Fischer, 1964, p. 108.)

[38] R. M. Rilke (1982) *The Notebooks of Malte Laurids Brigge*. New York: Random House, pp. 8–9. (*Die Aufzeichnungen des Malte Laurids Brigge* [1910]. Frankfurt: Insel, 1982, p. 13.)

[39] J.-P. Sartre (2000) *Nausea*. London: Penguin, p. 61. (*La Nausée* [1938]. In idem, *Œuvres Romanesques*, édition établie par M. Contat et M. Rybalka, Paris: Gallimard, Bibl. de la Pléiade, 1981, p. 48.)

[40] Cf. J.-P. Sartre (1947) M. François Mauriac et la liberté. In idem, *Critiques littéraires (Situations, I)*. Paris : Gallimard, p. 69.

[41] I. Svevo (1984) *Confessions of Zeno*. Harmondsworth: Penguin, p. 291. (*La coscienza di Zeno* [1923], Milan, Dall'Oglio, 1938, p. 369.)

[42] M. Proust (1976) *Le Carnet de 1908*. Paris: Gallimard (*Cahiers Marcel Proust 8*), p. 61.

[43] R. Musil, *Gesammelte Werke*, vol. VII, op. cit., p. 826.

[44] R. Musil, *Gesammelte Werke*, vol. V, op. cit., p. 1941.

[45] M. Proust (1970) *Remembrance of Things Past*, vol. XII. *Time Regained* (Part Two). London: Chatto and Windus, p. 262. (*A la recherche du temps perdu* [1913–1927], vol. IV [J.-Y. Tadié éd.]. Paris : Gallimard, Bibl. de la Pléiade, 1989, p. 474.)

[46] Ibid. (Ibid.)

[47] Cf. J.-P. Sartre (1979) L'Engagement de Mallarmé. In *Obliques* 18–19, special issue 'Sartre', p. 177.

[48] The problem of paradox in Kafka's works is discussed in A. L. Baum (1976) Parable as Paradox in Kafka's Erzählungen. In *MLN* 91.

[49] T. Todorov (1974) La Lecture comme construction. In *Poétique* 24, p. 421.

⁵⁰  H. Broch (1986) *The Sleepwalkers*. London/Melbourne/New York: Quartet Books, p. 200. (*Die Schlafwandler. Eine Romantrilogie* [1931–1932]. Frankfurt: Suhrkamp, 1978, p. 226.)

⁵¹  Cf. ibid., p. 217 (Ibid., p. 244.)

⁵²  K. R. Mandelkow (1962) *Hermann Brochs Romantrilogie 'Die Schlafwandler'.* Heidelberg: Winter, p. 76.

⁵³  I. Svevo (1962) *Confessions of Zeno*, op. cit., p. 326. (*La coscienza di Zeno*, op. cit., p. 414.)

⁵⁴  Cf. P. Robinson (1978) In C. Fonda (ed.), *Svevo e Freud. Proposta di interpretazione della Coscienza di Zeno*. Ravenna: Longo, p. 118.

⁵⁵  Cf. R. Barilli (1981) *La linea Svevo-Pirandello*. Milan: Mursia, pp. 43–50.

⁵⁶  R. Musil, *Der Mann ohne Eigenschaften*, in: idem, *Gesammelte Werke*, vol. I, op. cit., p. 229.

⁵⁷  Ibid., chapter IX: 'Erster von drei Versuchen, ein bedeutender Mann zu werden.'

⁵⁸  Ibid., p. 229.

⁵⁹  L. Pirandello (1992) *One, No One, and One Hundred Thousand*. New York: Marsilio Publishers, p. 71. (*Uno, nessuno e centomila* [1926]. Milan: Mondadori, 1985, p. 100.)

⁶⁰  Ibid., p. 42. (Ibid., p. 61.)

⁶¹  Ibid., p. 43. (Ibid.)

⁶²  Constructivist assumptions concerning an objective reality are discussed in H. J. Wendel (1990) *Moderner Relativismus. Zur Kritik antirealistischer Sichtweisen des Erkenntnisproblems*. Tübingen: Mohr, pp. 190–210.

⁶³  In this respect, the radical constructivists are right. Cf. E. von Glasersfeld (1991) Abschied von der Objektivität. In P. Watzlawick and P. Krieg (eds), *Das Auge des Betrachters. Beiträge zum Konstruktivismus*. Munich/Zurich, Piper, p. 23.

⁶⁴  L. Pirandello, *One, No One, and One Hundred Thousand*, op. cit., p. 42. (*Uno, nessuno e centomila*, op. cit., p. 60.)

⁶⁵  Pirandello's umorismo is commented on in S. Bartoli (1996) *Modernità nella novella di Luigi Pirandello e Arthur Schnitzler*. Milan: Marcos y Marcos, chapter I.3.

⁶⁶  Cf. H. von Foerster (1985) Das Konstruieren einer Wirklichkeit. In P. Watzlawick (ed.), *Die erfundene Wirklichkeit*, 3rd edn. Munich/Zurich: Piper , p. 40.

⁶⁷  W. Krysinski (1989) *Le Paradigme inquiet. Pirandello et le champ de la modernité*. Montreal: Préambule, p. 455.

⁶⁸  R. Musil, *Der Mann ohne Eigenschaften*. In idem, *Gesammelte Werke*, vol. I, op. cit., p. 250.

⁶⁹  The non-syntactic construction of Breton's *Nadja* is analysed in detail in G. Steinwachs (1971) *Mythologie des Surrealismus oder Die Rückverwandlung von Kultur in Natur*. Neuwied/Berlin: Luchterhand, chapter V: 'Paradigmatisches Schreiben'.

⁷⁰  J. Joyce (1971) *Ulysses* (1922). Harmondsworth: Penguin, p. 587.

⁷¹  Joyce's position between modernism and postmodernism is discussed in W. Erzgräber (2003) James Joyce: Zwischen Moderne und Postmoderne. In J. Alber and M. Fludernik (eds), *Moderne/Postmoderne*. Trier: Wiss. Verlag Trier, p. 107.

⁷²  R. Musil (1971) *Aus den Tagebüchern*. Frankfurt: Suhrkamp, p. 19.

⁷³  A. Breton (1972) *Manifestoes of Surrealism*. Ann Arbor: The University. of Michigan Press, p. 26.

⁷⁴  F. Jameson (1993) *Postmodernism, or, The Cultural Logic of Late Capitalism*. Durham: Duke University Press (1991), p. 173.

75 Cf. Ibid., p. 175.

76 Cf. Ibid., p. 324.

77 Cf. R. G. Renner (1988) *Die postmoderne Konstellation. Theorie, Text und Kunst im Ausgang der Moderne.* Freiburg: Rombach, p. 142: 'There is no doubt that, with these definitions, Musil departs from the orientations of classical modernity and projects forms of thought which pave the way for a postmodern constellation.'

78 J.-P. Sartre L'Homme et les choses. In idem, *Critique littéraires (Situations, I)*, op. cit., p. 305.

79 J. P. Sartre, Aller et retour. In idem, *Critiques littéraires (Situations, I)*, op. cit., p. 244.

80 F. Kafka (1965) In *Das Kafka-Buch.* Frankfurt: Fischer, p. 241.

81 R. Musil, *Aus den Tagebüchern,* op. cit., p. 128.

82 I. Svevo (1968) *Racconti, Saggi, Pagine Sparse (Opere III).* Milan: Dall'Oglio, p. 586.

83 Cf. for example G. Simmel (1890) *Über sociale Differenzierung.* Leipzig: Duncker und Humblot, and N. Luhmann (1980) *Gesellschaftsstruktur und Semantik. Studien zur Wissenssoziologie der modernen Gesellschaft,* vol. I. Frankfurt: Suhrkamp, p. 21: 'We set out from a nexus between *complexity* and *system differentiation.*'

84 H. Broch, *The Sleepwalkers,* op. cit., p. 472. (*Die Schlafwandler,* op. cit., p. 498.)

85 R. Musil (1952) *Der Mann ohne Eigenschaften.* Reinbek: Rowohlt, p. 1578.

86 T. Mann (1999) *Doctor Faustus. The Life of the German Composer Adrian Leverkühn as Told by a Friend.* London: Vintage Books, p. 45. (*Doktor Faustus. Das Leben des deutschen Tonsetzers Adrian Leverkühn erzählt von einem Freunde* [1947]. *Die Entstehung des Doktor Faustus* [1949]. Frankfurt: Fischer, 2001, p. 63.)

87 R. Musil *Gesammelte Werke,* vol. VIII, op. cit., p. 1412.

88 A. Camus (1965) *L'Homme révolté* (1951). In R. Quilliot and L. Faucon (eds), idem, *Essais.* Paris: Gallimard, Bibl. de la Pléiade, p. 478.

89 Cf. A. Camus, Révolte et servitude. In idem, *Essais,* op. cit., p. 762.

90 A. Rühling (1974) *Negativität bei Albert Camus.* Bonn: Bouvier, p. 231.

91 The relationship between Marxism–Leninism and Camus's philosophy is commented on in E. Tall (1979) Camus in the Soviet Union. Some recent emigrés speak. In *Comparative Literature Studies* 3.

92 F. T. Vischer (1922) Der Traum. Eine Studie zu der Schrift: *Die Traumphantasie von Dr. Johann Volkelt.* In idem, *Kritische Gänge,* vol. IV. Munich: Meyer und Jessen, p. 482.

93 M. Proust, *Remembrance of Things Past,* vol. XII. *Time Regained* (Part Two), op. cit., p. 240. (*A la recherche du temps perdu,* vol. IV, op. cit., p. 457.)

94 A. Breton (1937) *L'Amour fou.* Paris: Gallimard, p. 36.

95 K. Riha (1995) *Prämoderne, Moderne, Postmoderne.* Frankfurt: Suhrkamp, p. 245.

96 H. Hesse (1965) *Steppenwolf.* London: Penguin, p. 223. (*Der Steppenwolf* [1927]. Frankfurt: Suhrkamp, 1972, p. 209.)

97 A. Camus (1964) *The Outsider.* Harmondsworth: Penguin, p. 103. (*L'Etranger* [1942]. In idem, *Théâtre, Récits, Nouvelles,* textes établis et annotés par R. Quilliot. Paris: Gallimard, Bibl. de la Pléiade, 1962, p. 1198.)

98 The role of chance and contingency in Camus's *L'Etranger* is discussed in detail in E. Köhler (1973) *Der literarische Zufall, das Mögliche und die Notwendigkeit.* Munich: Fink, p. 86.

99 H. Hesse (1972) *Kurgast,* Frankfurt, Suhrkamp, p. 53.

100 Cf. G. Steinwachs, *Mythologie des Surrealismus,* op. cit., pp. 21–39.

[101]  H. R. Jauß (1991) Ursprünge der Naturfeindschaft in der Ästhetik der Moderne. In K. Maurer and W. Wehle (eds), *Romantik, Aufbruch zur Moderne*. Munich: Fink, p. 381.

[102]  F. Nietzsche, *Werke*, vol. V, op. cit., p. 327.

[103]  J.-P. Sartre (1948) *Qu'est-ce que la littérature?* Paris : Gallimard, p. 220.

[104]  J.-P. Sartre, *Nausea*, op. cit., pp. 185–186. (*La Nausée*, op. cit., p. 153.)

[105]  Ibid., p. 180. (Ibid., p. 148.)

[106]  J.-P. Sartre, *Œuvres romanesques*, op. cit., p. 1699.

[107]  F. Kafka, *The Trial*, op. cit., p. 10. (*Der Prozeß*, op. cit., p. 13.)

[108]  Cf. F. Kafka (1952) *Das Urteil und andere Erzählungen*. Frankfurt: Fischer, p. 79.

[109]  M. Krleža (1985) *Povratak Filipa Latinovicza* (1932). Split: Logos, p. 36.

[110]  Cf. H. Meter (1977) *Apollinaire und der Futurismus*. Rheinfelden: Schäuble, chapter II.4.

[111]  Cf. H. Bertens (1986) The postmodern Weltanschauung and its relation with modernism: an introductory survey. In D. W. Fokkema and H. Bertens (eds), *Approaching Postmodernism*. Amsterdam/Philadelphia: J. Benjamins, pp. 9–16.

[112]  T. W. Adorno (2000) *Negative Dialectics* (1966). London/New York: Routledge, p. 408.

[113]  T. W. Adorno (2005) *Minima Moralia. Reflections on a Damaged Life* (1951). London/New York: Verso, p. 244.

[114]  S. Mallarmé (1945) Crise de vers. In idem, *Œuvres complètes*, texte établi et annoté par H. Mondor et G. Jean-Aubry. Paris: Gallimard, Bibl. de la Pléiade, p. 368.

[115]  Cf. T. W. Adorno (1991) On lyric poetry and society. In R. Tiedemann (ed.), idem, *Notes to Literature*, vol. I (1958). New York: Columbia University Press, pp. 50–51.

[116]  Ibid., p. 52.

[117]  T. W. Adorno (1991) Short commentaries on Proust. In R. Tiedemann (ed.), idem, *Notes to Literature*, vol. II (1961). New York: Columbia University Press, p. 174.

[118]  R. Musil, *Der Mann ohne Eigenschaften*. In idem, *Gesammelte Werke*, vol. I, op. cit., p. 253.

[119]  T. W. Adorno, The Essay as Form. In idem, *Notes to Literature*, vol. I, op. cit., p. 9.

[120]  Cf. T. W. Adorno, *Negative Dialectics*, op. cit., p. 29.

[121]  Cf. S. Best and D. Kellner (1991) Adorno's proto-postmodern theory. In idem, *Postmodern Theory. Critical Interrogations*. London: MacMillan, p. 232: 'He vindicates otherness, difference, and particularity as consistently and brilliantly as any postmodern theorist.' However, the authors do overlook Adorno's critique of particularity.

[122]  T. W. Adorno (1997) *Aesthetic Theory* (1970). London: Athlone, p. 364.

[123]  Cf. P. V. Zima (2005) *Ästhetische Negation. Das Subjekt, das Schöne und das Erhabene von Mallarmé und Valéry zu Adorno und Lyotard*. Würzburg: Königshausen und Neumann, chapter IV.

[124]  M. Horkheimer T. W. Adorno (1997) *Dialectic of Enlightenment* (1947). London/New York: Verso, p. 19.

[125]  T. W. Adorno, *Aesthetic Theory*, op. cit., p. 331.

[126]  F. Kafka, In *Das Kafka-Buch*, op. cit., p. 252.

[127]  T. W. Adorno (1971) *Kritik. Kleine Schriften zur Gesellschaft*. Frankfurt: Suhrkamp, pp. 84–85.

[128]  Cf. T. W. Adorno, The Artist as Deputy. In idem, *Notes to Literature*, vol. I, op. cit.

[129]  W. M. Lüdke (1981) *Anmerkungen zu einer 'Logik des Zerfalls': Adorno-Beckett.* Frankfurt: Suhrkamp, p. 30.

[130]  H. U. Gumbrecht (1991) Die Postmoderne ist (eher) keine Epoche. In R. Weimann and H. U. Gumbrecht (eds), *Postmoderne – Globale Differenz.* Frankfurt: Suhrkamp, p. 369.

[131]  A. Moravia (2000) *The Time of Indifference.* Hanover (New Hampshire): Steerforth Press, p. 271. (*Gli indifferenti* [1929], Milan, Bompiani, 1966, p. 277.)

[132]  Ibid., p. 79. (Ibid., p. 84.)

[133]  Ibid., p. 245. (Ibid., p. 249.)

[134]  T. Bernhard (1986) *Auslöschung. Ein Zerfall.* Frankfurt: Suhrkamp, p. 645.

[135]  T. Bernhard (1979) In *Die Zeit*, 29 June 1979, p. 33.

[136]  R. Kock (1995) Postmoderne und dekonstruktive Sprachkritik in den frühen Prosatexten Frost, Zerstörung, Watten und Gehen von Thomas Bernhard. MA Dissertation, University of Münster, p. 45.

[137]  A. Breton (1965) *Arcane 17.* Paris: U.G.E., p. 76.

[138]  Cf. F. Nietzsche (1965) *Werke*, vol. III, op. cit., p. 73.

[139]  A. Schnitzler, *Dream Story*, op. cit, p. 68. (*Die Braut. Traumnovelle*, op. cit., p. 73.)

[140]  T. W. Adorno, *Minima Moralia*, op. cit., p. 49.

[141]  G. Benn quoted after W. Falk (1961) *Leid und Verwandlung. Rilke, Kafka, Trakl und der Epochenstil des Impressionismus und Expressionismus.* Salzburg: O. Müller, p. 409.

[142]  W. Falk, *Leid und Verwandlung*, op. cit, p. 409.

[143]  Ibid.

[144]  U. Eco (1984) *Reflections on the Name of the Rose.* London: Secker and Warburg, p. 67.

[145]  U. Eco (1984) *The Name of the Rose.* New York: Warner Books, p. XIII. (*Il nome della rosa.* Milan: Bompiani, 1980, p. 11.)

[146]  Ibid., p. 182. (Ibid., p. 163.)

[147]  W. Hüllen (1985) Erzählte Semiotik. Betrachtungen zu Umberto Ecos 'Der Name der Rose'. In R. Haas and Ch. Klein-Braley (eds), *Literatur im Kontext.* Sankt Augustin: Richartz, p. 128.

[148]  F. Kafka, In *Das Kafka-Buch*, op. cit., p. 241.

[149]  J. Fowles (1992) *The French Lieutenant's Woman.* London (1969): Picador, p. 54.

[150]  Ibid., p. 84.

[151]  Ibid., p. 85.

[152]  J. Becker (1983) *Felder, Ränder, Umgebungen.* Frankfurt. Suhrkamp, p. 141.

[153]  R. Barthes (1971) *Sade, Fourier, Loyola.* Paris: Seuil, p. 169.

[154]  J. Barth (1988) *Lost in the Funhouse.* New York (1968): Doubleday, p. 72.

[155]  Ibid., p. 77.

[156]  Ibid., p. 96.

[157]  A. Lindsay (1995) *Death in the Funhouse. John Barth and Poststructuralist Aesthetics.* New York: Peter Lang, p. 112.

[158]  J. Fowles, *The French Lieutenant's Woman*, op. cit., p. 398.

[159]  A. Robbe-Grillet (1959) *Dans le labyrinthe.* Paris: Minuit, p. 7.

[160]  Ibid., p. 9.

[161]  D. Bougnoux (1974) establishes a link between scientific fiction and structuralism: 'Approches de quelques lieux butoriens'. In *Butor. Colloque de Cerisy.* Paris: U.G.E. (10/18) , p. 349.

[162] T. Pynchon (1975) *Gravity's Rainbow*. London (1973): Picador, p. 134.

[163] Ibid., p. 701.

[164] This idea could be contested with W. Fluck: 'If someone argues therefore (. . .) that Pynchon doubts the sense of every construction of meaning, because everything that is part of civilization's entropy contributes to the consolidation of the existing order, then questions arise.' (W. Fluck (1992) 'Literarische Postmoderne und Poststrukturalismus: Thomas Pynchon'. In K. W. Hempfer (ed), *Poststrukturalismus – Dekonstruktion – Postmoderne*. Stuttgart: Steiner, p. 29.)

[165] T. Todorov (1981) *Mikhaïl Bakhtine. Le principe dialogique – suivi de Ecrits du Cercle de Bakhtine*. Paris: Seuil, p. 156.

[166] J. Becker, *Ränder, Felder, Umgebungen*, op. cit., p. 63.

[167] Ibid., p. 250.

[168] O. Wiener (1985) *Die Verbesserung von Mitteleuropa*. Reinbek: Rowohlt (1969), p. XXX.

[169] Ibid., p. L.

[170] M. Roche (1966) *Compact*. Paris: U.G.E. (10/18), p. 168.

[171] I. Calvino (1998) *If on a Winter's Night a Traveller*. London: Vintage Books, p. 3. (*Se una notte d'inverno un viaggiatore*. Turin: Einaudi, 1979, p. 3.)

[172] Ibid., p. 198. (Ibid., p. 197.)

[173] U. Schulz-Buschhaus (1990) 'Versöhnung mit dem Abenteuer. Zum erzählerischen Werk von Italo Calvino'. In G. Goebel-Schilling, S. A. Sanna and U. Schulz-Buschhaus (eds), *Widerstehen. Anmerkungen zu Calvinos erzählerischem Werk*. Frankfurt: Materialis Verlag, p. 23.

[174] Cf. R. Barthes (1984) La Mort de l'auteur. In idem, *Le Bruissement de la langue. Essais critiques IV*. Paris: Seuil, p. 61 and M. Foucault (1994) 'Qu'est-ce qu'un auteur'. In idem, *Dits et écrits 1954–1988*, vol. I. Paris: Gallimard, p. 793.

[175] H. R. Jauß (1989) Italo Calvino: 'Wenn ein Reisender in der Winternacht'. Plädoyer für eine postmoderne Ästhetik. In idem, *Studien zum Epochenwandel der ästhetischen Moderne*. Frankfurt: Suhrkamp, pp. 281–282.

[176] Ibid., p. 287.

[177] Cf. for example: P. Baroja (1952) *Camino de perfección. Pasión mística* (1902). New York: Las Américas Publishing Company.

[178] F. de Azúa (1986) *Historia de un idiota contada por él mismo o El contenido de la felicidad*, 17th edn. Barcelona: Anagrama, p. 29.

[179] Ibid., p. 31.

[180] Cf. A. Moravia (1960) *La noia*. Milan: Bompiani.

[181] F. de Azúa, *Historia de un idiota contada por él mismo*, op. cit., p. 68.

[182] Maria Cármen África Vidal's thesis according to which postmodernity has ceased to believe in art and in the artist is borne out by Azúa's novel: Cf. M. C. A. Vidal. *¿Qué es el posmodernismo?* op. cit., p. 43.

[183] F. de Azúa, *Historia de un idiota contada por él mismo*, op. cit., p. 101.

[184] Ibid.

[185] Ibid.

[186] Ibid., p. 115.

[187] Ibid., p. 119.

[188] Ibid., p. 123.

[189] Ibid.

[190] Ibid., p. 125.

[191] G. Flaubert (1979) *Bouvard et Pécuchet*. Paris: Gallimard, p. 443.

[192] Cf. F. Nietzsche (1990) *Beyond Good and Evil. Prelude to a Philosophy of the Future*. London: Penguin, p. 34.

[193] Cf. M. Janković (1999) Noch einmal zum Begriff der semantischen Geste. In V. Macura and H. Schmid (eds), *Jan Mukařovský and the Prague School*. Potsdam: University of Postdam, pp. 150–151.

[194] Ch. Ransmayr (1991) *The Last World*. London/Glasgow: Paladin/Grafton Books, pp. 100–101. (*Die letzte Welt* [1988]. Frankfurt: Fischer, 1995, pp. 169–170.)

[195] A. Camus, *Théâtre, récits, nouvelles*, op. cit., p. 120.

[196] Ch. Ransmayr, *The Last World*, op. cit., pp. 28–29. (*Die letzte Welt*, op. cit., p. 51.)

[197] Ibid., p. 287.

[198] A. Robbe-Grillet (1955) *Le Voyeur*. Paris: Minuit, p. 151.

[199] P. J. Johnson (1972) *Camus et Robbe-Grillet. Structure et techniques narratives dans 'Le Renégat' de Camus et 'Le Voyeur' de Robbe-Grillet*. Paris: Nizet, p. 39.

[200] P. Süskind (1986) *Perfume. The Story of a Murderer*. London: Penguin, p. 46. (*Das Parfum. Die Geschichte eines Mörders*. Zurich: Diogenes [1985], 1994, p. 57.)

[201] Ibid., pp. 46–47. (Ibid., p. 58.)

[202] Ibid., p. 245. (Ibid., p. 300.)

[203] Ibid., p. 247. (Ibid., p. 303.)

[204] J. Ryan (1991) Pastiche und Postmoderne. Patrick Süskinds Roman *Das Parfum*. In P. M. Lützeler (ed.), *Spätmoderne und Postmoderne. Beiträge zur deutschsprachigen Gegenwartsliteratur*. Frankfurt: Fischer, p. 99.

[205] P. Süskind, *Perfume*, op. cit., p. 71. (*Das Parfum*, op. cit., p. 89.)

[206] J. W. Goethe (1968) *Maximen und Reflexionen*, 2nd edn. Munich: DTV, p. 16.

[207] J. Becker (1972) Gegen die Erhaltung des literarischen status quo. In L. Kreutzer (ed.), *Über Jürgen Becker*. Frankfurt: Suhrkamp, p. 19.

[208] J. Becker, *Ränder, Felder, Umgebungen*, op. cit., p. 110.

[209] F. de Azúa, *Historia de un idiota contada por él mismo*, op. cit., p. 125.

[210] Cf. F. Furedi (2006) *Where Have all the Intellectuals Gone? Confronting 21st Century Philistinism*, 2nd edn. London/New York: Continuum.

[211] B. Brecht (1971) *Über Realismus*. Frankfurt: Suhrkamp, p. 70.

[212] F. de Azúa, *Historia de un idiota contada por él mismo*, op. cit., p. 22.

[213] Acceleration as a contemporary social phenomenon is analysed in great detail in H. Rosa, (2005) *Beschleunigung. Zur Veränderung der Zeitstrukturen in der Moderne*. Frankfurt: Suhrkamp.

[214] L. Goytisolo (1985) *Investigaciones y conjeturas de Claudio Mendoza*. Barcelona: Anagrama, pp. 25–37.

[215] E. Callenbach (1982) *Ecotopia Emerging*. Toronto/New York (1981): Bantam, p. 2.

[216] Ibid., p. 337.

[217] H. Tschachler (1990) *Ökologie und Arkadien. Natur und nordamerikanische Kultur der siebziger Jahre*. Frankfurt/Berne/New York: Peter Lang, pp. 353–354.

[218] M. Piercy (1983) *Woman on the Edge of Time*. London: Women's Press (1979), p. 375.

[219] J. Becker, *Ränder, Felder, Umgebungen*, op. cit., pp. 136, 173, 191, 212.

[220] Cf. P. Crowther (2000) *Critical Aesthetics and Postmodernism*. Oxford: Clarendon Press, 'Part Three', where the specific character of postmodern visual arts is analysed.

221 D. Harvey for example writes: 'High modernist art, architecture, literature, etc. became establishment arts and practices (. . .).' (D. Harvey (1995) *The Condition of Postmodernity*. Oxford: Blackwell [1990], p. 35.)

222 D. Borchmeyer (1987) Postmoderne. In D. Borchmeyer and V. Žmegač (eds), *Moderne Literatur in Grundbegriffen*. Frankfurt: Athenäum, p. 312.

223 T. Mann, *Doctor Faustus*, op. cit., p. 478. (*Doktor Faustus*, op. cit., p. 633.)

224 T. W. Adorno, *Minima Moralia*, op. cit., p. 50.

225 A critique of this stereotype expression is to be found in P. V. Zima (2007) *Deconstruction and Critical Theory* (2002). London: Turnshare, pp. 147–148.

226 T. W. Adorno, *Minima Moralia*, op. cit., p. 63.

227 T. W. Adorno, *Aesthetic Theory*, op. cit., p. 154.

228 Ibid.

229 J. H. Miller (1991) *Theory Now and Then*. New York/London: Harvester/Wheatsheaf, p. 126.

230 Cl. Simon (1960) *La Route des Flandres*. Paris: Minuit, p. 314.

231 P. de Man (1979) *Allegories of Reading. Figural Language in Rousseau, Nietzsche, Rilke, and Proust*. New Haven/London, p. 115.

232 G. Vattimo (1991) *The End of Modernity. Nihilism and Hermeneutics in Postmodern Culture* (1985). Baltimore: The Johns Hopkins University Press, p. 21.

233 R. Rorty (1995) *Objectivity, Relativism, and Truth. Philosophical Papers*, vol. I. Cambridge/New York: Cambridge University Press (1991), p. 207.

234 O. Wiener, *Die Verbesserung von Mitteleuropa*, op. cit., p. XXXIV.

235 F. Kafka, *The Trial*, op. cit., p. 166. (*Der Prozeß*, op. cit., p. 160.)

# Chapter 6

1 J. Habermas (1986) *Vorstudien und Ergänzungen zur Theorie des kommunikativen Handelns*. 2nd edn. Frankfurt: Suhrkamp, p. 504.

2 R. Musil (1952) *Der Mann ohne Eigenschaften*. Reinbek: Rowohlt, p. 1603.

3 N. Elias (1956) Problems of Involvement and Detachment. In *The British Journal of Sociology* 1, p. 252.

4 Cf. M. Foucault (1986) *La Pensée du dehors*. Paris: Fata Morgana.

5 R. Musil (1978) In A. Frisé (ed.), *Gesammelte Werke*, vol. VII. Reinbek: Rowohlt, p. 904.

6 D. W. Fokkema (1984) *Literary History, Modernism, and Postmodernism*. Amsterdam, Philadelphia: J. Benjamins, pp. 40–41.

7 Cf. Zima (1989) *Ideologie und Theorie. Eine Diskurskritik*. Tübingen: Francke, chapters IV and XII.

8 Cf. H. Albert (1975) *Transzendentale Träumereien. Karl Otto Apels Sprachspiele und sein hermeneutischer Gott*. Hamburg: Hoffmann und Campe, p. 147.

9 Cf. M. M. Bakhtin (1984) *Problems of Dostoevsky's Poetics*. Minneapolis: University of Minnesota Press, pp. 74–75.

10 E. Sapir, B. L. Whorf (1956) *Language, Thought, and Reality*. Cambridge, MA: The MIT Press, p. 134.

¹¹ The notion of *préconstruit* (*preconstruct*) is discussed by P. Henry (1975) Constructions relatives et articulations discursives. In *Langages* 37, March.

¹² T. S. Kuhn (1977) *The Essential Tension. Selected Studies in Scientific Tradition and Change*. Chicago/London: The University of Chicago Press, pp. XXII–XXIII.

¹³ Popper, K. R. (1970) Normal science and its dangers. In I. Lakatos and A. Musgrave (eds), *Criticism and the Growth of Knowledge*. Cambridge: University Press, p. 56.

¹⁴ Cf. J. Derrida (1987) Des Tours de Babel. In idem, *Psyché. Inventions de l'autre*. Paris: Galilée, and P. de Man (1986) *The Resistance to Theory*. Minneapolis: University of Minnesota Press, p. 91.

¹⁵ Cf. B. Croce (1973) *Estetica come scienza dell'espressione e linguistica generale*. 12th edn. Bari: Laterza, p. 76. Croce speaks of a 'new expression form'.

¹⁶ Within the framework of one and the same ideological (conservative, liberal) or theoretical (phenomenological, psychoanalytic) sociolect, an unlimited number of discourses can be generated. In everyday life, the sociolect is only present as an infinite number of real and potential *discourses*.

¹⁷ K. R. Popper (1963) *The Open Society and its Enemies, vol. II: The High Tide of Prophecy: Hegel, Marx, and the Aftermath*. London: Routledge and Kegan Paul (1945), p. 222.

¹⁸ J.-F. Lyotard (2004) *The Postmodern Condition: A Report on Knowledge* (1979). Manchester: Manchester University Press, p. 64.

¹⁹ J.-F. Lyotard (1989) In *Témoigner du différend. Quand phraser ne se peut*. Paris: Osiris, p. 119.

²⁰ W. Welsch (2000) *Vernunft. Die zeitgenössische Vernunftkritik und das Konzept der transversalen Vernunft*. 3rd edn. Frankfurt: Suhrkamp (1995), p. 877.

²¹ Ibid., p. 755.

²² Ibid., p. 700.

²³ Ibid., pp. 760–761.

²⁴ The function of relevance criteria and taxonomies in discourse is examined in P. V. Zima, *Ideologie und Theorie*, op. cit., chapter VII.

²⁵ Cf. W. Welsch (1990) Postmoderne oder ästhetisches Denken – gegen seine Mißverständnisse verteidigt. In G. Eifler and O. Saame (eds), *Postmoderne, Anbruch einer neuen Epoche? Eine interdisziplinäre Erörterung*. Vienna: Passagen, p. 247. (The postmodern problematic does allow for conservative reactions, some of which can be observed in Etzioni's moralizing critique. This is one good reason for not disqualifying Koslowski's conservatism as 'pseudo-postmodern'.)

²⁶ The relationship between intertextuality and alterity in Bakhtin's work is discussed by Julia Kristeva (1969) *Semeiotikè. Recherches pour une sémanalyse*. Paris: Seuil, p. 144.

²⁷ The thesis about the 'opacity of language' is developed in F. Schlegel (1967) Über die Unverständlichkeit. In idem, *Kritische Ausgabe*, vol. III. Paderborn: Schöningh, p. 364.

²⁸ Cf. L. Althusser, E. Balibar (1977) *Reading Capital* (1968). London: NLB.

²⁹ Cf. H. Lefebvre (1971) *L'Idéologie structuraliste*. Paris: Anthropos.

³⁰ Cf. for example: T. W. Adorno et al. (1972) *Der Positivismusstreit in der deutschen Soziologie*. Darmstadt, Neuwied: Luchterhand.

31  Cf. H. Albert (1980) *Traktat über kritische Vernunft.* Tübingen: Mohr, Siebeck, pp. 58–79.
32  Cf. O. Neurath (1981) Pseudorationalismus der Falsifikation. In R. Haller and H. Rutte (eds), idem, *Gesammelte philosophische und methodologische Schriften*, vol. II. Vienna: Hölder, Pichler, Tempsky, pp. 638–639.
33  M. Halbwachs (1972) *Classes sociales et morphologie.* Paris: Minuit, p. 150.
34  Ibid., p. 151.
35  K. Mannheim (1976) *Ideology and Utopia. An Introduction to the Sociology of Knowledge.* London/Henley: Routledge and Kegan Paul (1936), p. 270.
36  W. Dressler (1974) Der Beitrag der Textlinguistik zur Übersetzungswissenschaft. In V. Kapp (ed.), *Übersetzer und Dolmetscher. Theoretische Grundlagen, Ausbildung, Berufspraxis.* Heidelberg: Quelle und Meyer, p. 62.
37  The *seme* is defined as a general concept or *classeme*, holding together a class of semantic units, in A. J. Greimas (1979) *Sémiotique. Dictionnaire raisonné de la théorie du langage.* Paris: Hachette, p. 36.
38  Cf. Y. Lotman (1976) In D. Barton Johnson (ed.), *Analysis of the Poetic Text.* Ann Arbor: Ardis, p. 19.
39  The *idiolect* can be defined – with U. Eco – as the individual or private code of a speaker.
40  Cf. K.-O. Apel (1976) *Transformation der Philosophie*, vol. II. *Das a priori der Kommunikationsgemeinschaft.* Frankfurt: Suhrkamp, pp. 341–343.
41  Cf. for example: B. Martin, F. Ringham (2000) *Dictionary of Semiotics.* London/New York: Cassell.
42  P. Lorenzen (1974) *Konstruktive Wissenschaftstheorie.* Frankfurt: Suhrkamp, p. 118.
43  Ibid.
44  Ibid.
45  N. Luhmann (1991) Wie lassen sich latente Strukturen beobachten?. In P. Watzlawick and P. Krieg (eds), *Das Auge des Betrachters. Beiträge zum Konstruktivismus.* Munich: Piper, p. 70.
46  Ibid.
47  W. Welsch (1991) *Unsere postmoderne Moderne.* 3rd edn. Weinheim: VCH-Verlag, p. 306.
48  Cf. K. Salamun's analysis of the salient features of ideologies in K. Salamun (1988) *Ideologie und Aufklärung.* Vienna, Cologne, Graz: Böhlau, p. 105.
49  The nexus of irony, ambivalence and dialectics is described in P. V. Zima *Ideologie und Theorie*, op. cit., chapter X.
50  N. Luhmann (1976) Wahrheit und Ideologie. Vorschläge zur Wiederaufnahme der Diskussion (1962). In H.-J. Lieber (ed.), *Ideologie-Wissenschaft-Gesellschaft.* Darmstadt: Wiss. Buchgesellschaft, p. 53.
51  K. D. Bracher (1982) *Zeit der Ideologien. Eine Geschichte politischen Denkens im 20. Jahrhundert.* Stuttgart: DVA, p. 18.
52  I. Mészáros (1989) *The Power of Ideology.* London: Harvester, Wheatsheaf, p. 58.
53  Ibid.
54  Cf. D. Bell (1973) *The Coming of Post-Industrial Society. A Venture in Social Forecasting.* New York: Basic Books.
55  T. W. Adorno (2000) *Negative Dialectics* (1966). London/New York: Routledge, p. 8.

⁵⁶ The question concerning the value and the validity of different ideologies is discussed in P. V. Zima, *Ideologie und Theorie*, op. cit., chapter VIII.3.

⁵⁷ Cf. P. Bourdieu (1998) *Contre-feux*, Paris, Raisons d'agir, p. 68.

⁵⁸ Cf. L. Goldmann (1970) *Marxisme et sciences humaines.* Paris: Gallimard, pp. 13–15.

⁵⁹ P. M. Lützeler (1992) *Die Schriftsteller und Europa. Von der Romantik bis zur Gegenwart.* Munich: Piper, pp. 479–480.

⁶⁰ Those who consider 'Europe' mainly in an economic and financial perspective should ask themselves how long the member states of the EU will be able to afford 27 ministries of foreign affairs, 27 ministries of defence and countless embassies all over the world.

⁶¹ T. W. Adorno (2005) *Minima Moralia. Reflections on a Damaged Life* (1951). London/New York: NLB-Verso, p. 50.

# Bibliography

In this bibliography, only works dealing with 'modernity', 'modernism', 'post-modernity' and 'postmodernism' are quoted. Works by postmodern thinkers such as Lyotard, Baudrillard, Rorty or Vattimo are cited only if they are directly related to one of these topics. An extensive bibliography of 'postmodernism' covering the period from 1926 to 1994 was published by Deborah Madsen (1995) *Postmodernism. A Bibliography, 1926–1994* (Postmodern Studies 12). Amsterdam: Rodopi (662 pp.). Reflecting the structure of the book, the bibliography is divided into sections: 1. interdisciplinary studies and collective volumes; 2. sociology and politics; 3. philosophy and aesthetics and 4. literary criticism.

## 1. Interdisciplinary Studies and Collective Volumes

Alber, J. and Fludernik, M. (eds) (2003) *Moderne/Postmoderne*. Trier: Wiss. Verlag Trier.

Ankersmit, F. and Kibédi-Varga, A. (eds) (1993) *Akademische beschouwingen over het postmodernisme*. Amsterdam: Noordhollandse Uitgeversmaatschappij.

Bertens, H. (1995) *The Idea of the Postmodern*. London/New York: Routledge.

Bohrer, K. H. (ed.) (1983) *Mythos und Moderne. Begriff und Bild einer Rekonstruktion*. Frankfurt: Suhrkamp.

Connor, S. (1989) *Postmodernist Culture. An Introduction to Theories of the Contemporary*. Oxford: Blackwell.

Dowson, J. and Earnshaw, S. (eds) (1995) *Postmodern Subjects/Postmodern Texts*. Amsterdam/Atlanta: Rodopi.

Eifler, G. and Saame, O. (eds) (1990) *Postmoderne. Anbruch einer neuen Epoche? Eine interdisziplinäre Erörterung*. Vienna: Passagen.

Eysteinsson, A. and Liska, V. (eds) (2007) *Modernism* (2 vols.). Amsterdam/Atlanta: J. Benjamins.

Harvey, D. (1990) *The Condition of Postmodernity*. Oxford: Blackwell.

Huyssen, A. and Scherpe, K. R. (eds) (1986) *Postmoderne. Zeichen eines kulturellen Wandels*. Reinbek: Rowohlt.

Kamper, D. and van Reijen, W. (eds) (1987) *Die unvollendete Vernunft: Moderne versus Postmoderne*. Frankfurt: Suhrkamp.

Kaplan, E. A. (ed.) (1988) *Postmodernism and its Discontents. Theories, Practices*. London/New York: Verso.

Kemper, P. (ed.) (1988) *'Postmoderne' oder der Kampf um die Zukunft*. Frankfurt: Fischer.

Le Rider, J. and Raulet, G. (eds) (1987) *Verabschiedung der (Post-)Moderne? Eine interdisziplinäre Debatte.* Tübingen: Narr.

Picó, J. (ed.) (1988) *Modernidad y postmodernidad.* Madrid: Alianza.

*Postmodernism.* Special issue of *Theory, Culture, and Society,* vol. V, no. 2–3, 1988.

Renner, R. G. (1988) *Die postmoderne Konstellation. Theorie, Text und Kunst im Ausgang der Moderne.* Freiburg: Rombach.

Schmidt, B. (1994) *Postmoderne – Strategien des Vergessens,* 4th edn. Frankfurt: Suhrkamp.

Stierstorfer, K. (ed.) (2003) *Beyond Postmodernism. Reassessments in Literature, Theory, Culture.* Berlin/New York: De Gruyter.

Tew, P. and Murray, A. (eds) (2009) *The Modernism Handbook.* London/New York: Continuum.

Umbral, F. (1987) *Guía de la postmodernidad.* Madrid: Ed. Temas de Hoy.

Waugh, P. (ed.) (1992) *Postmodernism. A Reader.* London/New York: Edward Arnold.

Weimann, R. and Gumbrecht, H. U. (eds) (1991) *Postmoderne – globale Differenz.* Frankfurt: Suhrkamp.

Welsch, W. (1991) *Unsere postmoderne Moderne,* 3rd edn. Weinheim: VCH.

Welsch, W. (ed.) (1988) *Wege aus der Moderne. Schlüsseltexte der Postmoderne-Diskussion.* Weinheim: VCH.

## 2. Sociology and Politics

Arac, J. (ed.) (1986) *Postmodernism and Politics.* Manchester: Manchester University Press.

Aronowitz, S. (1987) Postmodernism and Politics. *Social Text,* no. 18.

Baudrillard, J. (1999) *L'Echange impossible.* Paris: Galilée.

Bauman, Z. (1987) *Legislators and Interpreters: On Modernity, Postmodernity and the Intellectuals.* Ithaca/Cambridge: Cornell University Press/Polity.

—(1992) *Intimations of Postmodernity.* London/New York: Routledge.

—(1997) *Postmodernity and Its Discontents.* Oxford: Blackwell.

Beck, U. (1988) *Gegengifte. Die organisierte Unverantwortlichkeit.* Frankfurt: Suhrkamp.

—(2007) *Weltrisikogesellschaft. Auf der Suche nach der verlorenen Sicherheit.* Frankfurt: Suhrkamp.

—(2008) *Risk Society. Towards a New Modernity* (1986). London: Sage (1992).

Bell, D. (1976) *The Coming of Postindustrial Society.* Harmondsworth: Penguin.

—(2000) *The End of Ideology. On the Exhaustion of Political Ideas in the Fifties* (1960), *with 'The Resumption of History in the New Century'.* Cambridge, MA: Harvard University Press.

Benhabib, S., Cornell, D. (1987) *Feminism as Critique. Essays on the Politics of Gender in Late-Capitalist Societies.* Cambridge/Oxford: Polity/Blackwell.

Berger, P. L., Berger, B., Kellner, H. (1974) *The Homeless Mind. Modernization and Consciousness.* New York: Random House, Vintage Books.

Best, S., Kellner, D. (2001) *The Postmodern Adventure. Science, Technology, and Cultural Studies at the Third Millennium.* New York/London: The Guilford Press.

Boyne, R. and Rattansi, A. (eds) (1990) *Postmodernism and Society.* London: Macmillan.

Callinicos, A. (1989) *Against Postmodernism. A Marxist Critique.* Cambridge: Polity.

Dickens, D. R. and Fontana, A. (eds) (1994) *Postmodernism and Social Inquiry.* London: UCL-Press.

Douzinas, C., Goodrich, P., and Hachamovitch, Y. (1994) *Politics, Postmodernity and Critical Legal Studies. The Legality of the Contingent.* London/New York: Routledge.

Endreß, M. (ed.) (2000) *Karl Mannheims Analyse der Moderne.* Opladen: Leske und Budrich.

Etzioni, A. (1968) *The Active Society. A Theory of Social and Political Processes.* London/New York: Collier/Macmillan/The Free Press.

—(1995) *The Spirit of Community. Rights, Responsibilities and the Communitarian Agenda.* London: Fontana Press.

Fechner, F. (1990) *Politik und Postmoderne. Postmodernisierung als Demokratisierung?* Vienna: Passagen.

Fern Haber, H. (1994) *Beyond Postmodern Politics.* New York/London: Routledge.

Fraser, N., Nicholson, L. (1988) Social criticism without philosophy: an encounter between feminism and postmodernism. In *Theory, Culture, and Society (Postmodernism),* vol. V, no. 2–3.

Galli, C. (ed.) (1991) *Logiche e crisi della modernità.* Bologna: Il Mulino.

Gehlen, A. (1988) Über kulturelle Kristallisation. In W. Welsch (ed.), *Wege aus der Moderne.* Weinheim: VCH-Verlag.

Giddens, A. (1990) *The Consequences of Modernity.* Cambridge: Polity.

—(1991) *Modernity and Self-Identity. Self and Society in the Late Modern Age.* Cambridge: Polity.

Gneuss, Ch. and Kocka, J. (eds) (1988) *Max Weber. Ein Symposion.* Munich: DTV, in particular: 'Max Weber und das Projekt der Moderne. Eine Diskussion mit Dieter Henrich, Claus Offe und Wolfgang Schluchter'.

Goodall, P. (1995) *High Culture, Popular Culture. The Long Debate.* St. Leonards, NSW: Allen & Unwin.

Gouldner, A. W. (1982) *The Dialectic of Ideology and Technology.* New York: Oxford University Press.

Hermand, J. (ed.) (1995) *Postmodern Pluralism and Concepts of Totality. The Twenty-Fourth Wisconsin Workshop.* New York/Berne/Paris: Peter Lang.

Hutcheon, L. (1989) *The Politics of Postmodernism.* London/New York: Routledge.

Jameson, F. (1989) Marxism and postmodernism. *New Left Review,* vol. 176.

Jameson, F. (1991) *Postmodernism, or, The Cultural Logic of Late Capitalism.* Durham: Duke University Press.

—(1998) *The Cultural Turn. Selected Writings on the Postmodern, 1983–1998.* London/New York: Verso.

Kellner, D. (2002) Postmodern War in the Age of Bush II. *New Political Science,* vol. 1.

Koslowski, P. (1988) *Die postmoderne Kultur. Gesellschaftlich-kulturelle Konsequenzen der technischen Entwicklung.* Munich: Beck.

—(1989) *Wirtschaft als Kultur. Wirtschaftskultur und Wirtschaftsethik in der Postmoderne.* Vienna: Passagen.

Koslowski, P., Spaemann, R. and Löw, R. (eds) (1986) *Moderne oder Postmoderne?* Weinheim: VCH.

Lasch, Ch. (1979) *The Culture of Narcissism.* New York: Norton.

Lash, S. (1990) *Sociology of Postmodernism.* London/New York: Routledge.

Lucas, D. (2009) *Crise des valeurs éducatives et postmodernité.* Paris: L'Harmattan.

Lyotard, J.-F. (1993) *Political Writings.* London: UCL.

McGowan, J. (1991) *Postmodernism and Its Critics.* Ithaca/London: Cornell University Press.

Mills, C. W. (1959) *The Sociological Imagination.* Oxford: Oxford University Press.

Mongardini, C. and Maniscalco, M. L. (eds) (1989) *Moderno e postmoderno. Crisi e identità di una cultura e ruolo della sociologia.* Rome: Bulzoni.

Münch, R. (1986) *Die Kultur der Moderne,* vol. I. *Ihre Grundlagen und ihre Entwicklung in England und Amerika.* Frankfurt: Suhrkamp.

—(1986) *Die Kultur der Moderne,* vol. II. *Ihre Entwicklung in Frankreich und Deutschland.* Frankfurt: Suhrkamp.

—(1992) *Die Struktur der Moderne. Grundmuster und differentielle Gestaltung des institutionellen Aufbaus der modernen Gesellschaften.* Frankfurt: Suhrkamp.

Nicholson, L. J. (ed.) (1990) *Feminism/Postmodernism.* New York: Routledge.

Niethammer, L. (1989) *Posthistoire. Ist die Geschichte zu Ende?* Reinbek: Rowohlt.

O'Neill, J. (1988) Religion and postmodernism: the Durkheimian bond in Bell and Jameson. *Theory, Culture, and Society (Postmodernism),* vol. V, no. 2–3.

—(1995) *The Poverty of Postmodernism.* London/New York: Routledge.

Rosenau, P. M. (1991) *Postmodernism and the Social Sciences.* Princeton: Princeton University Press.

Ross, A. (ed.) (1989) *Universal Abandon? The Politics of Postmodernism.* Edinburgh: Edinburgh University Press.

Ryan, M. (1982) *Marxism and Deconstruction. A Critical Articulation.* Baltimore/London: The Johns Hopkins University Press.

—(1988) Postmodern politics. In *Theory, Culture, and Society,* vol. V, no. 2–3.

—(1989) *Politics and Culture: Working Hypotheses for a Post-Revolutionary Society.* London: Macmillan.

Smart, B. (1992) *Modern Conditions, Postmodern Controversies.* London/New York: Routledge.

Tenbruck, F. H. (1990) *Die kulturellen Grundlagen der Gesellschaft. Der Fall der Moderne,* 2nd edn. Opladen: Westdeutscher Verlag.

Toulmin, S. E. (1992) *Cosmopolis: Hidden Agenda of Modernity.* Chicago: Chicago University Press.

Touraine, A. (1969) *La Société post-industrielle.* Paris: Denoël.

—(1992) *Critique de la modernité.* Paris: Fayard.

Vattimo, G. (1992) *The Transparent Society* (1989). Baltimore: The Johns Hopkins University Press.

Vester, H.-G. (1985) Modernismus und Postmodernismus – Intellektuelle Spielereien? In *Soziale Welt,* vol. 1.

von Beyme, K. (1989) Postmoderne und politische Theorie. In *Politische Vierteljahresschrift (PVS),* vol. 2.

—(2007) *Theorie der Politik im 20. Jahrhundert. Von der Moderne zur Postmoderne,* 4th edn. Frankfurt: Suhrkamp (1991).

White, H. (1982) The politics of historical interpretations: discipline and de-sublimation. In *Critical Inquiry,* no. 9.

Wilms, B. (1989) Postmoderne und Politik. In *Der Staat,* vol. 3.

Yeatman, A. (1994) *Postmodern Revisionings of the Political.* New York/London: Routledge.

Zimmerli, W. Ch. (ed.) (1988) *Technologisches Zeitalter oder Postmoderne?* Munich: Piper.

Zylberberg, J. (ed.) (1986) *Masses et postmodernité.* Paris: Klincksieck.

## 3. Philosophy and Aesthetics

Bauman, Z. (1993a) *Postmodern Ethics.* Oxford: Blackwell.

—(1993b) *Modernity and Ambivalence.* Oxford: Blackwell.

Benhabib, S. (1984) Epistemologies of postmodernism. In *New German Critique,* vol. 33.

Berman, M. (1982) *All That is Solid Melts into Air.* New York: Simon & Schuster.

Best, S., Kellner, D. (1991) *Postmodern Theory. Critical Interrogations.* London: Macmillan.

Buci-Glucksmann, Ch. (December 1985) La Postmodernité. In *Magazine Littéraire.*

Burgin, V. (1986) *The End of Art Theory. Criticism and Postmodernity.* London: Macmillan.

Caravetta, P. (1988) On Gianni Vattimo's Postmodern Hermeneutics. In *Theory, Culture, and Society,* vol. V, no. 2–3.

Crowther, P. (2000) *Critical Aesthetics and Postmodernism.* Oxford: Clarendon Press (1993).

Davis, D. (1977) *Artculture: Essays on the Postmodern.* New York: Harper & Row.

Déotte, J.-L. (1995) Die politisch-philosophische Situation: Die Postmoderne. In *Zeitschrift für Literaturwissenschaft und Linguistik,* vol. 97.

Dews, P. (1986) Adorno, post-structuralism, and the critique of identity. In *New Left Review,* vol. 157.

—(1987) *Logics of Disintegration.* London: Verso.

Ebeling, H. (1993) *Das Subjekt in der Moderne. Rekonstruktion der Philosophie im Zeitalter der Zerstörung.* Reinbek: Rowohlt.

Foster, H. (ed.) (1983) *The Anti-Aesthetic: Essays on Postmodern Culture.* Seattle: Bay Press.

Foucault, M. (1984) Nietzsche, genealogy, history. In P. Rabinow (ed.), *The Foucault Reader,* New York: Pantheon Books.

Frank, M. (1986) *Die Unhintergehbarkeit von Individualität. Reflexion über Subjekt, Person und Individuum aus Anlaß ihrer 'postmodernen' Toterklärung.* Frankfurt: Suhrkamp.

—(1988) *Die Grenzen der Verständigung. Ein Geistergespräch zwischen Lyotard und Habermas.* Frankfurt: Suhrkamp.

Frank, M., Raulet, G. and van Reijen, W. (eds) (1988) *Die Frage nach dem Subjekt.* Frankfurt: Suhrkamp.

Gane, M. (1991) *Baudrillard: Critical and Fatal Theory.* New York/London: Routledge.

Gargani, A. (ed.) (1985) *La crisi del soggetto. Esplorazione e ricerca del sé nella cultura austriaca contemporanea.* Firenze: S.E.S.

Garvin, H. (ed.) (1980) *Romanticism, Modernism, Postmodernism.* Lewisburg: Bucknell University Press.

Griffin, D. R. (1988a) *Spirituality and Science: Postmodern Visions.* Albany: State University of New York Press.

—(1988b) *The Re-enchantment of Science: Postmodern Proposals.* Albany: State University of New York Press.

Habermas, J. (1990) *Die Moderne – ein unvollendetes Projekt. Philosophisch-politische Aufsätze 1977–1990.* Leipzig: Reclam.

—(2005) *The Philosophical Discourse of Modernity. Twelve Lectures* (1985). Cambridge/Maldon: Polity.

Harland, R. (1987) *Superstructuralism: The Philosophy of Structuralism and Post-Structuralism.* London: Methuen.

Hekman, S. (1990) *Gender and Knowledge: Elements of a Postmodern Feminism.* Boston: Northeastern University Press.

Hoesterey, I. (1986) *Zeitgeist in Babel: The Postmodernist Controversy.* Bloomington: Indiana University Press.

Jay, M. (1989) The morals of genealogy: or is there a post-structuralist ethics? In *The Cambridge Review*, vol. 110, no. 2305.

Krammer Maynard, U. (1995) *Performing Postmodernity.* New York/Berne/Paris: Peter Lang.

Kellner, D. (1989) *Critical Theory, Marxism, and Modernity.* Cambridge/Baltimore: Polity Press/Johns Hopkins University Press.

—(1989) *Jean Baudrillard: From Marxism to Postmodernism and Beyond.* Cambridge: Polity.

Kellner, D. (ed.) (1989) *Postmodernism/Jameson/Critique.* Washington: Maisonneuve Press.

Kroker, A. and Cook, D. (1986) *The Postmodern Scene. Excremental Culture and Hyper-Aesthetics.* New York: Saint Martin's Press.

Lang, B. (1986) Postmodernism in philosophy: nostalgia for the future, waiting for the past. In *New Literary History*, vol. 18.

Lefebvre, H. (1962) *Introduction à la modernité. Préludes.* Paris: Minuit.

Lyotard, J.-F. (1992) *The Postmodern Explained to Children. Correspondence 1982–1985* (1986). London: Turnaround.

—(1993) *The Inhuman. Reflections on Time* (1988). Cambridge/Oxford: Polity/Blackwell.

—(1994) *Lessons on the Analytic of the Sublime (Kant's 'Critique of Judgment', §§ 23–29)* (1991). Stanford: Stanford University Press.

—(1999) *The Differend. Phrases in Dispute* (1983). Minneapolis: University of Minnesota Press.

—(2003) *Postmodern Fables* (1993). Minneapolis/London: Minnesota University Press.

—(2004) *The Postmodern Condition: A Report on Knowledge* (1979). Manchester: Manchester University Press.

Meschonnic, H. (1988) *Modernité modernité.* Paris: Verdier.

Milot, P. (1988) *La Camera obscura du postmodernisme.* Montreal: l'Hexagone.

Norris, Ch. (1990) *What's Wrong with Postmodernism. Critical Theory and the End of Philosophy.* London/New York: Harvester/Wheatsheaf.

—(1993) *The Truth about Postmodernism.* Oxford: Blackwell.

—(2000) *Deconstruction and the Unfinished Project of Modernity.* London: Athlone.

Palmer, R. E. (1976) The postmodernity of Heidegger. In *Boundary*, no. 2/4.

—(1977) Postmodernity and hermeneutics. In *Boundary*, no. 2.

—(1984) Expostulations on the postmodern Turn. In *Krisis*, no. 2.

Raulet, G. (1984) From modernity as one-way street to postmodernity as dead end. In *New German Critique*, vol. 33.

—(1986) Marxism and the post-modern condition. In *Telos*, no. 67.

Rorty, R. (1984) Habermas and Lyotard on Postmodernity. In *Praxis International*, no. 4/1.

—(1985) Le Cosmopolitisme sans émancipation (en réponse à Jean-François Lyotard). In *Critique*, no. 456.

—(1989) Philosophy and Post-Modernism. In *The Cambridge Review*, no. 110.

—(1999) *Philosophy and Social Hope*. London: Penguin.

Sadler, T. (1995) *Nietzsche: Truth and Redemption: Critique of the Postmodernist Nietzsche*. London: Athlone.

Schiwy, G. (1985) *Poststrukturalismus und 'Neue Philosophen'*. Reinbek: Rowohlt.

Silverman, H. J. (ed.) (1990) *Postmodernism – Philosophy and the Arts*. London/New York: Routledge.

Smith, H. (1982) *Beyond the Post-Modern Mind*. New York: Crossroad.

Trachtenberg, S. (ed.) (1985) *The Postmodern Moment. A Handbook of Contemporary Innovation in the Arts*. Westport/London: Greenwood Press.

van Reijen, W. (1994) *Die authentische Kritik der Moderne*. Munich: Fink.

Vattimo, G. (1991) *The End of Modernity. Nihilism and Hermeneutics in Postmodern Culture* (1985). Baltimore: The Johns Hopkins University Press.

Wallis, B. (ed.) (1984) *Art after Modernism: Rethinking Representation*. Boston: Godine.

Watson, S. (1984) Jürgen Habermas and Jean-François Lyotard: post-modernism and the crisis of rationality. In *Philosophy and Social Criticism*, no. 10.

Weber, S. (1986) 'Postmoderne' und 'Poststrukturalismus'. Versuch, eine Umgebung zu benennen. In *Ästhetik und Kommunikation*, no. 63.

Wellmer, A. (1993) *Zur Dialektik von Moderne und Postmoderne. Vernunftkritik nach Adorno*, 5th edn. Frankfurt: Suhrkamp.

Welsch, W. (1985) Postmoderne und Postmetaphysik. Eine Konfrontation von Lyotard und Heidegger. In *Philosophisches Jahrbuch*, vol. 92/1.

—(1987a) Heterogenität, Widerstreit und Vernunft. Zu Jean-François Lyotards philosophischer Konzeption von Postmoderne. *Philosophische Rundschau*, no. 34.

—(1987b) Vielheit ohne Einheit? Zum gegenwärtigen Spektrum der philosophischen Diskussion um die Postmoderne. In *Philosophisches Jahrbuch*, vol. 94.

—(2000) *Vernunft. Die zeitgenössische Vernunftkritik und das Konzept der transversalen Vernunft*, 3rd edn. Frankfurt: Suhrkamp (1995).

Welsch, W. and Pries, Ch. (eds) (1991) *Ästhetik im Widerstreit. Interventionen zum Werk von Jean-François Lyotard*. Weinheim: VCH-Verlag.

Zima, P. V. (2007) *Deconstruction and Critical Theory*. London (2002): Turnshare.

# 4. Literary Criticism

Arac, J. (1987) *Critical Genealogies: Historical Situations for Postmodern Literary Studies*. New York: Columbia University Press.

Azam, G. (1989) *El modernismo desde dentro*. Barcelona: Anthropos.

Ballesteros, J. (1989) *Postmodernidad: decadencia o resistencia*. Madrid: Tecnos.

Barilli, R. (1981) *La linea Svevo-Pirandello*. Milan: Mursia.

Barth, J. (1967) The literature of exhaustion. In *Atlantic Monthly*, no. 220.

—(1980) The literature of replenishment. Postmodernist fiction. In *Atlantic Monthly*, no. 245.

Barzun, J. (1943) *Classic, Romantic and Modern*. Chicago/London: University of Chicago Press.

Bennington, G. (1986) The question of post-modernism. In *ICA Documents* (London), no. 4–5.

Berger, A. and Moser, G. E. (eds) (1994) *Jenseits des Diskurses. Literatur und Sprache in der Postmoderne*. Vienna: Passagen.

Blau, H. (1987) *The Eye of the Prey: Subversions of the Postmodern*. Bloomington, Indiana University Press.

Borchmeyer, D. and Žmegač, V. (eds) (1987) *Moderne Literatur in Grundbegriffen*. Frankfurt: Athenäum.

Bradbury, M. and McFarlane, J. (eds) (1978) *Modernism 1890–1930*. Sussex/New Jersey: Harvester Press/Humanities Press.

Buccheri, M., Costa, E. (1995) *Italo Svevo tra moderno e postmoderno*. Ravenna: Longo.

Bürger, Ch. and Bürger, P. (eds) (1987) *Postmoderne: Alltag, Allegorie und Avantgarde*. Frankfurt: Suhrkamp.

Bürger, P. (2000) *Ursprung des postmodernen Denkens*. Weilerswist: Velbrück.

Calinescu, M. (1977) *Faces of Modernity: Avant-Garde, Decadence, Kitsch*. Bloomington, London: Indiana University Press.

Calinescu, M. and Fokkema, D. W. (eds) (1987) *Exploring Postmodernism*. Amsterdam/Philadelphia: J. Benjamins.

Cappuccio, E. (ed.) (1993) *Duchamp dopo Duchamp*. Siracusa: Tema Celeste Ed.

Chabot, C. B. (1984) The problem of postmodern. In *Etudes françaises*, vol. 20, no. 2.

Chvatík, K. (1996) Postmoderna jako sebekritika moderny. *Tvar*, no. 7.

Collins, J. (1989) *Uncommon Cultures. Popular Culture and Post-Modernism*. New York/London: Routledge.

Couturier, M. (ed.) (1983) *Representation and Performance in Postmodern Fiction*. Montpellier: Delta (Univ. Paul Valéry).

D'Haen, T. and Bertens, H. (1988) *Postmodern Fiction in Europe and the Americas*. Amsterdam/Antwerp: Rodopi-Restant.

Eagleton, T. (1986) Capitalism, modernism, postmodernism. In idem, *Against the Grain*. London: Verso.

—(1996) *The Illusions of Postmodernism*. Oxford: Blackwell.

Eco, U. (1984) *Reflections on the Name of the Rose*. London: Secker and Warburg.

Ellrodt, R. (ed.) (1983) *Genèse de la conscience moderne. Etudes sur le développement de la conscience de soi dans les littératures du monde occidental*. Paris: PUF.

Ette, O. (1998) *Roland Barthes. Eine intellektuelle Biographie*. Frankfurt: Suhrkamp.

Eysteinsson, A. (1990) *The Concept of Modernism*. Ithaca/London: Cornell University Press.

Ferroni, G. (1996) *Dopo la fine. Sulla condizione postuma della letteratura*. Turin: Einaudi.

Fiedler, L. A. (1972) *Cross the Border – Close the Gap*. New York: Stein and Day.

Fischer-Lichte, E. and Schwind, K. (eds) (1991) *Avantgarde und Postmoderne. Prozesse struktureller und funktionaler Veränderungen*. Tübingen: Stauffenburg.

Flaker, A. (1982) *Poetika osporavanja. Avangarda i književna ljevica*. Zagreb: Školska Knjiga.

Fokkema, D. W. (1984) *Literary History, Modernism, and Postmodernism*. (*The Harvard University Erasmus Lectures*, Spring 1983). Amsterdam/Philadelphia: J. Benjamins.

Fokkema, D. W. and Bertens, H. (eds) (1986) *Approaching Postmodernism*. Amsterdam/Philadelphia: J. Benjamins.

Fortier, F. (ed.) (1993) *La Fiction postmoderne*. Tangence, no. 39 (Quebec).

Frisby, D. (1985) *Fragments of Modernity. Theories of Modernity in the Works of Simmel, Kracauer and Benjamin*. Oxford: Blackwell.

Gablik, S. (1986) *Has Modernism Failed?* London: Thames and Hudson.

Giles, S. (ed.) (1993) *Theorizing Modernism. Essays in Critical Theory*. London/ New York: Routledge.

Gillespie, G. (2003) *Proust, Mann, Joyce in the Modernist Context*. Washington, DC: The Catholic University of America Press.

—(2006) *Echoland. Readings from Humanism to Postmodernism*. Brussels/Berne/ Berlin: Peter Lang.

Gottdiener, M., *Postmodern Semiotics. Material Culture and the Forms of Postmodern Life*. Oxford/Cambridge, MA: Blackwell.

Graff, G. (1979) *Literature Against Itself: Literary Ideas in Modern Society*. Chicago: Chicago University Press.

Grimminger, R., Murašov, J. and Stückrath, J. (eds) (1995) *Literarische Moderne. Europäische Literatur im 19. und 20. Jahrhundert*. Reinbek: Rowohlt.

Gullón, R. (ed.) (1980) *El modernismo visto por los modernistas*. Barcelona: Editorial Labor.

Hassan, I. (1971) *The Dismemberment of Orpheus. Toward a Postmodern Literature*. New York: Oxford University Press.

—(1987) *The Postmodern Turn. Essays in Postmodern Theory and Culture*. Columbus: Ohio University Press.

Hassan, I. and Hassan, S. (eds) (1983) *Innovation/Renovation. New Perspectives on the Humanities*. Madison/London: University of Wisconsin Press.

Hempfer, K. W. (ed.) (1992) *Poststrukturalismus-Dekonstruktion-Postmoderne*. Stuttgart: Steiner.

Howe, I. (1959) Mass Society and Post-Modern Fiction. In *Partisan Review*, no. 26.

Hutcheon, L. (1988) *A Poetics of Postmodernism. History, Theory, Fiction*. London/ New York, Routledge.

Japp, U. (1986) Kontroverse Daten der Modernität. In W. Haug and W. Barner (eds), *Ethische contra ästhetische Legitimation von Literatur. Traditionalismus und Modernismus: Kontroversen um den Avantgardismus*. Tübingen: Niemeyer.

Jardine, A. (1991) *Gynesis: Configurations de la femme et de la modernité*. Paris: PUF.

Jauß, H. R. (1989) *Studien zum Epochenwandel der ästhetischen Moderne*. Frankfurt: Suhrkamp.

Kibédi Varga, A. (ed.) (1986) *Littérature et postmodernité*. Groningen: CRIN, no. 14.

Kime Scott, B. (1995) *Refiguring Modernism. The Women of 1928*. Bloomington: Indiana University Press.

Kock, R. (1995) *Postmoderne und dekonstruktive Sprachkritik in den frühen Prosatexten Frost, Zerstörung, Watten und Gehen von Thomas Bernhard*. MA-dissertation, University of Münster.

Krauss, R. (1985) *The Originality of the Avant-Garde and Other Modernist Myths*. Cambridge, MA/London: The MIT Press.

Krysinski, W. (1989) *Le Paradigme inquiet. Pirandello et le champ de la modernité*. Montreal: Préambule.

Larrissy, E. (ed.) (1999) *Romanticism and Postmodernism*. Cambridge: Cambridge University Press.

Lawson, H. (1985) *Reflexivity: The Post-Modern Predicament*. La Salle: Open Court.

Leenhardt, J. (June 1992) La Querelle des modernes et des post-modernes. In *Futur antérieur ('Le Texte et son dehors')*.

Lewis, P. (2000) *Modernism, Nationalism, and the Novel*. Cambridge: Cambridge University Press.

Lindsay, A. (1995) *Death in the Funhouse. John Barth and Poststructuralist Aesthetics*. New York/Berne/Paris: Peter Lang.

Lodge, D. (1977) *The Modes of Modern Writing: Metaphor, Metonymy, and the Typology of Modern Literature*. London: Edward Arnold.

Lützeler, P. M. (ed.) (1991) *Spätmoderne und Postmoderne. Beiträge zur deutschsprachigen Gegenwartsliteratur*. Frankfurt: Fischer.

McCaffery, L. (1985) On modern and postmodern poetry. In *Contemporary Literature*, no. 4.

McHale, B. (1987) *Postmodernist Fiction*. London/New York: Methuen.

—(1992) *Constructing Postmodernism*. London/New York: Routledge.

Malmgren, C. D. (1985) *Fictional Space in the Modernist and Postmodernist American Novel*. Lewisburg: Bucknell University Press.

Marini Palmieri, E. (1989) *Modernismo literario hispanoamericano. Carácteres esotéricos en las obras de Darío y Lugones*. Buenos Aires: García Cambeiro.

Maurer, K. and Wehle, W. (eds) (1991) *Romantik, Aufbruch zur Moderne*. Munich: Fink.

Marshall, B. K. (1992) *Teaching the Postmodern. Fiction and Theory*. New York/London: Routledge.

Mazzani, G. (1988) *Postmoderno e la critica*. Roma: Guerini e Associati.

Mazzaro, J. (1980) *Postmodern American Poetry*. Urbana: University of Illinois Press.

Michaud, G. (1985) Récits postmodernes? In *Etudes françaises*, no. 3.

Moreno, J. (1988) Indiferente posmodernidad. In *Revista Muface*, no. 94.

Murphet, J. (2009) *Multimedia Modernism. Literature and the Anglo-American Avant-garde*. Cambridge: Cambridge University Press.

Neumann, G. (ed.) (1997) *Poststrukturalismus. Herausforderung an die Literaturwissenschaft*. Stuttgart: Metzler.

Newman, Ch. (1985) *The Post-Modern Aura. The Act of Fiction in an Age of Inflation*. Evanston: Northwestern University Press.

Nicholls, P. (1995) *Modernisms. A Literary Guide*. London: Macmillan.

Paterson, J. M. (1990) *Moments postmodernes dans le roman québécois*. Ottawa: Presses de l'Univ. d'Ottawa.

Poblet, F. (1985) *Contra la modernidad*. Madrid: Ed. Libertarias.

Porter, M. (1994) *Modernism*. Oxford: Oxford University Press.

*Postmoderna – Nova epoha ili zabluda*. Zagreb: Naprijed, 1988.

Quinones, R. J. (1985) *Mapping Literary Modernism. Time and Development*. Princeton: Princeton University Press.

Riha, K. (1995) *Prämoderne, Moderne, Postmoderne*. Frankfurt: Suhrkamp.

Ruiz Abreu, A. (1984) *Modernismo y generación del 98*. Mexico: Ed. Trillas.

Rull Fernández, E. (1984) *Modernismo y la generación del 98*. Madrid: Playor.

Schulz-Buschhaus, U. (1994) Postavanguardismo, non contra-avanguardismo. Intervista a Ulrich Schulz-Buschhaus. In V. Spinazzola (ed.), *Tirature '94*. Milan: Baldini e Castaldi.

—(1995) Critica e recupero dei generi – Considerazioni sul 'Moderno' e sul 'Postmoderno'. In *Problemi*, vol. 101.

Schulz-Buschhaus, U. and Stierle, K. (eds) (1997) *Projekte des Romans nach der Moderne (Romanistisches Kolloquium 8)*. Munich: Fink.

Schwartz, S. (1985) *The Matrix of Modernism: Pound, Eliot and Early 20th Century Thought*. Princeton: Princeton University Press.

Simard, R. (1984) *Postmodern Drama: Contemporary Playwrights in America and Britain*. Landham: University Press of America.

Spanos, W. (1982) *Postmodern Literary Hermeneutics*. Bloomington: Indiana University Press.

—(1987) *Repetitions: The Postmodern Occasion in Literature and Culture*. Baton Rouge: Louisiana State University.

Sterner, G. (1982) *Modernismos*. Barcelona: Labor.

Subirats, E. (1984) *La crisis de las vanguardias y la cultura moderna*. Madrid: Libertarias.

Surette, L. (1993) *The Birth of Modernism. Ezra Pound, T. S. Eliot, W. B. Yeats, and the Occult*. Montreal/London/Buffalo: McGill/Queen's University Press.

Taylor, B. (1987) *Modernism, Postmodernism, Realism: A Critical Perspective for Art*. Winchester: Winchester School of Art Press.

Tepe, P. (1992) *Postmoderne/Poststrukturalismus*. Vienna: Passagen.

Thiher, A. (1984) *Words in Reflection: Modern Language Theory and Post-modern Fiction*. Chicago: Chicago University Press.

Tono Martínez, J. (1987) *La polémica de la posmodernidad*. Madrid: Ed. Temas de Hoy.

Vidal, M. C. A. (1989) *¿Qué es el posmodernismo?* Alicante: Univ. de Alicante.

Wang Ning (March/June 1993) Constructing postmodernism: the Chinese case and its different versions. In *Canadian Review of Comparative Literature/Revue Canadienne de Littérature Comparée*.

Waugh, P. (1992) *Practising Postmodernism. Reading Modernism*. London/New York: Edward Arnold.

Weightman, J. (1973) *The Concept of the Avant-Garde: Exploration in Modernism*. Illinois: Library Press.

Wilde, A. (1981) *Horizons of Assent: Modernism, Postmodernism, and the Ironic Imagination*. Baltimore/London: The Johns Hopkins University Press.

Williams, R. (1989) *The Politics of Modernism. Against the New Conformists*. London: Verso.

Zavala, I. M. (1988) Bakhtin versus the postmodern. In *Sociocriticism*, no. 8.

Zima, P. V. (1998) Vers une construction du postmoderne. In *Neohelicon*, vol. XXV/1.

—(2001) *Das literarische Subjekt. Zwischen Spätmoderne und Postmoderne*. Tübingen/Basel: Francke.

—(2007) *Theorie des Subjekts. Subjektivität und Identität zwischen Moderne und Postmoderne*, 2nd edn. Tübingen, Basel: Francke (2000).

—(2008) *Der europäische Künstlerroman. Von der romantischen Utopie zur postmodernen Parodie*. Tübingen/Basel: Francke.

Žmegač, V. (1986) *Težišta modernizma. Od Baudelairea do ekspresionizma*. Zagreb: SNL.

Zurbrugg, N. (1993) *The Parameters of Postmodernism*. Carbondale/Edwardsville: Southern Illinois University Press.

# Index

Nerval, G. de 159, 186
Neurath, O. 227, 278n32
New Criticism 162
Nezval, V. 156
Nicholson, L. 32–3, 35, 244n73, 77
Niethammer, L. 239n40, 240n45
Nietzsche, F. 6–9, 15–16, 68, 71, 95–6,
    140, 146, 151, 160, 162, 209,
    241nn71–3, 250nn19, 24, 37, 43,
    254n148, 263n73–5, 264n78,
    266n144, 268nn12–14, 272n102,
    273n138, 275n192
  *Beyond Good and Evil* 195
  *Gay Science* 72
  *Morgenröte* 4
nihilism 8, 12, 136, 196, 216
noetic system 74, 140
nominalism 196
Norris, C. 56, 77, 247n184, 251n70,
    266n157, 267n164
Nouveau Roman 12, 136, 194, 201–2

object and subject, discrepancy
    between 128
objectification 19
objective chance 188
objectivity 227–8
  of dialectical cognition 101
  of truth 214
*objet trouvé* 187
Offe, C. 19
Oliva, A. B. 122–3, 126, 138, 182
O'Neill, J. 2, 37, 41, 45–6, 49, 238n5,
    245nn120, 122, 246nn137, 142
Oníz, F. de 8
openness 45, 161, 187
opposites, coincidence of 173
oppositional politics 35–6
organic solidarity 20
original and copy 97–8
Orphic Marxism 45
ortho-language 230
Osborne, T. 251n71
Other 88, 118, 124, 221, 231, 234

Pächt, O. 263n51
Pannwitz, R. 8
paradigm, theory of 223

paralogy 81, 105
Parent, C. 254n167
Pareto, V. 18
Parisian modernity 5
parody 152, 167, 194, 200–1, 204–5,
    214
particularization 16, 22, 38, 40, 53, 71,
    85–6, 88, 108, 120, 147, 181,
    239n37
  and extremes 107, 166
  feminism and 32
  and indifference 205
  of language and text 162
  postmodern 23, 36, 70, 75
  radical 34–5, 161–2, 164
  Rorty on 84
  and truth 216
Pasolini, P. P. 24, 242n28
Pérez Galdós, B. 14
periods *see* epoch
perspectivism 34–5
Petterson, B. 264n99
phrase regimens 106–7, 113
physis 74
Piaget, J. 86, 88, 253nn121, 128
Piercy, M. 152, 211, 213, 276n218
  *Woman on the Edge of Time* 212
Pirandello, L. 6, 30, 131, 135, 137,
    148–50, 179–80, 187, 196,
    270nn59, 64
Platonic repetition 164
Platonism 97–8
play 72, 90
pluralism 16, 83, 86, 88, 108, 135, 218
  aesthetic 121
  commercialized 122
  cultural 23, 44, 52, 158
  extreme 36, 40
  indifference and 200, 219
  Koslowski on 39
  of meaning 161
  modern 52
  postmodern 24
  radical 31, 39, 52, 66, 121, 162,
    166, 225
  and tolerance 157–8
  *see also* heterogeneity
political accountability 46

Lightning Source UK Ltd.
Milton Keynes UK
UKOW021902061111

181595UK00001B/4/P

9 780826 424020